Ben Jonson
and the
Poetics of Patronage

Ben Jonson
and the
Poetics of Patronage

Robert C. Evans

Lewisburg
Bucknell University Press
London and Toronto: Associated University Presses

Associated University Presses
440 Forsgate Drive
Cranbury, NJ 08512

Associated University Presses
25 Sicilian Avenue
London WC1A 2QH, England

Associated University Presses
P.O. Box 488, Port Credit
Mississauga, Ontario
Canada L5G 4M2

The paper used in this publication meets the requirements of the American National Standard for Permanence of Paper for Printed Library Materials Z39.48-1984.

Library of Congress Cataloging-in-Publication Data

Evans, Robert C.
  Ben Jonson and the poetics of patronage.

  Bibliography: p.
  Includes index.
  1. Jonson, Ben, 1573?–1637—Criticism and interpretation.   2. Authors and patrons—Great Britain—History.   3. Authors and patrons in literature.
I. Title.
PR2642.P39E94 1989   822'.3   87-42860
ISBN 0-8387-5136-9 (alk. paper)

Printed in the United States of America

For Ruth

Wer wüsste je— du und dein still geleucht—
Bänd ich zum danke dir nicht diese krone:
Dass du mir tage mehr als sonne strahltest
Und abende als jede sternenzone.
                    —Stefan George, "Danksagung"

Contents

Preface

This is a book about Ben Jonson as a "patronage poet" and about the impact of "micropolitics" on his writing. I have put these terms up front and in quotation marks for several reasons. First, I want to indicate that I am using them deliberately, not slipping them into the text accidentally when less awkward terms would do. Awkward they admittedly are, but I have decided nonetheless to use them, not because of any affection for self-generated jargon but precisely because no other terms convey more exactly the meanings I wish to communicate. I do not, for instance, want to call Jonson a "poet dependent on patronage," for the length of this phrase makes it awkward in its own way, and besides, it stresses his *dependency* in a manner that fundamentally simplifies the complex nature of his relations with superiors. ("Patronized poet" is plainly faulty.) By calling him a "patronage poet," I want to suggest that he was a writer whose life and works were radically conditioned by a culture rooted in hierarchical relations, and by using "patronage" as an adjective throughout this book, I want to imply that patronage during the English Renaissance was more than a matter of economic give-and-take, that it was basic to the period's life and *psychology* and crucially shaped Jonson's attitudes and experience. For this reason I sometimes use the word to designate social relations broader in scope than the specific connections between an aristocratic patron and his clients. In these instances I use it to refer to the complex network of hierarchical relations typical of that time. English offers ample precedent, of course, for sometimes treating nouns as adjectives: if there are bus drivers, auto mechanics, and management consultants, perhaps there can also be patronage poets.

But what about "micropolitics"? Surely some simpler term would do—"politics," perhaps? That word, however, still chiefly connotes ideological struggle, or conflict between economic classes or other large social groups. A study of Jonson's "politics" would probably concentrate on his attitudes toward major issues of public policy or governmental philosophy. However, I am interested in something simpler, more basic, more inevitable: in his struggle for *personal* power and status, in his competition on a *personal* level with other individuals. Whatever his larger "political" beliefs, whatever the larger ideological system in which he operated, "micropolitics" was an inexorable aspect of his life, as indeed it seems to be of nearly all lives. This inevitability is what makes it seem to me so fascinating and so worthy of study; and yet our language lacks a simple, convenient word to denote the exercise of individual power. ("Competition" emphasizes power relations mainly with rivals rather than also with superiors, friends, family members, and others.) This lack seems noteworthy in itself: it suggests that personal politics is a topic we do not often confront directly. Perhaps it also suggests that the topic makes us uncomfortable, that we do not like to face the full ramifications of thinking of ourselves as inescapably implicated in personal competition, in the struggle for personal power. Although politics and religion are two topics one is supposed to avoid in polite conversation, they seem much more openly and willingly discussed and debated than is the case with "micropolitics." Until recently (until, for instance, Foucault's exemplary insistence that "power" be studied in *all* its manifold complexity), that topic was usually left to a few social psychologists or to the authors of how-to-get-ahead-in-business manuals. Later in this book I shall discuss in more detail some possible reasons for this reticence; here I wish only to emphasize that I am (for the most part) unconcerned with Jonson's "politics," and that my *micro*political focus is deliberate.

This is a book largely about Jonson's poetry, although I also discuss the plays and the masques. If the space available were unlimited, I would have liked to delve more deeply into the details of the masques and dramas, exploring each of them in its individual uniqueness. Certainly Jonson's plays and aristocratic entertainments were vitally important to his career as a patronage poet. But Jonson was so prolific in both genres, and the works he produced in them are so richly complicated, that a full discussion of the plays and masques would have required a book-length treatment in itself. Yet to ignore them altogether in this book would have opened me—and rightly so—to charges of neglecting crucial aspects of his life and art. Thus I have included two chapters on these works, but those chapters are intended to be synthetic and synoptic, offering an overview of the impact of patronage on the masques and plays rather than providing detailed discussions of any single one of them. In both chapters I do try to discuss specifics (as, for instance, in my comments on *Sejanus*), but I do not attempt to provide "close readings" of entire works. Given my greater interest in examining the poems, this approach to the plays and masques seemed not only justifiable but sensibly pragmatic. Besides, the dramas and entertainments have been the object of some of the richest and most provocative criticism devoted to Jonson over the last several decades, whereas the poems have only recently begun to attract the same kind of intensely sustained scrutiny.

Central to my argument is the belief that Jonson's writings, and especially his poems, are far more complicated and intricate than has sometimes been assumed, and that studying them as micropolitical *performances* is one way of coming to grips with their full complexity as works of art. Jonson's reputation as a poet of the "plain style" has sometimes made his poetry seem less richly ambiguous than the works of his great contemporaries. Yet once his poems are viewed as frozen maneuvers, as instances of a highly self-conscious writer's highly public behavior, their fuller resonances can more easily be felt. Much of great value has been written about Jonson's literary and social ideals, about his exploitation of generic conventions, about his indebtedness to the great writers of the classical past. My focus, however, is on his immediate, *practical* context as a writer seeking to advance himself in a society permeated by the psychology of patronage relations.

Yet his writings, not his life, are my first concern. I am less interested in how he lived than in how the manner of his life intricately shaped the manner of his writings. Thus I have tried to examine many of his poems quite closely, paying attention to the connotations of individual words, to the placement of particular phrases, to the structures of specific passages. Some readers may think that sometimes I have not so much interpreted poems as tortured them, forcing them to reveal meanings they would not ordinarily communicate. My own feeling is (obviously) somewhat different. Since I believe that even the "simplest" instances of everyday behavior are full of complex, even contradictory implications; that their social meanings depend less on the performer's conscious intent than on the context in which he acts and on how his performance is interpreted and received by others; that a certain anxiety consequently underlies most social behavior; that all social acts are performances and that most are designed (whether consciously or not) to enhance or maintain the actor's power, it therefore does not seem to me implausible that Jonson's poems would be at least as complex as a conversation in a restaurant or a talk over the phone. In my examinations of his works, I have tended to look at the ways in which they are frankly (but not simplistically) self-serving. I have looked especially for the tensions, the insecurities, the ambiguities and ambivalences which seem to characterize his writing, however much he tried to pretend otherwise. Jonson strikes me as a writer much less in control of his writing than he wanted to be, and yet one who was acutely aware of the need for control and quite ingenious in attempting to impose it.

Of course, Jonson inherited many of the tactics he used from his poetic predecessors, both in the immediate and in the distant past. This fact raises the important issue of the conventionality of his art. The long tradition of literary patronage in European culture, combined with the pervasiveness of patronage relations in that culture generally, meant that few of the tactics he exploited were invented by him. But neither were they simply dead conventions or stale literary topoi which he merely mimicked. Indeed, one reason for studying his poems in their contemporary biographical context is to observe the ways he used conventions creatively, how his applications of old ideas and formulas might resonate with highly particular (perhaps even controversial) meanings for contemporary readers who knew details of his patrons' lives and circumstances now generally forgotten. The more we know specifically about Jonson's patrons, the more we can appreciate why he *chose* to adopt and adapt the particular conventions he selected in addressing them, and the more we can appreciate the kind and quality of originality his poems were capable of achieving.

Even using nonspecific epideictic conventions offered many practical, tactical benefits to a poet in Jonson's position. Praising a contemporary patron in language associated with great classical or medieval poets simultaneously complimented the patron in a subtle way; demonstrated the poet's learning; reminded the patron of poetry's antiquity and proven ability to cheat the effects of time; helped insulate the poet from suspicions of flattery; implied a link with readers astute enough to appreciate literary allusions; lent the poet's voice greater sanction and more timeless authority; allowed him to appropriate a valued tradition for his personal use; suggested a recognized standard by which his skills could be judged and his competitors (both past and present) could be assessed; allowed for a certain complexity of allusive nuance; implied the poet's acceptance of recognized traditions and his ability to extend and uphold them; indicated his competitive self-confidence but also an attractive reverence for honored forebears; and helped mediate and objectify the potentially complicated and touchy relations between egos whose interests did not always converge. In all these ways, literary topoi might contribute to a poet's pragmatic social *power.* Jonson drew on the conventions of patronage poetry not because his relations with patrons were simple or routine, but in part precisely because they were not and never could be. Many of the topoi he exploited may have been used by predecessors, but this hardly means that for Jonson they lacked specific personal relevance. Like proverbs or clichés, their very resilience depended on their perennial (and personal) applicability. Jonson turned to the writings of his great precursors—especially such Roman poets as Horace and Martial—not simply because they offered him literary forms to imitate but because they provided real-life models for his own complex dealings with social superiors.

Ample evidence suggests that the conventions Jonson exploited were more than literary tropes; they were practical tools useful for dealing with the everyday problems facing anyone who lived in the rigidly hierarchical culture of his day. Jonson used them with the cleverness and ingenuity of a great artist, but he was hardly unique in exploiting them. The fact that his rhetorical strategies are so often rooted in the particular conditions of his culture might seem to limit his poems' current relevance, but in fact just the opposite is true. The issues of competition, power, and self-assertion he confronted were (as he recognized) not radically different from the problems faced by his classical and medieval predecessors, nor are they radically different from the similar issues that confront us today. Macropolitical ideologies may shift and change, but micropolitics is inevitable and eternal: it is partly this fact that gives Jonson's poems their enduring relevance. This is important, since Jonson can sometimes seem (compared to such great contemporaries as Shakespeare, Donne, or Herbert) in danger of becoming a "dead" poet, read only by scholars as conversant with ancient conventions and mores as he. But anyone who has read Foucault, Goffman, Burke, or even Dale Carnegie will see that Jonson's poetry resonates with concerns, anxieties, and ambitions that are far from moribund. Indeed, one value of approaching his poems from a patronage perspective comes from recognizing the many ways in which one can speak (to paraphrase Jan Kott) of Jonson, our contemporary. Jonson's poems can seem both more vital and more complicated when we bear in mind the context in which they were written.

Like any work with a central defining theme, this book can perhaps be accused of being reductive, of forcing all of Jonson's works to jump through the same narrow hoop. This is an accusation I would (naturally) resist, although there is probably no way to resist it altogether without hopelessly blurring the focus of my argument. I cannot deny that certain words and phrases (such as "self-promotion") tend to recur in this book despite my best efforts to avoid undue repetition. However, this fact itself may indicate how limited and primitive our vocabulary is for discussing the kinds of micropolitical effects I have chosen to emphasize. I hope that the approach I take does help illuminate in new ways the detailed richness of Jonson's texts. However, my hope has also been to examine the particularities of his works without losing sight of their shared elements and strategies.

I realize that my focus on poets' self-interests (and, more to the point, on the tactical *effectiveness* of their works) may make some readers uncomfortable. However, my own feeling is that the more we acknowledge the universality and inevitability of micropolitics and of individual self-interest, the more we may be able to scrutinize our own motives and behavior with a certain humility, even humor. The implications of such an approach to Jonson's poetry need not be cynical or amoral, and could in fact prove precisely the opposite.

Chapter 1 of this study sketches the characteristics of the patronage "system" that helped condition conduct and attitudes in Jonson's day. It argues that patronage relations were so pervasive in his culture that hardly anyone could avoid being affected by the *psychology*, the habits of mind, those relations fostered. Yet it also emphasizes the tensions and contradictions between patronage ideals and actual practices, and stresses the uncertainty and anxiety those tensions provoked. Chapter 2 narrows the focus to Jonson himself, discussing his career and emphasizing that *all* his writings were intimately affected by his role as a patronage poet and that the two most important segments of his audience consisted of patrons and rivals, actual and potential. This chapter, at least in one section, is the most explicitly theoretical in the book; in it I try to offer some explanation and defense of the "dramatistic" approach to Jonson's writings (and to all human actions) that underlies my argument. The bulk of the chapter, however, is devoted to detailed discussion of several poems addressed to the Countesses of Rutland and Bedford. I take these works as test cases for proving out some of the assertions made earlier in this chapter and developed more fully later on. At the risk of seeming perverse, I also try to show how even such a gently appealing poem as the epitaph "On My First Sonne" can be looked at in terms of power. I chose this poem deliberately, not only because it is one of Jonson's best and most famous, but also because it may seem particularly resistant to the kind of approach this book pursues. For the same reason, I also look briefly at one of Jonson's best-known works about love, the "Celebration of Charis" sequence.

Chapter 3 raises issues of flattery and poetic freedom; it discusses the extent to which Jonson was—or could be—autonomous, arguing that although the appearance of independence was pragmatically important, his actual freedom was necessarily limited. The chapter discusses a number of works in which he confronts the issue directly, showing how he could turn it to his personal and artistic advantage and how the need to distinguish himself from flatterers could contribute to the subtlety and ambiguity of his works. Here and elsewhere, his ability to intimidate patrons, to play up to and play on their own insecurities and anxieties, is stressed. The second half of the chapter deals with a number of poems and incidents in which he seems to assert his independence most forthrightly and undeniably—but it shows how both the poems and the incidents take on a more complicated hue when placed in fuller biographical contexts.

Chapter 4, the longest section, is the heart of the book. It examines a variety of Jonson's poems to a variety of types of patrons, stressing the flexibility as well as the recurrent themes of his writings for superiors. In discussing his poems for King James, for instance, it indicates how Jonson could adopt a public role while nonetheless distinguishing himself from the public he claimed to represent, and how he could play on the King's insecurity to enhance his own power. This exploitation of a superior's insecurity is a theme also stressed in discussions of his poems to Sir Robert Cecil, the Earl of Pembroke, Sir Thomas Egerton, Francis Bacon, Bishop John Williams, and various members of the extended Sidney family. The chapter emphasizes that Jonson's patrons were themselves caught up in competitive struggles similar to the poet's own. It accentuates the paradoxes and contradictions of his tones and attitudes, disclosing his misgivings about competition yet emphasizing his need to compete. And it argues that examining the biographies of the patrons he addressed can help us better appreciate the intricacy and resonance of the poems addressed to them.

If patrons comprised Jonson's crucial audience, rivals were a close second: this is the argument of chapter 5. It stresses that rivals were probably his most attentive readers; certainly they were most alive to the micropolitical implications of his works. This chapter emphasizes the importance of patronage competition to the so-called poetomachia, one of the most significant and determining events of the poet's early career. The chapter also discusses some of his shorter satirical poems as well as his various satires on Inigo Jones and the famous "Tribe of Ben" epistle, emphasizing the ambivalence and tensions these poems reveal and the complex responses rivalry could (and can) evoke. Discussion of an attack on Jonson by George Chapman and of the ambiguities present even in elegies written to commemorate his death helps stress the competitive pressures with which he and his contemporaries had to cope.

Chapter 6 explores questions of power, self-promotion, anxiety, and competition in works where one might least expect to find them—in his poems on friends and friendship. This chapter attempts to complicate our view of the friendship poems by looking at them not so much as expressions of the poet's secure self-confidence and loftiest ideals but as competitive instruments, just as self-conscious, just as ambiguous in their own ways as any of his other works. The chapter opens by surveying classical and contemporary notions of friendship in order to suggest how these theories designed to explain and exalt friendship, far from offering Jonson a secure platform on which to build his poems, often exhibited the very tensions his own works could not elude.

Chapters 7 and 8 detail the various ways in which the patronage system affected the tones, themes, and tactics of Jonson's masques and entertainments and of his plays. These chapters show how he used his dramatic works to promote his individual interests and image, and argue that the circumstances that distinguished the plays and masques from the poems hardly insulated them from the pressures created by Jonson's continuing need to compete.

Acknowledgments

In writing this book I have benefited from the support of many people. I am especially grateful to Professor Anthony Low, whose encouragement, patience, and generosity with his time have made this a better book than it would otherwise have been. His careful and caring reading of the text helped improve both its substance and its style. My debt to him is greater than I can hope to repay. My editor, Ann Harvey, made numerous helpful comments. Professor David Riggs kindly allowed me to read a version of his forthcoming biography of Jonson just as my book was going to press. I am also grateful to Professors Frank Whigham, John Shawcross, Claude Summers, and Ted-Larry Pebworth, who read parts of my argument in other forms and who offered not only valuable suggestions but also the kind of encouragement that sustains and inspires. Whatever faults remain are my own. Professors Arthur Marotti, Russell Gill, John King, James Riddell, and George Szöny were kind in ways that may have seemed minor to them but meant a great deal to me.

My work was made easier by the very strong support I received from my university. I am particularly grateful to Pat Hill, Marion Michael, James Kenny, and Guin Nance. Among the friends and colleagues who helped me in numerous ways, I would like especially to thank Joe Crowley, Pat Bradley, Vivian Barfoot, Jeff Hyams, Ron Romanoff, Jean Gray, Steve Goodson, Gary Goodson, Rosemary Dills, and Mrs. Grace Waser. The Whitmans—Robert, Marina, Gretchen, and Beatrice—occupy a special place in my affections. Lawrence Danson, Lawrence Lipking, U. C. Knoepflmacher, Michael Goldman, Walter Evert, and Robert Gale all took the time to talk and to listen when that was what I needed most.

I am particularly grateful to the three teachers who most stimulated and nurtured my interest in Renaissance literature: to Robert Hinman, who sparked my first enthusiasm for the period and its texts; to Earl Miner, whose enormous kindness has been felt by all who know him; and to Alvin Kernan, whose generous and unstinting encouragement has meant so much to me and to this book.

My deepest thanks go to my wife, to our families, and to my friend Jim Barfoot, who all provided the most caring sustenance I could have wished.

When I first began work on an early version of this project more than seven years ago, the critical landscape appeared much different than it appears today. It seemed very important then—in the face of the enormous influence still exercised by the old New Criticism, and in response to the growing influence of deconstruction—to insist on the importance and legitimacy of reading literary texts from an explicitly historical perspective. In recent years, the need for polemics on this point has abated, thanks to the increasing prominence (especially in Renaissance studies) of what is usually called "the New Historicism." When I began, Stephen Greenblatt's seminal work on *Renaissance Self-Fashioning* had only recently been published; it was soon followed by Richard Helgerson's masterful study, *Self-Crowned Laureates*. In the years since, these works have been joined by books and articles by a number of other writers whose ways of thinking about literature and history have provided a powerful stimulus for my own. These include Leah Marcus, Don Wayne, Frank Whigham, Jonathan Dollimore, Daniel Javitch, Wayne Rebhorn, Alan Sinfield, David Norbrook, Annabel Patterson, Louis Adrian Montrose, Jonathan Goldberg, Stephen Orgel, Arthur Marotti, and Leonard Tennenhouse. Others could be mentioned, and I have tried to acknowledge my debts more fully in my notes. Even where I sometimes depart from their emphases, my work has profited greatly from the theoretical perspectives and analytical insights these authors have provided.

My work has benefited from the support of a number of organizations and institutions and the people associated with them. I am grateful to the Whiting Foundation, the Newberry Library, the American Council of Learned Societies, the Folger Library, the National Endowment for the Humanities, and the Huntington Library for fellowships in support of my research. Work on this project was also supported in part by the Research Grant-in-Aid program at Auburn University at Montgomery. In addition, I wish to thank the editors of the following journals for permission to reprint portions of articles that first appeared in their pages: *Texas Studies in Literature and Language; Renaissance and Reformation; Renaissance Papers;* the *College Language Association Journal;* and the *Iowa State Journal of Research;* a full listing of these articles is given in the bibliography.
Finally, I owe very special thanks to Claude Summers and Ted-Larry Pebworth for allowing me to use several portions of a long article of

mine entitled "'Games of Fortune, Plaid at Court': Politics and Poetic Freedom in Jonson's Epigrams," which is scheduled for publication in their anthology *The Muses Common-weale: Poetry and Politics in the Earlier Seventeenth Century*. I am similarly grateful to Professors David G. Allen and Robert A. White for permission to include in this book the substance of my essay "'Inviting a Friend to Supper': Ben Jonson, Patronage, and the Poetry of Power," which was accepted for publication in a collection resulting from the Fifth Citadel Conference on Literature.

Ben Jonson
and the
Poetics of Patronage

1

Introduction: Poets and the Psychology of Patronage

The impact of patronage on English Renaissance literature seems all the greater when one recognizes that literary patronage was only one aspect of a much larger, far more comprehensive system of patronage relations. Patronage, broadly defined, was the central social system of the era. It dominated political life and permeated the structure of the church and universities. Its influence on the economy was enormous, and the assumptions behind it were reflected in religious thought, in cosmological speculation, and in the organization and daily detail of family life. Painting, architecture, music—all the arts and not just literature were affected by a patronage culture so pervasive that no individual or sphere of life could entirely escape its effects.[1] The connection between poetry and patronage, then, involved more than how writers were paid, the ways they made their livings. It involved, more fundamentally, how they lived their lives. The patronage system was more than simply a means of organizing the economy or of structuring politics, of arranging social life or of thinking about one's relations with God. Because it was all these things, it was also a psychological system: the assumptions behind it inevitably affected how people thought about themselves, others, and their mutual interactions. Patronage, or one's place in the various interlocking patronage networks, went far toward defining not only one's social status but also one's self-esteem. Finding a secure and respected niche in the patronage system meant more than ensuring a healthy income. It meant winning an opportunity to participate most fully, most *really*, in the life of one's time.

In its broadest sense, the patronage system was simply the translation into practical social terms of the grand hierarchical "Elizabethan World Picture"—that set of assumptions, grounded in notions of subordination and degree, by which society was ordered and its place in the universe explained. With God the Father at the head of an enormous chain of subordinate relationships, with the monarch as God's vicegerent on earth and as a father to his people, and with individual fathers as little sovereigns, minor masters of their own families and households, Renaissance culture formed a web of patriarchal relations. Authority was vested in powerful, mostly older male figures, who exercised it over properly deferential inferiors. Gaining power meant propitiating those who held it, and at every level one's most important relations were less with equals or peers than with superiors and subordinates. "Horizontal" relations—friendships, for instance—were not insignificant; for one thing, they could provide some relief from the pressures of competition. But the relief could never be total, the alternative never complete: no friendship, however satisfying, could in itself assure one a secure place in the social hierarchy. And one's friends, of course, also participated in the same system. Connections with them might, in fact, be useful in winning or maintaining patronage, but the relation with the patron was of prime importance. Indeed, the very fact that friendships could provide some refuge from competitive pressures suggests how the patronage system could psychologically color relations seemingly separate from it. Even the link between man and wife was conceived less as a partnership of equals than as a subordination of the woman to her husband. In theology, politics, and domestic relations, hierarchy was the rule and patronage its reflection in practical life.[2]

Ideally patronage relations were grounded in reciprocity: the inferior's service earned the superior's reward. But the translation from theory to practice was inevitably imperfect. Relations among individuals are always more complicated in fact than in abstraction. While in theory the system reflected the hierarchical order of the universe, in practice it created numerous opportunities for tensions, contradictions, suspicions, and resentment. By its very nature it involved the accommodation of egos with different, sometimes contradictory interests. The patron was not simply an influence on those beneath him; they also sought to influence the patron. The actual operation of the "system," then, was neither simple nor rigidly systematic; relations among its participants were likely to be complex and dialectical rather than straightforwardly causal. The opportunities for irony, ambiguity, paradox, and equivocation existed not only in the literary works to which patronage relations gave birth, but in the relations themselves. And these complexities characterized not only the literal give-and-take between patrons and clients, but the equally important dealings between clients competing with each other for support. The pervasiveness of patronage relations, combined with the frequently conflicting interests of their various participants, helped ensure that the system could never run completely smoothly, could never satisfy all those who took part in it. It was a system built on expectation and apprehension, on the deepest hopes and fears. Recognizing this can help us better appreciate the emotional and intellectual intricacies of the lives and literature it helped produce.

The patronage system during the English Renaissance was firmly rooted in traditions of domestic patriarchy that had dominated European culture for many centuries. Indeed, patriarchy's long history and conjunction with patronage gave them both the sanction of apparent timelessness. When people in the Renaissance read about people in the past, they glimpsed a world not radically different from their own. It was a world in which power was most often wielded by older males, frequently literal fathers, often fathers nominal or symbolic (patrons; popes). The close association between patronage and patriarchy helped give the former psychological resonance and social legitimacy; it made alternatives more difficult to conceive.[3] But it also invested the system with emotional overtones that colored dependents' expectations. A patron—ideally, at least—was more than someone who happened to possess power; he was expected to exercise that power benignly, to reward merit, recognize true virtue, and requite devoted service. In theory there should have been as little antagonism between superiors and those beneath them as between fathers and sons. The idea that social relations might be grounded in the competing self-interests of relatively autonomous individuals, that patronage connections might reflect free-market conditions in which persons sold their services to the highest bidder and in which calculations of personal profit were more important than noblesse oblige or deferential subordination—such ideas had little place in the explicitly formulated dogma of the time.

The system's emotional and intellectual connotations helped authorize and justify it, helped make it seem to reflect something larger and more permanent; but like most ideals they also implicitly dramatized the disparity between reality and themselves. Many of the tensions and contradictions between patronage in theory and in practice were inevitable. But they were also exacerbated by the high expectations the theory helped create. The dissatisfaction that often dominates contemporary comments is less often directed at the system itself than at the shortcomings of individual superiors who failed—or were felt to have failed—to live up to an ideal standard. Calls for the overthrow of the system were far less frequent than the desire for its reform, and misgivings about the system as such were far less common than discontent with particular patrons.

Nevertheless, changes in every aspect of English Renaissance life inevitably affected the system in numerous ways, and helped eventually to decrease its importance. It is easy to exaggerate the impact of the changes, to underestimate the psychological durability of the assumptions on which the system rested. It is equally easy to underestimate the persistence and pervasiveness of patronage relations themselves, to simplify historical events, processes, and personalities by viewing them teleologically—in terms of what they led to rather than in the context of their time. Changes in the political patronage system and in the political attitudes that conditioned it, for instance, were probably neither as radical nor as rapid as has sometimes been suggested.[4] Changes in thinking about the relations between man and God or between man and state, which eventually helped produce significant alterations in patterns of church and secular authority, were often supported by patrons or by those dependent on patronage. Differences of faction were at least as important as different ideologies, the conflict of personalities often as significant as the clash of ideas. Changes in one aspect of the patronage system, moreover, need to be viewed from the larger perspective of the system as a whole. The growing economic independence of the professional writer thanks to theatrical capitalism and other factors, for instance, should not lead us to exaggerate the possibilities of genuine intellectual or artistic license, or to suppose that because his main income derived from the stage a writer was exempt from the influence of the patronage system.[5] No matter how he earned his living, every individual was still implicated, in countless ways, in a society permeated by patronage relations and shaped by assumptions conducive to them.

Yet however cautiously we should describe historical changes, there seems no denying that the factors making for change were numerous. The proliferation of print, the growth of capitalism, the rise of ever-purer forms of Protestantism, the increasing centralization of political power—all of these forces inevitably affected the tone and conduct of patronage relations. But since these forces themselves evolved in contexts variously shaped by patronage, they were themselves influenced by it. The interaction was inevitably complex and dialectical. The growing power of individual fathers over their families, for instance, meant that the father became psychologically an even more important figure than he had been in the past. Like the patrons with whom the child would someday have to deal, he enjoyed a position that could inspire genuine affection and loyalty as well as uncertainty and apprehension. Benefits were his to dole out or withhold; pleasing him was both psychologically and pragmatically important. In households across the country, youngsters had their first tastes of a dependency and subordination that would, in various guises, last a lifetime.[6]

For many children, dependence on substitute father-figures began even before their childhoods ended. Whether placed under the care of tutors or apprenticed to "masters"; whether educated by schoolmasters or instructed in the homes of wealthy relatives or family friends; whether educated later by different masters at the universities or Inns of Court, young men throughout the country quickly learned that the deference and service they owed their natural fathers was also expected by figures whose influence over their futures was in some ways equally strong. They learned not only facts or skills but a whole mode of life, a whole manner of behavior and set of expectations. Maturation involved initiation in countless ways into the rites and requirements of a system permeated by patronage relations. Many fathers themselves recognized this, and some left written instructions to their sons advising them how to cope. These writings often acknowledge or imply the competitiveness latent in the system, its stress on reputation, and the ambiguity of relations between superiors and their dependents.[7] Thus by the time he reached maturity and was ready to enter more directly into the quest for place and status, the child had already been exposed for many years to the psychology of patronage. His subordinate status encouraged dependency, but his need to compete could promote more self-centered, self-assertive impulses. Both the dependency and the competition helped make his situation inherently insecure, and could often lead to apprehension, mistrust, and jealousy. All these factors became even more important when the stakes increased, when the grown child entered most fully into the struggle for patronage.

The central arena for such struggle was undoubtedly the court. Although only a tiny segment of Englishmen ever directly vied for status there, they were the intellectual and social elite, the articulate class who participated most fully in running the country and whose allegiance was crucially important. No social segment stood apart from the court's authority; no other institution rivaled it in power or preeminence.[8] The men and women who competed there were often themselves the most powerful figures in other spheres of life or in other areas of the country, while the government bureaucracy offered numerous opportunities to those of lesser birth who were skillful, ambitious, or well-connected. Influence or a place at court automatically heightened one's psychological and pragmatic status; loss of favor there could be devastating economically and in social and self-esteem. For all these reasons, competition was that much more frenetic. Along with the church, the universities, and the legal system, the court was one of the great centers of social power and social competition.

Given the pervasiveness of patronage relations in English Renaissance society, it hardly seems surprising that the period's literary culture was also heavily influenced by patronage concerns. In part this was because the literary system was itself fundamentally rooted in patronage: many writers depended for protection, promotion, prestige, and a substantial part of their incomes on the support and encouragement of interested superiors. But the impact of patronage on Renaissance literary culture goes much further and deeper. It is precisely because literary patronage was not an isolated or peculiar arrangement, precisely because it reflected and replicated in one sphere the patterns of thinking and behavior dominant in society at large, that its effects on literature seem so potentially complex, important, and far-reaching. By the time a child became old enough to decide to become a poet or writer, he had already been exposed for years to the typical habits of mind, the conventional ways of acting and reacting that a patronage culture engendered. Depending on patrons to help support his writing would be only the latest instance in a routine of psychological and practical dependence on superiors to which he had long become accustomed. And since many of the greatest writers thought of themselves not as writers per se but as amateur authors or as aspirants in some other part of the larger patronage system, the system's general importance seems all the greater.[9]

No writer in the England of Elizabeth, James, or Charles could be wholly free of patronage influences because no person in that culture could be wholly independent of the larger patronage system. Neither the wealthy aristocratic amateur, who needed no outside money to finance his writing; nor the professional dramatist, who earned most of his income by writing for the stage; nor even the gentleman amateur, who may have circulated his poems simply among friends or fellow wits—none of these could be entirely untouched by the psychology of a culture grounded in assumptions of theoretical hierarchy and practical subordination. Of course, the particular impact of the patronage system on a particular writer, his specific response to the problems and opportunities it presented, would be affected partly by his individual personality and partly by his social rank or economic circumstances. But because there were broad similarities between experiences at every level of the system, there were also broad similarities between the various challenges posed and the various responses they evoked. The wealthy aristocrat was still subordinate to someone and in competition with his peers; the professional dramatist wrote for an audience whose most influential members were likely to be his social superiors and those dependent on them, while his plays were always subject to the censor and were often performed at court; the gentleman amateur still knew that his poems could affect his reputation, how people thought about and reacted to him. One need not have been a professional writer, then, to be affected by the concerns, anxieties, pressures, and stimulations of a patronage culture. The practical problems and theoretical issues it posed were essentially concerned with power—winning it, keeping it, feeling and conferring its legitimacy. They were, therefore, relevant to every member of society, especially to those who ventured to express (and thus expose) themselves on paper.[10]

Literary patronage was obviously most important to those writers who thought of themselves *as* writers and who depended on superiors for income, advancement, or protection. During the Renaissance the number of such writers sharply increased, placing a growing burden on a system of literary patronage inherited from the middle ages. Writers themselves felt the stress most acutely, and to many, talk of a literary patronage "system" might have seemed naive, suggesting a more smoothly operating mechanism than ever existed in their own experience. Indeed, part of the fault writers found with the system was its very lack of systematization: its largely arbitrary, improvisational character meant that service, no matter how devoted or unstinting, led not always nor automatically to reward. There were, in fact, two systems of literary patronage during the Renaissance: an ideal version, grounded in perfect reciprocity and noblesse oblige, that existed mostly in the minds and imaginations of the writers; and the often imperfect, inadequate, frustrating, or uncertain arrangements they encountered in everyday life. Contrasting the second with the first—a habitual practice—only increased their dissatisfaction and discontent. But the very irregularity and unreliability they complained about was one of the actual system's most typical features, and helped underscore the subservient relationship of writer to patron that the system actually fostered.[11]

Paradoxically, however, it is only when one pulls back from a focus on literary patronage *per se* to a concern with the larger system that the full implications of patronage for literature become clear. Viewing patronage as a *psychological* system suggests that nearly every work written during this time might be, in some sense, a poem of patronage. It suggests that few texts could escape being conditioned or affected by the ways of behavior and habits of mind a patronage culture encouraged. It implies that nearly every text has some political dimension or aspect, even as it also stresses the importance of *micro*politics instead of focusing exclusively on larger questions of ideology. Since nearly every work presents, implicitly or explicitly, an image of the author who created it, nearly every work has some effect on the author's status in the patronage hierarchy. And this seems true whether the author consciously intends that effect or not. From this perspective, a text need not flatter a patron—or, indeed, even be addressed to a patron—to function as a patronage poem; it need not explicitly solicit money, protection, or position. An effective patronage approach to Renaissance poetry would assume that few Renaissance texts could help being touched in some way by a social system so pervasive and inescapable.

Instead of focusing on the author's intentions, such an approach would emphasize instead the effects and effectiveness of any particular work in promoting the author's social standing. More important, it would explore not only how any given text might potentially affect its author's status, but also how a culture rooted in patronage might help dictate the detailed texture, structure, and meaning of the work itself. Instead of viewing texts simply as vehicles for the expression of large political ideas, it would attempt to look at them as micropolitical acts or *performances*. And it would attempt to show how the complexities, ambiguities, and tensions inherent in the patronage system could be reflected in the minute characteristics and aesthetic strategies of particular works.

2

Jonson and the Poetics of Patronage

Like Spenser, Ben Jonson was touched by patronage at an early age. Spenser's father, a gentleman of modest means, had been able to educate his sons with help from a wealthy family. In Jonson's case the need was more extreme. His father, he claimed, had "Losed all his estate under Queen Marie, having been cast in prison and forfaitted." Eventually released, he became a preacher, then died a month before Jonson's birth in 1572. His widow remarried, but the match—to a bricklayer—later embarrassed Jonson. He preferred to think of himself as "a Ministers son," and spoke with pride of his grandfather, "a Gentleman" who had "served King Henry 8." He appropriated the coat of arms of the Johnstone family, but seems to have dropped the "h" from his name to distinguish himself from run-of-the-mill Johnsons. He complained that he had been "brought up poorly," and might have faced a future of bricklaying had he not been "putt to school by a friend."[1]

That help proved decisive. Like Spenser under Richard Mulcaster at the Merchant Taylor's School, Jonson learned from his tutor William Camden the social no less than intrinsic value of a humanist education. Schooling enhanced both his ambition and his means of advancement.[2] How might his life have evolved had he been able to continue his education at college or the Inns of Court? The question is moot. Whether from lack of money or for some less obvious reason, he eventually had to withdraw from school—and this time no patron intervened. For a while he took up bricklaying, but detested it. Later he served with the army in the Low Countries, where (he claimed) he had killed a man. Back in England, he married Anne Lewis, started a family, and then—perhaps from financial need—drifted into involvement with the burgeoning English theater. At first an actor, he was soon able to put his education to practical use writing plays for the London stage. But he could never have been content as a popular dramatist merely. It would be more dignified—and more profitable—if his writing could attract the support of wealthy aristocrats. His first known contacts with important people, and his earliest preserved poems to them, date from this time.[3]

Over the next thirty years Jonson became perhaps the most spectacularly successful patronage poet of his era. House-guest of well-connected nobles, perennial author of holiday masques, recipient of royal grants of money and sack: he had become by middle age a fixture at the Jacobean court. He achieved the kind of fame and influence that always eluded Spenser, and although his fortunes diminished in his final years, at his death a parade of nobles escorted him to the grave. Many of his best poems were addressed to patrons, and many more deal explicitly with patronage as a theme. During the course of his long career he met many of the typical challenges and fulfilled most of the common functions of the patronage poet. His work represents, to an unsuspected extent, a repertoire of responses to patronage pressures and influences. Yet discussion of the impact of patronage on his writing has rarely been as complicated or extensive as the impact itself.

For this his success is partly responsible. If any Jacobean poet benefited from patronage, he did. Compared to others (Donne, for instance) his rise was meteoric and his status secure. Year after year he won lucrative commissions to write masques for James's court, so that in time his prosperity became almost its own best guarantee. Aspiring courtiers who noted his favor with the King employed him to help win or maintain similar status for themselves. And if his writing could enhance the prestige of one aristocrat, he was likely to win the attention and encouragement of others. The more he became known and regarded at court, the more likely he was to continue flourishing there. His experience with patronage can thus seem at first unproblematic—hence uninteresting and comparatively unimportant.

But this account of his career is defectively simple. It substitutes the long view of literary history for Jonson's day-to-day *lived* experience. Looking back on his life from a distance of several centuries, it is much easier for us than it ever was for him to take his literary and social success for granted. Historical hindsight imposes a shape and thus a seeming inevitability on his career—an inevitability of which *he* was inevitably ignorant. His early years seem to have impressed on him how uncertain and unpredictable life could be—the extent to which good fortune and status could depend on chancy contingencies or luck. And his later experience as a competitor for patronage only reinforced that lesson. He sought patronage for the same reasons others did—to enhance his social and financial security—but he had the extra motive of winning back some of the status and self-esteem his father's death and his mother's remarriage had denied him.

Jonson's struggle for social acceptance was thus more than pragmatically important; it was psychologically imperative. It was waged, moreover, in the face of recurrent, sometimes rancorous competition. Even a short list of his competitors—men he seems to have threatened or felt threatened by—reads like a Who's Who of Jacobean letters: Alexander, Brome, Chapman, Daniel, Day, Dekker, Jones, Marston, Overbury, and (most conjectural and controversial of all) Shakespeare. Not all these men directly competed with him for patronage, but his relations with none of them can be entirely separated from patronage concerns. Nor were all his challengers themselves historically important: some rate footnotes only for having quarreled with him, while the names of others—some of those he attacks in his *Epigrammes*, for instance— cannot be recovered. Yet the impact of such competition was immense, and no assessment of him as a patronage poet can afford to ignore it. His patronage works include not only those addressed to patrons, but those directed against his rivals for their attention.

Even if Jonson had had no competitors to worry about, his position as a patronage poet would still not have been entirely secure. Although more profitable and respectable than writing for the stage, patronage dependency was dependency nonetheless, and carried its own hazards. Indeed, in certain respects the transition from the stage to the court could leave a poet more exposed to uncertainties and anxieties than before. A play might fail in the theater because it did not please, but a poet might fail at court if his personality were unpleasant. And even the theater was in many ways simply another arena for patronage competition.[4] Because the patronage system during this period was tied so intimately to the predilections and characteristics of individual patrons, it lacked many of the checks and balances, the institutional safeguards, typical of the more impersonal patronage practiced, for instance, by private foundations and government endowments in twentieth-century democracies. At any time, for any reason, a patron could take offense, lose interest, lose influence, or die. A poet could win the favor of a noble lady along with the jealousy of her husband. He could anger a patron by angering the patron's friend, while words innocently meant could easily be misinterpreted and held against him. He could be used by an aristocrat while the aristocrat lived, then abused by the man's enemies when the patron died. These are not fanciful suppositions—all happened to Jonson at one time or another, and in most cases more than once. Poetry was never as important to patrons as to poets, nor was the poet's actual social position ever as exalted as poets wished. Unlike suitors with political or economic benefits to confer, poets had relatively less to offer and were thus relatively less secure. Even success, if it came, could breed anxieties of its own. The more patrons accepted Jonson, the more his dependence on them grew and thus the more their possible rejection would have meant, financially and psychologically. By the closing years of James's reign, no one was more aware than Jonson himself of how unusual his position was: this was reason enough both to doubt its security and to fight to maintain it.

These twin sources of anxiety—the inherently unstable nature of the relationship between poet and patron, and the inevitable fact of continuous competition for patronage support—arguably had a profound, even determining influence on his life and art. Coupled with the uncertainties of his early years, such anxieties must have affected in minute fashion how he thought about, executed, and presented each of his works. Of course, almost all writers will, with different degrees of self-consciousness, need to anticipate possible audience reactions. For the patronage poet, however—and for Jonson, in particular—such considerations must have been far more important than we can easily appreciate today. For him, each work was quite literally a calculated risk; he could never confidently predict how superiors or competitors might react to it, yet he knew that their reactions could fundamentally determine his future. Thus, his work was invested with an immense amount of psychic energy and tension; a patronage perspective on those works can help return some of that energy to us.

Yet the idea of Jonson as a fundamentally anxious poet has received relatively little emphasis. Even when it has been mentioned, it has often been dealt with in such a way as to underplay its significance. To stress that the audience he was necessarily most responsive to was comprised primarily of patrons and potential patrons, of competitors and potential competitors; to argue that when he wrote, distributed, or printed a work he had to take the possible reactions of these readers into account— such an emphasis might seem to compromise the image he presents of himself as a poet fundamentally secure, self-confident, and independent of social pressures. And to compromise that image might seem to undermine his importance. Many of Jonson's readers, influenced by Romantic assumptions of poetry as self-expression, frequently express a mild contempt for any poem that suggests too clearly its concern with patronage; for these readers his "begging" poems, or the official verse he churned out under Charles, make an embarrassing coda to the apparent independence of his earlier career. At the same time, they tend to be embarrassed by his personal feuds. Both reactions implicitly acknowledge a fact he himself could hardly ignore: that his acceptance depended (and often *still* depends) very much on the right kind of *self-*presentation.

The image Jonson presents of himself is often highly attractive, and much of the best modern criticism has been devoted to explicating its intricacies. Bluff Ben the plain speaker, disinterested champion of virtue, custodian of traditional values, advocate and learned patriarch of English classicism, righteous counselor to king and court, friend to Donne and Selden, jovial headmaster at the Mermaid Tavern, father to a numerous Tribe: these are only its most familiar and lovable facets. It is easy to see how this image would have been useful to him, and also why it would appeal to modern readers. To the extent that it continues William Gifford's reaction against the image of Jonson as Shakespeare's malignant antagonist, it is not only more charitable but also closer to the truth. And to the extent that it undercuts notions of Jonson as (in George Parfitt's colorful phrase) a male "whore to the Stuart court," its appeal is understandable. Neither of these negative views does justice to the real complexity of his position.[5]

At the same time, we need to resist the understandable temptation to take him entirely on his own terms, to accept the moral categories he proposes and use them to frame our discussion of his work. When in the *Epigrammes* he skewers an unnamed satiric butt by branding him corrupt and venal, we can perhaps regard this simply as evidence of his concern for society's moral health. When, however, he makes similar charges against Inigo Jones—an artist we know and value—or when Chapman accuses Jonson of the same crimes, the situation suddenly turns murky. As long as Jonson's victims are anonymous, as long as they seem historically "unimportant," as long as they have left no rebuttals, or as long as the attack's circumstances remain unclear, it is easy to accept his account with a clear conscience. But when the antagonist's identity *is* known, or when he is clearly Jonson's rival, or when the moral issues are less clear-cut because the circumstances are more available and more complicating, our instinct simply to side with Jonson is harder to justify.

Our standard ways of dealing with his rivalries—glossing over them with a sense of embarrassed regret for all parties involved, explaining them as chiefly due to intellectual differences, minimizing their importance by stressing their conventional aspects—have the effect, if not the intent, of "transcendentalizing" him and his art, of underemphasizing the powerful passions at the heart of these quarrels. Criticism cannot (and fortunately need not) decide whether Jonson was right about the allegedly whorish "court pucell" or whether she was right about him; whether he was right about Jones's character or whether Chapman was right about Jonson's. But we must find ways to deal with the competitive energies such quarrels evoked.[6]

Yet our standard concepts of poetry—whether we like to think of it as didactic instruction, personal expression, the congealed spirit of its culture or age, or the free play of signifiers—have offered little room for thinking of it in terms of self-promotion and individual advantage. Until recently, the idea seemed a bit distasteful, for however "sophisticated" or "critical" or "distanced" our attitudes toward other conventional verities, the urge to enshrine the poet as a creative culture-hero, somehow set apart from and above ambition, remained strong. Nurtured over the centuries by poets themselves, this urge still exercises an understandable appeal for many readers as well. It helps account for the fact that some discussions of poetic anxiety tend to focus less on the poet's relations with contemporary competitors than on mental wrestlings with intellectual forebears.[7] It partly explains why studies of poets and politics so frequently concentrate on their subjects' ideological commitments, or on major shifts of historical thought, rather than on the day-to-day power relations that consume so much of the energy and attention of so many ordinary people. (This tendency is especially puzzling in view of the fact that what might be called "micropolitics"—the power relations between people in everyday life—continue no matter what particular macropolitical or ideological system a culture embraces.) In Jonson's case, the urge to idealize poets makes sense of the tendency to present his quarrel with Jones as chiefly an aesthetic disagreement, and in almost every case it has led to an emphasis on ideas in and of themselves while neglecting their tactical serviceability—the ways people use ideas against or direct them toward each other, and why. Of course, to reduce human activity *merely* to power relations, to a concern with social prestige or self-esteem, would be false; but (as recent trends in criticism imply) the power dimension must become part of any total explanation.

Any behavior (no matter how "genuine" the actor's commitment) necessarily involves a tactical element. Each of us must compete to a greater or lesser extent with others offering attractive, persuasive, or convincing self-presentations. The competitive context ensures that these presentations will also function as self-promotions, although individuals themselves will usually have little incentive to think of their presentations in such terms.[8] Ironically, it is usually the actor's rival—himself, of course, also an actor—who will be most alert to the tactical features and effectiveness of the other's presentation. Perceived threat hones sensitivity, and competitors are more likely to feel threatened by another's ingratiatory tactics than are the tactics' targets, since such tactics implicitly affirm a superior's power.[9] But a rival's evaluation of his competitor's motives is likely to be no more completely reliable than the actor's own assessment, for while the rival will tend to see the actor's behavior in terms of selfish advantage and thus ascribe it to "base" motives, the actor himself will tend to think of it in terms of larger, "impersonal" standards. Thus Jonson's rivals depict him as proudly ambitious, while he sees himself as an exemplar of virtue.[10]

Neither the actor's nor the rival's assessment is wholly trustworthy, although both may contain elements of truth. The actor may indeed act to advance some larger purpose, but by doing so he also advances a particular positive self-image. Even if he intends to act selflessly, he inevitably presents the positive *image* of someone intent on acting in a selfless way. Every social act is inescapably part of one's social *acting* or public performance. Rivals will rightly notice its tactical advantages, how it enhances the actor's power, but there is no necessary reason to accept their ascription of it to "base" motives. Yet, by the same token, we must also be wary of completely accepting the actor's own account. The status of his behavior as one term of a power relationship is, however, an objective fact that can be described neutrally, with no need for moral evaluation of anyone involved.

This neutral approach lends itself well to a consideration of Jonson's relations with his patrons, where we must resist the temptation to take his own assessments for granted. His remarks to Drummond, that he esteemed no man for the name of a Lord, and that he would not flatter though he saw Death (H&S 1:141), have an appeal that is hard to resist. Our reluctance to consider Jonson as a flatterer can sometimes lead to an almost compulsive insistence on his moral independence, and in some cases he can even be depicted as an heroic challenger of authority. As the ensuing survey of his life and works will suggest, however, the evidence for this interpretation of his behavior is not as strong as has sometimes been suggested.[11]

Jonson seems usually to have been careful to avoid offense. In his relations with superiors, he seems less often to have been an accuser than the accused, a fact that would tend to make his dealings with them even more anxious. This is not to suggest that he was simply their tool, nor is it meant to paint a negative moral portrait. Both the view that emphasizes his independence and the view that sees him as a toady tend to overlook the true complexity of his position. Both seem concerned to depict him in some moral light; both imply assumptions about the kind of independence he *should* have exercised and thus ideals of behavior he either exemplified or failed to attain. Both tend to obscure the extent to which he necessarily served *himself*—the extent to which his works can be viewed in terms of personal strategy and tactics. Of course, emphasizing power relations cannot explain *every-thing* about his writing, and indeed, once we begin to think of literary works as instances of behavior, their implications can come to seem as complex—sometimes even as apparently contradictory—as human beings themselves. Emphasizing the strategic significance and aspects of Jonson's works is simply one approach worth pursuing further—one that can perhaps even prove more neutral, more objective, than some others because it requires us neither to promote the poet nor to denigrate him. Instead, it is an approach that sees power as an inevitable and inherently fascinating aspect of human relations.

Yet such an approach to Jonson's works is likely to seem unsavory. The poet as self-discoverer, as self-presenter, as maker and wearer of masks—these are exciting, attractive ideas. They appeal to a benign humanistic sense of man's protean possibilities and essential independence. But the poet as self-promoter (not simply a promoter of ideals he happens to embody, but a man constrained yet driven by the personal need to compete): about this there is something almost ugly. It seems to raise again the old issue of poetic sincerity—the idea that unless the poet speaks from his heart, his verse is somehow suspect or flawed. This idea is easier to belittle than to abandon. Even the view of the poet as masquer—as one who explores and tries on different identities— rarely assumes that his adoption of different roles may reflect a need or desire for power. Assuming such a need might seem to entail also assuming a view of him as cold, calculating, and cynically manipulative—in which case his power to shift identities might seem less a tribute to human freedom than a means of undermining it.[12]

There is, however, no need to associate poetic self-promotion—or indeed self-promotion of any kind—with conscious deception or cynical calculation. Other resources being equal, the best competitor in any power game is likely to be the person least conscious of the game as such, the one most sincerely committed to (and involved in) his role. His performance is likely to convince others precisely when it convinces himself; his absorption in the role gives him an advantage over the less committed, even though increasing his power may be the furthest thing from his mind. The analyst of power relations must be careful not to ascribe to the actor the analyst's own awareness of the tactical advantages of different self-presentations. The actor may or may not be aware (there are strong incentives to suppress or disguise such awareness), and if he is aware, the degree of his self-consciousness may vary. If the image he presents reflects his own self-image, then his need to have it accepted—thus his need to accept it himself and to promote most effectively its acceptance by others—becomes all the greater. And it is with the tactics he uses to promote that acceptance that the analyst (or critic) must be concerned.[13]

Even those works in which Jonson seems least concerned with impressing patrons cannot be entirely divorced from patronage ambitions.

Whether writing "love" poetry or poems to colleagues, whether celebrating God or lamenting some personal loss, whether writing masques for the court or plays for the public theaters, he could never forget that any work—especially if it were printed or acted—might become widely known by those capable of furthering or retarding his career. Even his poems on friends—justly admired for their apparently forthright plainness—cannot be entirely separated from patronage concerns. Although acceptance by wits and literary coteries was obviously important (both for self-esteem and because such allies heightened chances of patronage success), their acceptance alone could not ensure the security of his career and status. For Jonson the crucial audience consisted of patrons, actual and potential; but in addressing them he also had to consider the reactions of present and possible rivals. Thus a patronage perspective concretizes any approach to his works that emphasizes the "audience" or "reader."

Anxiety about patrons and rivals hardly explains everything about Jonson as a patronage poet; carefully examining his career will show just how manifold his response to his role could be. But such anxiety should neither be overlooked nor underestimated; even when not openly acknowledged, it seems to have helped shape and condition his writings. Usually the two strands of pressure are inseparable, an assertion neatly illustrated by one of his earliest datable poems, the "Epistle to Elizabeth Countesse of Rutland" (*For.* 12). Examining the poem provides an insight into his career at the crucial point when he was attempting to make the transition from writer of popular plays to genuine "poet" with an appeal to more sophisticated tastes.[14] And it also provides an opportunity to begin examining the various devices and strategies he used in his dealings with patrons and rivals.

Indeed, in many ways the Rutland "Epistle" is an exceptionally representative example of Jonson's patronage poetry. Partly because of its length and partly because of the complicated circumstances from which it was born, it incorporates a surprising number of the tactics and techniques he used most frequently in appealing to patrons. Its precise balance of deference and self-assertion creates an intriguing complexity of nuance and tone. The "Epistle" shows Jonson asserting his distance from competitive anxiety and ambition in order to make himself a more effective competitor, even as it betrays evidence of the very anxiety and ambition he claims to disdain. It shows him using humor to suggest his freedom from fear and thus enhance his attractiveness and power, and it also indicates how appeals to objective religious ideals could promote his subjective, competitive interests. Reflecting his own insecurity, the "Epistle" exhibits some of the ways—and some of the reasons why—he played up to, played on, and played with his superiors' insecurities.

Condemning distrust, it nonetheless fosters it. It demonstrates how technical skill and poetic virtuosity could contribute to a writer's power, and how, by allying himself with classical precedent, a poet could both sanction his poems and protect them. It also raises interesting questions about why and to what extent a patronage poet might prove a poetic innovator. And it indicates how a poet, unlike some other artists dependent on patronage, could use his work to explicate its own value and achievement.

The Rutland "Epistle" is characteristic for other reasons, as well. In it, Jonson uses his ostensible lack of power to create a powerful image; he emphasizes his supposed isolation to underscore his independence *and* dependability. He puts his own ego and character at center stage, even while attempting to moderate and counteract the impression of egotism this threatens to convey. He praises his patrons' virtue to pressure them, using compliment not simply to teach but to intimidate. He emphasizes the values he and they ostensibly share, but also uses those values to threaten their reputation and social credit. He claims victim status, but partly to enhance his power. Depicting himself as the prey of envious malcontents, he thereby asserts his own importance and prestige. In these and other ways, the "Epistle" reveals not only his poetic skills but also his competitive resourcefulness. For him, both talents necessarily went hand in hand.

Elizabeth Sidney, daughter of Sir Philip (and, according to Jonson, "nothing inferior" to her father in poetry [H&S 1:138]), had become Countess of Rutland sometime early in 1599. Her husband Roger Manners, the fifth Earl, was young, impetuous, widely-traveled, and well-connected.[15] In the years immediately before and after their marriage he was one of the kingdom's wealthiest men, but also one of its biggest spenders. By one reckoning, at least, his "rate of expenditure was almost certainly higher than that of any other private individual in the country, exceeded only by that of one or two of the great courtiers and officials dependent on royal favors for their support."[16] Jonson was well aware of the size of the Rutland fortune, as his tactful reference to it in the poem suggests. As her father's daughter, the new Countess could be expected to appreciate the value of poetry; as her husband's wife, she was well placed to express that appreciation tangibly. One of the fascinations of the epistle—presented as a gift on New Year's Day, 1600—is to observe how subtly and skillfully Jonson distances himself from economic motives, all the while inviting financial reciprocation.

Wealth, in fact—its use and abuse—provides the keynote to the poem's long, seemingly-sprawling, but tightly-controlled opening sentence:

Madame,
Whil'st that, for which, all vertue now is sold,
   And almost every vice, almightie gold,
That which, to boote with hell, is thought worth heaven,
   And, for it, life, conscience, yea, soules are given,
Toyles, by grave custome, up and downe the court,
   To every squire, or groome, that will report
Well, or ill, onely, all the following yeere,
   Just to the waight their this dayes-presents beare;
While it makes huishers serviceable men,
   And some one apteth to be trusted, then,
Though never after; whiles it gaynes the voyce
   Of some grand peere, whose ayre doth make rejoyce
The foole that gave it; who will want, and weepe,
   When his proud patrons favours are asleepe;
While thus it buyes great grace, and hunts poore fame;
   Runs betweene man, and man; 'tweene dame, and dame;
Solders crackt friendship; makes love last a day;
   Or perhaps lesse: whil'st gold beares all this sway,
I, that have none (to send you) send you verse.

$$(1-19)^{17}$$

The accomplishment of this passage is easy to underestimate: more than simply satirical, it blends and balances a number of tones and attitudes, suggesting the poet's intimate familiarity with the techniques of self-promotion while asserting his distance from them. Combining moral abstraction and concrete detail, it communicates a vivid sense of the frantic competition for patronage at the Elizabethan court, and in the very texture and movement of the verse underscores the anxious uncertainty that competition engendered. By cleaning up and smoothing over its halting, spasmodic punctuation, modernized editions rob the passage of much of its force, while a critical tendency to emphasize its harshness overlooks its countervailing humor and thus simplifies our understanding of how it both presents and promotes the poet.[18] Jonson does more than merely attack the courtiers' obsession with patronage, reputation, and gold; he makes fun of it, claims implicitly to be above it, and thereby obscures his own necessarily similar concerns. By seeming to demonstrate an ability to stand back and describe such courtly competitiveness with a mixture of disgust and wry detachment, he presents a more attractive—in part because more potent—self-image, paradoxically enhancing his own competitive position.[19] Although he claims to disdain the struggle he depicts, his poem functions partly as a weapon in it.

The first two lines exemplify the inspired craftsmanship of the opening passage and of the work as a whole. "Whil'st that" initiates a dependent clause, which the reader has no reason to expect will last as long as it does, and which therefore becomes more and more audaciously effective with each added line. Yet this technique is only the most obvious instance of how Jonson manipulates the reader's movement through the poem. "Whil'st that, for which, all vertue now is sold" implies the seriousness of the corruption he is about to describe, as well as his own moral probity and ethical concern; yet the very next clause— "And almost every vice"—suggests how skillfully he can modulate his tone, how effectively he can balance acerbic criticism with understated humor. When he reveals the target of his criticism, "almightie gold," his daring pun at once depicts the competing courtiers as idolators, anticipates the religious language of the ensuing couplet, and helps prepare for the ironic conclusion of the whole opening passage.

The punning, however, is less important than the way the poem's very syntax reenacts the anxious uncertainty and distrust the competition for patronage both generates and manifests. Gold "Toyles, by grave custome, up and downe the court"—a phrase that suggests both actual physical movement and an entire social hierarchy infected with avarice. Hopeful clients dish out payments "To every squire, or groome, that will report / Well, or ill, onely, all the following yeere, / Just to the waight their this dayes-presents beare." By inserting commas after "well" and "ill" and then by inserting the apparently superfluous "onely," Jonson achieves a masterful ambiguity. Will the squires and grooms report well of those who bribe them, or ill? The bribers cannot really be sure: when self-interested ambition replaces genuine trust and reciprocity, social relations are calculated with an eye to private advantage merely. Since neither client, intermediary, nor patron has any but his own interests at heart, real security becomes practically impossible. Indeed, Jonson's line admits another (but complementary) interpretation: it may suggest that clients bribe intermediaries to report well of them but ill of their rivals. In either case, Jonson manages to communicate convincingly in the verse itself the fitful insecurity patronage relations could involve.

He underlines this insecurity twice again before the passage concludes—first, when, punning on the adjective, he remarks that gold "makes huishers serviceable men, / And some one apteth to be trusted, then,"—and now the other shoe drops—"Though never after;" (9–11) and second, when he tells the Countess that money "makes love last a day"—the line ends with a semi-colon; then the thought resumes: "Or perhaps lesse" (17–18). He thus demonstrates his technical virtuosity while implying that he himself is so distant from frantic anxiety that he feels able to mock it. Indeed, although he emphasizes the uncertainty of the client faced with unreliable intermediaries and patrons, part of his "strategy" is to expose the "real" motives and practices of most of those scrambling for patronage. He turns a spotlight on the swarming under-side of the Elizabethan social system, and part of the effect of this scrutiny must be to make the young Countess and her peers both aware and wary of the machinations of most of those seeking their support. Paradoxically, in a poem that satirizes competitive distrust, it is partly to Jonson's advantage to make his own patrons as uncertain as possible about the intentions and behavior of potential rivals. Despite its tone of ethical aloofness, his poem cannot really stand above the fray it mocks; however "genuine" and "sincere," its tone functions most effectively as a tactic in the struggle it disdains.

Jonson is aided by the fact that a poem, unlike other patronage gifts or works of art, can literally interpret its own worth—in part by devaluing the worth of its competition. The fact that he has (or claims to have) no influential intermediary, for instance, comes to seem a positive advan-tage, since intermediaries are depicted as far from trustworthy. The mere fact that their favor can be bought suggests the worthlessness of their opinions, while their exploitation of clients implies their ability to deceive superiors as well. Jonson's directness becomes in this context, then, not indelicate arrogance but testimony to his forthright honesty. Unlike other clients, who work furtively behind the scenes to influence the opinions of patrons by bribing intermediaries, he is willing to make his plea public.

That is why the technique of the long suspended sentence, all leading up to the emphatic stress on his act of giving, is such a brilliant tactic. The metrically-emphasized "I," on which all the preceding clauses depend, gives the passage its long-postponed semantic and syntactical stability. It is as if Jonson means to contrast his own solidity with the flux the poem so effectively mimics. The tactic allows him to imply, rather than assert, his own opposition to everything just described, and it paradoxically turns his lack of gold into a strong recommendation both of his character and of the gift he presents. At the same time, it allows him to suggest his own need in a way that seems less self-serving than complimentary. Just as he distinguishes himself from other clients, so he invites the Countess to distinguish herself from patrons obsessed with gold. The poem's claim that she is unlike other patrons can only be validated by her proper reaction. There is a sense, in fact, in which Jonson's position is analogous to that of the squires or grooms who accept money for favorable reports; but his poem's praise can only be effective if the Countess responds as he expects.[20]

Indeed, the means Jonson uses to manipulate the Countess is one of the poem's most interesting aspects. At one point, for instance, he combines explicit disdain for gold—"this drosse" (27)—with clever insinuations that gold would be a proper reciprocation for his gift. His reference to "noble ignorants" who over-value gold (28) follows hard upon an earlier reference to its power to give "peasants birth" (26). In the latter case he distances himself from those whose social standing depends on distributing gold to superiors; attacking them, the former bricklayer asserts his own claim to gentility and respect. Similarly, by attacking "noble ignorants," he demonstrates his power to ridicule anyone, the Countess potentially included. The ideal of devaluing gold can thus ironically be seen partly as a strategy for extracting it from her.

By claiming to *know* his offering will win the Countess's "grace" (30), Jonson compliments her virtue while also making it even more difficult for her to respond differently. His certainty here contrasts with the uncertainty earlier ascribed to other patronage relationships, but it also pressures her to respond appropriately. The word "grace" suggests that her response will be freely undertaken, and thus underplays the coerciveness of Jonson's rhetoric; but it also looks back to the poem's earlier use of religious language, soft-pedaling any sense that he expects a monetary response and allowing him to compliment her by comparing their relation to that between a religious devotee and his deity. He thus reverses the earlier image of other suitors idolatrously serving gold.

Religious language continues in lines 31–34, when Jonson exclaims what a sin it would be against Sidney's spirit to think that the Countess did not inherit his love of poetry. It is one of the poem's most masterful passages. The apparent exclamation, "what a sinne," momentarily invites the Countess to imagine herself as the sinner; the full clause seems naturally to call for a continuation such as, "would it be if you did not inherit . . . ." But the clause that does follow shifts the burden of sin to an unnamed someone who could even "thinke" this about her. For an instant, then, Jonson is able to intimidate the Countess very subtly, conjuring up the memory of her father and thereby suggesting what *he* would do, in the process complimenting both Sidney and the Countess herself, but only insofar as she lives up to his example. Moreover, by implying that she has inherited her father's love of the muses (although that issue is, in fact, still undecided), he provides further justification for addressing her: her putative devotion means that she has also inherited (and merited) the attention of such poets as himself.

This same kind of equivocation is apparent when Jonson tells the Countess that her father's "skill / Almost you have, or may have, when you will" (33–34). "Almost" is the key word: by including it, he moderates his praise of her only to enhance his praise of her father, thereby protecting himself from charges of flattery while also suggesting that his opinion of her skill is thoughtfully weighed and thus of greater worth. In fact, in his empirical study of ingratiatory behavior, Edward Jones found that compliments were more effective when comparative rather than absolute; the ingratiator thus establishes his own high standards, while the person he seeks to influence accepts the compliment as hard-won.[21] Paradoxically, those poems in which Jonson seems to adopt a somewhat independent line toward his patrons may have been especially effective in winning their support. Since patrons could never be sure of a client's sincerity, clients who risked affronting them to express "genuine" opinions may have competed more effectively.

Effective for different reasons is Jonson's ensuing comment that in poetic skill "wise *Nature* you a dowrie gave, / Worth an estate, treble to that you have" (35–36). This statement reiterates his position that riches alone are relatively worthless, obliquely reminds the Countess (and others) of her ability to be generous, and yet also functions as a compliment: the greater one imagines her wealth to be, the greater one's assessment of her poetic skill. Moreover, by implying that she herself has received gifts from Nature, he invites her to prove similarly generous. Such equivocation runs throughout the poem. When he encourages her to "thinke what store / The world hath seene" of those who naively trusted in beauty, blood, or riches (38–39), the imperative warns her not to make the same mistake. Yet since he has already credited her with an interest in poetry, the invitation to "thinke" also calls attention to the values they ostensibly share. Supposedly, she has no need to learn the lesson the poem teaches. Instead, he seemingly invites her to review what she already knows. In one sense, the ensuing passage about poetry's value (41ff.) thus functions simply as a reminder—in theory, at least, superfluous; but, in another sense, it functions more ominously to warn her.

There is no need to rehearse the extended justification of poetry that Jonson now offers; all the arguments would have been familiar even if the Countess had read no more widely than her father's own *Apologie*. It is impossible to say, of course, whether Jonson intended her to notice any such similarity, especially since the ideas expressed both in his poem and in Sidney's treatise are almost anonymously conventional. His claims for poetry here are thus safely decorous; they raise no uncomfortable or embarrassing questions about the tact of praising one's own talents and skill. But the poem's conclusion is more interesting; there the mastery of tone seems to falter momentarily under the pressure of competition, although the old assurance is finally recovered. But the poet's small miscalculation is significant: it spotlights the anxieties that condition the whole poem, illustrates the risks involved in the strategy the poem pursues, but suggests through contrast Jonson's generally successful avoidance of such mistakes elsewhere in his work.

This final portion of the poem begins well enough. Jonson concludes a catalogue of historical and mythical figures by asserting that they have been memorialized by no other than "*Poets*, rapt with rage divine," and then turns to the Countess, continuing, "And such, or my hopes faile, shall make you shine. / You, and that other starre, that purest light, / Of all Lucina's traine; Lucy the bright" (64–66). The inclusion of Lucy, Countess of Bedford, in a poem addressed to the Countess of Rutland is a curiosity to be discussed presently; for the moment, it is worth concentrating instead on the immediately following lines:

> Who, though shee have a better verser got,
> (Or, *Poet*, in the court account) then I,
>   And, who doth me (though I not him) envy,
> Yet, for the timely favours shee hath done,
>   To my lesse sanguine *Muse*, wherein she'hath wonne
> My gratefull soule, the subject of her powers,
>   I have already us'd some happy houres,
> To her remembrance; which when time shall bring
>   To curious light, the notes, I then shall sing,
> Will prove old Orpheus act no tale to be:
>   For I shall move stocks, stones, no less than he.
>
>   (68–78)

The rival poet's identity must have been clear enough to all involved; unfortunately, for that very reason it has been lost to us. Although Jonson may have been referring to Samuel Daniel, most scholars agree that the rival was probably Michael Drayton, with whom he was still uncomfortable almost thirty years after the Rutland poem was written.[22] Knowing precisely to whom he alludes, however, is less important than emphasizing the significance of such rivalries in his works generally as well as the ways the works themselves confront the challenges such rivalries presented.

In claiming to hope, for instance, that "onely *Poets*, rapt with rage divine" will memorialize the Countesses, Jonson invites us to think of him as precisely such a poet, while at the same time suggesting that he would not resent—would indeed welcome—talented competition. "Competition," in fact, hardly describes the kind of cooperation he magnanimously seems to envision.[23] This maneuver allows him to deny envying his rival; instead his disdain ostensibly springs from a low opinion of the rival's verse and from a concern that his patrons be worthily celebrated. But is this strategy entirely successful?

Frequently in the Renaissance a writer's claim to be envied asserts and advertises his importance. Jonson had much more to fear from simple indifference than from competitors' hostility, since the jealousy of rivals was a clear measure of his social significance and poetic skill.

Other writers would have little reason to be bothered by—or to bother with—a poet insufficiently talented or powerful enough to threaten their own interests. Hate, paradoxically, is one of the most intensely social emotions: being hated means being paid the uncomfortable but perversely flattering tribute of serious attention.[24] Jonson's fear of envious criticism must frequently have been accompanied by the pleasure of feeling important enough to provoke it. Seeking a patron's protection from envy thus testified not only to the patron's power but to the poet's notability. Moreover, the posture of self-defense against unmerited attack was inherently attractive: it allowed the patron to view his support of the poet as ethical rather than as merely self-serving, and it allowed the poet to preempt any allegations about his own possible envy. Curiously, the more convincingly he depicted his victimization, the more effectively he might compete.[25]

Jonson's attempt to make Drayton the guilty party in the Rutland epistle fails rhetorically, however, for two reasons—each, interestingly, related to our perception of his power. His casual (literally parenthetical) accusation that his rival envies him was probably intended to suggest a lack of serious concern. But its very brevity prevents him from particularizing his claim and thus hampers his chances of winning much sympathy. Indeed, the fact that it occurs in a passage obviously concerned with loss of patronage makes his position and motives seem not only suspect but *weak*. His own denial that he envies Drayton further undermines his disinterested pose. Our earlier sense of a poet loftily above the fray begins to unravel here; the earlier sense of his potency, security, and certainty begins to break down, and an unattractive note of desperation enters, if only for a moment. Jonson's use of first person, which had earlier suggested so effectively his integrity of voice, here reveals risks of its own—risks we might otherwise have overlooked. Paradoxically, his stumble highlights the expertness of the poem's tone elsewhere and helps us appreciate the difficult task Jonson originally set for himself.

At the same time, the stumble suggests how fully the whole poem is conditioned by the concerns that boil to the surface here. Only when the threat becomes uncomfortably immediate does Jonson falter, but the sense of such threat must have been a powerful shaping force behind every work he composed. To poets who had been trained to think of themselves as servants of society, and who recognized that the only practical way to influence society was to influence those who controlled it, much more than a loss of money was at stake in the failure to win significant patronage. Individual poems, including this one, were probably less often designed simply to solicit funds than to establish or maintain relations with powerful patrons, relations probably as important to the poet's self-conception as to his pocketbook. Being accepted and rewarded by a patron meant, at least in part, that a poet had won public, authoritative recognition of his very status *as* a poet, so that the quest for patronage became much more than a search for financial reward—although it was inescapably and undeniably that. It became, perhaps more importantly, a pursuit of self-validation. If Jonson does seem envious of his rival here, if energies seem released which even the poem's otherwise accomplished form cannot control, perhaps it is because he recognized, at a deep level, how much more than money was at risk. Erving Goffman notes that the desire for social status involves "not merely a desire for a prestigeful place but also a desire for a place close to the sacred center of the common values of society." In Jonson's society, that place was the court—a place "where reality was being performed."[26]

To emphasize the psychological importance of patronage is not to suggest that the poet was completely dominated or incapacitated by his dependency. Although the poet greatly depended on the patron for self-validation and self-esteem (especially in the face of competition), the patron to a lesser extent also depended on the poet to enhance his own reputation in the face of competition with rivals of his own. A skillful poet could take clever advantage of these concerns. Jonson's inclusion of the Countess of Bedford in his poem to the Countess of Rutland allows him, for instance, to set up a kind of quiet, understated competition between the two women to see which will prove the more deserving. If this reading seems unnecessarily complicated or even cynical, it may be worth pausing, before pursuing it further, to examine a poem (*Ep.* 84) addressed to the Countess of Bedford in which the same tactic is employed a little more obviously, although with equal skill:

> Madame, I told you late how I repented,
>   I ask'd a lord a buck, and he denyed me;
> And, ere I could aske you, I was prevented:
>   For your most noble offer had supply'd me.
> Straight went I home; and there most like a *Poet*,
>   I fancied to my selfe, what wine, what wit
> I would have spent: how every *Muse* should know it,
>   And Phoebus-selfe should be at eating it.
> O *Madame*, if your grant did thus transferre mee,
>   Make it your gift. See whither that will beare mee.
>
> (1–10)

This is, of course, a much slighter poem than the Rutland "Epistle," and its objective is more immediate, more practical, and much less important. Yet Jonson himself seems to have fancied the work: Drummond mentions it as one the poet particularly liked to quote. Simply as a work of "art," it is hard to imagine why he would have been so proud of it; but as an example of how one could skillfully manipulate a patron (itself an artful undertaking), it becomes easier to understand how a poet who valued poems in such terms could think so highly of it. Seen in this way, it is sophisticated indeed.[27]

Jonson uses the first quatrain to contrast clearly—for the Countess and for anyone else to whom he or she might show or quote the poem—the unnamed lord's niggardliness and her own spontaneous generosity. Since the works of Renaissance poets were often "published" long before they were ever actually printed and sold, manuscript circulations or readings in small groups could be far more significant in establishing a poet's reputation than merely selling copies of a printed book—especially if the intimate audience consisted of those who shaped society's tastes and values. Manuscript publication and readings also meant that a poet could control—or try to control—his work's distribution more effectively than if it were widely published in print. Proper interpretation might then depend on the context the poet established during his reading. This point becomes especially significant when considering Jonson's attacks on unnamed malefactors. Thus, although the lord is unnamed in the epigram's printed version, there is every reason to suspect that when Jonson read the poem or showed it around, his audience was informed of his target's identity.[28]

Jonson claims that while the unnamed lord had denied his specific request, the Countess granted his desire before he could even appeal to her. He puns with the initial rhyme-words, "repented" and "prevented," seeming to suggest at first that *he* has something to feel sorry about, until it emerges that the unnamed lord is at fault. Similarly, in claiming he was "prevented" from beseeching the Countess, he momentarily seems to imply that someone stopped him, until it becomes obvious that the Countess anticipated his need before he could voice it. The first pun emphasizes the lord's stinginess, the second the Countess's generosity. But Jonson not only compliments Lucy; he also reminds her of his power to affect her own reputation. Just as he probably revealed in conversation the unnamed lord's illiberality, so her failure to fulfill her grant could produce the same result. Indeed, the very poem that now compliments her would then stand as a potentially public rebuke; the clear distinction it establishes between the Countess and the lord would collapse, and she might even seem *more* culpable, since she would not simply be denying a request but reneging on a promise. The epigram thus illustrates James Tedeschi's point that moral and social norms—such as abiding by one's word—tend to be invoked by the less powerful to deal with those over them. (He also notes, however, that such norms are not *formed* by the weak, but by the strong to protect themselves from one another.) Here and elsewhere, Jonson uses norms to intimidate patrons by threatening them with a possible loss of face. By violating the very norms they depend on, they risk making themselves more vulnerable.[29]

In a sense, then, the Countess herself holds the key to how the epigram will be interpreted: depending on how she acts it will either, as presently written, speak well or ill of her. Jonson allows her to prove herself more worthy than the lord, yet the poem pressures her to seize the opportunity lest she be thought even less worthy. Explaining the poem's effect in such terms, however, risks underemphasizing how subtly the effect is achieved. It risks failing to notice how skillfully Jonson employs humorous self-deprecation—his presentation of himself as a somewhat silly, wine-guzzling poet with an over-active imagination—to minimize any overt sense of threat while making himself as lovably attractive a potential recipient as possible. He explicitly holds out the promise of public gratitude if she fulfills her grant, and his willingness to print the poem suggests that the epigram itself discharges that promise. Yet the poem reminds both the Countess and the lord of the poet's power, while also demonstrating his ability to play competing interests off against each other to enhance his own.

The sense of competition Jonson engineers in the Rutland "Epistle" is much more subtle, partly because there is no clear-cut opposition for him to exploit. The two Countesses had much in common: both were young, both were daughters of famous patrons, both moved in the same social circle, and both had husbands allied to the Earl of Essex. Undoubtedly they were friendly—otherwise it would have been sheer folly to link their names so closely. But the very factors that made them such natural allies may also have contributed to an underlying rivalry. One need not assume any Machiavellian intentions on Jonson's part to notice that by mentioning the Countess of Bedford's patronage of the "better verser," he not only implicitly criticizes her but also provides the Countess of Rutland the perfect opportunity to prove herself a more discriminating patron. At the same time, by promising to sing the Countess of Bedford in a poem on worthy ladies, he asserts his continuing loyalty despite her recent neglect, while also giving the Countess of Rutland further reason to encourage him to make her own role in such a poem at least as prominent as Lucy's. Meanwhile, his elaborate promise to celebrate the Countess of Rutland in his projected poem provides Lucy an added incentive to continue her patronage, which he seems to have felt was threatened. Referring to his future poem thus allows him to compliment both patrons while also mildly intimidating each. The sheer complexity of nuance and implication in these lines reminds one of Tedeschi's point that in power relations, one mode of influence is seldom used exclusively, even though a single tactic usually sets the tone of any given encounter. Lines like these also prove that Jonson's complimentary poems seem "inert" only when viewed primarily as poems of *statement*. When one emphasizes, on the other hand, the anxious milieu from which they were born and the apparently conflicting tendencies of deference and self-assertion they embody, their emotional and aesthetic complexity seems far more apparent.[30]

Referring to his projected poem also allows Jonson to work in one final—this time more generalized and more successful—attack on poetic rivals (79–92). His reference to the "tickling rimes" and "common places, filch'd" of other poets (87–88) perhaps functions as a more carefully veiled parting shot at the rival mentioned earlier. If so, then it also functions as another implicit warning to the Countess of Bedford, implying that while she wastes her patronage on such versers, the Countess of Rutland will be celebrated by a worthy poet. As interesting as this attack on his rivals, however, are the claims made for Jonson's own art—claims that themselves seem responsive to the pressures generated by patronage competition. The reference to his "strange *poems*" (81) suggests that he is innovating in an English context while following classical tradition—precisely the sort of assertion we might expect a patronage poet to make. His need to distinguish himself from competitors would encourage claims to innovation, but it would also prevent his innovations from becoming too idiosyncratic. Both eccentric self-expression and stale conventionality could leave one open to rivals' criticism. The trick was to innovate while also claiming the sanction of some acknowledged authority. Generic traditions often provided such a standard; observing them offered a means of protecting oneself from attack. Innovation *within* a tradition, rather than its wholesale overthrow or rejection, was likely to be fostered by the competitive milieu from which patronage poetry was born.[31]

For many Renaissance poets the best way to innovate conservatively was to revivify classical genres. In fact, only a few years before Jonson's Rutland poem, Thomas Lodge claimed to have achieved just such a feat by revivifying the verse epistle, while Jonson himself made similar claims about the epigram and other classical kinds.[32] Depicting contemporary experience and persons through a classical lens allowed a poet to pay his patrons a subtle compliment while also advertising his skill. The "strange *poems*" Jonson cites are thus not strangely unique or original—the kind of claim one might expect from a modern poet. At the same time, to protect himself against precisely the kind of charges about uninspired borrowing or plagiarism he levels against his rivals, he claims that his own poetry will be "such as flies / From braines entranc'd, and fill'd with extasies" (89–90). While this assertion sharply contrasts Jonson with other poets, it also risks seeming more than a little immodest. Indeed, the problem of using poems to proclaim one's abilities without seeming merely boastful was one almost all patronage poets faced, and Jonson's various solutions to it are often ingenious.

In an epigram to the Countess of Rutland, for instance (*Ep.* 79), he seems not only to recognize the problem but to play with it. The apparent audacity of its first line ("That *Poets* are far rarer births than kings") is immediately and wittily checked by the opening half of its second ("Your noblest father prov'd"), as Jonson turns what might have seemed egotistical self-assertion into praise not only of the lady's father but of the lady herself. In fact, he goes even further, turning his praise of her father into a humble assertion about himself (no poet, he claims, has ever equaled Sidney's accomplishment [2–4]), while also turning Sidney's lack of male children into a clever compliment to the Countess (5–9). The poem's facility, the ease with which Jonson creates problems and then undoes them, wins the admiration one might have resisted granting him had he done nothing more than simply claim it (as the first line seemed to do). Like many of his patronage poems, this one is less a string of assertions or requests than a *performance* in which the poet sets and then meets technical and semantic challenges, *demonstrating* his accomplishment while often in the very act of asserting or minimizing it, and thus illustrating a kind of *sprezzatura* that enhanced his attractiveness to possible benefactors.

In the conclusion to the Rutland "Epistle," Jonson uses some of the same tactics exploited in the epigram, turning his claim for his own poetic ability into an assertion about the Countess's father that also allows him to bring Rutland himself into the work. Poetic ecstasies, he claims, were "Moodes, which the god-like Sydney oft did prove, / And your brave friend, and mine so well did love" (91–92). The reference to Rutland's enthusiasm compliments the Earl's taste as much as Sidney's verse, and indeed there is some evidence for the claim.[33] What is more surprising, however, is the picture Jonson paints of his own relationship with Rutland, not only when he calls him his "friend" but when he continues that the Earl,

> . . . wheresoere he be, on what dear coast,
> Now thincking on you, though to England lost,
> For that firme grace he holdes in your regard,
> I, that am gratefull for him, have prepar'd
> This hasty sacrifice, wherein I reare

A vow as new, and ominous as the yeare,
Before his swift and circled race be run,
My best of wishes, may you beare a sonne.

(93–100)

When the poem was printed in the 1616 folio, these lines were omitted; in the years since its composition, Rutland had been rumored to be impotent, and the matter still occasioned humor when Jonson visited Drummond six years after the Earl's death.[34] By that time he seems to have felt justified in defaming Rutland, who had at some point developed his own contempt for versers. As Drummond records Jonson's version of events,

> Ben one day being at table with my Lady Rutland, her husband comming in, accused her that she keept table to poets, of which she wrott a letter to him which he answered   My Lord intercepted the letter, but never chalenged him.[35]

The anecdote is interesting not only as evidence of the intimacy a poet could enjoy with his patron but of the tension it could provoke. It would be useful, but unfortunately seems impossible, to determine just when Rutland adopted this attitude. Knowing this would allow us to say with more assurance whether Jonson, by calling the Earl his "friend" in the epistle's conclusion and by claiming to have written it partly to voice the Earl's own feelings, was writing with assured knowledge of the Earl's good will, or whether the lines represent an anxious attempt to placate an unsympathetic reader. In either case, the glancing reference to the poem as a "hasty sacrifice" helps call final, understated attention to its real accomplishment and skill.

The insecurity underlying this poem and the others just considered is hardly unusual in Jonson's work; indeed, it is far more common than has sometimes been admitted. It arises from uncertainties inherent not only in his own position but in the entire patronage system, which fostered in most participants a strong competitive anxiety. Whether implicit or explicit, whether between poets seeking patronage or between patrons themselves, this competition characterized the whole milieu to which Jonson's poetry necessarily responded. From one perspective, his entire career can be seen as a process of coping with its challenges. His patronage poetry is frequently complex and full of tensions, as he attempts to satisfy his own needs while adapting himself and his art to others' demands and interests (in both senses of that term). His work for patrons often seems least interesting when it is most conventionally prescribed, yet the conclusion of the Rutland epistle suggests the problems he could create by failing to adapt his strongest emotions to the exigencies of his art. Whenever he spoke in his own voice—or invited his readers to assume that he did—he took risks.

In this sense the patronage poet's role was much more "exposed," much more inherently hazardous, than that of more anonymous artists such as painters, artisans, or musicians. All the arts could be used to celebrate patrons, but literature by its very nature could do more. A poem could be used not simply to extol the interaction between writer and patron, but also to comment on their relationship, to manipulate its nature and direction. In other arts, the relation between artist and benefactor occurred mostly outside the work (however indirectly and insistently it might impinge on it). Studying the relation thus becomes mainly a problem for biography. But in many of Jonson's poems the relation continues—is negotiated—*within* the work. The epigram about the promised buck is a slight but striking example. There, as in other works, Jonson exemplifies Erving Goffman's observation that often the most successful servant is the one who seizes the initiative, who acts to set the terms (insofar as he can) of the relation with his superior.[36] The epigram suggests in a rather blatant way what seems more subtly true of numerous other patronage poems: a view of the poem as a compromise, an accommodation of egos. But precisely because this accommodation is carried out *within* or *through* the work, it becomes more than simply a matter for biography. It becomes a problem for aesthetics and criticism, a matter with definite implications for the success—and the successful understanding—of the poem *as* poem.

As a vehicle for carrying forward the writer's interaction with his patron, a poem offered definite advantages. To a much greater degree than "spontaneous" conversation or the contacts of "everyday life," its tactics or structures could be calculated or premeditated. Indeed, it is precisely a poem's studied, artful nature that makes a genuinely literary-critical approach to patronage verse possible. But because the poem *was* more stable than the fluid give-and-take of ordinary discourse, it was also in some ways more dangerous. The very ability to give a thought lasting shape and expression—which was one of the poet's chief claims to importance—meant that a tactical mistake in a poem would be far from easy to correct or forget. A conversational slip might be erased in the very next moment by a smile, a glance, an explanatory phrase. But a blunder committed to paper was both easier to recollect and harder to revoke. Jonson's enemies often mocked lines he had written just months previously or many years before.

Paradoxically, the poem's very effectiveness as an instrument for self-promotion meant that the writer who used it most obviously for that purpose was perhaps least likely to succeed. Not only did he make himself an easier target for antagonists; he was also more likely to arouse the suspicions or disdain of the person addressed. Thus, studying patronage poetry often means studying strategies of indirection and implication. This is less true—there is less reason for it to be true—of poems aimed at rivals. There Jonson can afford to speak more bluntly. Even in those poems, however, he was writing for a larger audience than any particular antagonist. Just as, when addressing a patron, he had constantly to be aware of possible rivals and rivalries, so in attacking an enemy he could never forget the image he presented to a wider world.

The micropolitical implications of Jonson's poetry can be glimpsed even—or perhaps especially—in those works where they seem least obvious or which seem to resist them most strongly, such as the lovely epitaph "On My First Sonne" (*Ep.* 45). Perhaps no other poem by Jonson is more universally admired, and perhaps no other seems so remote from issues of power, self-promotion, and patronage. Here, as in few other works, Jonson seems to speak most simply, most directly, most obviously from the heart, with the least degree of deliberate self-consciousness:

> Farewell, thou child of my right hand, and joy;
>   My sinne was too much hope of thee, lov'd boy,
> Seven yeeres tho'wert lent to me, and I thee pay,
>   Exacted by thy fate, on the just day.
> O, could I loose all father, now. For why
>   Will man lament the state he should envie?
> To have so soone scap'd worlds, and fleshes rage,
>   And, if no other miserie, yet age?
> Rest in soft peace, and, ask'd, say here doth lye
>   Ben. Jonson his best piece of *poetrie*.
> For whose sake, hence-forth, all his vowes be such,
>   As what he loves may never like too much.
>
> (1–12)

This is one of Jonson's most powerful poems precisely because it seems least obsessed with power. It presents one of the most attractive and irresistible images of him precisely by seeming unconcerned with self-presentation. Its practical, social effectiveness is enhanced by our sense of being privileged to a very private moment, our sense that here Jonson is relatively unconcerned with achieving a social effect. Although an epitaph does have, by its very nature, a social purpose, and although it does reflect the larger values of Jonson's society, this poem is so powerful precisely because its public, didactic function does not seem primary. Its peculiar impact allows us to ascertain more clearly the different kinds of effectiveness—or, as in the conclusion of the

Rutland epistle, the failures to be effective—evident in Jonson's other poems.

Set among the satiric epigrams and poems of praise, the epitaph on Jonson's son lends his voice a tone of sincerity and powerful feeling. It expresses a deep yet delicate love that enhances the intensity and credibility both of the courtly compliments and of the cynical satires that surround it. Whereas Jonson can sometimes seem most interested in praising the powerful, in commending those best positioned to help him, this poem and his other epitaphs, especially the ones on children, display his commitment to values higher than power alone. But for that reason they promote his pragmatic appeal and social status. Ironically, this poem confessing his deeply-felt lack of power is one of his most powerful in every sense. Rooted in a profoundly personal loss, its effectiveness nonetheless depends on its ability to make us share that deprivation, to empathize and identify with the poet to an extent never quite aroused by the satires or complimentary works. Although in the epitaph Jonson speaks most intensely and intensively for himself, he also voices common feelings and fears. Our sympathy can never be completely selfless, and indeed its force is magnified by our realization that all people will suffer losses similar to Jonson's. The threat to his power voiced so eloquently here is a threat anyone can take to heart.

Jonson exposes himself in the epitaph in a fashion rare in his works; he betrays an impotence he usually seeks to disguise. When powerlessness does sometimes flare out in his poems (as in the "Ode to Himselfe," the "Tribe of Ben" epistle, or the satires on Inigo Jones), our reaction is often less likely to be sympathy than embarrassment. In those poems the sense of impotence can seem unattractive, and Jonson's attempts to deny it or put a good face on it can seem self-serving or strained. Those poems express powerlessness but reflect the poet's personal ambition, whereas the epitaph on his son promotes his power by seeming to transcend any interest in it. In the conclusion to the Rutland epistle, Jonson's sense of threat had marred the work's self-confident tone; in the epitaph, however, the threat and the sense of straining against it lend the poem its tense and forceful appeal. Elsewhere Jonson denies being motivated by envy; here he pursues envy of a kind (and in a way) we can only admire (6). His confession of weakness, by enhancing our sense of his inner strength, can only promote his social standing. Even the severest rival would be hard put to attack this poem, which is indeed (in every respect) nearly impervious to criticism. It practically forces readers to take it on its own terms, challenging them to respond to it with the same tact and subtlety it embodies. Any approach that seemed to sully the work by raising issues it ignores would run the risk of seeming crass and crude, threatening the reader's standing and (even worse) perhaps his self-regard. In its own way, the epitaph is far more intimidating than any of Jonson's blustering prologues or satirical barbs.

"On My First Sonne" celebrates a relationship rooted in love and therefore all the more appealing in a society in which such relations between adults would have been complicated or rare. It exalts a relation free of any hint of envy or rivalry, one in which Jonson was the patron, the superior, the giver and provider. Clearly the poem also recognizes his subjection to a greater power, but that power is not presented as exploitative or self-serving. The Lord who exacts tribute is himself a loving Father with only the best interests of his sons at heart. Jonson has offered up this "best piece of *poetrie*" to the one patron fully capable of appreciating it.

Jonson's epitaphs—especially the ones on children—enhance his power by wrestling with issues that seem to transcend the political.[37] Such poems make us temporarily forget the ambitions and struggles of the here and now, reducing these concerns to their "proper" importance and offering a reprieve from the necessity of thinking about them. The epitaphs remind us of our inevitable mortality, but they thereby also suggest that micropolitical issues which seem so important today will in the long run seem insignificant. Thinking of death can prove a great antidote to ambition, but it can also spur the desire to achieve temporal fame. In either case, the poems in which Jonson confronts death help promote his social standing. In them he becomes a spokesman not only for the life and memory of the deceased but for the values of the larger community. The very conventionality of such poems is part of their skill, part of their purpose, part of their power, but at the same time, it helps highlight any special achievement or innovation by a specific poet. Since epitaphs strongly imply his religious convictions, they strengthen his social position by making him seem more disinterested, less self-serving than in poems from many other genres.

If Jonson's poems on death are inevitably implicated in micropolitics, can the same be said of another class of works seemingly free of such concerns—his poems on love? Perhaps an answer can best be sketched by looking very briefly at one of his most famous meditations on that subject, the sequence titled "A Celebration of Charis" (*Und.* 2). Although this series of ten poems is (for my present purposes) too extensive and complex to discuss in any detail, there may, in fact, be some merit in suggesting how such a sequence as a whole—on such an apparently unJonsonian topic as romantic love—may have served his interests as a patronage poet.[38] However one chooses to interpret the meanings of its individual components, the entire series would have benefited Jonson's standing in any number of ways. First, it displayed his range, showing that the poet who once felt compelled to explain "Why I Write Not of Love" (*For.* 1) could indeed handle with great aplomb a topic of perennial interest at court. The "Charis" poems show his ability to teach by delighting rather than simply by severe satire, and they also exploit the jolly "Ben" persona to play on—and thus enhance—his status as a public figure. The self-mocking tone of the sequence makes the poet seem more appealing than when (as in some of the early "comical satyres") he seems to take himself too seriously. They exhibit his playful side, and by suggesting his social ease and security, they help create it. The poems reveal a comfortable familiarity with courtly manners even while suggesting a critical distance from them, implying a commitment to ideal behavior while insinuating the ways many courtiers fall short. The speaker's foolishness suggests the deeper wit and wisdom of his creator, as Jonson insinuates an amused detachment from the follies he describes. Yet he does not distance himself completely, or smugly put himself on a higher plane, and the sense of self-mockery that pervades the poems helps make them, ironically, almost invulnerable to criticism. Because the sequence seems to have no overt political designs, because it seems primarily playful, it is all the more politically effective. Here as in the epitaphs, works seemingly unconcerned with the poet's power help (for that reason) to promote it.

Whether addressing patrons, enemies, friends, the courtly audience of a masque, the broader audience of a play, a fictitious lover, or even the memory of a dead child, Jonson's texts are always affected by his status as a poet writing in a hierarchical society. They are nearly always colored by the intense self-consciousness of an author performing before an audience of patrons, rivals, and peers. Even when (as in the epitaph on his son) his voice seems unimpeachably "sincere," or even when (as in the "Charis" sequence) his tone seems most cleverly playful, the effects of his words cannot be divorced from competition for social standing. The traces of power are everywhere embedded in his writing.[39]

3
Issues of Flattery and Freedom

Flattery is the occupational hazard of any writer who depends on patronage, and no one was more aware of this than Jonson. He could hardly help being aware: throughout his career, his antagonists either snidely insinuated or openly charged that his success resulted from sycophancy, that his skills as a poet were less highly developed than his abilities as a time-server. Flattery—and hypocritical flattery at that—is one of the chief charges leveled against him in Thomas Dekker's *Satiromastix*, that ferocious and crucial early assault on his character and conduct. Dekker presents Jonson, under the guise of "Horace," as an unscrupulous lickspittle whose public adulation of his patrons masks an attitude of cynical contempt and conscious exploitation. John Weever, at around the same time Dekker's play was written, implied that Jonson was "one of those that if a man can find in his purse to give them presently, they can find in their hearts to love him everlastingly," and he further charged that "few" were "corivals with [Jonson] in the love of silver" (H&S 11:363). Years later, John Eliot charged that one of Jonson's poems had "basely flatter'd e'en the worst of men" (H&S 11:406), while in another assault he implied that Jonson's flattery had been rewarded with "A certain sum of forty pound in gold" (H&S 11:406). After the poet died, one eulogist, John Taylor, took pains to assert that Jonson had "serv'd two Kings, with good integrity," that his "Royall pension" was "true pay," and that he was "No *Mammons man*, no base extortioner, / He lov'd not gold and silver" (H&S 11:426–27). Similarly, Robert Meade, in a volume of elegies whose tone is almost more defensive than simply celebratory, implied that Jonson was "Free from base *flattery*" and that his careful judgment kept his "*Bayes* / From the suspition of a *vulgar praise*" (H&S 11:471). Jonson himself ridiculed the oily flattery of such dependents as Sejanus and Mosca, and in his *Conversations* with Drummond he mocked preachers who used their sermons for flummery or self-promotion (H&S 1:142). He insisted that he himself had "never esteemed of a man for the name of a Lord," and he further proclaimed that "he would not flatter though he saw Death" (H&S 1:141).

Although we need hardly take the allegations of Jonson's enemies completely seriously, they do suggest how important it was to avoid even the appearance of sycophancy. The danger of being ridiculed as a toady must have helped subtly color his self-consciousness and his public behavior. Repeatedly his works betray a concern with flattery. He worries not only that friends might flatter or that flatterers might effectively compete against him but also that he himself might be mistaken for a flatterer. The problem of distinguishing between appearance and reality, so central to Renaissance literature generally, seems especially important in Jonson's poetry of patronage. If he sometimes seems unsure that others share his ability to distinguish the true from the false, he seems even more uneasy about the prospect that his own performance might be misinterpreted. He attacks duplicity but must not seem duplicitous himself. And in fact his attacks helped serve that purpose.

Yet satire and invective were only two of the methods at his disposal. Paradoxically, his need to distinguish himself from flatterers could often contribute to his works' tonal subtlety and ambiguity. Although he sometimes deals with the problem by using a style that seems straightforward and plain, even the works exhibiting this style reveal intriguing complexities when examined more closely. At other times he adopts the voice of impersonal morality, as if he speaks less for himself than for his culture's central values. Yet however sincerely he spoke with that voice, its tactical effectiveness should not be ignored. Sometimes he speaks with attractive modesty, with humorous self-deprecation that confirms his patron's power while enhancing his own. Such modesty was particularly effective because it was especially invulnerable. At other times, however, he seems almost the opposite of modest, almost deliberately assertive. In poems adopting this stance, he seems to guarantee his words' integrity by staking his reputation on them. His stubborn and flamboyant self-respect made it harder to believe him capable of flattery.

Ironically, though, the very tone that makes him seem to stand above the fray also makes him a more effective competitor. His need not to seem to debase himself in trying to prove appealing is closely tied to his need to appeal. Jonson disdains flattery—and the appearance of it—not only for moral reasons but because an obvious flatterer would prove a highly ineffective suitor. No patron could really trust him; no antagonist would need to take him seriously. He would be an easy target for attack. The poet's self-conscious concern to avoid seeming a flatterer might reflect his respect for himself, for his patrons, or for general moral precepts, but it almost inevitably also reflected a concern with his practical social standing.

For Jonson, therefore, the problem of praising rightly was acute, and it enhanced the self-consciousness that characterizes his poetry. His praise, to be effective, had to be convincing—not only to those he commended but to a wider audience as well. To be valuable, it had to seem sincere. Jonson and his patrons both benefited from the appearance that he enjoyed a measure of independence in his dealings with them. Paradoxically, the more convincing his autonomy seemed, the more effective a subordinate he could be, and thus the more effectively he could bolster others' power. His independent image made him a more valuable and attractive dependent. And his need to cultivate that image, combined with his awareness of the real limits to his authority, made him highly attuned to the subtle nuances of power his works conveyed.

In various poems written over a wide span of his career, Jonson explicitly confronted the possibility that he might be a flatterer. Intriguing not only because they openly raise an issue he often finessed, these poems also suggest some of the tactics at his disposal for dealing with this especially ticklish problem. Indeed, his very willingness seemingly to face the issue squarely was one of his best and most potent tactics; the self-confidence it implied might bolster others' trust in his essential integrity. Sometimes, in fact, his attitude seems bold almost to the point of provocation. An epigram written late in his life (*Und.* 66), for instance, congratulates Queen Henrietta Maria on the birth of the prince who would someday rule as Charles II:

> Haile *Mary*, full of grace, it once was said,
>   And by an Angell, to the blessed'st Maid,
> The Mother of our Lord: why may not I
>   (Without prophanenesse) yet, a Poët, cry,
> Haile *Mary*, full of honours, to my Queene,
>   The Mother of our Prince? When was there seene
> (Except the joy that the first *Mary* brought,
>   Whereby the safetie of Man-kind was wrought)
> So generall a gladness to an Isle,
>   To make the hearts of a whole Nation smile,
> As in this Prince? Let it be lawfull, so
>   To compare small with great, as still we owe
> Glorie to God. Then, Haile to *Mary*! spring
>   Of so much safetie to the Realme, and King!
>
>   (1–14)

The first half of the opening line is doubly daring. It catches the reader off-guard by seeming to risk the "prophaneness" it subsequently disavows, even while reminding readers of the Queen's controversial Catholicism. Despite Jonson's claim about the joy that greeted the prince's birth, even this event—which occurred during a period of rising tensions between the King and many of his subjects—was not unattended by misgivings and strife. Charles had already promised "that once the Queen was brought to bed none of the nurses or rockers would be Catholics," and after the birth he was prevailed on to substitute a Protestant governess for the Catholic he had originally chosen. One hapless Puritan "who threw doubt on the Prince's parentage was hung, drawn, and quartered for his pains."[1] Here, as in so many of Jonson's poems of patronage, what seems at first simply celebratory turns out to be implicit political rhetoric. By reminding his patrons of their insecurity even while seeming to ignore it, the poet implies his own usefulness as an ally.

Although Jonson anticipates objections to his unconventional praise, he wittily fashions the poem precisely out of his attempt to justify it. The poem is simultaneously festive and argumentative; its final lines sum up its tribute even while concluding its logical development. The potentially offensive phrase is repeated thrice—evidence of Jonson's willingness to strike a provocative stance, but also of his confidence in the poem's ability to demonstrate the proposition on which it rests. The repetitions give the poem an incantatory quality, but each reiteration also marks a new stage in the work's syllogistic progression. By the end of the epigram, Jonson argues that his praise of the Queen indirectly praises God. If the poem has been successful, the third repetition of "Haile . . . *Mary*" should seem neither brazen nor flattering but perfectly apt. Although ostensibly concerned with the prince's birth, the epigram's real interest comes from seeing whether the poet can pull off his self-imposed challenge. From one perspective, the poem seems focused less on an external event than on its own dynamics, yet its poetic intricacy is inseparable from its social effectiveness.

The epigram to Henrietta Maria was written near the end of Jonson's life, but throughout his career he openly and repeatedly confronted the problem of flattery. "To the Ghost of Martial," for instance (*Ep.* 36), demonstrates not only a finesse similar to that exhibited in the poem just examined, but also an ability to turn compliment into a kind of delicate assertiveness:

> Martial, thou gav'st farre nobler *Epigrammes*
>   To thy Domitian, than I can my James:
> But in my royall subject I passe thee,
>   Thou flattered'st thine, mine cannot flatter'd bee.
>
> (1–4)

The pride Jonson professes in James makes him seem attractively humble, while his initial humility toward Martial is dissolved—or at least transformed—by the poem's developing logic. Yet its transformation preserves its appeal: James, not Jonson, is credited with making Martial seem the lesser poet. Similarly, James is also credited with the poet's inability to flatter; even if flattery were his intention (Jonson implies), James's excellence would make it impossible since no praise could be too high. At the same time, he suggests that James would reject any flattery offered him. While this compliments the King, it also instructs him, pressuring him to merit Jonson's confidence. Paradoxically, in the very act of proclaiming his inability to flatter, Jonson offers praise that is at once extravagant, delicately implicit, and equivocal. Similar tact is evident in his attitude toward Martial. Although initially he commends his predecessor's poems as "farre nobler" than his, in the end he attempts to force the reader to acknowledge the *moral* superiority of his own verse. To dispute this claim would be (according to the terms the poem establishes) to defame not Jonson but the King. Rather than responding to the potential charge of flattery with lame or conspicuous self-defense, he turns its very possibility into an occasion for further compliment.

In another epigram, "To Thomas Earle of Suffolk" (*Ep.* 67), Jonson again attempts to dispose of the charge by raising it explicitly and by turning the tables, challenging his readers rather than openly defending himself. The poem illustrates how he could manipulate the reading experience, how this poet of the "plain style" could use equivocation to display his skill, insinuate meaning, and attempt to guide the responses of general readers and of patrons in particular:

> Since men have left to doe praise-worthy things,
>   Most thinke all praises flatteries. But truth brings
> That sound, and that authoritie with her name,
>   As, to be rais'd by her, is onely fame.
> Stand high, then, Howard, high in eyes of men,
>   High in thy bloud, thy place, but highest then,
> When, in mens wishes, so thy vertues wrought,
>   As all thy honors were by them first sought:
> And thou design'd to be the same thou art,
>   Before thou wert it, in each good mans heart.
> Which, by no lesse confirm'd, then thy kings choice,
>   Proves, that is gods, which was the peoples voice.
>
>   (1–12)

The poem's opening is nicely ambiguous, reflecting credit on both Suffolk and Jonson. The opening sentence at once objectively comments on the "men" it mentions and subtly coerces the "Most" who doubt the truth of praise. Read in one sense it initially seems to distinguish the "men" from the "Most": since men *have* ceased to do praise-worthy things, it might seem reasonable for most people to distrust praise. Yet on second glance the sentence implies that those who suspect all praise do so because they are themselves incapable of worthy acts. This tactic could be used disarmingly against a wary patron, but its main target seems to be skeptical readers in general. Since they do nothing worthy themselves, they cannot conceive either of true merit in others or of genuine appreciation of it *by* others. The poem implies that Jonson's true praise is almost as rare and commendable as the true worth it extols.

Twice he plays with the notion that of all Suffolk's merits, the greatest is that Suffolk himself is not hungry to have them rewarded—that instead his virtues make others ambitious *for* him. There is a paradoxical quality about the seventh and eighth lines, in which Suffolk's virtues are said to have "wrought" certain effects, but in which all of that verb's usual suggestions of conscious intent have been stripped away. Again, others are described as having "sought" honors—but not for themselves. Jonson toys here with the standard expectations engendered by contemporary competition: that seeking could only be self-seeking, that a man of Suffolk's rank must have been driven by personal appetite. In fact, he teases the reader with such expectations in line nine: "And thou design'd to be the same thou art." Here the verb at first seems active, as if to imply that Suffolk did pursue a calculated goal. But line ten reverses this, making the verb passive and making others, again, the chief designers of Howard's good fortune.[2] Given the real mechanics of Renaissance patronage, Jonson no doubt underplays the true extent of Suffolk's ambition (just as he minimizes his own).

More interesting than his self-presentation, however, are his attempts to make it persuasive. By implicitly contrasting "good" men with the suspicious, suspect "Most," Jonson invites readers to identify themselves with one category or the other. There is no question with which side *he* identifies; but if the reader makes the same choice, he automatically grants Jonson rights as his spokesman. In fact, the status of the poet's voice in the final lines becomes cunningly vague. On the one hand presenting himself as simply part of the larger "peoples voice," Jonson at the same time becomes the means by which that voice achieves concentrated articulation. This fusion of voices contributes to the powerful concord the poem cultivates. Just as the King's choice of Howard simultaneously enacts the desires of the people and the will of God, so Jonson's poem ostensibly unites the voices of God, king, people, and poet. The psychological appeal of such harmony must have been profound. To assent to it, to imagine oneself as part of such concord, would have been immensely satisfying. But it would also mean relinquishing any right to question Jonson's motives as celebrant. The problem of flattery is successfully dealt with only if he can persuade readers that *his* voice subsumes their own. Although in one sense self-effacing, this ploy for that very reason helps to augment his personal power. Moreover, the physical fact of the poem serves, in and of itself, to remind Suffolk that while others may *wish* him a high place and honors, Jonson and the King (in different ways) are the figures most capable of helping him *realize* those goals. In this as in other poems in which Jonson adopts the role of popular spokesman, then, one paradoxical effect of his work is to suggest a subtle but important distinction between his own voice and the voices he claims to represent.

As the epigram to Suffolk suggests, self-effacement was often the most effective means of self-promotion. The more genuinely modest a poet seemed, the more effectively he might assert and achieve his interests. Humble deference enhanced the patron's power while practically obligating a gracious response. Moreover, convincing modesty made the poet less vulnerable to criticism from antagonists. At other times, however, Jonson insists openly on the importance of his own role and voice. While such insistence ran the risk of seeming proud and thus left him open to attack, it also signaled his unwillingness to submit entirely to the patron's domination. In part, such assertiveness was sanctioned by tradition, by literary convention, and by his culture's moral code—and thus proved less easy for patrons to resist or for rivals to criticize. And yet it must also have appealed to many patrons suspicious of subtle ingratiation. Bluff-spoken Ben may have seemed as attractive to them as to many modern admirers, who often share his concern to distance him from the charge of flattery.

Once, however (and in one of his most famous poems), Jonson did openly admit to such charges. Whatever its narrower historical and biographical contexts, "To My Muse" (*Ep.* 65) is interesting both for its complexity and for the solid information and pungent commentary it provides on the temptations and dangers of patronage competition. The sense of attraction to a "great image" (4) that turns out to be devoid of substance; the dilemma of winning the animosity of some powerful figures by winning the support of others; the anxiety that present acceptance might prove unstable; the atmosphere of distrust, in which friendship can be as ephemeral as fortune: the poem communicates all this economically yet effectively. But it does more than comment on such problems; it attempts to cope with and exploit them. Despite the disillusionment it emphasizes, it does not—cannot—reject the patronage system entirely: this much is clear from the closing couplet but is implied by the poem's very existence. Rejecting one patron, it seems partly designed to interest others, functioning as an apology, a defense, and a bid for renewed acceptance. Its simultaneous confession and rejection of flattery is intimately tied to the poet's need to compete:

Away, and leave me, thou thing most abhord,
    That hast betray'd me to a worthlesse lord;
Made me commit most fierce idolatrie
    To a great image through thy luxurie.
Be thy next masters more unluckie *Muse*,
    And, as thou'hast mine, his houres, and youth abuse.
Get him the times long grudge, the courts ill will;
    And, reconcil'd, keepe him suspected still.
Make him loose all his friends; and, which is worse,
    Almost all wayes, to any better course.
With me thou leav'st an happier *Muse* then thee,
    And which thou brought'st me, welcome povertie.
Shee shall instruct my after-thoughts to write
    Things manly, and not smelling parasite.
But I repent me: Stay. Who e're is rais'd,
    For worth he has not, He is tax'd, not prais'd.

                             (1–16)

    The poem's humor, its device of blaming the muse, its telling reference to the poet's youth—all these distance Jonson from responsibility for an idolatry he now claims to deplore. But in fact the poem's humor, which has received little attention, is extremely ambiguous and complex. On the one hand the bluster publicly checks and tempers the intense emotion and fear aroused by the betrayal, loss of face, and potential loss of status the poem deals with. Jonson uses humor to distance himself from the more frightening possibilities the situation poses; certainly he uses the poem's wit and hyperbole to help defuse his readers' potentially harsh judgments. His comic exasperation makes him seem more sympathetic, more appealingly humble. Blaming the muse in a tone of exaggerated indignation, he accepts some responsibility without admitting full or precise guilt, playfully (if self-consciously) deflecting humiliation and embarrassment and thus defusing some of the threat he felt. Beneath the joking lurks an undercurrent of real fear and apprehension with which the humor helps him cope. Suggesting his self-respect and self-security, it asserts his power; but it also insinuates his vulnerability, implicitly confessing his need to defend himself, even if rather circuitously. The humor is at once "manly" (14) and somewhat disingenuous.

    Accusing the muse allows Jonson to accept some blame while deflecting most; he is presented chiefly as an "unluckie" victim (5), betrayed to and by a lord whose worthlessness contrasts with the worthy example set by the repentant poet. Seeming at first to accept blame, he in fact re-assigns it: repenting his banishment of the muse, he ends by claiming that his earlier praise is a kind of implicit censure. Yet although the final couplet at first appears to exonerate the poet, it is not nearly as assertive as it seems, since it functions as one last rationale, one last submission to the pressure to explain. Significantly, Jonson cannot even identify his target; although the poem forthrightly declares the lord worthless, it necessarily bows to his superior power. Despite its rejection of him, he still exerts some control. The epigram's purpose, however, seems less to destroy the patron's reputation than to salvage Jonson's. Supposedly he is wiser now, still committed to the values of his youth but more mature and thus potentially an even more attractive client.

This is a poem haunted by fear of betrayal—comic betrayal by a "muse," more serious betrayal by patron and friends, betrayal also of self and ideals. Jonson's stratagems imply a keen awareness of the micropolitical context in which his confession would be read and reacted to; the poem suggests both a need to confess and a need to preserve and re-assert his power so as not to give his enemies an opening to exploit his weakness. His confession is also a concession to the very self-interest he attacks. No doubt prompted partly by conscience, the poem also responds to more mundane concerns for reputation and position at court (7). Addressed to an imaginary muse, it is actually aimed at a broader audience of real superiors and rivals, antagonists and potential allies. Seemingly obsessed with the past, its real fixation is on the present and future, on Jonson's damaged standing and the need to repair it.

"To My Muse" suggests how the very permanence of writing that gave the poet power, allowing him to claim he could immortalize, could also prove a corrosive danger. Once circulated or printed, Jonson's poems could not easily be recalled, recanted, or denied, however embarrassing they might later seem. There is no way to banish an earlier muse: as the final lines imply, she must be acknowledged. The best he could hope was to affect how people read him. This is why his poems so often call attention to their own features—not because they are self-contained but precisely because they are not. Although on the surface he seems unusually in control of his medium, in fact his poems often betray intense anxiety about how they might be misconstrued and turned against him. Far from exulting in the free play of language, he genuinely feared it. Losing control over his words meant losing power—a threat he confronts in "To My Muse." The poem attempts to guide readings of his earlier writing, to re-assert his threatened authority over his texts. In the final lines he pretends those texts are self-adjusting: poems that *seem* complimentary are supposedly satirical if only read correctly. But this is an important *if*: in attempting to guide reactions to his work, Jonson tacitly acknowledges that poems *cannot* correct themselves, that his meaning (less the product of texts than of interpretations) is socially determined and therefore subject to political contention. Jonson depended not only on patrons but on the presumptive goodwill of readers in general, and both kinds of dependence fostered apprehension. And while both might prompt him to flatter or curry favor, they could also encourage him openly to reject flattery and distance himself from the charge. "To My Muse" asserts his independence in a way designed to enhance his appeal to those on whom he depended.

Jonson's experiences inevitably bred a sensitivity to the nuances of power in a society rooted in patronage. Although his own power depended on participating in that society, there must have been times when he tired of its demands and longed for a measure of freedom. A little-noted passage in the *Conversations*, for instance, reports that he knew "by Heart" an intriguing poem by Sir Henry Wotton; indeed, a transcript in his handwriting still exists, and the poem's theme suggests why he so admired it. "How happy is he borne, or taught," it begins, "That serveth not anothers will!" After then listing the various advantages of self-possession, it concludes: "This man is free from servile bandes / Of hope to rise, or feare to fall; / Lord of himselfe, though not of landes: / And having nothing, yet hath all" (H&S 1:135, 157). But however alluring Jonson found this stoic ideal, he seems to have been unfitted to realize it both by temperament and by his practical need to compete. His actual autonomy was more limited than he often claimed. Realizing this fact can help us better appreciate what his poetry is about, the kinds of practical functions it served and the actual challenges it attempted to meet. Realizing this can also help us better appreciate how tensions between poetic ideals and social realities contributed to his work's intricacy and richness. And it can prevent us from judging his poetry harshly if it sometimes falls short of the lofty, autonomous standards he often claimed for it, since the very usefulness of such claims derived partly from their practical, tactical effectiveness.

Because individuality of thought and expression is a central value in modern liberal cultures, it is much easier for modern writers than it ever was for Jonson to express themselves freely—a fact worth remembering when the temptation to judge him arises. However complicated the actual positions of individual authors, the *claim* to independence is fundamental to the modern Western writer and reflects the romantic presumption that the source of poetry is neither the external world nor external doctrines; rather, that source is the shaping, creative imagination of the artist himself. Since we tend to think of the poet as the source of truth, of truthful insights, or at the very least of true beauty, any constraint on his free expression seems to violate his essential function. His freedoms are theoretically protected in part simply because he lives in a democracy; but they also seem particularly relevant to his role. Whereas a modern poet might win internal fulfillment and even external affirmation by challenging his culture's values, in a patriarchal, authoritarian society the very possibility of strictly internal fulfillment was more difficult to imagine.

Thus, however much Sidney or other Renaissance theorists might speak of the poet as a *vates* or claim that he ranged freely within the zodiac of his own wit, or however much Jonson might like to boast of the poet's rarity or compare his role to a king's, in practical terms his role was highly circumscribed. He might indeed be a prophet, but his prophecy could safely be only Christian; he might fancy himself a kind of law-giver, but his prescriptions had better conform to official morality. Even comparing the poet to a king paradoxically implies acceptance of the poet's subordinate role, since it suggests that kings are the most powerful and prestigious earthly figures. Jonson's position was crisscrossed by a network of obligations to superiors, and while his relations with them could not be free of tension, his behavior was inseparable from his dependency. It would be anachronistic to claim that he felt completely oppressed by his position, but it seems naive to think that he ever felt wholly satisfied with it in practice.

There are, of course, poems in which Jonson seems not only to claim but to demonstrate his autonomy. Important precisely because they seem to contradict the view of his circumstances just outlined, they can seem to imply that he enjoyed more liberty than we might otherwise assume. Like a number of intriguing incidents in his career, they seem to exemplify an attractive freedom, a willingness to take risks, that enhances respect for Jonson by enhancing our sense of his *self*-respect. But also like those incidents, they lend themselves to appealing interpretations that run the risk of being simplistic. Examined more closely, both the works and the events take on a more clouded hue. Set in their actual contexts, they seem in fact to illustrate not so much the poet's autonomy as the ambiguities of his situation and the difficulties of assessing precisely the "correct" meaning of crucial aspects of his life and works.

It is true, for instance, that Jonson was imprisoned for several months in 1597, presumably for his part-authorship of *The Isle of Dogs*. This lost play was suspected by the Privy Council of containing "very seditious and sclandrous matter," and some of the actors were ordered punished for "theire Leude and mutynous behavior" (H&S 1:217). But Jonson's exact responsibility is unclear, and the play's contents are even more mysterious. Recent investigations have tied the work to political frictions within the court, to rivalries between competing factions.[3]

Indeed, it seems generally worth remembering that much of the period's satire was political in several senses of the term. Often written not simply to comment on controversial issues but to advance the interests of a particular court faction, it thereby promoted the personal interests of the poet with that faction and its allies. A poet took political positions not in a vacuum but in a context defined by the competing interests of powerful individuals and groups. When he insinuated criticism of one prominent figure or openly praised another, he did so within a context itself shaped and permeated by competition among the powerful.

Many of the incidents in Jonson's career that seem at first to suggest unbridled independence dissolve into complexities when examined more closely, and nearly all suggest the various ways in which he was implicated in contemporary power politics. His troubles over *Sejanus* are a good case in point. Apparently he was called before the Privy Council by the Earl of Northampton, who accused him "both of popperie and treason" (H&S 1 : 141). But Philip J. Ayres's thorough examination of the affair suggests that the Earl may have perceived the play as covert satire of his own recent maneuverings against Sir Walter Ralegh, one of his chief courtly rivals. According to Ayres,

> Whether or not [Northampton] knew Jonson to be a Catholic, he could claim that *Sejanus,* in its perceived support of Ralegh, was not only treasonable but "popish," since the charges against Ralegh [in the controversial trial that shortly preceded the first performance of the play] were "that he did conspire, and go about to deprive the king of his government, to raise up sedition within the realm, to alter religion, to bring in the Roman superstition, and to procure foreign enemies to invade the kingdom."[4]

These charges were largely manufactured, and Ralegh won wide sympathy as a victim of political persecution engineered by his enemies. Ayres implies that Jonson did not consciously intend any satire, but he also notes that "Northampton would have had no reason to know that Jonson had been laboring over his scholarly piece for a year or two" before Ralegh's trial.[5] Northampton, in other words, may have glimpsed a topical application the poet never intended. But perhaps Ayres is wrong; perhaps the play excited no suspicions at all in connection with Ralegh's trial. Perhaps it was seen instead, as some have suggested, as an allusion to the earlier fall of the Earl of Essex, or to contemporary political espionage and manipulation. As with numerous other events in Jonson's career, the surviving evidence provides us with frustratingly little to go on. What, precisely, Jonson himself may or may not have intended *Sejanus* to imply or allude to is unclear and is likely to remain so. What *is* clear, however, is how liable a poet in his position could be to the suspicions and charges of offended superiors. More than once during his career, Jonson found himself in trouble because of others' allegations. In the *Discoveries* he comments on this explicitly:

> It is true, I have beene accus'd to the Lords, to the King; and by great ones: but it hap'ned my accusers had not thought of the Accusation with themselves; and were so driven, for want of crimes, to use invention, which was found slander: or too late, (Being entred so farre) to seek starting-holes for their rashnesse, which were not given them. And then they may thinke, what accusation that was like to prove, when they, that were the Ingineers, fear'd to be the Authors. . . . Nay, they would offer to urge mine owne Writings against me; but by pieces, (which was an excellent way of malice) as if any mans Context, might not seem dangerous, and offensive, if that which was knit, to what went before, were defrauded of his beginning; or that things, by themselves utter'd, might not seeme subject to Calumnie, which read entire, would appeare most free. (H&S 8:604–05)

As Annabel Patterson notes, the passage reflects "a long life of insecurity, of being misunderstood."[6] But perhaps what is most surprising is that in spite of such accusations, in the long run Jonson's fortunes rarely faltered; his unparalleled rise seems to have been almost unaffected by the occasional predicaments he faced. In the passage quoted above, in his letters, and elsewhere, he evinces a confident assurance of his essential innocence, and the record does seem to indicate that his enemies were usually unsuccessful in making their charges stick. Their accusations seem hardly at all to have retarded his rise. Thus, during or not long after the time he was accused about *Sejanus*, he was probably nonetheless living in the household of one of his most important early patrons, Lord D'Aubigny (H&S 11:576–77). Not long after, he was commissioned to prepare an entertainment for James's coronation, and a few months later was assigned to write a private entertainment for presentation before the King and Queen. By the end of the year, he was busily at work on his first court masque. The following year, *Sejanus* itself was allowed to appear in print, accompanied by a host of tributes from other writers who apparently saw no danger in associating themselves with a work once suspected (by at least one powerful figure) of advocating treason. All these facts suggest that the charges leveled against Jonson did little to damage his standing at court, his success in winning patronage, or his support from those seeking influence themselves. It seems plausible to surmise either that the charges were baseless or that whatever political stances he adopted in his work hardly offended all those who possessed the power to aid him. Indeed, in assessing this and similar incidents in his career, it always seems worth asking to which larger political or factional interests he may have been appealing when he wrote what might otherwise seem simply provocative.

Just as curious as his problems with *Sejanus* are the accusations and brief jailing he faced in 1605 for his part-authorship of *Eastward Ho*. The play was apparently staged without the prior knowledge or approval of the responsible court officials, who seem to have been temporarily absent from London. George Chapman, one of Jonson's collaborators, later denied any deliberate plan to circumvent their authority, explaining that the play was "much importun'de" and that its authors felt that "nothinge it contain'd could worthily be held offensive."[7] In this they were mistaken. Two clauses—perhaps improvised by the actors—were interpreted as anti-Scottish satire. Jonson, remembering and perhaps embellishing the outcome years later, told Drummond that

> he was delated by S[ir] James Murray to the King for writting something against the Scots in a play Eastward hoe & voluntarly Imprissonned himself w[ith] Chapman and Marston, who had written it amongst ym. the report was that they should then had theirs ears cutt & noses. (H&S 1:140)

The idea that Jonson, "in a characteristically magnanimous gesture . . . voluntarily committed himself to prison as a display of solidarity with his collaborators" is attractive, but it finds little support in the contemporary documents; nor is it even certain that Marston was imprisoned at all.[8] Jonson seems to have felt sure that he could prove his innocence if given a chance; in a series of letters—one definitely to Robert Cecil, the others probably to the Countess of Bedford, to Lord D'Aubigny, and to the Earls of Suffolk, Montgomery, and Pembroke—he pleads less for mercy than for the right to be examined (H&S 1:193–200). The letters, themselves fascinating displays of rhetoric, exhibit many of the very tactics he often drew on in his poems. They suggest how extensive his contacts with members of the aristocracy were at this time, and also how useful such contacts could prove. Although he owed his imprisonment to the anger of certain powerful figures, he probably owed his quick release partly to the helpful intervention of others. In both cases the incident must have further emphasized his dependency. His regained freedom was gratifying, but the episode cannot have increased his deeper sense of security.

Not long after his release, Jonson was able to return the assistance figures like Cecil had presumably given him. The Gunpowder Plot, a Catholic conspiracy to blow up Parliament and kill the King, had just been exposed on 5 November 1605. Two days later, Jonson received a warrant from the Privy Council to act as an intermediary in investigating the incident (H&S 1:203). What is intriguing is that Jonson, a Catholic himself, should have been trusted in this way at a time when many of his co-religionists were under the most intense suspicion. In part he must have been chosen precisely because of his religion and because of his contacts with prominent Catholics. Indeed, less than a month before the plot's discovery, he had dined at a party given by Robert Catesby, one of the leading conspirators. Both factors may have made him a logical choice to represent the Council. But it is unlikely that he would have been chosen to serve in any capacity if Cecil (with his wide network of spies) had had any reason to suspect his loyalty. The fact that he was so trusted so soon after the *Eastward Ho* affair should perhaps caution us against exaggerating its significance. This is especially the case when we remember that in the months following his imprisonment, he was nonetheless still commissioned to write *Hymenaei*, his second masque for the court.

At first glance, Jonson's Catholicism may seem another sign of his daring independence, and certainly he made little attempt to hide his faith. Soon after his conversion he wrote a poem Cecil must have read in which his sympathies were obvious, and the year before the Gunpowder Plot he publicly commended a book by Thomas Wright, the famous priest who may have converted him (H&S 11:124–25; 128–129).[9] Despite occasional harassment—from unfriendly potentates like Northampton, from lower-level authorities, and from rivals eager to exploit any potential embarrassment—Jonson seems to have viewed his Catholicism as no serious impediment to his aspirations. Certainly his success suggests that it was not. His faith, however much it may have made for some uncertainty and insecurity, does not seem to have much retarded his career. In April of 1606, it is true, he was cited before the Consistory Court at London for failing to attend church regularly, for failing to take communion, and for attempting to seduce youths to the popish religion. He disputed the first and last charges, and responded to the second by explaining that although he had indeed refused communion (because of a "scruple of conscienc' "), he was "nowe uppo[n] better advisement . . . determined to alter" (H&S 1:221). He requested that the court appoint several "learned men" with whom he could confer about the matter, and promised "to Conforme him selfe according as they shall advise him & p[er]swade him" (H&S 1:221). When—or even whether—he was persuaded remains unclear, but apparently the whole issue was eventually dropped. Herford and the Simpsons speculate that some "powerful influence . . . may have intervened" on his behalf. In any case, they note, the "court was plainly disposed to throw the burden of proof upon his accusers" (H&S 1:43). In the months following these troubles, Jonson's literary and social status nonetheless continued to improve. July saw the performance of another royal entertainment, and, probably later that same year, *Volpone* was presented before audiences at Oxford and Cambridge.

Jonson's difficulties about his religion follow a pattern repeated several times during his rise. More than once he stood suspected of having transgressed his authority, of having dangerously asserted his freedom. But these suspicions nearly always proved insubstantial, and at any rate seem hardly to have affected his progress. Three incidents may serve as brief examples. Thus, a few years after the investigation just mentioned, he was in trouble again, this time in connection with *Epicoene*. The charge—that a passage in the play maligned Lady Arabella Stuart— seems almost certainly to have been groundless (H&S 5:143–47), but the incident reinforced his sense of how vulnerable he was to "the certaine hatred of some, how much a man's innocency may be indanger'd by an uncertaine accusation" (H&S 5:161). Once again his professions of innocence seem bolstered by his continued success in the immediate aftermath of the episode. The commission to write *Prince Henry's Barriers* may or may not have preceded *Epicoene*'s first performance (H&S 1:146), but certainly the commission for *Oberon* (the masque for the following year) postdated his supposed slur on this woman of royal blood. The allegations concerning *Epicoene*, like other charges leveled at other times, seem to have been both baseless and inconsequential. In October 1628, for instance, Jonson was questioned about some verses circulating in support of John Felton, the assassin of Buckingham, the King's friend and favorite. He vigorously denied having written them, and professed "uppo[n] his christianity & hope of salvation" that he had never even made a copy. He swore that when he first read them he "condemned" them, and that he regarded them with "detestation" (H&S 1:242). Apparently the authorities were satisfied; there is no record of further action. Surely Charles would have been unlikely, only a year and a half later, to increase Jonson's pension substantially if he had doubted the poet's innocence. And finally, when Jonson and the Master of Revels fell under suspicion for indecent language in *The Magnetic Lady*, they were eventually absolved in full. An investigation implicated the actors instead.[10] In the months following these accusations *A Tale of a Tub* was ordered performed at court, and Jonson was commissioned to compose *Love's Welcome at Bolsover*. Thus, although all three incidents might at first glance seem to illustrate Jonson's willingness to provoke official displeasure, they instead seem to illustrate the unrelenting uncertainties and instability of his position. They suggest vulnerability more clearly than insouciant self-assertion.

Yet there are poems in which Jonson does seem to throw caution to the wind, poems in which he seems to assert himself in ways we might not expect. His notorious "Epigram on the Court Pucell" (*Und.* 49) is an intriguing case in point. According to Jonson himself, the poem attacks Cecilia Bulstrode, one of Queen Anne's ladies-in-waiting and a cousin and close friend of the Countess of Bedford. Bulstrode owed her influence not only to these connections but to her involvement with the group of courtiers, writers, and wits the poem describes. James E. Savage has detailed the connections between the "newes" writing depicted in the epigram's opening and an elaborate courtly game that led to the publication of a collection of "conceited newes" items. These writings tend to share an emphasis on intellectual and stylistic wit; they do not report news *per se* but provide clever, often moralistic observations. The published collection contains one item attributable to Cecilia Bulstrode, but the virtuous thoughts she expresses there ("That the most feare the worlds opinion, more than Gods displeasure. That a Court-friend seldome goes further than the first degree of charity. That the Divell is the perfectest Courtier. . . . That sinne makes worke for repentence of the Divell. . . . That all this is newes only to fools") hardly suggest the court whore Jonson's poem describes.[11] Perhaps the contradiction is precisely his point: perhaps he means to highlight her hypocrisy. Whatever the case, his poem seems quite daring for the explicitness and savagery of its satire against a superior. Equally interesting are the ways it exploits the ideals and language associated with proper patronage relations. Biographically intriguing, the epigram also seems poetically rich and tactically complex:

> Do's the Court-Pucell then so censure me,
>   And thinkes I dare not her? let the world see.
> What though her Chamber be the very pit
>   Where fight the prime Cocks of the Game, for wit?
> And that as any are strooke, her breath creates
>   New in their stead, out of the Candidates?
> What though with Tribade lust she force a Muse,
>   And in an Epicoene fury can write newes
> Equall with that, which for the best newes goes
>   As aërie light, and as like wit as those?
> What though she talke, and cannot once with them,
>   Make State, Religion, Bawdrie, all a theame?
> And as lip-thirstie, in each words expence,
>   Doth labour with the Phrase more then the sense?
> What though she ride two mile on Holy-dayes
>   To Church, as others doe to Feasts and Playes,
> To shew their Tires? to view, and to be view'd?

What though she be with Velvet gownes indu'd,
And spangled Petticotes brought forth to eye,
　　As new rewards of her old secrecie?
What though she hath won on Trust, as many doe,
　　And that her truster feares her? Must I too?
I never stood for any place: my wit
　　Thinkes it selfe nought, though she should valew it.
I am no States-man, and much lesse Divine,
　　For bawdry, 'tis her language, and not mine.
Farthest I am from the Idolatrie
　　To stuffes and Laces, those my Man can buy.
And trust her I would least, that hath forswore
　　In Contract twice, what can shee purjure more?
Indeed, her Dressing some man might delight,
　　Her face there's none can like by Candle light.
Not he, that should the body have, for Case
　　To his poore Instrument, now out of grace.
Shall I advise thee, *Pucell?* steale away
　　From Court, while yet thy fame hath some small day;
The wits will leave you, if they once perceive
　　You cling to Lords, and Lords, if them you leave
For Sermoneeres: of which now one, now other
　　They say you weekly invite with fits o'th' Mother,
And practise for Miracle; take heed,
　　This Age would lend no faith to *Dorrels* Deed;
Or if it would, the Court is the worst place,
　　Both for the Mothers, and the Babes of grace,
For there the wicked in the Chaire of scorne,
　　Will cal't a Bastard, when a Prophet's borne.

　　　　　　　　　　　　　　　　　　　　(1–46)

Jonson focuses less on the content of the Pucell's news-writing than on its literal conceitedness—on its egotistical purpose of promoting her image as a wit. What she writes seems less important to him than the prestige and influence her writing brings her. And what threatens him is precisely her ability to use that influence against him—to "censure" him and to prevent him from responding. The "censure" of a social equal would be less menacing not only because it would carry less weight, but also because it would be easier for Jonson to retaliate. In answering her challenge, in refusing to remain silent, he makes immediate claims on our sympathies, both by presenting himself as an underdog and by letting "the world see" (2) the forthright courage of his response.

Yet his response may have been less daring than the poem itself suggests. Drummond's notes indicate that far from challenging her directly or circulating the poem for all the world to see, Jonson instead planned to show it only to those who could be trusted not to show it to

Bulstrode. And in the final analysis, his caution was wise (if ineffective): according to Drummond, "that piece of the Pucelle of the Court, was stollen out of his pocket by a Gentleman who drank him drousie & given Mistress Boulstraid, which brought him great displeasur" (H&S 1:150).[12] Apparently he never intended his target actually to see the poem but instead planned to circulate it strategically, damaging her reputation while denying her access to the physical evidence of his satire. By neglecting to name her explicitly in the poem, he made it easier to deny any personal application. And by keeping the poem from her, he made it all the harder for her or her friends to confront him directly. The rumors and innuendoes generated by his readings would pose a less tangible but (perhaps for that very reason) more menacing threat. Rumors can always be repudiated by their source, but Jonson seems to have found the physical text more difficult to deny.[13] The "great displeasur" he suffered seems to have involved some temporary loss of favor with the Countess of Bedford (H&S 11:130–31). Considering Bulstrode's greater power, his furtiveness in circulating the poem is difficult to blame. But the facts of that circulation should be kept in mind when we try to assess the poem's tone or to generalize about the independence Jonson could display.

Independence is an issue the epigram explicitly raises, claiming that because Jonson has "never stood for any place," he is free of the Pucell's influence. Yet the circumstances of the poem's circulation suggest that he feared her enough to be less than completely forthright in attacking her. By proclaiming his own independence, he lampoons the self-interest of the other writers and intellectuals who pay her so much regard. Indeed, he presents their relations with her as a parody of the ideal relations between poet and patron. Like the ideal patroness, the Pucell is a writer herself, but her talents are labored rather than inspired; her wit is only simulated ("like wit" [10]), and instead of incarnating the muse, she homosexually rapes her (7). She provides no real inspiration to the writers who surround her, encouraging them only to engage in demeaning wit combats that Jonson, in overtones at once animalistic and sexual, compares to cock fights.[14] The ideal of trust and concern between writer and patron gives way to frantic and degrading competition, in which the competitors are treated as merely expendable by their self-indulgent patron. "[A]s any are strooke," Jonson reports, "her breath creates / New in their stead, out of the Candidates" (5–6). The lines are wonderfully effective: they exploit the insecurity of her attendants even while simultaneously conceding and satirizing her real social power. And the irony of comparing the Pucell to a divine being whose breath is literally creative is all the more potent for being left implicit.

Although it derides the wit combats the Pucell sponsors, Jonson's poem is part of just such a contest. Attacking her pompous self-display, it displays Jonson's wit. Indeed, its rigidly-structured but smoothly-flowing opening—with its anaphoristic clauses and devastatingly brief reversal—may parody while also excelling the typical form of the typical "newes" item. Thus Jonson not only mocks but mimics, in both cases asserting his own superiority. Far from renouncing the game it satirizes, the poem plays it quite effectively. Jonson implicitly presents himself as the champion and defender of the same moral and intellectual ideals the Pucell violates, a tactic that allows him to elevate his tone and make his satire seem motivated by more than simply spite or wounded pride. Unlike her, he ostensibly refuses to exploit weighty political and religious topics as grist for his own mill. His avowed refusal to commit "Idolatrie / To stuffes and Laces" helps emphasize by contrast not only the Pucell's shallowness but also the idolatry of the divines and others who pay her so much deference and attention (27–28). At the same time, his claim that "bawdry" is "her language, and not mine" cannot quite disguise the extent to which his own poem is shot through with sexual satire and innuendo (26).

But this sexual emphasis is hardly gratuitous: by depicting Bulstrode as a whore, Jonson suggests how easy it is for relations rooted in dependency to become prostituted, to become calculating and manipulative. He communicates this sense of social corruption partly through a kind of linguistic corruption, in which references to "statesmen" and "divines" remind us of the gap between those titles and many of the men who bear them; or in which it is possible to speak, somewhat oxymoronically, of "[winning] on Trust" (21); or in which it makes sense to say, paradoxically, that the Pucell's "truster feares her" (22). Fear, ultimately, is at the heart of the relations he describes, and although he claims freedom from it, his whole elaborate assault is partly an attempt to cope with the threat she poses.

The closing lines turn this sense of uneasiness against the Pucell herself, seeking to undermine confidence in her own security. Earlier Jonson had suggested that she regarded her suitors as dispensable, but the final passage (especially 37–39) reverses that coin by highlighting her own vulnerability. Jonson's solicitous concern for her "fame" (36) seems all the more cutting since his own poem so effectively undermines it. In advising her to "steale away" while she still enjoys some modicum of respect, he implicitly threatens her, insinuating the damage his poem can wreak while also suggesting that it simply repeats rumors already current (40). The effect is to give her a good dose of her own medicine, to make her as anxious about public censure and alienation as Jonson seems to have been when he began the poem. Of course, the wits or lords will hardly abandon her because of belated moral misgivings; instead, and as always, their decisions will be rooted in self-interest. The Pucell will thus fall victim to the very narcissism she incarnates. Exposed and excoriated, she will be subject to the same "scorne" (45) she now directs against Jonson.

The poem's last lines, thick with religious imagery (including a submerged allusion to the virgin birth), not only remind us of the Pucell's irreverence but supply a comprehensive perspective from which the corruption of the entire court can be judged. Although Jonson mocks "Divine[s]" and "Sermoneeres" (25; 39), his poem implicitly discharges the functions they ignore. Opening with a reference to the Pucell's specific censure of Jonson, closing with a reference to a more generalized scorn, the epigram achieves a symmetry that places the incident from which it sprang in a more meaningful perspective. Jonson presents himself not as a single man maligned (perhaps with good reason) by a particular aristocrat, but as a beleaguered champion of virtue. What might have seemed simply an isolated exchange in a personal feud is thus transmuted into an opposition with all the interest and significance of the enduringly typical.

This superior note of prophetic admonition is compromised a bit when we remember how and with what results the epigram was circulated—how it was stolen from Jonson's pocket in a moment of drunken stupor, and the "great displeasur" he experienced when the Pucell was actually confronted with it. Whether this phrase refers to his own embarrassment, to some retaliation on her part, to a loss of favor with the Countess of Bedford, or to some other result or combination of these, what does seem plain—from Jonson's own words—is that at the time of Bulstrode's death at the Bedford estate in August 1609, his relations with her were still a matter of some discomfort.

Ironically, when she died, Jonson was one of a number of poets approached by George Garrard to compose verses in her memory. The resulting epitaph (*U.V.* 9) is not one of his better efforts, but it so completely contradicts his earlier assessment that what it lacks in literary merit, it more than makes up in biographical curiosity. Praising Bulstrode as "a Virgin" who "might have claym'd t'have made the Graces foure" (3; 6), it claims that "She was earthes Eye: / The sole Religious house, and Votary, / W[i]th Rites not bound, but conscience" (9–11). In an accompanying note to Garrard, Jonson makes relatively modest claims for the poem, taking some pride in it but admitting that his "invention hath not cooled so much to judge" (H&S 8:372). Nowhere, however, does he discuss the most intriguing question the poem poses: how could he so drastically and quickly reverse himself? Did he sincerely regret his earlier attack? If so, then it is difficult to understand, as Herford and the Simpsons have noted, why he not only preserved the poem but read it to Drummond almost a decade later (H&S 11:131). Perhaps, more deviously, he reasoned that his praise would seem so hyperbolic that it would actually redound to her discredit. This position has been supported by contending that Jonson's use of the conditional mode in effect undercuts the praise he offers, deliberately suggesting that what Bulstrode *might* have been, she was not.[15] But this argument neglects those statements of praise—the majority—that are undeniably indicative and declarative.

Perhaps Jonson was partly motivated by the dictum, "de mortuis, nil nisi bonum." But the simplest explanation, and the one most in keeping with Renaissance decorum, is that in the epitaph the writer speaks not in his own voice but in an anonymous tone dictated by the occasion and by the nature of his commission. His own views are irrelevant: what matters is that he say the appropriate thing, as his role as a public poet requires. In responding so promptly and competently to his friend's sudden request, he demonstrated the kind of responsible craftsmanship that must have been exceedingly useful to him as a patronage poet. And in fact, the final lines of his note suggest that he may have had patronage explicitly in mind as he was writing. After mentioning his sadness at Bulstrode's death, he continues: "Would God, I had seene her before that some [that] live might have corrected some prejudices they have had injuriously of mee." Herford and the Simpsons suggest that he may have been thinking of his relations with the Countess of Bedford (H&S 11:131). Perhaps he viewed the epitaph as a way of making public amends for his earlier attack, in which case one of his motives may have been to placate a woman far more important to him than the one whose death he commemorates.

The whole Bulstrode episode, in fact, suggests the kinds of constraints he operated under in dealing with superiors—how difficult it was to criticize them openly, how circumscribed his independence could be. Although he could recite his satire in private conversation with Drummond, while Bulstrode lived he had to be more circumspect. His righteous stance—"let the world see" (2)—is at odds with what we know about the poem's actual circulation, and just as we need to be wary of uncritically accepting the epigram's claims, so it seems dangerous to over-estimate the poetic license Jonson enjoyed in his career as a whole. The idea of such freedom was as attractive to him as it may be to us, but for that very reason we should guard against assuming it too easily, against confusing an appealing ideal with the everyday realities he had to confront and cope with.

The epigram "To Sir Henry Nevil" (*Ep.* 109) has invited this kind of idealization, especially since Jonson himself encourages it. The poem begins by asserting that its muse is one that "serves nor fame, nor titles; but doth chuse / Where vertue makes them both" (2–3). Neville himself is praised as one who does not seek "miseries with hope" (5), one who does not pretend to serve "the publique, when the end / Is private gaine" (7–8). Instead, he strives "the matter to possesse, / And elements of honor, then the dresse" (9–10). As in many of his poems of praise, the qualities Jonson ascribes to his subject are implicitly ascribed to himself. Just as Neville is too scrupulous to make "private gaine" his ruling passion (8), so Jonson implies the same about his own relations with Neville, while his praise of his patron's selflessness helps promote his own self-interests. But however much the poem tries to distance Neville from the scramble for preferment, it inevitably reflects his involvement in the pursuit of power. Whether intended primarily to console him for some momentary setback, to enhance his competitive standing, or both, it necessarily served some purpose in relation to the patronage system in which Neville was inescapably implicated, and which he could not afford to ignore.

This reading—stressing how the epigram serves the mutual patronage interests of both author and subject—seems to contradict what Jonson's editors have had to say about Neville's social standing. Ian Donaldson, for instance, follows Herford and the Simpsons in reporting that Neville, an "MP from 1584 to 1614, ambassador to France 1599–1600, had been imprisoned in the Tower and heavily fined for his involvement in Essex's plot; though released in 1603, he remained out of royal favour." Similarly, William Hunter, after noting Neville's imprisonment, adds that he "was not in James's favor because of his sympathy with the popular party." And from such information Edward Partridge draws the reasonable (and appealing) conclusion that "it could not have been profitable to praise [Neville] since he was apparently as out of favor with James as he had been with Elizabeth." Partridge concludes: "Something about Neville's courage and integrity, and his refusal to knuckle under to either Elizabeth or James may have caught Jonson's admiration; something certainly caught his poetic interest."[16] The appeal of this reading is that it seems to confirm the image Jonson presents in the poem of both Neville's and his own essential independence. To praise a man so clearly out of favor thus comes to seem an act of clear and disinterested principle, and Partridge's statement that "it could not have been profitable" can even imply that Jonson did so at some risk to his own standing.

But Neville's actual place in the Jacobean hierarchy was more complicated than brief notes can suggest. His involvement in Essex's plot may have been partly motivated by his ambition to replace Robert Cecil as Secretary. When the plot failed, he went to the Tower; but after James's

accession he was released, and his hopes of becoming Secretary re-
vived. Again, however, Cecil stood in his way, and it may have been
frustrated ambition as much as anything else that eventually led to his
involvement with the so-called popular party. Never, though, did he
become a full-fledged opponent of James or the court; his power derived, in fact, from his position as a middleman, as someone who could
serve as a bridge between the court and Commons. But he never quite
gave up his aspiration someday to serve the King as Secretary.[17]

That opportunity seemed to present itself early in 1612, as Cecil's
health deteriorated. Months before he actually died, rumors were already circulating that Neville might replace him, and although Neville
at first publicly denied any interest in the office, with the help of
powerful allies he spent the next year and more campaigning for it.
Eventually the post was once again withheld from him—apparently in
part because of "too much soliciting" by Neville's supporters. But at the
time when Jonson's *Epigrammes* volume was entered in the Stationers'
Register in the spring of 1612, it must have seemed anything but
unprofitable to publish praise of Neville. This is not to say that Jonson's
motives were opportunistic or expedient; the poem may have been
written years before it was printed. It is only to argue that Neville's
status—and consequently Jonson's relations with him—were more complicated than either the poem, its editors, or its commentators sometimes imply. If Neville was as clearly out of favor as some notes suggest,
it is unlikely that he would ever have been taken so seriously for so long
as a candidate for such a prestigious office. And it is worth wondering,
too, whether Jonson could have afforded to praise such a man in print if
he had really been so utterly disliked by the King.[18]

Just as Jonson's role probably prevented him from praising freely
whomever he might "chuse," so it also seems to have kept him from
attacking odious superiors openly, even if they attacked him first. His
satires are usually nameless not only because, as has often been
claimed, he was more concerned to reprehend vice than to malign the
vicious, but perhaps also for the more practical reason that personal
attacks could be personally risky. The events surrounding the Pucell
epigram indicate how Jonson could seek to circumvent such risks. But
although the poem scrupulously mentions no names, when he read it
he could (and obviously did) make its target clear.[19]

Other poems suggest that he pursued this same strategy. His satirical
epigrams thus derived part of their real force from the social context in
which they were *presented*; much of their impact depended less on
what they said than on what was said about them—and to whom. The
epigram to the Countess of Bedford about the promised buck (*Ep.* 84),
for instance, depends partly on the guilty lord's knowledge that Jonson

has been talking behind his back. The poem mentions no name but makes clear that the poet does. Indeed, its effectiveness as an appeal to Lucy depends on her recognition that although she benefits from such gossip, she might just as easily be its victim. The Rutland "Epistle," with its more public (but for that reason more subtle) brand of intimidation, provides another example of this strategy. And one of Jonson's most famous, most curt, and most curious epigrams—"To My Lord Ignorant" (*Ep.* 10)—provides another still:

> Thou call'st me *Poet*, as a terme of shame:
> But I have my revenge made, in thy name.
>
> (1–2)

From one perspective this poem lays bare Jonson's relative impotence, for while the lord he mentions could attack him by name, the epigram implicitly concedes his inability to retaliate in kind, at least in writing. The poem may claim to take revenge by naming the lord, but realistically speaking this was precisely what it could not do. Jonson seems caught between the need to assert his dignity and the risk of lapsing into harmless, ridiculous bluster. He copes by turning the problem, apparently, to his own advantage, implying that the lord's anonymity (except in the abusive title) is itself a kind of revenge. Unlike the admirable figures whose names occupy other pages of the *Epigrammes* volume, the ignorant lord's name is forever lost, unremembered by posterity. This is revenge of a sort—the sort especially likely to appeal to poets and critics, who tend to take poetry more seriously than do such men as Jonson's lord. But when the poem's social context is recalled—when one reflects that it was probably first published from Jonson's own mouth—another aspect of its revenge, and of the second line's meaning, becomes clear. Surely when he spoke the poem, Jonson identified its target, just as he identified the Pucell; surely the epigram's first and most important readers knew who was meant. And surely it is this kind of *social* revenge that would have truly threatened a man otherwise so contemptuous of poets.[20]

Jonson thus revenges himself not only by branding the lord "ignorant" or by refusing to name him in print (both relatively ineffectual tactics), but by naming him so as to do the most damage. If the lord's identity had truly been known only to Jonson, the poem's retaliatory effectiveness would have been practically nil. In any of his personal satires, it must have been this interplay between text and context that was of most concern to the targets themselves. Ironically, the most potent revenge he could inflict on such antagonists could be inflicted not by his words alone but only by words embedded in precisely the kind of gossip for which the targets are often faulted.

In a later and more elaborate poem, Jonson again seems to confront the problem of dealing with social superiors for whom he has little real respect but whose power and status make their judgments difficult to ignore. In the elegy beginning "Let me be what I am" (*Und.* 42), his first concern is to defend himself against the jealousies of "Fathers, and Husbands" who suspect his praise of their "Daughters and . . . Wives" (11; 19). Such suspicions may in fact have been a problem for Jonson, if comments recorded by Drummond can be believed.[21] Yet despite the elegy's humorous tone and its emphasis on the special trials and vexations of writing verse to women, the poem implicitly raises larger and more fundamental questions—questions about the poet's possible independence and about the nature of his attitudes toward some of the superiors with whom he had to deal. Combining mock self-deprecation with satiric ferocity, the elegy evolves from a defense of the poet's motives into an attack on the unnamed antagonists who question them. In the opening lines, Jonson turns their suspicions to public advantage, depicting such misguided reactions as convincing testimony to his own poetic skills:

> Let me be what I am, as *Virgil* cold;
>   As *Horace* fat; or as *Anacreon* old;
> No Poets verses yet did ever move,
>   Whose Readers did not thinke he was in love.
> Who shall forbid me then in Rithme to bee
>   As light, and active as the youngest hee
> That from the Muses fountaines doth indorse
>   His lynes, and hourely sits the Poets horse?
> Put on my Ivy Garland, let me see
>   Who frownes, who jealous is, who taxeth me.
> Fathers, and Husbands, I doe claime a right
>   In all that is call'd lovely: take my sight
> Sooner then my affection from the faire.
>   No face, no hand, proportion, line, or Ayre
> Of beautie; but the Muse hath interest in:
>   There is not worne that lace, purle, knot, or pin,
> But is the Poëts matter: And he must,
>   When he is furious, love, although not lust.
> But then consent, your Daughters and your Wives,
>   (If they be faire and worth it) have their lives
> Made longer by our praises. Or, if not,
>   Wish, you had fowle ones, and deformed got;
> Curst in their Cradles, or there chang'd by Elves,
>   So to be sure you doe injoy your selves.
> Yet keepe those up in sackcloth too, or lether,
>   For Silke will draw some sneaking Songster thither.

> It is a ryming Age, and Verses swarme
>   At every stall; The Cittie Cap's a charme.

$$(1-28)^{22}$$

These lines are masterful in several respects. The opening phrase reads at first like an exasperated plea for poetic independence, as if the poet chafes under the burden of external expectations. This sense of the phrase lingers and helps color the tone of the rest of the work, but it soon becomes clear that its primary meaning is more explanatory than defiant, more concessive than contemptuous. "Although I am as fat as Horace and as old as Anacreon," Jonson says in effect, "some readers still insist on seeing my 'love' poems as expressions of personal feeling." Here and throughout, he balances agitated self-assertion with attractive modesty. His use of the "fat old Ben" persona is at once disarming and appealing, allowing him to make claims for himself far more effectively than if he had offered more bald or peremptory assertions. It allows him, for instance, to link himself with great classical predecessors, yet in a way that playfully minimizes any vanity or undue self-importance. By mocking his own appearance, he not only makes himself appear more attractive and deprives critics of an obvious weapon, but he also renders their jealousies more ridiculous. Their suspicions result not from his physical allure but from their innate egotism, but they are also a tribute to the power and beauty of his verse.

The poem effectively suggests, in fact, that because his critics' apparent concern for their daughters and wives merely reflects self-concern and conceit, they hardly differ from the scheming "Songster[s]" they despise (26). Jonson sets himself apart from both groups, distinguishing himself from poetic competitors who praise women merely to advance themselves and from such females' equally self-interested relatives. Jonson alone, the poem suggests, appreciates their true beauty and merit. By highlighting the self-interests of others, he de-emphasizes his own and the ways this poem promotes them. Yet concern about his use of poetry for self-advancement—and not simply or even necessarily about his real romantic attitudes—was probably at the heart of much of the "jealousy" he attacks. The poem's satiric double-thrust, its assault both on other poets and on unnamed but hostile superiors, suggests that more important matters were involved than merely his affections. It suggests that some aristocrats, like the possibly fictional one he attacks, regard women in purely external (even baldly economic) terms. Just as the "sneaking Songster[s]" either cannot or will not appreciate more than women's outward trappings, so the unsavory aristocrat treats his own wife and daughter like the voyeur we later discover him to be (59–

64). His attitude, in its unhealthy tendency to make others the objects of his detached but self-absorbed amusement, denies any possibility of genuine trust and community.

Jonson suggests that such aristocrats are as much obsessed with appearances and outward status as those who serve them (26). His claimed indifference to these values allows him, paradoxically, to advertise his social prominence; he draws attention to his courtly standing (29–36) even while suggesting his disinterest in using it for selfish gain. He asserts his importance in a way that seems non-threatening. Despite his satiric tone and announced liabilities as a lover, Jonson emerges from the elegy as the figure most capable of love, most able to relate to others sincerely. Yet his public self-defense seems less concerned with his traits either as lover or love poet than with his general trustworthiness as a member of the social hierarchy. Lust was a less important charge than insubordination. However contemptuous Jonson may have felt toward the individual aristocrat he attacks (if, indeed, any single person *is* aimed at), he could not afford to ignore the kinds of suspicions and charges the poem confronts. Such accusations would undermine the credibility and effectiveness of any poet dependent on patrons, because at root they challenged the motives of his writing, suggesting that he used it chiefly for private gain. Whether or not this poem was written with an actual superior in mind, its disgust with the writer's vulnerability to suspicions from above seems real enough. Yet the fact that Jonson could never have dared to name his target openly (at least not in his text) is part of the silent significance of this poem.

Appreciating the contexts of Jonson's writing seems crucial to appreciating the complexities both of his works and of his social position. The more we know about the conditions that helped shape his works, the less likely we are to judge his character hastily. The more closely we examine the issues of independence and flattery in his works, the more problematic they seem. As both the Pucell epigram and the poem to Neville suggest, our views of Jonson's "freedom" need to regard more than simply the words on the page; they need to be anchored, as far as possible, in the specific facts of particular situations. In most cases those facts are lost to us, but enough survive to warn us away from any simple assertion that the poet was either wholly autonomous *or* completely subservient. In assessing his disdain for flattery, we need to ask how such disdain might actually have promoted his interests as a dependent; in dealing with his satire on superiors, we need to ponder its circumstances and the ways it might have advanced his and others' power. While appreciating the real limits to his authority, we nonetheless need to consider how nearly all his works promote or defend it.

For Jonson, issues of power were acute precisely because he operated in a patronage culture. His place was by definition subordinate; he did not enjoy the luxury either of safely asserting full autonomy or of ignoring others' influence. Poets' dependence was a fact of life and had been for centuries. It therefore seems unwise to exaggerate the degree to which they felt oppressed: they did not necessarily share more modern assumptions about personal freedom, and since many assumed (as many moderns do not) that true, "objective" values were possible, they could at least hypothesize a power structure that mirrored legitimate truths. Today, as confidence in the likelihood of determining objective values erodes, external power is increasingly viewed as coercive, but it is important not to project our own assumptions onto an earlier age. Jonson's view of himself as a servant of society seems to have been more than simply a rationalization (although it may have been partly that). It was undoubtedly also the heartfelt conviction of a writer who could hardly conceive of his value in other terms.

Yet, while Jonson was probably not a free spirit oppressed, neither was his adaptation to the demands of his role wholly unproblematic. However sincerely committed he may have been to his society's larger values, plenty of evidence indicates that he sometimes chafed at his subordination to the real and fallible persons whose power made them especially responsible for implementing those values. The fact that he and his contemporaries may have shared certain broad, "objective" ideals did not necessarily minimize the potential for interpersonal struggle or even for dissatisfaction with particular figures who should theoretically have commanded deference. Wide agreement about the ideal characteristics of a social role may in fact expose those attempting to discharge it to even more criticism (or to resentment or suppressed contempt) than if no such agreement exists. Similarly, the presumption that objective values do exist, that one can know what they are and embrace them, may make the participants in power struggles that much more determined and dogmatic. When all values are uncertain, one may be less likely to identify one's own position with the "truth" or with "right"; but when most people adhere at least nominally to the same ideals, conflicts are perhaps even more likely to have a personal or tactical edge.

That Jonson wrote in a society whose structure and ideology were relatively well-defined by no means implies that his role was un-troubled or secure. The impulses to romanticize his situation by view-ing him either as an oppressed crypto-democrat or as an unperturbed servant of God or country should both be resisted. So, by the same token, should any tendency toward automatic cynicism, whether this means viewing him as a toady or as a schemer. Both reactions may reflect more our own preoccupations than the complexities of his real position. "Dependence," writes Arnold Hauser, "is the precursor of every attachment and loyalty, as well as of every uprising and aggression."[23] Jonson's undeniable dependence made him neither a rebel nor a marionette, but it inevitably made issues of power central to what and how he wrote. Since his most important audience consisted of figures who enjoyed more power than he, his attitudes toward them were likely to be even more ambivalent than those most writers feel toward their readers.[24]

4
Poems for Patrons

The crucial fact about Jonson's poetry is that it was written with an audience very clearly in mind. Unlike the Romantic or modern poet, who may write chiefly to express his feelings, to create an autonomously beautiful object, or to offer a unique insight into reality, Jonson could never afford to forget that his first obligation was to his readers. In part this fact reflects the central rhetorical emphasis of Renaissance poetics, the assumption (derived from Horace) that the purpose of poetry was either to teach or to please, and ideally to do the first by doing the second. Certainly Jonson endorsed this view; indeed, he twice translated the *Ars Poetica* and wrote a commentary on it (subsequently lost). The Horatian formula, especially as it was given a didactic emphasis by Renaissance interpreters, provided poets and poetry a defensible social function. Horace's treatise may itself have been addressed to patrons and partly for that reason may have been useful to Renaissance poets seeking a model for their own accommodations to the demands that their subordinate position imposed on them. But the patronage situation inevitably complicated the relatively simple Horatian dictum. Jonson's "Panegyre" to James, written to celebrate the King's opening of Parliament in 1604, is a stunning example: adopting the role of spokesman for the nation, he nonetheless also subtly distinguishes himself from his fellow countrymen. Acting in one sense to legitimate the King's power, he thereby also helps legitimate his own social role. His poetry may teach by pleasing, but its teaching is not disinterested. And the situation is further complicated by the fact that what and how he taught were matters he could not determine entirely on his own.

As a patronage poet, Jonson did not so much create values as affirm values already widely recognized and accepted. Creative in a different sense than a Romantic or modern poet, he sought less to discover new truths than to make old ones freshly persuasive. His usefulness both to society and to individual patrons was promoted by creativity of this kind. More recent poetic ideals—such as discovering truth, creating beauty, or expressing one's innermost feelings—can all be justified as ends in themselves. They suggest a more private conception of poetry than Jonson's, one that assumes less automatically the poet's need to communicate. Often in modern poetics the poem seems simply a transcript of a prior imaginative state, an attempt to capture a personal experience more intense, more real and valuable than the poem that endeavors to express it. But the patronage poem—however broadly or narrowly the term is defined—always presupposes the poet's awareness of an audience and the inevitability that his work will affect not only them but also their attitudes toward its author. Whether he simply reflects his culture's values, attempts to persuade others to embrace them, or tries to convince a particular patron of his personal worthiness, Jonson is always more or less conscious that he is writing for someone else.

The poem addressed explicitly to a superior, which might be called the essential or archetypal patronage poem and which makes up such a large part of Jonson's output, has no real counterpart in recent writing. Neither the Romantic lyric nor its Victorian heirs, neither symbolism, expressionism, imagism, nor more recent notions demand such a radical accommodation to another ego. In Jonson's poetry the terms of that accommodation are frequently complex and multifaceted and help contribute to the poem's power as a work of art. His preoccupation with his audience, far from stifling his creativity, more often than not promotes it. The challenges he meets and faces in his poems of patronage are not only the ones he sets for himself but the ones set *for* him by his circumstances.

Written for superiors who could reward, punish, or damagingly ignore him, for rivals who might criticize, or for friends who might offer assistance or relief from competitive pressures, Jonson's patronage poetry simply as rhetoric seems bound to have been multilayered and entangled. Even a poem of "plain" statement was inevitably more than that, for the statement it made concerned not only itself but its author's image and his attempt to project it. Poems of "direct address" can become the most indirect and complicated of all, for in them the poet most clearly confronts another ego and exposes his image to attack or rejection.

Poems to King James

Precisely when or how Jonson first came to James's attention cannot be said. The monarch may have heard of him early in his reign from Sir Robert Cotton; or from Queen Anne and Prince Henry, spectators at the 1603 *Entertainment at Althrope*; or from the various aristocrats whose favors Jonson had courted over the preceding years; or from the Scottish nobleman Esme Stuart, Lord Aubigny, with whom Jonson may have been living at this time (H&S 11:576–77). Or perhaps he knew that Jonson and his friend, Sir John Roe, had been ejected from the court for misbehaving during a performance of Samuel Daniel's *Vision of the Twelve Goddesses* (H&S 1:39). Or, more ominously, he may have known that Jonson had been summoned before the Privy Council to defend *Sejanus*. Whatever the cause of the accusations against that play, Jonson's reputation seems to have escaped unscathed: when arrangements were being made to celebrate the King's opening of Parliament in March 1604, Jonson was one of two poets chosen to write speeches and songs for delivery at the various triumphal arches through which the royal procession would pass. (Ironically, the other poet was Jonson's old nemesis, Dekker, who later could not resist the temptation to gibe at him for using the occasion to display his knowledge of the classics; see H&S 7:67, 77–79, and 10:386–88). A few weeks later the King and Queen witnessed *A Private Entertainment*, written by Jonson and commissioned by Sir William Cornwallis. A little more than a year after James's accession, then, Jonson had begun to achieve the kind of official recognition that had eluded him under Elizabeth.

The speeches for James's procession are of little interest today, he took full advantage of the opportunities they presented. As Dekker recognized, the occasion provided the perfect background for self-display. Shortly after delivery, the speeches were rushed into print, with copious annotations as unspoken but eloquent evidence of their author's learning. The same quarto also included a work of far more lasting value. Jonson's "Panegyre" to James (H&S 7:113–17) is important not only as one of the first English examples of this prestigious genre but as an accomplished poem in its own right, one in which Jonson both fulfilled and exploited his public role. Acting both as servant of and spokesman for the public, he enhanced his own power by helping to legitimate and shape the King's. In the "Panegyre," he helped fashion not only one man's role but the larger institution of kingship.[1]

The "Panegyre" has a mythic resonance uncharacteristic of Jonson's poems. In part its manner, tone, and imagery are dictated by its circumstances and genre, but Jonson does more than go through prescribed and conventional motions. The work has a metaphorical density, a sense of movement within an unfolding unity. James stands at the center of intersecting spheres, an axis around whom the poem, his kingdom, and even the universe ostensibly revolve. Yet this celebration of his power is insistently checked by a countervailing emphasis on the threats he faces. The "Panegyre" exalts harmony, but its exaltation is

informed and intensified by an underlying awareness of potential discord. An opening passage comparing the King to the rising sun is
immediately countered by references to private sins and to "forraine
malice, or unnaturall spight" (29). Here and throughout, the poem
exalts the patron even as it plays up sources of insecurity. In the
"Panegyre" as in many of his works, Jonson underscores his own
usefulness by reminding his superiors of their power's real limits.

Throughout the poem, Jonson implicitly claims to voice moods and
attitudes others feel but are unable to articulate. He speaks for the
people while implying his distinction from them. His references to
their extreme reactions—to their mute rapture and excited shouting—
point up by contrast the skill and measured accomplishment of his own
response; yet his poem incorporates those reactions even as it transcends them. As a master of words who can give lasting sense and
shape to significant events, the poet enjoys an attractive and powerful
mystique. The King may summon up and focus enormous energies, but
only the poet (Jonson implies) can give them permanence. His work
both recreates and reenacts the harmony it celebrates. It helps fashion
and perpetuate the power it extols.

Harmony from discord is one of the poem's central themes, which
helps account for its frequent use of paradox. By describing the people's
eyes as "covetous," for instance (34), Jonson reverses the word's typical
connotations, using it to describe their genuine love for James. Similarly, his comparison of the "amorous" City's preparations to those of
"ambitious dames, when they make feast, / And would be courted" (52–
53) not only reminds readers of his own role in preparing the festivities
but also distinguishes the selfish ambition of the dames from the City's
genuine affection. Even the muted competition between London and
Westminster (55) signals a shared determination to honor James. Indeed, the poem often reverses terms associated with competitive strife,
yet without wholly depriving them of their original overtones. Although the work implies that the King's influence dissolves social and
intellectual contradictions, here as elsewhere the emphatic celebration
of a patron's powers insinuates the poet's.

In the poem's longest section, Jonson deals with James's responsibilities to his subjects, as explained by the goddess Themis (77–108).
What is fascinating is the passage's heavy emphasis on contemporary
social pressures. The monarch, Jonson implies, is especially susceptible to the self-consciousness engendered by the system he heads.
Through Themis, the poet evokes and plays on James's "feare / In
publique acts what face and forme" he bears (87–88), even as the
present work suggests the poet's usefulness in shaping such appearances. Themis, at once the poet's mouthpiece and ostensibly an aspect

of the King's own nature, exemplifies Jonson's decorous fulfillment of his role, as she instructs the King in virtues he supposedly already possesses. When the poem shifts from what she says to what James ostensibly knows (109ff.), there is little break in continuity. Just as Jonson earlier gave Themis words to speak, now he credits James with attractive thoughts. A new kind of concord makes it difficult to distinguish poet from goddess from King.

Jonson repeatedly demonstrates the architectonic skills that give the poem its convincing coherence. When he mentions, for instance, a previous monarch "Whose necessary good 'twas now to be / An evill king" (116–17), the paradox looks back to previous examples. But while those paradoxes had refurbished suspect terms, making covetousness and ambition seem virtuous, in this instance "good" is perverted and debased. Similarly, the paradox of one wickedness befriending and defending another (120) gains further force when juxtaposed with the "friendly temper'd" cooperation mentioned earlier (71–72). The "Panegyre" owes much of its impact to its self-containment, with its different parts resonating with or playing off against each other. At other times, however, it draws on sources of energy outside itself, as when James's coming is implicitly likened to Christ's ("a fate / Was gently falne from heaven upon this state; / . . . a father they did now enjoy / That came to save, what discord would destroy" [135–38]). The allusion's muted nature makes it all the more effective; James's position is rendered more legitimate by being bracketed with his culture's central myth. Yet the poem's final lines introduce new insecurity just when the celebration becomes happiest and most intense:

> And this confession flew from every voyce:
> *Never had land more reason to rejoyce.*
> *Nor to her blisse, could ought now added bee,*
> *Save, that shee might the same perpetuall see.*
> Which when time, nature, and the fates deny'd,
> With a twice louder shoute againe they cry'd,
> *Yet, let blest* Brit[t]aine *aske (without your wrong)*
> *Still to have such a king, and this king long.*
>
> (155–62)

Although the passage nearly fuses the voices of people and poet, a distinction remains. The people long for the continuance of present "*blisse*"—whether this means merely the holiday spirit, the deeper harmony behind it, the King who evokes it, or all these. Yet Jonson refuses to sentimentalize: the holiday must inevitably pass, the harmony must partly deteriorate, the King himself must someday die. Just when we might have expected him to declare the occasion's transcendent significance, he skillfully reintroduces a note of disharmony, dis-integration, and death. Only the present poem lends the event any measure of permanence, not only by preserving it on paper but by recreating and reviving for each participant the mood and energy of that day. When the final line implores that Britain may always have "*such a king, and this king long,*" the King referred to is not only the historical James but the James whose image has been partly fashioned by this poem. The line compliments the King while also impressing on him the necessity that "*this king*" always be "*such a king*"—the kind of King the poem claims he is and helps him appear to be. James may be the source and focus of the harmony the poem celebrates, but it is through Jonson's words that that harmony continues to live. The Latin tag with which the poem concludes—"*Solus Rex, & Poeta non quotannis nascitur*"—is neither an excrescence nor an afterthought but instead an explicit statement of what the whole poem implies: "Only the king and the poet are not of everyday birth."

This idea was important to Jonson; he uses it frequently in soliciting the support of a monarch who had demonstrated an early interest in poetry. In one of his most carefully crafted epigrams (*Ep.* 4), he exploits the comparison so as to compliment James while enhancing his own standing. Here again, though, praise of the King's power also insinuates his need:

> How, best of Kings, do'st thou a scepter beare!
>   How, best of *Poets*, do'st thou laurell weare!
> But two things, rare, the Fates had in their store,
>   And gave thee both, to shew they could no more.
> For such a *Poet*, while thy dayes were greene,
>   Thou wert, as chiefe of them are saide t'have beene.
> And such a Prince thou art, wee daily see,
>   As chiefe of those still promise they will bee.
> Whom should my *Muse* then flie to, but the best
>   Of Kings for grace; of *Poets* for my test?
>
>   (1–10)

Using parallel syntax and structure to underscore the King's parallel accomplishments, Jonson exploits the monarch's pride in his literary achievement to help improve and ensure his own social status. To the extent that James was willing to accept in his own case Jonson's high valuation of the poet's role, he had logically to value similarly the role of poets in general. Jonson's compliment, then, actually magnifies his own importance; far from demeaning him, his praise promotes recognition of his own significance. And yet the need to praise implies his subordinate position.

By describing James's talents as themselves gifts of fate, Jonson augments the prestige of poets but also implies the King's own dependence. Both men have been gifted with poetic ability: all that distinguishes them is James's further gift of preeminent social power. By emphasizing how much the King himself owes to gifts of fortune, Jonson at once compliments him and reminds him (and others) of his capacity to share those gifts more widely. Such understated pressure is typical of the poem's subtlety. Thus, Jonson idealizes the union of poetic and political power while making it clear that James himself can no longer effect that union on his own. Praise of the King thus turns into muted advertisement of Jonson's own talent and availability. James *can* reunite both powers, but only by invoking assistance. Indeed, in the final lines Jonson draws on his earlier dual tribute to imply that as both poet and King, James is also best equipped to act as patron. As a poet, he can judge writers' merits; as a King, he can grant the worthy the "grace" they deserve. Jonson's willingness to submit himself to James's "test" insinuates a final compliment, but it also suggests confidence that his poetry can withstand even the most exacting scrutiny. Here, as elsewhere, he turns public humility into canny self-assertion. Indeed, the entire poem illustrates how complex the implications of his praise could be, how well he could use it to play up his superiors' deficiencies and yet how much his need to do so suggests his own insecurity. The King may have served unseen "fates," but the powers Jonson depended on could in some ways be far more capricious.

Poems to Robert Cecil

In the process of becoming James's most important deputy, Robert Cecil accumulated even more power and wealth than his father, Lord Burghley, had amassed under Elizabeth. Already extremely influential during the closing years of the old Queen's reign, Cecil had helped assure a smooth transition to the new regime (and his own continued prominence) by conducting secret negotiations with the Scottish King. When James took command, Cecil's assistance was not forgotten. He was allowed to keep his former offices as Master of the Wards and Secretary of State but was also made, in rapid sequence, first a baron, then a viscount, then Earl of Salisbury in May 1605. One of Jonson's poems may have been written to commemorate this last elevation; another was more certainly written to celebrate his appointment, in 1608, as Lord Treasurer. Although remembered more as a sly political tactician and skillful statesman than as a patron of letters, Cecil seems in fact to have been one of the most significant of Jonson's aristocratic contacts.[2]

It was natural for Jonson to cultivate Cecil's attentions: like his father before him, he had become perhaps the central figure, after James, in the entire patronage system. His own wealth and influence depended extraordinarily on the monarch's trust and favor; but as long as he enjoyed these, he could be invaluable as an intermediary or benefactor.[3] Jonson had already had some contact with Cecil while Elizabeth ruled; under James, however, their relationship became more intimate and their dealings more frequent. Four times between 1606 and 1609, Cecil commissioned Jonson to write speeches or entertainments for presentation before the King, a fact highly suggestive about Jonson's favor with James, even so early in his reign.[4] Cecil was nothing if not an adept courtier; he would have been unlikely to have chosen Jonson, and chosen him repeatedly, had he not been confident the King would be pleased.

Although Jonson was handsomely compensated, he may never have felt entirely comfortable with the Earl. "Salisbury," Drummond recorded him as saying, "never cared for any man longer [than] he could make use of him" (H&S 1:142). By the time of this comment, the Earl had been disgraced and dead for a good while, and it had become fashionable to derogate him. But if the remark bears at all on Jonson's earlier attitude, it suggests a distrust and disrespect he could not express openly in his poems—a possibility that makes their subtler implications all the more interesting to contemplate.[5]

Whatever his later attitudes or however he may have "really" felt about Cecil over the course of their long relationship, in the years immediately following James's accession, both men proved variously and mutually useful. Jonson's poems helped burnish Cecil's reputation, while Cecil's lucrative commissions handsomely supplemented Jonson's income. But the trade-offs could be even more practical. Thus, Cecil may have helped Jonson in 1605 in connection with *Eastward Ho*, while Jonson soon returned the favor by assisting his investigation of the Gunpowder Plot (H&S 1:194–96; 40–41). Even *Hymenaei*, his second masque, promoted Cecil's interests. Performed in January 1606, its immediate purpose was "the auspicious celebrating of the Marriage-union, betweene *Robert*, Earle of *Essex*, and the Lady *Frances*, second Daughter to the most noble Earle of *Suffolk*" (H&S 7:207). Reporting home, however, the Venetian ambassador succinctly explained the wedding's political purpose:

> Six months later another daughter of [Suffolk] is to marry a son of Lord Salisbury. The object is to reconcile the young Earl of Essex to Lord Salisbury if possible. Essex is but little the friend of Salisbury, who was the sole and governing cause of the late Earl's execution. Nothing is more earnestly desired by Salisbury than not to leave this

legacy of hatred to his son . . . [yet] there is no doubt but that, when the Earl of Essex is a little older, suggestions and persuasions to revenge will not be wanting. Lord Salisbury hopes by creating ties of relationship to cancel the memory of these ancient enmities; many, however, are of opinion that this is too feeble a medicine for so great an ill. (H&S 10:465)

This fascinating report communicates the anxiety courtly existence could induce even in so powerful a figure as Cecil. And it also suggests how symbolic forms—whether marriages, masques, or occasional poems—could be used to cope with insecurity and tension. Both wedding and masque functioned in part politically, not so much celebrating an antecedent harmony as attempting either to fashion concord out of conflicting interests or to impose it on them. Jonson's masque helps legitimate the marriage by lending it symbolic weight, yet here as elsewhere it seems important not to take his art entirely on its own terms. *Hymenaei* conveys little sense of the real social and political tensions from which it was born. Instead it transfigures them, rendering them symbolically but thereby disguising and simplifying them. Cecil's opponents must have viewed the masque less as a compelling vision of concord than as an elaborate rhetorical ploy. It asserts harmony but could not guarantee its achievement. Like Jonson's poems, the masque could never really transcend political struggle, only continue it by other means.[6]

Cecil's power coincided with deep apprehension and insecurity. His unusual prominence inevitably made him the target of envy and dissatisfaction. Like Jonson, the higher he rose, the more he came to count (financially and psychologically) on the benefits of his position, especially since his fortunes depended more than most on the King's sufferance. Occasionally he defended himself publicly against detraction, and it has even been argued that Jonson may have assisted him in these efforts.[7] In one fascinating document on "The State and Dignity of a Secretary of State's Place, with the Care and Peril Thereof," Cecil himself outlined the special precariousness and dangers of his position. "All officers and counsellors of princes have a prescribed authority by patent, by custom, or by oath," he writes; ". . . only a secretary hath no warrant or commission, no, not in matters of his own greatest particulars, but the virtue and word of his sovereign." Thus "the secretary's life [is] his trust in the prince. . . . all that he hath to trust to . . . is, that his prince will be *semper idem*." While numerous foreign and domestic enemies hate secretaries, "Their fellow-counsellors envy them, because they have most free and easy access to princes." "[T]he place of a secretary is dreadful," Cecil continually emphasizes, "if he serve not a constant prince," and he compares the counsels kept between sovereign and secretary to "the mutual affections of two lovers," with all the ambivalence that phrasing implies.[8] For all his power, Cecil suggests here and elsewhere his keen awareness of its limits. Certainly Jonson could sympathize: both men depended on patrons for economic and psychological support; both achieved a prominence so unusual that it might easily prove unstable; both were troubled by rivals; both were vulnerable to court politicking; neither could find an alternative to participating in the patronage system.

Recognition of Cecil's vulnerability is important not only in understanding the context of Jonson's poems but in achieving distance from them, so that features that might normally pass unnoticed stand in greater relief. Indeed, in reading these or any of his poems addressed to superiors, it is worth contemplating how his and his patrons' rivals might have reacted. These were the readers who would scrutinize the poems most carefully; viewing them as threats, they would be alive to each word, alert to each rhetorical strategy and micropolitical tactic. They would read closely, reacting less to the poet's total canon than to the nuances of each individually circulated work. And in this they provide an analytical model worth imitating. The poems to Cecil form an intriguing if unintended sequence, interesting for the larger problems it raises. Individually, the poems are less interesting as versified moral statements than as highly complex, highly self-conscious *performances*. Abstracting them from their immediate contexts inevitably simplifies them. Studying them closely means paying attention not only to what they say but to what they *do*. Epigram 43, for instance, does more than comment on the possible charge of flattery; it enacts a highly complex, finely nuanced response, combining equal measures of defensiveness and subtle aggression:

> What need hast thou of me? or of my *Muse?*
>   Whose actions so themselves doe celebrate;
> Which should thy countries love to speake refuse,
>   Her foes enough would fame thee, in their hate.
> 'Tofore, great men were glad of *Poets:* Now,
>   I, not the worst, am covetous of thee.
> Yet dare not, to my thought, lest hope allow
>   Of adding to thy fame; thine may to me,
> When, in my booke, men reade but Cecill's name,
>   And what I write thereof find farre, and free
> From servile flatterie (common *Poets* shame)
>   As thou stand'st cleere of the necessitie.
>
> (1–12)

By implying that Cecil needs no praise, Jonson simultaneously praises him, makes his praise seem more genuine, assumes a humble stance that balances his later proud distinction between himself and "common *Poets*" (11), and plants the question of need all the more firmly in the patron's mind. By claiming that Cecil's actions celebrate themselves, by implying that there is no (and can be no) disjunction between act and interpretation, the poem insinuates the extent to which Cecil's acts are precisely subject to others' reactions. The epigram itself is one such interpretation: despite its denials, its very existence points up the distinction between action and explication, between doing and being seen to do. Yet the poem also allows Cecil to think of any return he might offer as itself freely given rather than extracted because of need.

By reminding Cecil that in the past "great men were glad of *Poets*" (5), Jonson also reminds him that patrons as well as writers can be judged by exacting standards. Here as throughout, he implicitly intimidates Cecil, threatening his reputation even while seeming to defend it. Repeatedly he questions the real security of Cecil's status. Although he mentions foreign enemies, domestic antagonists obviously posed a far more immediate threat. Indeed, he explicitly raises the possibility that Cecil's own countrymen might refuse to honor him. Although he presents himself as a kind of spokesman for his countrymen's affection (distancing himself again from the charge of flattery), he and Cecil both knew that many despised and distrusted the Earl. By subtly reminding Cecil of his vulnerability to ill fame, Jonson goes a long way toward answering the poem's initial question.

Even while indicating Cecil's need, Jonson alludes to his own dependence, yet in ways that simplify and minimize it. Claiming to be "covetous" of Cecil (6), he immediately and cleverly subverts the word's obvious connotations. Although the succeeding reference to "hope" (7) at first seems to reinforce those common meanings, the next line alleges that what the poet *really* covets is only the opportunity to augment Cecil's fame. Selfishness, deflected into selflessness, is then deflected again: Jonson now claims that it is the *poet* who will benefit from association with Cecil (8–9)—a statement at once humble, true, complimentary, and, in the following lines, cunningly qualified. Balancing modesty and self-assertion (and thereby using modesty as a *means* of self-assertion), the closing passage affords a prime example of Jonson's tact. Line 9 seems to complete the syntax of the assertion about Cecil; but then the sentence continues. The final lines make it clear that Cecil's name will add fame to Jonson's book less because of its appearance than because of the poet's response. Celebrating the Earl's importance, Jonson re-insinuates his own. It is not simply the fact of their association but its quality (partly determined by the poet) that will add to the reputations of both.

Yet the final lines inevitably simplify Jonson's response. Emphasizing the single issue of avoiding flattery, they ignore the more clever means by which the poem intimidates and manipulates the patron. They de-emphasize each party's real needs and exaggerate the autonomy of both. They stress the relationship's ethical aspects while obscuring its micro-political dimensions. They accentuate the poet's virtue rather than his power or its limits, but this simplification itself works precisely to his political advantage.

The epigram implies that common poets have nothing to offer Cecil: indeed, patronizing them would threaten his reputation, giving his enemies openings for derision and disdain. Yet the very self-respect Jonson exhibits makes him a more attractive and useful dependent. For all its lofty language, his appeal is partly utilitarian and pragmatic. Although the poem's conclusion seems to parallel the opening idea of freedom from necessity, it actually undercuts surface symmetry, rein-forcing the implicit distinction between Jonson and his competitors. Cecil needs no flatterers, but this (he suggests) is different from not needing Jonson, who is free from "common *Poets* shame" (11)—mean-ing a shame common to poets and one to which common poets are prone. Predicting fame for the poet if he avoids flattery, the poem offers itself as evidence that he merits such renown and thereby helps him achieve it. Jonson's need to avoid seeming to flatter reflects his need to prove appealing.[9]

Another epigram to Cecil (*Ep.* 63) confronts some of the same issues, this time in a more tightly controlled structure. Here the rhetorical questions used so effectively in the earlier work help organize the entire poem:

> Who can consider thy right courses run,
>   With what thy vertue on the times hath won,
> And not thy fortune; who can cleerely see
>   The judgement of the king so shine in thee;
> And that thou seek'st reward of thy each act,
>   Not from the publike voyce, but private fact;
> Who can behold all envie so declin'd
>   By constant suffring of thy equall mind;
> And can to these be silent, *Salisburie,*
>   Without his, thine, and all times injurie?
> Curst be his *Muse,* that could lye dumbe, or hid
>   To so true worth, though thou thy selfe forbid.
>
> (1–12)

The opening questions explicitly characterize Cecil, but implicitly they present Jonson both as morally perceptive and as responsible enough to act on his perceptions. Although the questions pretend to generality, implying that anyone would feel compelled to praise Cecil's merit, in fact they highlight Jonson's specific act. Typical of the poem's unforced resonance is its claim that Cecil's advancement depended not on "fortune" (3), not on luck, chance, or ambitious scheming, but simply on his virtue. Inevitably this simplifies his rise,[10] but the simplification works to Jonson's advantage precisely by insinuating the alternatives it so studiously excludes. Certainly Cecil's competitors realized (and resented) that his status derived in large part from his good "fortune" of having had a powerful father determined to ensure his prominence. Thus, Jonson's words are much more specific, much more tactical and defensive than they initially appear. They imply that Cecil would have achieved his status despite the head start given him by his father's influence and wealth (another meaning of "fortune"). The poem, with its casual references to winning and "envie" (2; 7), obliquely mirrors a highly charged micropolitical context. Yet it obfuscates the very ambitions it plays upon, reflects, and epitomizes.

Jonson's calculated anonymity makes his praise seem almost an emanation of the "publike voyce" (6) to which Cecil is ostensibly indifferent, but which even so powerful a politician could hardly afford to ignore. The anonymity deflects attention from Jonson's personal motives; instead the poem is offered as an automatic, almost compulsive response to the patron's virtues. By repeatedly asking who could resist praising Cecil, the poet presents his own praise as natural and unforced; yet the insistent questions not only imply his defensive self-consciousness but also remind Cecil that many doubted the merit Jonson credits him with. The questions even imply that some who did recognize his virtues might nonetheless maliciously deny them. Thus the act of praise that Jonson depicts as so natural, necessary, and spontaneous appears, at second glance, far more problematic—a fact that enhances the value of his efforts. Although the epigram presents itself as the freely offered but inevitable response to Cecil's virtue, on closer examination it seems tightly tangled in the complex *realpolitik* of Jacobean courtlife.[11]

The poem's complexities result from the dialectic between its contexts and its language. The reference to Cecil's "equall mind" (8), for instance, illustrates the deceptive simplicity of Jonson's style. The adjective implies adequacy and fitness: Cecil is equal to his responsibilities. But his mind is also "equall" in its balance and justness: his fairness supposedly makes "envie" (general discontent as well as hostility aimed specifically at him) far less likely to occur. Raising the possibility of envy even while praising Cecil for diminishing it, Jonson again insinuates the usefulness of his own praise. The poem celebrates Cecil's adequacy but intimates his need for support. It praises his

mind's "constant suffring" (8)—nicely suggesting both unceasing attentiveness and the toll such attentiveness exacts. It exalts his mind as
"equall" (suggesting an almost Stoic composure and unruffled inner
security) even as it reminds him of the challenges and threats he faces.

If taken seriously, the poem would encourage others to praise Cecil—
at least other poets, to whom the last lines seem particularly addressed.
Competitively non-competitive, they challenge silent rivals even as
they advertise Jonson's own freedom from envy. By renouncing political
motives, he enhances his political position. Although the epigram
presents itself almost as a compulsive response to Cecil's virtues, it is at
the same time highly structured, consciously and artfully fashioned.
Supposedly it balances deeply felt emotion and mature deliberation,
yet the deeper and more complex tension at its heart is a tension
between praise (reflective or spontaneous) ostensibly innocent of selfish calculation, and the micropolitical savvy the poem so clearly exhibits, even in pretending not to. Whether Jonson was fully conscious of
this tension seems less important than the effects—and effectiveness—
of his words.

The impassioned final couplet draws strength from (but also releases)
the tension built up by the preceding questions. Again the lines characterize both poet and patron. Jonson uses Cecil's supposed indifference
to his reputation precisely to enhance his standing, while his own
commitment to virtue is ostensibly so deep that he risks Cecil's displeasure in order to praise him. The poet does concede some self-
interest, but his words sanitize and disinfect it. Although "his . . .
injurie" (10) may be one result of failing to honor Cecil's virtue, clearly
this means injury to larger social values and to himself as their representative. Still the line is unexhausted, since "his" may refer both to the
unnamed "who" and to King James, mentioned a few lines before.
Certainly the poem, in honoring Cecil, honors also "The judgement of
the king" that "shine[s]" in him (4), both in the sense that Cecil's power
reflects James's sagacity and in the sense that Cecil's wisdom mirrors the
King's. Failing to honor Cecil would therefore also injure James. Neither
reading of "his" takes precedence: the brief confusion works to Jonson's
advantage, even suggesting a harmony between his own interests and
those of his sovereign. Just as Cecil and Cecil's honors reflect honor on
the King, so does Jonson in honoring Cecil. The ambiguous "his"
implies concord between poet, patron, and patron's patron while also
illustrating how Jonson's epigrams often achieve a dense yet canny
complexity.

The poem that immediately follows this one (Ep. 64) was written to
commemorate Cecil's appointment in 1608 as Treasurer, an event for
which Jonson also wrote one of the four entertainments commissioned

by Cecil, as well as an epigram "upon a plate of Gold" in tribute to
Cecil's father (H&S 8:185). In being named Treasurer, Cecil not only
succeeded to the powerful office Burghley had once held but also
tightened his grip even more firmly on the reins of Jacobean patronage.
The preferment vastly increased his official influence while also opening up many new opportunities for private gain. Lawrence Stone calls
the treasurership "the highest and most lucrative office of all" and
remarks that dual mastery of the exchequer and Court of Wards gave
Cecil "control of strategic economic decisions affecting large numbers
of wealthy and influential people, who were prepared to conform to the
custom of the times and offer 'gratuities' in order to influence policy."[12]
Yet his new position also brought new perils; the power to please some
would inevitably alienate others. As Treasurer he would have to juggle
the competing claims of private interests and the public good, of Parliament and the King. And even more than before he would be besieged by
clamoring suitors. Jonson's poem nicely catches and exploits this sense
of harried siege:

> Not glad, like those that have new hopes, or sutes,
>   With thy new place, bring I these early fruits
> Of love, and what the golden age did hold
>   A treasure, art: contemn'd in th'age of gold.
> Nor glad as those, that old dependents bee,
>   To see thy fathers rites new laid on thee.
> Nor glad for fashion. Nor to shew a fit
>   Of flatterie to thy titles. Nor of wit.
> But I am glad to see that time survive,
>   Where merit is not sepulcher'd alive.
> Where good mens vertues them to honors bring,
>   And not to dangers. When so wise a king
> Contends t'have worth enjoy, from his regard,
>   As her owne conscience, still, the same reward.
> These (noblest Cecil) labour'd in my thought,
>   Wherein what wonder see thy name hath wrought?
> That whil'st I meant but thine to gratulate,
>   I'have sung the greater fortunes of our state.
>
> (1–18)

As skillful technically as its predecessor, this poem's tone is more
urgently personal. Jonson cleverly communicates the sensation of being
bombarded by selfish aspirants by piling one kind of claimant on top of
another and then suddenly restarting the catalogue just when it seems
to falter, as if it will never stop. He distinguishes himself both from new
supplicants (whose fickle loyalties derive from Cecil's new position) as
well as from "old dependents" (a phrase emphasizing the patron's
obligations rather than the service due him [5]). His poem reminds

Cecil of their long relationship while demonstrating that it can still be mutually fruitful. By referring, in fact, to the poem as "these early fruits / Of love" (2–3), Jonson not only claims to act from different motives than the other suitors but speaks of the poem with an attractive modesty that counterweights his later bolder assertions about its worth. Yet the fruits may be "early" in still another sense. By inviting comparison with the apparently similar "new hopes, or sutes" of his rivals, he suggests that the cases are in fact very different. He labors throughout to distinguish himself from his competitors, projecting on them the very self-interest inevitably expressed and advanced by his own poem.

Jonson's "fruits / Of love" ostensibly grow out of a more natural relation between patron and client than is typical of the contemporary "age of gold" (4), the contrast in images reinforcing the contrast in values. In fact, however, the opposition between "fruits / Of love" (suggesting vitality and nature) and mere "gold" (implying dead materialism) points to a more fundamental contrast central to the poem's meaning and internal tensions. It is a contrast between the artificial and natural, less important for categorizing images than for categorizing behavior. Jonson repeatedly implies that his own behavior is natural and spontaneous while that of his rivals is artificial and forced. Yet *his* behavior is inevitably also tinged with calculation and artifice; his poem is as carefully contrived as their appeals for favor. However much he tries to distinguish himself from his rivals, his language is insufficient to do so; it cannot enforce distinctions but can only assert them. It cannot prove his difference but merely claim it. He implicitly contrasts his and his rivals' language: theirs is groundless. Unanchored in virtuous selves that might guarantee its integrity, it is simply a political instrument. But how can Jonson's words prove themselves any different? They cannot, although differences might very well exist. Any social use of language involves similar apprehension and frustration: one can never know *for sure* that others' words are rooted in responsible, benevolent selves or express sincere intentions, nor can one ever. finally prove *through language* the integrity of one's own words. Jonson's poems confront this problem repeatedly, but despite their confident pronouncements and discriminations, they do not so much solve as finesse it. His language is inevitably political, perhaps especially when it claims not to be.

Jonson distinguishes the "age of gold" from a more healthy and natural "golden age" in which art was held "A treasure" (3–4), playing with terms related to Cecil's new office both to rebuke the avarice of other suitors and to pressure Cecil himself to demonstrate allegiance to higher values. As in many of his poems to superiors, the ideal standard Jonson asserts here is as effective in judging the patron as anyone else.

Not only does the "golden age" provide that standard in this poem; so, implicitly, does the behavior of Cecil's own patron, the King. The opening catalogue of clamoring suitors is answered by a later catalogue that enumerates the countervailing virtues associated with James's providence. By presenting him as a wise King who "Contends t'have worth enjoy, from his regard, / As her owne conscience, still, the same reward" (13–14), Jonson compliments James while also drawing attention to their similar social roles. Both actively honor true worth: the verb "contends" makes the monarch seem more than a passive endorser of other men's goodness; like Jonson, he is its vigorous promoter. Both poet and King display their wisdom in honoring Cecil; neither exhibits any conflict between private motive and public act. James, Cecil, and the poet are implicitly united: Cecil's conscience, the King's honors, Jonson's poem—all endorse the same behavior. In all three, the conflict between appearance and reality implied earlier is supposedly resolved. More important, however, the reference to James reminds Cecil of his own dependence on the King's generosity. The epigram delimits his power even while celebrating its attainment, at the same time implying that if Cecil truly believes he has been rewarded for his virtues, he is obligated similarly to reward them in others (including the poet). The very poem that celebrates his freedom from danger becomes itself a threat to his reputation if he fails to respond to it properly.

In fact, the whole issue of "danger" is dealt with ambiguously. Jonson says that Cecil's virtues have earned him honors, not dangers, but both men knew that with the Earl's new status came heightened hazards as well. In the years following his appointment, Cecil became increasingly unpopular and ultimately began to lose influence with the King; his position offered new opportunities but also exposed him to greater resentment and blame. In fact, shortly before his elevation he remarked to an associate that his new office "was a perilous place, for if the Treasurer consents to monopolies and to all the numberless devices for concealment and the proposals of new taxation he gains for himself the people's ill will and their curses; and if he resists the same he will be made odious to the suitors and perhaps to the King."[13] These comments provide a powerful context for the epigram's cunningly blithe assessment of the dangers he faced. Although ostensibly minimizing those dangers, Jonson reviews and exploits them.

As in some of his other poems to Cecil, he implies that the epigram is less the result of conscious intent than of the patron's benign and inadvertent inspiration. Cecil, in fact, comes to seem a kind of muse whose influence helps the poet surpass his original plans. Ascribing almost talismanic powers to Cecil's influence, Jonson thereby intimates his own skill, just as reference to his labored intentions highlights the finished work's smooth success (15). Yet he immediately credits Cecil for whatever success the poem achieves, implying that he inspired the tribute to James, who is chiefly responsible for (and therefore one of) "the greater fortunes of our state" (which can mean not only "our nation" but also, more generally, "our circumstances and condition"). If the first part of the poem defined the poet's intentions, the final couplet returns to that question but astutely claims that thanks to Cecil's inspiration, those intentions have been excelled. We are invited to note the adroitness of the song just as the singing stops.

Examined closely, Jonson's epigrams to Cecil suggest a density of texture and implication not usually associated with this poet of the "plain style." They incorporate the ambiguities of his dependent status; they are shot through with paradoxes and contradictions, some of which he exploits, some of which he is powerless to control. Like many of his other works, they suggest how he could manipulate the resources of language to advance his own interests, but they also reveal how his language itself gestures toward and epitomizes the enigmas and dilemmas of his social position, how works that initially seem assertive and certain nonetheless disclose apprehension and multivalency. Jonson's poems are far more paradoxical than is sometimes assumed. The epigrams to Cecil embody tensions between humility and self-assertion (often using humility *as* assertion). They claim to speak for others but employ a unique voice and advertise a special role. They celebrate the patron's strength but suggest his weakness. They confess dependence but imply power, just as they imply strength while disclosing vulnerability. They extol acts as self-sufficient even as they insist on and demonstrate the interpreter's power to give acts public significance. They reveal their own micropolitical contexts while ostensibly commending values and virtues that transcend them. Poised between idealism and pragmatism, morality and force, they exhibit tensions between spontaneity and art, compulsion and calculation, improvisation and design. They accentuate one kind of necessity (poetic "inspiration") while de-emphasizing others (economic need, social dependence). They counterpoint virtue and ambition without quite being able to enforce the distinction. They use humor to cope with fear, and imply guilt while shunning blame. They are competitively noncompetitive, projecting on others the inevitable self-interest they themselves epitomize. They seem to focus on the patron but subtly call attention to themselves. They disclose Jonson's misgivings about dependency as well as his inability to break free; they attack aspects of patronage even while seeking to win it. They imply concord between poet, patron, patron's patron, and the broader public while simultaneously revealing the complexities and tensions these relationships embody.

The Epigram to Pembroke

As the poems to Cecil suggest, the fact that Jonson's patrons were themselves caught up in patronage networks bears importantly on his own dealings with them. They, too, were involved in the struggle for status; they, too, were responsible to superiors and troubled by rivals. Like Jonson, they too sought relief from the anxieties competition created, and like him, they promoted images of themselves that made them more effective competitors. Their reputations were as much a concern as their financial security, and both were subject to similar uncertainties. Their experiences with patronage frequently resembled his, and his ability to address familiar issues or play on familiar anxieties probably contributed both to his success and to the complexity of his works.

One of Jonson's best-known patrons—and a man to whom he addressed one of his best and most characteristic poems—was William Herbert, third Earl of Pembroke. Their relationship may have begun as early as the 1590s, when Jonson was involved with the acting company patronized by the Earl's father. They had a number of mutual contacts— Cecil and the Countess of Bedford were only two—and, during the *Eastward Ho* debacle, Pembroke was one of the aristocrats to whom the poet turned for help. Jonson seems to have competed with Samuel Daniel for Pembroke's support, and must also have been troubled by the Earl's encouragement of Inigo Jones. It has been suggested, however, that it was partly thanks to Herbert's influence that Jonson and Jones were able to work together at all, since he fostered both without specially favoring either. His importance as a patron is suggested by the fact that he received more dedications in the early seventeenth century than any other aristocrat, royalty only excepted. To him Jonson dedicated both *Catiline* and the *Epigrammes* volume, in each case appealing to the Earl to vindicate him from the malicious reaction which in the first instance he had already experienced and in the second he expected would ensue.[14]

By the time the play and poems were published in the 1616 folio, Pembroke was Lord Chamberlain; two years later he became Chancellor of Oxford; and in 1620 he became Lord Steward. Each new office enhanced his capacity as a patron or conduit of patronage. Apparently through his influence, for instance, Jonson received his honorary Oxford M.A.—a circumstance that later seems to have rankled George

Chapman (H&S 1:234–35; 11:406–12). As Lord Chamberlain, Pembroke was involved in supervising the theaters and also had a hand in producing the court masques. In his conversations with Drummond (himself probably patronized by the Earl), Jonson reported that "every first day of the new year he had [20 pounds] sent him from the Earl of Pembroke to buy bookes" (H&S 1:141). He had many reasons, then, not only to feel gratitude for the Earl's past favors but to continue to seek his support.[15]

In his only epigram to Pembroke (*Ep.* 102), however, Jonson does not so much seek support as give it. Although the poem, with its neat division of humanity into the virtuous and the vicious, invites consideration in abstractly moral terms; although it constitutes a prime text for those critics concerned with issues of "naming" in Jonson's verse; and although in writing it he seems to have had in mind a number of passages from classical sources—in spite of all this, it seems a mistake to divorce the poem from its immediate historical context. Besides being a beneficent patron and a good man, Pembroke was also very powerful and important politically. Brother of one of James's favorites and himself a favorite of the Queen; an ally of Cecil, with influence of his own in Parliament; a proud man, who would resort to violence rather than brook a slight to his status—such a person was likely to win antagonists as well as admirers. Clarendon would later claim that "no man had ever wickednesse to avow himselfe to be [Pembroke's] enimy."[16] But Jonson's poem—with its reference to envious adversaries, its depiction of Herbert "besieg'd with ill / Of what ambition, faction, pride can raise," and its closing concern for the commonwealth's safety—suggests a more complex situation:

> I doe but name thee Pembroke, and I find
>   It is an *Epigramme*, on all man-kind;
> Against the bad, but of, and to the good:
>   Both which are ask'd, to have thee understood.
> Nor could the age have mist thee, in this strife
>   Of vice, and vertue; wherein all great life
> Almost, is exercis'd: and scarse one knowes,
>   To which, yet, of the sides himselfe he owes.
> They follow vertue, for reward, to day;
>   To morrow vice, if shee give better pay:
> And are so good, and bad, just at a price,
>   As nothing else discernes the vertue' or vice.
> But thou, whose noblêsse keeps one stature still,
>   And one true posture, though besieg'd with ill
> Of what ambition, faction, pride can raise;
>   Whose life, ev'n they, that envie it, must praise;

That art so reverenc'd, as thy comming in,
    But in the view, doth interrupt their sinne;
Thou must draw more: and they, that hope to see
    The common-wealth still safe, must studie thee.

                                                    (1–20)

It would help to know when the poem was written, but dating it precisely seems impossible. Presumably included in the quarto *Epigrammes* probably published in the spring of 1612, its political references suggest that it may have been composed within the preceding three or four years. In 1608 Pembroke began to be appointed to important administrative positions; in 1611—the same year he received the dedication to *Catiline*—he was named to the Privy Council and quickly became active in its inner circle.[17] After 1611 he was a force to be reckoned with in national politics, and he soon became a dominant member of the strongly Protestant, anti-Spanish faction. Another of Jonson's patrons, Sir Thomas Egerton, was a member of this group, which supported Sir Henry Neville's ambitions to succeed Cecil as Principal Secretary. The faction opposed to Pembroke's was led by the Earl of Northampton, who had earlier accused Jonson of "popperie and treason" and who later became (in Jonson's own words) his "mortall enemie" (H&S 1:37; 141). Ironically, Northampton himself was suspected of secret Catholic sympathies; his support for closer ties with Spain made his conflict with Pembroke inevitable. Already in 1605 there was evidence of a rivalry between them, and their relations do not seem to have improved with time. In the court politicking that followed Cecil's death, Northampton was anxious to exacerbate tensions between Pembroke and Robert Carr, the new royal favorite. In one letter to Carr, he calls Pembroke a "Welsh juggler"; later, he sneeringly alludes to the dead and discredited Cecil, encloses a critical poem about him, and stresses Cecil's regard for Pembroke—who, he cryptically speculates, "is likely to prove an alchemist."[18]

None of this proves that Jonson had this antagonism in mind when he composed his epigram, although that possibility certainly exists. What does seem undeniable is that Pembroke *did* have enemies, and that at the time the poem was probably written, circulated, and first printed, its references to faction, ambition, pride, and envy could be taken quite literally and specifically. If any reader chose to interpret them this way, that was of course the reader's doing. In the dedication beseeching Pembroke's protection for the *Epigrammes*, after all, Jonson would later deny explicitly—and perhaps even sincerely—that any of his satires were aimed at particular targets.

It was partly to Jonson's rhetorical advantage, of course, to present the opposition between Pembroke and his unnamed antagonists in general moral terms—as a clear opposition between good and evil. By presenting Pembroke as the victim of factionalism, he denies the reader any opportunity to consider the Earl himself as a factional leader; by ascribing ambition to the Earl's opponents, he downplays the possibility that ambition might be one of Pembroke's motives; by depicting those opponents as envious, he makes Pembroke seem all the more principled and virtuous. And he makes his own allegiance to Pembroke seem less self-interested, less vulnerable to the suspicions of others or of the Earl himself. Understanding the poem in abstractly moral terms works to the advantage of both Jonson and his patron; viewing it as at least in part a political document, responsive to particular circumstances and personalities, makes for a more complicated reading. Thus, although it expresses disdain for the kind of market-oriented competitiveness in which individuals sell their loyalties to the highest bidder, and although it exalts in contrast relations rooted in genuine trust and mutuality, Jonson's epigram is itself affected by the pressure it attacks. It is itself a bid for new and continued patronage; it helps Jonson sell and promote both himself and his patron and can itself be seen as a response to the demands of the patronage marketplace. However much Jonson insists on the concord between author and patron and however much he attempts to embody that concord within and through the poem, his epigram inevitably betrays evidence of the self-interests of both parties.

To say that the poem has roots in Jonson's self-interest and imply that it also plays on Pembroke's is not to suggest that it is somehow dishonest or "insincere." The poem works tactically, it promotes the poet's power, but there is no need to attribute Machiavellian motives to its author. In fact, there is every reason to believe that Jonson truly wanted to see his relations with Pembroke and other patrons in ideal terms, as grounded in reciprocal loyalty and respect. He would not want to think of himself as consciously exploiting his patrons, not only because thinking this would rob his performance of its conviction and thus diminish its persuasiveness, but also because such thoughts could not help but remind him of his patrons' far greater capacity to exploit their dependents. The rhetoric of oneness he uses with such authority and self-assurance to celebrate his link with Pembroke can be seen as a means of coping with his fundamental insecurity. The ideal terms he uses to depict the connection are tactically effective but also anchored in his deepest longings and desires. His poems do not simply comment on or react to the tensions inherent in his position; they embody those tensions. The tensions are embedded in them.

Jonson subtly emphasizes and promotes the ideal concord between poet and patron through the epigram's very structure, opening with "I" and closing with "thee" to give it a neatly symmetrical, circular shape, as if to suggest the reciprocity it celebrates. The poem emphasizes that relation's importance to both parties, especially in view of the hostility and threats the work details. Its structure underscores one of its central meanings—that poet and patron can be mutually useful, mutually helpful, and indeed that in some ways Pembroke needs the poet as much as the poet needs him.

Ambiguities in the opening lines help illustrate this point. By claiming that Pembroke's name itself is an epigram full of rich significance and meaning, Jonson gives the name almost "talismanic" importance, as if a certain compelling and self-evident power resided within it, as if it embodied Pembroke's self-sufficiency and functioned as a kind of muse that evoked a meaning the poet only elaborates.[19] It is as if Jonson did "but name" Pembroke, and the poem sprang forth fully-fledged in response. But of course, this very modesty helps highlight the accomplishment and necessity of his own work, helps stress how much more than merely "naming" he and his poem actually do. Although there is a sense in which the poem simply unfolds or explicates the rich meaning implicit in Pembroke's name, the epigram more than merely celebrates the name's practical and symbolic power. It helps create that power, maintains and defends it, and thereby (paradoxically) also subtly undermines and qualifies it, thus enhancing the poet's own importance. The implications of Jonson's phrasing subvert the surface meaning of his lines in such a way that, far from undermining our sense of his skill, they actually promote the power of the author *vis-à-vis* his patron.

The first few lines describe Pembroke in a manner that reflects and defines the qualities of Jonson's own work and of Jonson himself. Calling Pembroke's name an epigram "of" and "to" the good suggests that the same is true of the present epigram, and it suggests interesting connections between poet, subject, and audience. Jonson's own epigram is "of" the good not only because it deals with a virtuous subject but because its author is implicitly depicted as a good man. Similarly, the poem is "to" the good not only because it is addressed specifically to Pembroke but because Jonson projects a broader audience who are presumed to share Pembroke's (and the poet's) values. Through deft shadings of syntax, he already begins implying the sense of virtuous community explicitly called for at the end of the poem. He seems to play with the epigram genre's conventional association with antithesis, using the antithesis between good and evil not only as a central theme but as a defining element of structure: the poem progresses from an emphasis on duality and opposition to an emphasis on the still oneness and moral stability Pembroke supposedly exemplifies. At the same time Jonson tactically exploits this stress on duality and conflict to enhance

Pembroke's instability and insecurity, to underscore his consciousness of the threats he faces and thus undermine the calm self-assurance that the poem so effectively attributes to him. Ironically, it was not to Jonson's advantage to make his superiors feel completely secure and wholly self-sufficient. His own power and security depended partly on making the most of others' insecurities. The epigram suggests how he could exploit the nuances of language and structure to do just that.

It is not only by manipulating his own language, however, that Jonson attempts to guide the responses of his patron and broader audience. He also adapts and manipulates the language of others. For instance, his assertion that both the bad and the good are "ask'd" in order to comprehend Pembroke is indebted to Seneca's description of Cato (H&S 11:22). Through a number of such allusions to classical texts, Jonson situates Pembroke's virtue in a larger historical context, providing a sense of perspective to remind us that the struggle between vice and virtue is ancient and continuous. At the same time, such allusions distance us from thoughts of Pembroke the politician and factional leader. Because he is implicitly depicted as the latest in a long line of moral heroes, the contemporary political aspects and ambiguities of his position are de-emphasized and obscured. The allusions function partly as "sincere" tribute, partly as tactical ploys.

They function, also, to characterize Jonson, reminding us of the role past writers have played in championing and perpetuating the memory of great men, and thus of the extent to which such writers exemplify the same courage they praise. The allusions subtly compliment Pembroke while subtly enhancing the image of the poet. They also extend the range of such references as the one in line 6, to "all great life," thrusting it backward to encompass men like Cato, who was as morally and socially "great" in his age as Pembroke is now. The allusions give added force even to such an apparently simple word as "yet" (8), suggesting that even after all these centuries, even after all the great examples of the past, some men still, incredibly, are undecided about the values to which they owe allegiance. By adopting and adapting the language of other writers, Jonson gives greater resonance to his own.

Pembroke is presented in the poem both as a figure whose allegiance is tested and as one to whom allegiance is due—both as someone who stands to profit financially from astute (if immoral) commitments and as one who can engineer the profits of others. On first reading, it is not at all clear, for instance, to whom Jonson refers when he claims that "scarse one knowes, / To which, yet, of the sides himselfe he owes. / They follow vertue, for reward, to day; / To morrow vice, if shee give better pay" (7–10). Following lines make it obvious that he has Pembroke at least partly in mind. Unlike the unnamed "they,"

Pembroke's commitment to virtue is not financially variable; he cannot, Jonson implies, be bribed to ally himself with the vicious "side" against the good. The poem thus suggests that other men of his social status *could* be—a suggestion easy to accept when one remembers that the real rewards of high office rarely came from the usually nominal salaries involved but from the monies and other gifts suitors were willing to offer influential officials to advance their particular interests.

Jonson hardly implies that Pembroke spurned such gratuities; to refuse them would have been most unusual in view of contemporary political realities.[20] But he does suggest that Pembroke's fundamental commitment to virtue could not be affected by perquisites, gifts, or promises, whether from suitors, from peers, or from the few figures more powerful than he. Indeed, by claiming that "all great life / Almost, is exercis'd . . . in this strife / Of vice, and vertue" (5–7), Jonson suggests that the general, universal struggle between good and evil is especially crucial to men of Pembroke's class. One's allegiances in this struggle determine whether one is truly (morally) great or simply "great" in social standing. Celebrating Pembroke's ethical stature, Jonson mocks the mere "greatness" of his patron's rivals. Although he claims that the age could not have "mist" Pembroke in the "strife" the poem describes, and although the word "mist" primarily suggests Pembroke's indispensability to the triumph of good, it also insinuates one function of the present poem itself: to ensure that Pembroke's role does not go unnoticed, unheralded, or misunderstood. In this case, virtue is hardly its own reward. For all Jonson's distancing insistence on the larger struggle between the good and the bad, the poem's most immediate context was micropolitical. The struggle most immediately relevant was the one between Pembroke and his peers.

Just as the poem distinguishes Pembroke from the mercenaries among his own class, it also draws attention to the broader body of mercenaries beneath him—the clients Pembroke and other patrons supported. In connection with such clients, words like "pay" and "price" are apt, and when Jonson speaks of "sides" he not only refers to moral categories but anticipates the later reference to faction. One implication is that just as Pembroke faces a choice between vice and virtue, so do all who might potentially serve him; but the poem implies that *their* decisions will often be far less predictable or reliable than his own. Thus, when Jonson writes that "scarse one knowes, / To which, yet, of the sides himselfe he owes," the word "scarse" does double duty, suggesting not only the meaning "one hardly knows" but also the meaning "hardly one knows." The first meaning implies a general and essential indecisiveness, a lack of firm commitment to any overriding principle of virtue; the second connotes the relative isolation of the few

good men who do exist. "Owes" at once wittily foreshadows the ensuing language of the marketplace, suggests an opposing sense of much
deeper obligation, and also intimates the idea of open acknowledgment,
of a publicly avowed commitment.

All these meanings work to Jonson's particular advantage as a client
addressing his own patron. In the same way that he distinguishes
Pembroke from the vicious generally but especially from vicious aristocrats, so he implies his own distinction from corrupt and avaricious
suitors. The clever pairing of "one" and "he" with "They" (7–9) underscores this difference: at first Jonson speaks momentarily in general
terms, as if even he might be fallible; but the shift to "They" implicitly
exempts him. Like Pembroke, his own virtue keeps "one stature still"—
"still" implying "even now," implying "always," and also implying
"calmly, with quiet self-assurance." Unlike the other suitors described,
Jonson's own commitment to virtuous service is ostensibly permanent
and public; this very epigram is the most visible possible evidence of
his willingness openly to "owe" himself to one side and against the
other. His language stressing Pembroke's virtuous isolation actually
helps advertise his own public stance.

The shift to Pembroke inaugurated in line 13 is the poem's structural
turning point and coincides with the shift away from its earlier emphasis on conflicting dualities to a new emphasis on unity, on dualities
overcome. Words such as "stature" and "posture" give Pembroke's virtues an almost physical solidity, while the reference to his "true posture" suggests the calculated posturings of the corrupt. Moreover,
Jonson's praise of Pembroke for remaining upright "though besieg'd
with ill" also reflects well on a poet willing to ally himself openly with
the enemy of powerful forces motivated by "envie," "ambition, faction,
[and] pride" (14–16). The poem implicitly distinguishes between Jonson's own supposedly natural, spontaneous (yet highly skilled) praise
of Pembroke and the backhanded praise he receives from others—praise
rooted in the envy his antagonists feel for him. Jonson's words obscure
the subtle senses in which his own praise of patrons was something less
than a free offering, the senses in which it was shaped, dictated, and
compelled by his given status in the patronage hierarchy. Pembroke's
opponents react to the Earl's power with envy because they feel threatened by it. Jonson's position was more paradoxical. For him, a patron's
power was at once the guarantee of his own standing and the potential
cause of its loss. In this and in other poems, he claims to celebrate
another's power freely, confidently, and disinterestedly. Yet one function of the poem is also to manage that power, to control and direct it, to
contain any sense of its threat. Far from being mere exercises in tired

conventional praise, poems like this were originally charged with intense psychic energy.

Jonson implies that Pembroke's antagonists' envy is itself a kind of praise, reflecting through negation Pembroke's worth and value; so strong is his virtue (Jonson suggests) that it compels tribute even from his enemies. And yet, as in Epigram 43 to Salisbury, this clever notion is highly ambiguous and works to Jonson's distinct advantage. True, the envy of Pembroke's enemies paid tribute to his power. He had no need to fear the envy of the impotent, since their envy ironically testified to his own importance. But Jonson's phrasing reminds us that some very powerful men also envied and disliked Pembroke; their animosity, while it reflected his power, also threatened it. Here as elsewhere, then, the very words that seem to acclaim Pembroke's power also indicate his vulnerability.

Like the later assertion that Pembroke "must" draw more followers to his side, the reference to praise from Pembroke's adversaries credits him with an almost mythic power even as it underscores his real and practical need for the poet's assistance in shaping his public image. The word "must" calls into question the same power it exalts, helping to suggest the epigram's own role in making the Earl literally more attractive (19). Similarly, the claim that those who "hope to see / The common-wealth still safe, must studie thee" (19–20) draws attention to the poem's own part in rendering Pembroke a possible object of study and emulation. Of course, Pembroke could be "studied" in the flesh, as the clever reference to his "comming [into] the view"—with its overtones of courtly entrance—makes clear. But the poem itself, now nearing completion, offers another and far more stable means for Pembroke to project his influence, not only on his contemporaries but on future generations as well. It is implicitly presented as a product of the very study and moral scrutiny it attempts to evoke. Similarly, it exemplifies the movement toward Pembroke it calls for and predicts, even while insinuating its ability to help make that movement more likely.

While the epigram pays tribute to the patron's antecedent stability and centeredness, it helps to create that stability, to remove Pembroke's image from the flux and contentiousness of day-to-day political maneuvering and to frame a stature it claims he already possesses. At the same time, the poem reviews and exploits all the sources of Pembroke's insecurity. Part of the paradox of the work is that it is itself significantly unstable. At the least, its claims to stability seem increasingly problematic the more they are scrutinized. There is, for instance, no way for Jonson finally to enforce or prove through his language the distinctions he draws between Pembroke and his enemies or between the poet and rival suitors. Those distinctions may exist, but the poem alone can neither verify nor substantiate them, only assert them. In its middle lines, it implicitly gestures toward the complexities of distinguishing truly between good and evil: "They follow vertue, for reward, to day; / To morrow vice, if shee give better pay: / And are so good, and bad, just at a price, / As nothing else discernes the vertue' or vice" (9–12). This is humorously paradoxical: of course, Jonson implies, to follow virtue "for reward" is not really to follow virtue, and it is just as effectively ironic to suggest that price can be used as a criterion for discerning between good and bad. The poem mocks such notions and satirizes moral confusion; here and throughout, it suggests that distinctions between good and evil can easily be made. The epigram is grounded in the presumption that it is not only possible to distinguish but that one is obliged to do so. It presents itself as the instrument and product of such disinterested distinctions.

But how can the poem authenticate its claims? How can we know from reading it that its assertions about Pembroke, his antagonists, the poet, and itself are true? There seems no easy answer to this question, and Jonson does not so much confront as sidestep it. To do otherwise would paralyze the poem. At its heart the epigram tacitly reveals an impasse and incapacity inherent in Jonson's epideictic language. In his seminal article on the *Epigrammes*, Edward Partridge writes that Jonson

> was moved more by what was actually happening than by what one could imagine happening. Fancy is finally less moving to him than fact. More important than the talismanic significance of Pembroke's name is its designative function: it points to a man who actually lives, who does certain verifiable things, who has a particular character and historically accountable relationships. Jonson, one must see, had an historian's sense of the holiness of fact.[21]

As a characterization of the poet's aesthetic this rings true. But it also follows Jonson in simplifying the difficulties involved in separating "fact" from interpretation. Jonson does seem to imply that "facts" are neutral and compelling and can guarantee his poems' veracity. But this assertion only begs the question. How can one know that Jonson's interpretation of the "facts" of Pembroke's life, behavior, and motives is "accurate"? It may be, but how can one know for sure? Evidently Pembroke's antagonists saw the same "facts" altogether differently. Beneath the certain, assertive referentiality of Jonson's language lurk disturbing possibilities. The insistent bluntness of his phrasing helps mask the difficulties inherent in his project. The claim that Pembroke's virtue is manifest and obvious finesses the extent to which all traits are subject to interpretation. The connection between Jonson's words and the "facts" they claim to re-present is inevitably more tenuous and elusive than he suggests. Although the epigram presents itself as the simultaneous product of inspiration ("I find / It is an *Epigramme*" [1–2]) and of intense moral scrutiny ("must studie thee" [20]), both assertions simplify the difficulties involved in *proving* the truth of praise. Even as the poem pays tribute to supposedly objective, verifiable virtues that ostensibly transcend politics, it thereby engages in political persuasion and promotes the political interests of both its patron and its maker. The poem's status as a transcript of "objective" reality may be in doubt, but its status as a political document is not.

Jonson's praise of Pembroke implicitly reflects credit on his own character and capabilities and on the particular accomplishment of his own work. The poem sets both poet and patron apart and magnifies their importance, but its enhancement of the poet's image never seems overbearing or indelicate; indeed, part of its point is to indicate the poet's usefulness, his serviceability. Ironically, it was partly Jonson's skill in declaring his allegiance to Pembroke that would make him attractive to other potential patrons. By displaying his creativity and calling attention to the achievement of his work, he not only advertised his talents to a wider audience but demonstrated pragmatically his utility, his capacity to participate in truly reciprocal relationships. Yet he did so in a way that seems to focus attention almost solely on the patron—a skill which in itself exemplifies his talent. Although patronage poetry in general is often associated with bald or craven flattery, Jonson's performance shows how richly equivocal and complex it could frequently be. It is poetry that displays its maker's wit while challenging and complimenting its reader's intelligence.

The epigram to Pembroke demonstrates as well as any poem Jonson ever wrote how effectively the poet could play on the anxieties and concerns of his superiors to enhance his own security. Asserting and attempting to promote Pembroke's power, the poem also skillfully and subtly questions it. One effect is to remind the Earl of his own need, his own lack of independence and autonomy. Aristocrats as well as writers were inevitably caught up in the same competition for assured status—status that could never be assured precisely because it was subject to competition. The uncertainty at the heart of the patronage system (and at the root of the writer's own relative social weakness) thus paradoxically provided poets a potential source of strength in their dealings with superiors. At the same time, the Pembroke epigram may inadvertently point toward a deeper, more fundamental impasse or instability at the heart of Jonson's attempts to use poetry as an ethical instrument. Viewed in abstract moral terms, the poem is a memorable statement of Jonson's deepest values; viewed from the perspective of patronage, it is also a highly complicated tactical *performance*, a work born from and deeply responsive to the micropolitical pressures inherent in his social position and role. And those pressures, by contributing to the complex tone and resonance of the poem, enhance its interest as a work of art.

Poems for the Sidney Circle

Whatever their other differences, the poems to James, Cecil, and Pembroke are intriguingly similar in one respect: all variously exploit their recipients' different insecurities. The "Panegyre" reminds James of his highly conspicuous position and of the pressures it imposed. It insinuates his mortality and the potential for discord within his kingdom even as it implies its own and its author's usefulness in coping with these problems. Ostensibly celebrating James's power, it partly undermines and questions that power. Although it seems to proclaim the poet's deference and to accept his dependency, in some ways it functions as canny self-assertion. Similarly, the poems to Cecil praise him in ways that subtly indicate the threats he faced. The very extravagance of Jonson's overt praise enhances our sense of the patron's insecurity: no one was better-positioned than Cecil himself to recognize the disparity between Jonson's optimistic assertions and the real complexities of Cecil's status. Similar tensions characterize the epigram to Pembroke. Thus, many of Jonson's poems to patrons play on his superiors' vulnerability and anxiety. It is a recurrent note, and one that complicates his works. Thus in one of his most famous treatments of the ideals and problems of patronage, the "Epistle to Sir Edward Sacvile" (*Und.* 13), he not only satirizes unsatisfactory superiors but also heightens the anxieties of patrons of all sorts by detailing their risks of being deceived by their own dependents. The poem pays tribute as much to Jonson the recipient as to Sackville's sensitive generosity.

Various poems to various members of the Sidney circle also exploit insecurities even while seeming to extol power and good fortune. Thus the lengthy poem "To Sir Robert Wroth" (*For.* 3), which contrasts the relaxed atmosphere of his country house, Durrants, with the corruptions and frenetic competitiveness of city and court, nonetheless evokes the real competitive threats Wroth and others like him faced. Durrants supposedly provides refuge from competition, but the poem's many references to contentious ambition help complicate and darken its celebratory mood. They remind Wroth that he could never completely escape courtly pressures, and indeed they imply the poem's value in burnishing his public image. Although the poem explicitly disdains competitive social relations, it promotes Wroth's (and the poet's) ambitions and interests. Thus, its opening contrasts other social gatherings—

a "Sherriffes dinner," a "Maiors feast," but especially a night of courtly masquing (6; 9–10)—with revels enjoyed at Durrants. The other gatherings ironically contradict the ideal mood and purposes of festivity. Rather than dissolving social barriers, rather than enhancing community and celebrating shared interests, they become arenas for petty self-assertion. Wroth's feasts, on the other hand, supposedly inculcate an easy familiarity in which rigid distinctions are temporarily relaxed. Yet "temporarily" is the crucial word, for the respite is inevitably circumscribed by the very pressures it rejects. Its preciousness is defined and intensified by its rarity.

This is especially true of the *poet's* ability to enjoy and participate in the freedom his work exalts. The poem begins by proclaiming that Wroth is "blest" either "by choice, or fate, or both" with an ability to "love the countrey" (1–2). On the one hand these words make Wroth's freedom seem a tribute to his character, to his exercise of free will. His chosen lifestyle reflects well on his personality. But the words also remind us that his freedom partly resulted from the very good fortune of having been born into social and economic circumstances that permitted him a relatively independent choice. "Blest," perhaps, with certain predispositions, Wroth was also "blest" with the liberty to follow them—a liberty that Jonson, for instance, did not possess to nearly the same degree. Wroth's freedom could never be absolute (as the poem itself makes clear), but it was still greater than most people's.

The poem's opening emphasis on Wroth's blessings anticipates its concluding stress on his relations with God, who is described as a kind of patron who "always gives what he knowes meet; / Which who can use is happy" (98–99). In His solicitous concern for those beneath Him—"To him, man's dearer, then t[o]'himselfe" (96)—God stands as a model whom, from the evidence the poem provides, Wroth already emulates to some extent. But His presence in the poem also gives greater sanction to the lesson Jonson teaches; it reminds Wroth of his own place in the larger scheme of things. This order, with God at its head, provides an alternative to the corruption the poem depicts; from this fact Wroth could take some encouragement. But that order also provides a standard against which Wroth's behavior is judged; from this fact he, and all others "blest" with earthly power, might take pause. The conclusion of the poem mixes celebration of Wroth's good fortune with a countervailing recognition of its ultimate ephemerality. Life itself can be seen from this perspective as comparable to the masques mentioned earlier, as in one sense simply a "short braverie of the night" (10); but the tone of the conclusion, far from suggesting despair, tries to persuade the reader to make the best use of what is, after all, "a thing but lent" (106).

The deliberate ambivalence of this poem helps promote Jonson's interests in a number of ways. By praising Wroth's character and values, Jonson identifies with them and thus makes *himself* seem more attractive. When he attacks those who "flatter vice, and winne, / By being organes to great sinne" (85–86), he implicitly contrasts their behavior with his own role in publicizing Wroth's virtue. But by reminding Wroth of his vulnerabilities, he also enhances his own power. The poem illustrates how effectively he could play on competitive pressures even while seeming to disdain them. It exploits the ambitions of its patron even while embodying Jonson's. [22]

Much the same seems true of "To Penshurst" (*For.* 2), his most famous celebration of an estate and of the family associated with it. Penshurst was owned by Sir Robert Sidney, Wroth's father-in-law and Pembroke's uncle. Support from patrons like these was as important, in its own way, as support from the King or from dominant political figures like Cecil; and indeed, each kind of patronage fed and sustained the others. The more favor Jonson found with James, the more he was likely to win from courtiers like Cecil or from aristocrats like the Sidneys. Similarly, the more opportunities the latter provided him to display his talents and the more access they provided to the inner circles of the court, the more he might increase his standing with the King. "To Penshurst" illustrates, as well as any poem he wrote, his sensitive awareness of these multiple audiences. Ostensibly addressed to Penshurst itself, it actually addresses the estate's owners, challenges their rivals, and appeals to the King whose judgment could determine the social worth and status of them all. Celebratory, it is also subtly argumentative. Mythic in imagery and resonance, it is also charged with micropolitical energy. Disdainful of competitive ambition, it promotes the interests of recipients and author alike. Openly confident, it nonetheless exploits and embodies the very insecurities it claims to transcend.

J. C. A. Rathmell has shown how closely the poem reflects the actual details and ambience of life at Penshurst. But Rathmell also shows how complicated and uncertain Lisle's social position was. His private correspondence during the early Jacobean period is full of financial anxieties and an acute sense of his need to compete for status. Conscious, on the one hand, that he was living beyond his means, Lisle at the same time felt impotent to effect real economies. In one letter to his wife, he worries that "If my ill-willers should know in what state I were, it were subject enough for them to laugh at me forever. . . . I must confesse I am at my wits end."[23]

Despite (or perhaps because of) this financial desperation, Lisle thought seriously from time to time of expanding or remodeling his estate. Huge and ornately elaborate "prodigy houses" had recently been springing up, their enormous expense offset by their value as status symbols. More than vanity was involved, for the King was more likely to visit houses whose magnificence did credit to his own. Built originally in the fourteenth century, Penshurst had developed haphazardly since then. New construction was undertaken not in accordance with an encompassing and consistent plan, but rather "to suit the needs and taste of the family as it grew."[24] However much affection Lisle himself felt for the estate, he knew it could not compete with the houses of various other courtiers. His hopes for large-scale remodeling fell through for lack of funds, and his plans to expand the park (James was an avid hunter) similarly came to naught. Jonson's poem makes little explicit reference to Lisle's difficulties or anxieties, although as Rathmell suggests, he could hardly have been unaware of them. More than polite, this silence is eloquent, and is full of implications for the poem's function and meaning.

Jonson's opening claim that Penshurst is not "built to envious show" not only emphasizes the contrasting opulence of the prodigy houses but implies something suspect about the motives behind them. Such houses are "envious" both in the sense that they elicit envy and in the sense that eliciting envy is what they are designed to do. Their purpose is not to inspire genuine admiration but to exact acknowledgment of their owners' power. Their relation to anyone viewing them is implicitly contentious and competitive. Unlike Penshurst, they express not so much their owners' secure self-confidence as their need to feel superior or their fear of seeming weak. This, indeed, is a third sense in which such houses are "envious": they not only elicit envy and are designed to provoke it; they also express the envy their owners feel for others. Prodigy houses are built not for their own sakes but to be compared with other homes. Thus, although they seem to embody concretely and undeniably their owners' status and self-assurance, they are monuments to deep anxieties and fears.

In contrast, Jonson implies that Penshurst and the Sidneys have a center of value within themselves, secure and inviolable. While the prodigy houses are "grudg'd at"—while they wrest the envious tribute they were designed to win—Penshurst is genuinely "reverenc'd" (6). Jonson's own attitude toward the other houses seems grudging not in the sense of envy or resentment of their splendor (since that would pay them the recognition their owners expect) but in the sense of disdainful ridicule. He mocks their features and their notoriety; yet that notoriety obviously concerns him. His very defense of Penshurst suggests that the Sidney estate was not so universally "reverenc'd" as the poem claims, nor was the general attitude toward prodigy houses so disdainful as he might have wished. His own poem manifests much of the same concern with reputation and renown that it attacks. Seeking to enhance the renown of Penshurst, it must disparage the renown of rival estates. Thus it implies the same competitive mentality the other houses enshrine. His praise amounts to an attempt to improve Penshurst's reputation, using words, since Lord Lisle could neither hope nor afford to improve it by using more material means. The good fortune and security Jonson associates with the estate is less an objective datum than a tactic for dealing with the insecurity, the sense of threat, he chooses to underplay.

Jonson himself most clearly enacts the reverence his poem proclaims. By announcing from the start that that attitude is general, he attempts to make his praise less suspect, less vulnerable to charges of flattery. By means of the poem, he becomes the spokesman for most of the figures it mentions: the owners, their neighbors, visitors, and dependents, who all share a love for the estate, who all supposedly participate in the harmony it symbolizes and sustains. Yet Jonson's voice is hardly anonymous, nor is his presence invisible. He interjects himself not only to advertise his close connections with the Sidneys but to guarantee his praise. His panegyric implicitly develops from and reflects his own experience of the harmony it celebrates. His poem is as much a free tribute to his patrons, as much a natural outgrowth of the concord the poem embodies, as the gifts presented by the "officious" fish or, less whimsically, by "the farmer, and the clowne" (36; 48).

Jonson emerges as a bit of a clown himself—bibulous, even humorously gluttonous, but also innocent of courtly guile or false sophistication. More than merely decorous, the very simpleness of this persona helps highlight the skillfulness and accomplishment of the poem. Here, as so often in his work, his willingness to poke fun at himself helps promote his serious interests. His frank concession of appetite, like the ambition of the neighboring farmers to display their marriageable daughters, is benignly non-threatening. He takes pride that the same food and drink Lord Lisle consumes is "also mine" (64) and asserts that he is treated so well at Penshurst that it is almost "As if thou, then, wert mine, or I raign'd here" (74). Yet neither statement betrays covetous egotism; both reflect Jonson's modesty, his deferential regard for hosts willing to treat him and other guests with such unusual thoughtfulness. Paradoxically, by announcing the obligation he feels to the Sidneys for their kind treatment of him, he partly discharges it; his confession of public gratitude pays back their hospitality. From one perspective his act reasserts some claim to individual power and initiative; his ability to thank them so elaborately and imaginatively implies his own value and thus his freedom from utter dependence. From another perspective, however, the poem reinforces larger patterns of social reciprocity by reaffirming the poet's sense of obligation. Indeed, one of the qualities Jonson celebrates about Penshurst is that the gifts received there are (supposedly) not felt as threats but as free expressions of love. Although gift-giving can often underscore the benefactor's superiority over the recipient, Jonson implies that at Penshurst this is not the case. Instead, social concord ostensibly reigns there. Thus, in the same way that he expresses no overt jealousy of the abundance and comfort the Sidneys regularly enjoy, so the server who gives Jonson his meat feels no envy for the poet's good fortune (67–78). A recurring theme in his works and in those of other patronage poets, envy is here presented less as a simple moral defect than as an inevitable consequence of the need to compete. "To Penshurst"—although it responds to that need—celebrates a world from which such competition and its attendant anxieties have supposedly been eradicated. This aspect of the poem's vision is one of its most appealing—and thus, paradoxically, helps make it in every sense more politically competitive.

Although Jonson presents the arrival of the King and Prince as a surprise, their presence in the poem is hardly accidental. They complete the hierarchical scheme—from plants to animals, from peasants to poets to patrons—the poem so carefully constructs. Moreover, "To Penshurst" must have been written partly with the King in mind, not only because it might remind him of the hospitality he received there, but especially because his opinion of a country house (as expressed by his eagerness to visit it) would most determine its status and prestige. Jonson's description of the King's visit is crucial to his object of improving Penshurst's reputation; the King's praise of the estate impressively corroborates his own. That James's visit was unanticipated may have been simple fact, but Jonson adapts this circumstance to one of his chief themes—that life at Penshurst is spontaneous but well-ordered, uncalculating but well-prepared. The fact that the Sidneys did not expect the King's arrival makes their treatment of him all the more genuine and impressive—and also, not incidentally, explains why the "cheare" they offered him was not even greater than it was (82).

Jonson's treatment of the visit manifests the same spontaneity it describes. At one point the poem seems to shift gears, to revise itself in mid-sentence, as Jonson makes us privy to his own act of poetic creation: "What (great, I will not say, but) sodayne cheare / Did'st thou, then, make 'hem!" (82–83). The lines themselves achieve an effect of suddenness, while Jonson's use of "great" (even as he ostensibly refuses to use it) leads one to wonder whether his tone is genuinely apologetic or cunningly modest. A few lines later this sense of spontaneity is achieved again, when the poem seems to finish its catalogue of Penshurst's virtues, only immediately to resume it: "These, Penshurst, are thy praise, and yet not all" (89). It is as if the poem, like the high-swolne *Medway*" (31), cannot quite contain itself, as if the vigor and vitality it depicts affects even its own form and structure. The "These," which are Penshurst's praise, refer, obviously, to the various praise-worthy features Jonson has just highlighted, but the word can also refer to the praises he has spent most of the poem uttering.

Indeed, the final lines seem as intent on calling attention to the poem's importance in enhancing the estate's reputation as on summing up its qualities. "Now," Jonson concludes, ". . . they that will propor-tion thee / With other edifices, when they see / Those proud, ambitious heaps, and nothing else, / May say, their lords have built, but thy lord dwells" (99–102). "Now"—that is, now that his poem exists as an example, now that it has altered perceptions and made it possible to see so much else in Penshurst—false comparisons are much less likely. Size or "proportion" alone (Jonson puns wittily in the verb) will no longer seem as important as the less tangible features his poem exalts. These closing lines abruptly remind us that even in its most celebratory moments, the poem's purpose has been comparative and argumen-tative—and now the consummation of its argument has been reached. It stands both as a challenge to those who might evaluate Penshurst and as a reminder to Jonson's patrons of the important role his poem would likely play in the outcome of any such comparison.

Comparisons of a different sort are the central concerns of another of Jonson's poems to a Sidney. In his "Ode. To Sir William Sydney, on his Birthday" (For. 14), Jonson plays on the young man's sense of his need to compete not only with contemporaries but also with illustrious an-cestors. He highlights others' great expectations of Sidney and exploits these both to pressure him and to imply his own usefulness in helping Sidney define and achieve his goals. His tone is clearly didactic, and in fact the work may have grown out of Jonson's service to the Sidneys in a more official capacity than poet. In that case, it provides interesting evidence for speculation about how service in the larger patronage system may have affected a poet's self-conception and public stance. In any case, the poem is intriguing for the skill with which Jonson man-ages, in a work so clearly addressed to another person, to focus atten-tion so squarely on his own role and voice, transforming a joyous celebration into an event of greater weight and significance and thereby enhancing his own importance. And he does all this in a poem prob-ably designed to make an impression on a wider and more important audience than Sidney alone.

William was Robert Sidney's eldest son, and Rathmell cites a letter suggesting that Jonson may have served the young man as a tutor.[25] The "Ode" was probably written in November 1611, when William turned twenty-one. He had been knighted earlier that same year, but by the end of the following year he was dead. At the time Jonson wrote, however,

William was Sir Robert's heir apparent, although he was also apparently something of a disappointment to his family. His academic record at Oxford had been undistinguished, and he had hurt his standing at court by a rash and violent display of anger.[26] Against this background, Jonson's serious advice hardly seems platitudinous.

The ode's stanzaic form has been called the most complex used in any of Jonson's poems, and its subtle contribution to the work's tone and meaning has been rightly praised.[27] But less attention has been paid to the poem's larger movement, its passage from one sense of time, place, and mood to another, and then back again. As the poem opens, Jonson stands somewhat apart from the merriment and festivity he describes; his pensive silence contrasts with the boisterous conviviality of the other celebrants. His move to bridge this gap only renders it more distinct: the ode's middle stanzas are meditative, thoughtfully serious. The reader's sense of the present and consciousness of the party and of the other participants recede. Jonson and Sidney come to the fore; the poem pulls back from the birthday and places the anniversary in the larger context of past and future. Foretelling a time when "all the noyse / Of these forc'd joyes, / Are fled and gone" (17–19), Jonson creates such a moment in the very midst of the ode. Thus Sidney already, in the poem itself, is "with his best *Genius* left alone" (20). More than merely a tutor, Jonson becomes almost an attendant spirit—yet not one who protects his charge from the challenges he faces. The friendly, benign striving "t[o]'advance / The gladnesse higher" (5–6) mentioned in the opening stanza is gradually replaced by an emphasis on more serious self-exertion: "Your vow / Must now / Strive all right wayes it can, / T[o]'out-strip your peeres" (23–26). The implied competition is most obviously ethical: Sidney must strive to become the best person he can be. But the lines inevitably also suggest the less pleasant aspects of the competitive life now inaugurated by his transition to adulthood. The middle stanzas make it clear that the birthday celebration's festive mood provides only a temporary respite from the weighty challenges facing him, from his inevitable involvement in a competition for reputation not only with his contemporaries but with his ancestors as well. Jonson claims merely to "tell" what "This day / Doth say" (13–14), but his poem creates the significance it reports. He credits the examples of Sidney's ancestors with the ability to teach the young man "how" to live up to what will be expected of him (48); but it is Jonson's poem that stresses the more important preliminary lesson that such expectations exist.

In the last stanza the poem's focus shifts back to the festivities, back to the present place and moment with their "smiling fire" and bright love. But Jonson's tone is almost prayerful; the benediction in the final stanza, which highlights the poet's vatic role, also re-emphasizes the challenge the whole poem has posed: "So may you live in honor, as in name, / If with this truth you be inspir'd, / So may / This day / Be more, and long desir'd" (51–55). But if the ode has been successful, we should recognize that the meaning of "This day" already *is* more (54). Its significance has already been enlarged, deepened, and transformed by the poem itself. Although the poem partially devalues the party's importance, it should help intensify Sidney's experience of that event. Yet "This day" refers not just to the present anniversary of Sidney's birth but to all future anniversaries as well. If Sidney will only permit the ode's truth to inspire him, all his future birthdays can have more than quotidian or even temporarily festive meaning; they can become anniversaries commemorating his ever-renewed and renewing determination to meet the public and private demands that being a Sidney imposes. The poem's action—in simplest terms, the redeeming of time—will then have been transferred to (and realized in) Sidney's life. Just as the poem pulls back from the present to view it from the perspective of future and past, so will Sidney's perspective on each of his own present moments be transformed and broadened by the ode. Ironically, at the same time that it devalues this present moment in Sidney's life, urging him to take a more encompassing view of it, the poem memorializes and enshrines that moment, makes it even more a public and personal milestone. So long as the poem continued to exist and to be read, the high expectations it voiced would be part of the standard by which Sidney's performance would be judged. The poem not only makes Sidney aware that such expectations exist but itself embodies them.

Jonson can speak frankly for several reasons: because he is older than Sidney; because he implicitly adopts the role of Sidney's "best *Genius*," who has the young man's true interests at heart; because of his probable real-life role as Sidney's tutor; but also because he writes as much with Robert as with William Sidney in mind. Lord Lisle cannot have been displeased with Jonson's teachings, and in offering them Jonson cannot have been unmindful of this fact. Although he had an obvious reason to be interested in William's future development as an aristocrat and potential patron, his more immediate interest must have been in gratifying his present benefactor. Lisle's presumed approval of Jonson's counsel gives it greater sanction and persuasiveness. Although William's death, a little more than a year later, cut off whatever expectations Jonson may have entertained concerning his support, it hardly rendered his poem meaningless. Indeed, posthumously printed, the "Ode" stands as a mute, poignant tribute to the dead youth—a memento of the high hopes men had for him, of happier times past, and of the poet's important place in his brief life.

Not all of Jonson's poems for the Sidney circle cast him in such an essentially serious role. But nearly all his patronage poems, including those for the Sidneys, manage to display his talents and promote his interests even while seeming to focus on those he addresses. Often he exploits his superiors' vulnerabilities, as in the poems to Wroth, to Penshurst, and to young William. But his tone can also be less weighty, and part of the point of looking at works written for an extended family is precisely to appreciate his range. Examining them can also suggest how variously his concrete relations with his patrons could affect the style and stance of his poems. The "Ode" exemplifies this, but so does Jonson's "Song. That Women are but Mens shaddowes" (*For.* 7), a slight poem which seems at first to have nothing to do with patronage. However, remarks recorded by Drummond provide an intriguing context. "Pembroke and his Lady discoursing," Drummond wrote, "the Earl said the Woemen were mens shadowes, and she maintained [them], both appealing to Johnson, he affirmed it true, for which my Lady gave a pennance to prove it in Verse, hence his Epigrame" (H&S 1:142).[28] "Pembroke," of course, was William Herbert, Earl of Pembroke and nephew of Robert Sidney. Both the incident Drummond describes and the resulting poem suggest attractive, warm relationships among all the parties involved. The work itself displays Jonson's wit, tact, and sure decorum—all qualities obviously useful to him as a patronage poet. Although Jonson takes Pembroke's side in the dispute, the "Song" never once suggests anything more than playful antagonism. The fact that it *is* a song, that it grows out of a real-life game and translates its sportiveness into poetry, helps lend it an assured poise, a delicate deference. But the "Song" assumes an added interest since it is the only one of Jonson's poems whose subject we *know* to have been "set" by a patron.[29]

Like some of the masques, the "Song" demonstrates Jonson's ability to write competently on command and to handle skillfully a theme few might immediately associate with him. Pembroke himself seems not only to have fancied but to have written poems on love, and a number of works composed by Jonson during the second half of James's reign—the period of his closest association with the court—take love as their theme.[30] Whether this is coincidence or whether Jonson was influenced by the tastes of those around him is impossible to say, although it is worth noting the testimony of his "Sonnet, To the Noble Lady, the Lady Mary W[ro]th" (*Und.* 28). She was the daughter of Lord Lisle and wife of Sir Robert Wroth, but she was also an accomplished sonneteer, and most of her lyrics probably date from the decade when Jonson's involvement with the court was most intense.[31] In his own sonnet, Jonson extravagantly praises the effects her works have had on him, claiming that since copying them out, he has become "A better lover, and much better Pöet" (4). There may be an element of self-mockery here, as there frequently is when Jonson writes about love. But however much fun he pokes at himself as a lover, as a patronage poet he undoubtedly recognized the advantages of being able to write verse on such a perennially popular theme. Thus in the opening line of the sonnet to Lady Wroth he calls attention to the fact that he has previously written about love—an assertion that establishes his qualifications as a judge of her verse even while paving the way for the deferential compliment that follows.

Jonson demonstrates a similar ability to insinuate his own gifts while praising another's in one of his several epigrams to Lady Wroth (Ep. 105), in which he insists repeatedly that anyone would notice the resemblances he draws between her and various classical goddesses. This tactic proclaims the objectivity of his homage even as it underscores the fecundity of his own wit and inventiveness while preserving a modest tone:

> Madame, had all antiquitie been lost,
>   All historie seal'd up, and fables crost;
> That we had left us, nor by time, nor place,
>   Least mention of a *Nymph*, a *Muse*, a *Grace*,
> But even their names were to be made a-new,
>   Who could not but create them all, from you?
>
> (1–6)

Although Jonson credits Lady Wroth with restoring in her self "all treasure lost of th'age before" (20), it is largely through the action of his poem that this restoration is achieved and, perhaps more important, is made publicly manifest and permanent. If by the end of the work she indeed seems "*Natures Index*" (19), it is thanks in no small part to Jonson's poem. The epigram illustrates one of its own implications: the importance of the poet in keeping alive the memories of significant figures and events. Without the written records left by poets and others, the names and remembrance of those mentioned in the epigram would indeed be lost. Jonson stands in much the same relation to earlier poets as Lady Wroth stands in relation to the graces, muses, and nymphs those poets praised. As she incarnates their beauty, so Jonson restores in himself the talent and creativity earlier bards embodied. That the poet's ability to eternize his subject is a long-established literary convention does not make it any less an important social determinant.

Like all his poems for the Sidneys (indeed, like all his patronage poems), the epigram for Lady Wroth constitutes a subtle advertisement for its author. However dissimilar in other respects, all of Jonson's writings inevitably present an implicit or explicit image of the man who made them. Whatever adopted role he emphasizes in particular works (whether it be the likable tippler in "To Penshurst," the champion of virtue in the poem to Robert Wroth, the sage counselor in the ode for William Sidney, the sly wag in the song for Lady Pembroke, the self-mocking lover in the sonnet to Lady Wroth, or the exalting celebrant in the epigram just discussed), in all these works Jonson crafts a public image even as he shapes his poems. The poems to the Sidneys illustrate the variety of roles he could adopt, but they also suggest how all the images implicit in his works come together to constitute a multifaceted self-portrait. While the poems suggest the diversity of his relations with the different members of one of England's most important and influential families, they also exemplify the sheer complexity of roles and stances his social position could encourage. Single poems were less important in themselves than as parts of a larger mosaic in which all the roles Jonson adopted helped constitute a unified and appealing self-portrait.

Jonson's poems for the Sidney circle reveal an impressive variety within continuity. They show him dealing subtly and effectively with the different members of a single extended family, and they suggest how important his relations with such families must have been in promoting his career and cementing his stature. Winning the support of such a family must have enhanced his sense of security in a way that dealing with a single, isolated patron could never equal. Gaining entree into such a circle might potentially mean gaining access to a far-flung network of connections and influence, but it could also provide the opportunity to establish durable links with different generations of the same family—links that might conceivably last a poet's lifetime. Jonson's possible service as a tutor to William Sidney may seem to us to have been a somewhat inglorious way for a great poet to support himself, but Jonson must have seen it as an opportunity to serve Lord Lisle in a highly visible capacity while also establishing a valuable relation with his heir. William's early death dashed any private hopes Jonson may have entertained of him, but it is interesting to speculate about the potentialities Jonson would have seen in such a relationship. What seems true of the "Ode" to William seems true of all of his works for the Sidney circle: in addressing a poem to any single member of it, he must have been conscious of its effects on his standing with the circle at large.

Poems to Egerton, Bacon, and Williams

A different sort of variety within continuity is exhibited by an unplanned series of poems Jonson addressed, over a number of years, to three men who served as Lord Keeper of the Great Seal, one of the kingdom's highest judicial offices. These poems—to Thomas Egerton,

Francis Bacon, and John Williams—are worth scrutinizing for a number of reasons. They provide fascinating insights into the court milieu in which Jonson operated, especially into its uncertainties and competitive insecurity. They illustrate how he could use connections with the powerful to promote his own and others' interests. They suggest the intriguing similarities of background, ambition, and general experience he often shared with his patrons, and they exemplify his talent for appealing to superiors of differing temperaments, circumstances, and idiosyncrasies.

Egerton's highly successful career suggests how (and how far) one might rise in the larger patronage system through the right combination of talent and powerful connections. Like Jonson, Egerton was largely a self-made man who nonetheless depended on the encouragement and support of superiors. He began life as an illegitimate son, but his father acknowledged him and ensured him a good education. At Oxford he developed an appreciation of learning that afterward led him to patronize scholars and encourage scholarship, but it was his later legal studies that most clearly shaped his subsequent career. When his Catholic sympathies threatened to block his chance to practice law, he abandoned them and conformed to Anglican usage. Admitted to the bar in 1572, he eventually attracted the attention of the Queen, who in 1581 appointed him Solicitor General. For the next two decades further honors and offices followed, until in May 1596 he became Lord Keeper of the Great Seal.[32]

The power—but also the precariousness—of Egerton's status depended on the Queen's continuing favor. Lacking noble blood, great hereditary wealth, or the support of family or faction, he was perhaps even more aware than most courtiers of the insecurities his position entailed. But he also exhibited a shrewd ability to strengthen his standing whenever possible. He used his official influence to help powerful figures who could help him, embarked on a steady program of land acquisition, and made a series of useful marriages. His wedding in 1600 to Alice Spenser (a noted patroness) allied him "to some of the most powerful families in England."[33] By the turn of the century, the one-time illegitimate commoner could anticipate a brood of grandchildren born of noble blood. Egerton's good fortunes continued under the new regime. Soon after James's succession he was promoted to Lord Chancellor and created Baron Ellesmere, and from then until his death in 1617 he remained one of the King's most trusted and effective servants.

Jonson's *Epigrammes* contains a brief but striking poem (Ep. 74) which, while praising Egerton as a judge, implies the poet's role in judging Egerton. It carefully weighs the facts of his temperament and behavior and then pronounces a public verdict on his character. Jonson emphasizes the poem's highly logical structure through such devices as parallel phrasing, a thoughtful distinction between legal wisdom and legal skill, and suspended grammatical constructions presumably leading to a crowning logical and syntactical conclusion. It is as if the poet were himself a lawyer meticulously marshaling evidence, less to move the reader emotionally than to convince him with reason. This logical tone helps make the final lines' imagistic leap all the more startling and witty. Suddenly Jonson moves from painstakingly sensible (even prosaic) assessment to mythopoeic allusion, in which Egerton's conscience is said to have become the new home of Astraea, the virgin goddess of justice. The wit of the final couplet stems from the fact that if one has been willing to take seriously the poet's carefully weighed judgment of Egerton's own "weigh'd judgements" (1), then the epigram's conclusion—however surprising—should seem neither extravagant nor simply empty flattery. The poem's logical, argumentative structure gives it a greater sense of objectivity than it might otherwise have possessed. At the same time, by reenacting Egerton's own judicious method of thinking, it pays the patron a far more subtle compliment.

When, toward the end of his life and suffering under the strain of illness, Egerton asked to be allowed to lay down the burdens of office, James at first resisted. Later he agreed, but only on condition that Egerton resume his duties when his health improved. As further evidence of his esteem the King promised to bestow an Earldom on the old judge, but within two weeks Egerton was dead. Shortly before this, Jonson addressed to him two epigrams. The title of the first, "To Thomas *Lo: Elsmere, the last Terme he sate Chancellor*" (*Und.* 31), suggests that it was written sometime during or just prior to January 1617. In both poems, Jonson asks Egerton to look favorably on the case of someone identified in an accompanying note simply as "a poore man." Besides their aesthetic value, the epigrams are interesting as evidence of his capacity to intercede poetically with a patron on behalf of a third party:

> So, justest Lord, may all your Judgements be
>   Lawes, and no change e're come to one decree:
> So, may the King proclaime your Conscience is
>   Law, to his Law; and thinke your enemies his:
> So, from all sicknesse, may you rise to health,
>   The Care, and wish still of the publike wealth:
> So may the gentler Muses, and good fame
>   Still flie about the Odour of your Name;
> As with the safetie, and honour of the Lawes,
>   You favour Truth, and me, in this mans Cause.
>
>   (1–10)[34]

As in Jonson's first poem to the Lord Chancellor, the syntax of this one is skillfully suspended; all meaning and judgment hinge on the crucial last couplet and its final words. Both poems implicitly liken judge and poet, and both works judge as much as they commend. Although the second begins with what might seem the baldest flattery, the validity of its praise is made to turn on Egerton's particular decision in this case. Both men knew that the case would indeed be one of Egerton's last—that it would in *fact*, not just in the poem's fiction, be a kind of summing-up of his qualities as a jurist. Egerton himself, by his reaction to Jonson's plea, had it within his power to determine whether "the gentler Muses, and good fame / [would] Still flie about the Odour of [his] Name" (7–8). The poem's references to Egerton's "enemies" and serious ill health make the usefulness of its praise all the more obvious. Depending on his decision, the poem would serve either as testimony to, or as ironic commentary on, Jonson's avowed faith in his good judgment. When the poem was written it was intended as praise; whether it will "still" function in that way is implicitly one of the issues it asks him to decide.[35]

In the end, Egerton is urged to support the "poore man's" cause both out of principle and as a personal favor. This closing juxtaposition of the public and private brings the poem full circle and achieves (potentially—since all depends on Egerton's decision) a symmetry with its opening lines. There Jonson had punned on the double sense of "Judgements," the ideal coalescence of private conviction and public decree, a blending of Conscience and Law.[36] Until the final line, the poem focuses almost exclusively on the future, but the last words suddenly shift to the presence and urgency of "this mans Cause." The last line's monosyllabic nouns are strung out like discrete and equidistant cells, Egerton alone possessing the power to fuse a vital link between them.

The sense of immediacy which closes this epigram also dominates its sequel (*Und.* 32), which begins by asserting that "The Judge his favour timely then extends, / When a good Cause is destitute of friends, / Without the pompe of Counsell" (1–3). Although this work contains no explicit reference to the poet, its tone nevertheless seems personal and urgent. Jonson shifts from the preceding poems' general praise to the details of the specific case; implicitly adopting the role of counselor, he directly pleads with the judge and maligns the opposition's integrity. He plays on Egerton's personal indignation by accusing his opponents of boasting about their perjury. But the poem suggests that thanks to Jonson's intervention, this "good Cause" is not entirely "destitute of friends" (2). Jonson's aid is charitable (6) in every sense of the word, while his mocking reference to "the pompe of Counsell" highlights his own blunt eloquence.

Jonson depicts his effort as not only one of assisting his friend but of helping to prevent Egerton's deception and embarrassment. In the final couplet, however, he gives Egerton credit for not really needing such assistance: "When this appeares, just Lord, to your sharp sight, / He do's you wrong, that craves you to do right" (15–16). "When" implies a subtle compliment, as if the Chancellor's penetration of duplicity can almost be taken for granted. At the same time, "When" also suggests the poem's role in making Egerton's "sharp sight" possible. As in other poems, Jonson credits his superior with already knowing (or, in this case, inevitably discovering) what the poem so earnestly elaborates. Line 16 is richly ambiguous in a different way. On the one hand the wrong-doers mentioned are those who crave justice when they know their cause is false. But the line can also be interpreted to mean that once Egerton perceives the truth of Jonson's claims, any further need to persuade him to act justly would be both superfluous and somewhat insulting. This second meaning, paradoxically, itself functions as persuasion, pressuring Egerton into responding as Jonson hopes. But the tactic is all the more effective for being broached as an implicit compliment.

The epigram's closing reference to the possibility of having to "crave" Egerton "to do right" (16) brings the poem full circle, reminding us of its opening emphasis on timely "favour" (1). To speak of impersonal justice as reflecting the judge's "favour" might seem paradoxical, but the phrasing implies that simple justice cannot be simply assumed. It results not from the smooth, mechanical functioning of an anonymous system but reflects the personal goodness of powerful men charged with interpreting and applying the law. This epigram, like so many others by Jonson, implicitly concedes that abstract ideals can only be realized by the individual (often fallible) men and women who control the levers of social influence. By emphasizing Egerton's crucial role in ensuring justice, Jonson potentially pays him a great compliment; but the poem also implicitly holds him responsible if justice miscarries.

Egerton's death opened the way for Francis Bacon to succeed him, in March 1617, as Lord Keeper and then, less than a year later, also as Lord Chancellor. These appointments helped fulfill deep-rooted and long-standing ambitions, and seemed especially satisfying after years of frustration, uncertainty, and complicated political maneuvering. Unlike Pembroke (who largely inherited his influence) or Egerton (whose rise was relatively swift and unencumbered), Bacon knew from childhood not only the appeals of power but also the effects of its loss. His own career can largely be seen as a struggle to regain—or surpass—the status once possessed by his father. In that sense, he and Jonson may have been similarly motivated. Bacon's interest in Egerton's offices had been formed years before the latter's death and seems to have reflected more important desires than simple ambition. His father had served as Lord Keeper under Elizabeth, who took to calling Francis "the young Lord Keeper." But when Nicholas Bacon suddenly died, his son just as suddenly found himself facing "a problematical future." Paul Kocher writes that in the uncertain years that followed, "Bacon tended to revert to the foundation of his security and self-esteem, which was the figure of the long-dead Lord Keeper. . . . [T]he older man's reputation was, in a sense, part of his son's stock in trade."[37] Exactly how early he conceived the hope of succeeding to his father's office cannot be said, but an entry in his private journal makes it clear that thoughts of occupying another of Egerton's positions—the Lord Chancellorship—had occurred to him already in 1608.[38] The year before, after more than a decade of frustration and disappointment, he had been named Solicitor General, but further significant advancement was stalled until after Cecil's death in 1612.

With Salisbury gone, Bacon's prospects improved. He maneuvered to have himself appointed Attorney General, and in the process had his old rival, Sir Edward Coke, removed as Lord Chief Justice of the Court of Common Pleas and "elevated" to a more prestigious but less powerful position. In 1616, Bacon played a prominent role in evicting Coke from his new office, and then shortly thereafter, with assistance from Buckingham (the new royal favorite), became Lord Keeper at last.[39] When Coke sought to arrange a marriage between his daughter and Buckingham's brother, Bacon worked to thwart the plan. He assumed that Buckingham and the King would also oppose the match, but in this he miscalculated. Attempts to explain himself only exacerbated their anger; in the end, only abject submission prevented Buckingham from punishing him severely. Once Bacon had capitulated, Buckingham proved willing to forgive—perhaps realizing (as Bacon must have, too) that the Lord Keeper's narrow escape made him even more dependent than before on the favorite's good graces.[40]

The next few years brought added honors. In January 1618 Bacon was appointed Lord Chancellor, and in July was created Baron Verulam. On the occasion of his sixtieth birthday, on 26 January 1621, a party was held at York House, his new residence, where he had been born and where his father had lived when he was Lord Keeper so many years before. The celebration was made all the merrier by Bacon's knowledge that he would be created Viscount St. Albans the next day—far surpassing the status even his father had achieved. Jonson was present, and the poem he delivered not only reveals his clever ability to exploit a present occasion but also achieves greater impact by drawing on the deeper themes, aspirations, and ironies of his subject's life.

For Bacon as perhaps for no other patron, Jonson seems to have felt an intellectual respect verging on awe. He prided himself on his comprehension of the Lord Chancellor's difficult *Novum Organum* and kept a copy in his library (H&S 8:592). The attraction of associating with Bacon went beyond the allure of his power and prestige: Jonson had mingled with the powerful and prestigious for many years now. It was rather, Jonson wrote, "that he seem'd to mee ever, by his worke, one of the greatest men, and most worthy of admiration, that had been in many Ages" (H&S 8:592). To have won the support and respect of such a figure must have produced a special satisfaction, must have enhanced the poet's own sense of self-esteem. This was not the least of the gifts a patron could give, and Jonson seems to have believed that Bacon could give it abundantly.

There was, of course, a more practical side to their relationship, and its significance should not be minimized. Bacon was by his own confession a proud man, and was ambitious, too, with a keen sense of the dignities of his new status and a pronounced appetite for self-display. Although he had suffered financial hardship in his youth, when he became powerful he showed a careless disregard for money and proved willing to spend it lavishly to enhance his status at court.[41] Moreover, throughout his life Bacon showed himself keenly aware of the various roles writing could play in building and sustaining a courtly reputation. Some of his own earliest public service involved commissioned writing of propaganda, while many of his other writings seem originally to have been composed partly to win, maintain, or regain political status. Jonathan Marwill demonstrates convincingly how closely Bacon's intellectual activities were tied to his practical ambitions; here, as in the case of other Renaissance writers, no neat distinction between the active and contemplative lives seems possible.[42]

Various evidence suggests that by the time Jonson attended the sixtieth birthday celebrations at York House, he and the Lord Chancellor had been friendly a good while.[43] Whether Jonson was expected to produce a poem to commemorate the event or whether the work was entirely his own idea cannot now be known, nor can it be said whether he was compensated for his efforts. Perhaps the opportunity to play so prominent a role in festivities celebrating so prominent a figure seemed compensation enough. In any case, he demonstrates a clever ability to make the most of the possibilities the occasion presented.

> Haile, happie *Genius* of this antient pile!
> How comes it all things so about the[e] smile?
> The fire, the wine, the men! and in the midst,
> Thou stand'st as if some Mysterie thou did'st!
> Pardon, I read it in thy face, the day

> For whose returnes, and many, all these pray:
> And so doe I. This is the sixtieth yeare
> Since *Bacon*, and thy Lord was borne, and here;
> Sonne to the grave wise Keeper of the Seale,
> Fame, and foundation of the English Weale.
> What then his Father was, that since is hee,
> Now with a Title more to the Degree;
> *Englands* high Chancellor: the destin'd heire
> In his soft Cradle to his Fathers Chaire,
> Whose even Thred the Fates spinne round, and full,
> Out of their Choycest, and their whitest wooll.
>   'Tis a brave cause of joy, let it be knowne,
> For 't were a narrow gladnesse, kept thine owne.
> Give me a deep-crown'd-Bowle, that I may sing
> In raysing him the wisdome of my King.
>
> (1–20)

Reminiscent in some ways of his earlier "Ode" to Sir William Sidney, this poem (*Und.* 51) nevertheless importantly differs. Oddly enough (considering its genre), the Sidney "Ode" seems somehow less "public" than this one, more intimate in conception and execution, less celebratory than cautionary. While that poem urges a young man to equal the grand examples set by his forebears, this one has nearly the opposite intention.[44] Significantly, it presents Bacon as having already lived up to—indeed, as having surpassed—the example that meant most to him; Jonson's reference to his patron's "Title" (12) reminds us that while Sir Nicholas had been Lord Keeper, his son was that and Lord Chancellor, too. And the word also momentarily suggests his membership in the peerage as Baron Verulam and then as Viscount St. Albans. These, again, were distinctions Sir Nicholas never attained.

While the Sidney "Ode" emphasizes the diligent effort needed to attain public greatness, the emphasis of the poem to Bacon is instead on the seeming naturalness and inevitability of his rise. Jonson's lines convey little sense of the Bacon who emerges from the letters and from other contemporary evidence—the frustrated, struggling courtier, ambitious for status but unsure of its attainment, inspired (but also somewhat intimidated) by his father's success, adept at (but also the victim of) political intrigue, proud and increasingly powerful yet fundamentally insecure. The poem mythologizes his rise and legitimizes his position, offering no hint of the struggle, infighting, and anxiety that attended them. Bacon's prospects when he was Sidney's age were in some ways far gloomier than Sidney's; his career had developed slowly, haltingly; he no sooner succeeded to his father's old office than he was threatened with humiliation and the prospect of its loss. Jonson's poem, with its allusions to destiny and fate, papers over these sources of conflict and tension, not only because it would be indecorous to mention them, but also because the poem is as much concerned with assuring Bacon's future as it is with celebrating his past. By naturalizing and legitimizing Bacon's power, by making it seem more a birthright than the fruit of calculated service and political contention, Jonson helps render it more convincing, harder to question or subvert. The poem must have appealed deeply to Bacon's own strong sense of destiny and family; in a way, Jonson simply takes over and ratifies a theme Bacon had done the most to develop and perpetuate. Hailing him as his father's son was a double tribute: it praised him by mirroring his own favorite notion of himself, but it also signaled that that notion had by now become an integral part of his public legend.

As interesting as the poem's larger strategies is its local texture. Sometimes the phrasing is most meaningful when it seems most awkward.[45] When Jonson mentions, for instance, "the day / For whose returnes, and many, all these pray: / And so doe I," we momentarily stumble over the syntax. But the very "clumsiness" of the lines emphasizes their component parts. That added thought—"And so doe I"— asserts the common purpose Jonson shares with the other guests even as it highlights the unique form his own wish takes. Jonson himself, through this very poem, best fulfills the injunction of its final lines: " 'Tis a brave cause of joy, let it be knowne, / For 't were a narrow gladnesse, kept thine owne" (5–7; 17–18). When he calls for a "deep-crown'd-Bowle, that I may sing / In raysing him the wisdome of my King" (19–20), his use of "may" only underscores the fact that such singing is what he has already done and is doing. "In raysing him" is similarly suggestive: most obviously it refers to James's acts of elevating Bacon; but by immediately following the verb "sing," the phrase also briefly suggests Jonson's act of raising (and praising) Bacon through the poem. His song at once sums up the wishes of the other celebrants, articulates them, but, precisely by doing so, distinguishes itself from them. As in the Sidney ode, only the poet can lend transcendent significance to an essentially ephemeral and "narrow gladnesse."

Jonson's wit manifests itself in a number of particular details. Referring to the "happie *Genius* of this antient pile," for instance, anticipates the later reminder that Bacon's new residence was also his birthplace; the reference associates his brief tenure there with the structure's antique grandeur. At the same time, by addressing the imaginary *"Genius"* so intently and so vividly that his real presence seems simply to be taken for granted, Jonson invites us to notice the senses in which he himself (as in the Sidney poem) fulfills the functions of that role. And if, once again, the lines that immediately follow seem clumsy or ambiguous, it seems worth pausing to wonder why Jonson chose not to make them more smooth or clear. "This is the sixtieth yeare," he announces, "Since *Bacon*, and thy Lord was borne, and here; / Sonne to the grave wise Keeper of the Seale, / Fame, and foundation of the English Weale" (7–10). The staggered phrasing of line 8 may at first seem merely slipshod, but in fact it serves to recapitulate the major transformations of its subject's career, from "*Bacon*" the private citizen to Bacon "thy Lord," from his birth "here" to his triumphant return to the same place. The words "Fame, and foundation of the English Weale" are obviously applicable to Bacon's father, but for a moment, at least, Jonson seems to be using them to continue his description of the son—an ambiguity intensified by the parallel positioning of "Sonne" and "Fame." Whether consciously calculated or not, the confusion works to the poem's advantage, emphasizing on another, subtler level the explicit comparisons between Bacon and Sir Nicholas. For an instant we can't be sure which of the two the words describe, and even on reflection their reference to one rather than the other seems less than completely certain.

Within a few months after Jonson's poem was written, Bacon's career lay in ruins. Fined, disgraced, stripped of his offices and nearly deprived of his titles, barred from public employment and exiled from the court, his fall had been shockingly swift and precipitous. A parliamentary committee investigating judicial corruption turned up charges that he had accepted bribes; in no time the number of accusations ballooned from two to twenty-eight. At first Bacon tried to defend himself, but when that proved pointless he admitted his guilt and beseeched his judges' mercy. He hoped to escape merely with the loss of the Lord Keepership, but Parliament was in no mood to be lenient. Only the votes of Buckingham's faction and of the bishops prevented the House of Lords from divesting him completely of his membership in the peerage. And yet despite his humiliation, Bacon did not relinquish all hope of recovering at least part of his former status. Denied avenues of purely political advancement, he turned instead to his pen as an instrument of self-promotion. Although he never regained his earlier stature, neither did he lose power completely. In 1622 he was granted an annuity of 1200 pounds, and altogether he received "about two thousand a year, a sum higher than most noblemen could count on." Fully pardoned in 1624, when he died in 1626 he was more respected than one would have thought possible only a few years before.[46]

Almost as unexpected as Bacon's fall was the selection of John Williams as the new Lord Keeper. Williams had been Egerton's chaplain and protégé, but otherwise he had scant acquaintance with the law. The fact that he was only thirty-nine and also a cleric made him an unlikely and (in some quarters) an unpopular candidate, but James was impressed by his intelligence and chose him even though Buckingham clearly was pushing another man's suit. James's favorable impression of Williams dated back at least a decade, when the young cleric had preached a sermon before him that seems to have pleased them both. "I had a great deal of court holy water," Williams subsequently wrote to a kinsman, "if I can make myself any good thereby."[47]

Like Egerton's, Williams's rise was relatively steady. He was patronized by both Egerton and Bacon, and after another sermon before the King in 1619, his fortunes improved dramatically. When the Deanery of Salisbury opened up, Williams received it (despite, once more, Buckingham's support for another candidate). Then, in 1621, the King promoted him to the bishopric of Lincoln. Like Bacon, however, he eventually suffered a dramatic fall. Both his advance and his decline illustrate not only the importance of royal backing but also the growing importance of the favorite's favor. Like Bacon, Williams discovered that Buckingham's power could neither be ignored nor easily resisted. More than anything else, however, it was James's death that sealed his fate. Like Jonson, he soon discovered that his position in the new reign was suddenly less certain, and there may even be reason to think that Jonson's poem lamenting Williams's fall reflects the poet's own insecurity at the time. The poem, moreover, raises intriguing questions about Jonson's tone, about the extent of his license to criticize, about his possible motives for addressing Williams at such a time and in such a way, and about how the poem was actually circulated. Fascinating on all these counts, the epigram is also an important work in the transition from the Jacobean to the Caroline periods of Jonson's career.

Williams seems to have been wary of courting Buckingham very assiduously, both because he worried that his support might prove inconstant and because he doubted that Buckingham's own status could long endure. It was James himself who suggested that Buckingham's friendship was worth pursuing, and Williams was not slow to act on the advice. He was instrumental in smoothing the way for Buckingham's marriage to the Earl of Rutland's daughter, and afterward he proved valuable as an advisor on parliamentary matters. But when, as Lord Keeper, he proved less than completely subservient, the favorite began to lose patience, and by 1625 was determined to cut him down. James's death early that spring had helped make Williams more vulnerable, since Charles shared Buckingham's attitude in this as in other matters. Unlike Bacon, however, Williams stood guilty of no obvious offense and seemed confident that he could survive. In the end, a purely technical pretext was found, and on 25 October he lost his office even more suddenly than he had gained it.[48] An untitled poem in the *Under-wood* volume (61) has often been assumed by Jonson's editors to have been prompted by this dismissal:

> That you have seene the pride, beheld the sport,
>   And all the games of Fortune, plaid at Court,
> View'd there the mercat, read the wretched rate
>   At which there are, would sell the Prince, and State:
> That scarce you heare a publike voyce alive,
>   But whisper'd Counsells, and those only thrive;
> Yet are got off thence, with cleare mind, and hands
>   To lift to heaven: who is't not understands
> Your happinesse, and doth not speake you blest,
>   To see you set apart, thus, from the rest,
> T[o]'obtaine of God, what all the Land should aske?
>   A Nations sinne got pardon'd! 'twere a taske
> Fit for a Bishops knees! O bow them oft,
>   My Lord, till felt griefe make our stone hearts soft,
> And wee doe weepe, to water, for our sinne.
>   He, that in such a flood, as we are in
> Of riot, and consumption, knowes the way
>   To teach the people, how to fast, and pray,
> And doe their penance, to avert Gods rod,
>   He is the Man, and Favorite of God.
>
> (1–20)

Never before had Jonson so emphatically praised a man so obviously out of favor; given the circumstances, his last line seems particularly daring. With this poem as with so many others, however, we need to know much more about the facts of circulation before we can speculate intelligently about Jonson's intention. Was the poem widely published, or was it shown only to Williams and his circle, who could be relied on not to betray the poet's trust? Was Jonson's decision to leave "the Bishop" unidentified prompted by prudence or by some far simpler consideration? Did he identify himself as the work's author, or was his name also omitted? When—precisely—was the poem written? Immediately after Williams's dismissal, for instance, "[his] friends were confident that he would eventually rise again to some other great place. They believed, or Williams had told them, that the Duke, in bringing about his fall, had acted from fear rather than hatred."[49] If the epigram dates from this period, then its veiled allusion to the favorite (and indeed, its very existence) seems less risky, more comprehensible. "It was soon plain," however,

> that Williams was to be pursued even at [his estate] Buckden by the Duke's rancour and the King's displeasure. A commission was ap-

pointed to investigate his conduct and report whether any charge could be brought against him. That expedient failed; the commission could find nothing culpable in his past career. But he was continually watched and spied upon; it was reported that he kept a state unbecoming a 'cashiered courtier,' and that the Bishop's palace at Buckden was a rallying-place for those who bore a grudge against Buckingham.[50]

If the poem was written under the circumstances and at the time these sentences suggest, then it seems far more provocative. Perhaps neither supposition is correct. Unfortunately, it is doubtful that we will ever know. Yet however uncertain the poem's precise context, its skill is certainly worth remarking. The first two couplets, for instance, cleverly balance the trivial with the deadly serious, the former quality at once offsetting and intensifying the latter. At first glance the court seems merely an arena where "games" are "plaid"—*for* fortune, but also *by* Fortune. Through the simple equivocation of "of," Jonson manages to suggest that the participants at once are players and are played with— seekers after fortune but also her potential victims. The sense of "sport" that dominates the first couplet is radically attenuated in the second, with its imagery of bargaining that is doubly cheap but deadly treacherous. If the opening distich focuses with wry irony on the corruption of individual courtiers, the second draws out the implications of their chicanery for the state as a whole. The "rate" they are willing to accept in exchange for their perfidy is both economically and morally "wretched," while the poem's reference to "the Prince" not only exempts Charles from any responsibility for the dishonesty surrounding him but implies the unshakeable loyalty both of the poet and of the poem's subject. No mention is made of Charles's role in sanctioning Williams's dismissal, which is indeed presented not as a dismissal at all. When Jonson asks "who is't not understands / Your happinesse, and doth not speake you blest, / To see you set apart, thus" (8–10), he depicts Williams's fall as a kind of election to a higher grace. In adopting this sanguine attitude, he consoles Williams the individual while also bolstering the threatened reputation of Williams the public man. God becomes an alternative Patron, Williams His ideal servant; the relationship between this King and this "Favorite" obliquely mirrors—but also shows up—the one between Charles and Buckingham.

Loyalty to a generous benefactor, as much as daring and righteous indignation, may have prompted Jonson's poem. Williams had always been a learned man friendly to learned men, and he continued his patronage even after his fall. Although disgraced, he enjoyed a hefty income, and used much of it to entertain the nobles, gentry, and intellectuals who frequently visited his estate. It is not hard to believe that

Jonson was one of those who enjoyed his hospitality and munificence, and in fact there is documentary evidence of Williams's concurrence in a gift of 5 pounds in 1629 "to Mr. Benjamin Jhonson in his sickness & want" (H&S 1 : 244–45). Jonson's praise of the fallen bishop, then—while at first glance a purely altruistic and perhaps even defiant act on behalf of a discharged courtier—proves more complicated on closer inspection. At the time Jonson probably wrote, Williams was still both wealthy and powerful and had not altogether given up hopes of someday reentering that "glorious miserye and splendid slaverie" from which he had so recently been freed.[51] Perhaps the poem, with its tone of frustrated indignation, also reflects Jonson's personal concerns about the changes the new reign might bring to his own standing and security at court.

By the end of the Jacobean period, Jonson could look back over twenty years of involvement in the patronage system. The contempt he expresses in the Williams epigram for the system's corruptions may seem simply conventional. But the disgust may also reflect real misgivings, born of a long and intimate acquaintance with the court. Such satire, however, represents only one of the many elements of his complex response to the demands of his social role. As even the few poems surveyed in this chapter suggest, the various challenges posed by the competition for patronage encouraged him to respond in various but always creative ways, contributing to his work's rich resonance. The different styles and roles, techniques and tactics he adopts can all be seen as partly conditioned by his awareness of the most important audience for whom he wrote. His plain diction is often balanced by understated deftness—either because he feels the need to insinuate meaning that might be too dangerous to express openly (as, perhaps, in the poem to Williams), or simply in order to complicate and deepen his praise. Although patronage poetry in general is often associated with bald or even craven flattery, Jonson's performance shows how richly equivocal it could be.

His patronage poetry could be playfully delicate (as in the song for Pembroke and his lady), defiantly righteous (as in the appeals to Egerton), sneeringly sarcastic (as in the poem on Wroth), or full of fawning praise that nonetheless magnified his own importance (as in the epigram to Wroth's wife). It provided Jonson the opportunity to display his command of various genres and to exploit classical precedents to define and give poetic structure to contemporary patronage experiences. If, at bottom, its fundamental impulse is self-promotion, it nevertheless demonstrates the manifold means by which this goal could be pursued. The claim that Jonson's poetry is to a large extent self-advertising is neither reductive nor simplistic; instead it is one method of coming to grips with the full complexity of his achievement.

Jonson could present himself both as a clown and as a celebrant whose words lent dignity to and derived dignity from his subject (as in "To Penshurst"). In the poems to William Sidney and to Bacon, as in the "Panegyre" to James, he seems part of a common effort but also distinct: his relationship with the patron seems both exemplary and unique. If in the ode to Sidney he seems almost to lecture the young man he addresses, in the poem to Bacon his role is more nearly priestly; and in both works good humor is balanced by deeper seriousness. In various poems, for various reasons, Jonson either bolsters and consoles patrons whose power seems threatened (as in the poem to Williams); celebrates patrons whose power seems confirmed (the poems to Cecil and Bacon); or attempts to undermine the confidence of patrons in other clients partly to promote the success of his own suits (the first epigram to Cecil; the epistle to Sackville). Although he sometimes champions courtiers whose status seems at risk, they are almost always men still powerful enough to lend him useful help. Sometimes he subtly magnifies the danger the patron faces to play on the reader's sympathies (as in the epigram to Pembroke); at other times, however, he minimizes or downplays its seriousness, either to console his patron or to nourish his reputation and prospects for recovery (the epigram to Williams).

Often Jonson depicts the corruption of the court while still distancing himself, his particular patron, and his royal patron from it—despite the intimate involvement of them all in the courtly system. He can use a poem simultaneously to ratify or to undermine a patron's reputation, and can make his praise of others reflect specifically on himself. Some poems are distanced from the immediate concerns of the practical world (such as the song to Pembroke and his lady), others intimately caught up in and responsive to it. If in some poems he paints starkly detailed pictures of social corruption (the poem to Wroth), in others he ignores or glosses over important facts, either from decorousness or prudent discretion. He celebrates an ideal world in which self-serving competition and self-promotion are unnecessary, all the while using that celebration to promote his own and his patrons' interests. He demonstrates an ability to play on the general concerns of all patrons (as in the epistle to Sackville) and on the particular concerns of specific individuals (such as Bacon).

Examining the lives of his patrons shows how pervasive patronage concerns were. His superiors were almost inevitably caught up in the same kinds of anxieties and ambitions as Jonson himself, and it may have been partly his own familiarity with the feelings competition engendered that allowed him to exploit those feelings so skillfully when addressing others. The poems discussed in this chapter help illustrate the sheer variety of *kinds* of patrons he could address: young men at the start of their careers (Sidney), older men at high points (Bacon; Cecil) or at climaxes (Egerton); others caught up in the day-to-day struggle to maintain power (Lisle) or who had lost power but hoped to recover (Williams); patrons officially able to assist him (Pembroke); wives of patrons, important mainly as appendages to their husbands (Lady Pembroke), and other patronesses important in their own rights (Lady Wroth); older patrons who had already done him favors (Cecil), or prospective patrons capable of assisting him in the future (Sidney); patrons related to one another either through family ties (the Sidneys, Wroths, and Herberts) or through patronage connections of their own (Egerton, Williams, Bacon). By the end of his Jacobean career Jonson had addressed a wide variety of different kinds of patrons and had met in varying ways the numerous challenges and demands that being a patronage poet had set for him. Like any poet, he found himself continually confronted with blank paper, and therefore with the need to make choices. And his role as a poet writing for patrons helped fundamentally to determine, in matters large and small, the kinds of choices he made.

5

Poems on Rivals and Rivalry

Precisely because relations with patrons were so important, Jonson's dealings with antagonists and competitors were almost equally significant. Rivals, paradoxically, probably constituted his most attentive and interested audience, since they stood to gain or lose the most from his failures and successes. The attention they paid him was perversely flattering: it was a tribute—but also a latent threat—to his real social power. Jonson wrote with a high degree of self-consciousness not only because his words would be read by superiors, but because they would be vulnerable to attack from antagonists as well. Every poem he wrote presented an implicit image of him for public scrutiny; every poem was in some sense both an advertisement and a calculated risk. The "Epistle" to the Countess of Rutland, with its flawed concluding tone, exemplifies as well as any of his works the kind of heightened self-consciousness these twin pressures could produce.

The Rutland "Epistle" was probably written near the end of 1599, in the midst of an extremely important transitional period in his career. During this time he sought increasingly to define and present himself as a serious Poet, one who deserved the respect and patronage of the intellectual and social elite. Nearly every work he wrote at this time can be seen as part of an effort to fashion a distinctive role and image acceptable to those who could most affect his status as a serious public author. Each new work must have seemed particularly important to him precisely because of its newness: its chief function was less to confirm his reputation than to establish it.

Rarely in his career was Jonson quite as vulnerable as now, or for quite the same reasons. The insecurities and uncertainties he experienced during this time derived largely from his status as a new poet, one who had yet to carve out a niche for himself in the literary and social hierarchy. Although tensions would also arise years later, when the unusual eminence he had obtained by then seemed threatened, in these early days he was far more exposed: he possessed neither the extensive social contacts nor the tested literary experience that afterward proved so useful in coping with the dangers of his position. If literary records are any indication, his rivalries with other writers were particularly intense at this time, when he must have seemed a more inviting and less protected target than in his later heyday under James. His scramble to promote himself encouraged the ill-will of antagonists, but because he could not foresee his eventual success, the struggle to obtain it no doubt seemed all the more pressing and important. The works he wrote during this period must have been invested with a particularly intense energy and with a self-consciousness sharpened by a driving need to compete.

Perhaps the most crucial and determining event in Jonson's life during this period was the "poetomachia"—his publicly-staged mud-slinging match with Thomas Dekker and John Marston, which extended over several years and a number of different plays. Jonson's *Poetaster* is the best-known product of this dispute, but that play was itself conceived as a preemptive strike against Dekker's ferocious *Satiromastix*, a work apparently designed to embarrass Jonson in front of the most influential and important segment of his audience at a critical juncture in his career. Indeed, a concern with patronage seems central both to the tactical purpose and to the thematic unity of the work. In *Satiromastix*, both Horace the poet (closely patterned after Jonson) and the leading patron seem selfish and corrupt; both fall short of the lofty ideals associated with their roles. Each selfishly undermines the trust and reciprocal regard so crucial to the healthy functioning of a hierarchical society. Dekker seizes one of Jonson's favorite ideas—that true kings and true poets possess similar gifts and comparable responsibilities—and exploits it to great satiric effect.[1]

In the years before *Satiromastix* was written, Jonson's efforts to win aristocratic patronage and to establish himself as a poet worthy of aristocratic support had been particularly intense. His earliest known poems of patronage, including the Rutland epistle, date from around this time, as does one of his few surviving acrostics, the epitaph on Margaret Ratcliffe, Queen Elizabeth's favorite maid of honor. (In *Satiromastix*, Horace's pride as a writer of acrostics is mocked explicitly; see 1.2.90). Also during this period, the Lord Chamberlain's men staged the first performance of *Every Man Out of His Humour*. In that work's controversial original conclusion, an actor impersonating the Queen was acclaimed by another in terms that even Jonson seems later to have considered a bit too fulsome (H&S 3:602–03).

One of his most curious patronage poems also dates from around this time—his "Ode to the Earl of Desmond." Apparently his first attempt to meet the demands of one of the most public, prestigious, and poetically elaborate of all Renaissance genres, the Desmond "Ode" marks an important stage in his effort to be taken seriously (both by superiors and by competing writers) as a Poet in the fullest sense. It seems to have been widely read in the months after it was written; in *Satiromastix*, Dekker not only alludes to Jonson's pride in his ability as a writer of odes (1.2.92) but actually burlesques the language of the poem itself.[2] All the evidence suggests, then, that by the summer of 1601 (when *Satiromastix* was probably written), Jonson's patronage ambitions were well known, and the controversy over the original ending of *Every Man Out of his Humour* only publicized them further. Whatever their other motives, Dekker and Marston must have seen their play as an opportunity to hit their rival where it would hurt most, not only by mocking his behavior as a patronage poet but by seeking "to untruss him" (as John Davies of Hereford noted) before an audience of "Knights and Lords."[3] Jonson himself had already inadvertently damaged his reputation among influential circles when his *Poetaster* had been produced and failed earlier in the year, and Dekker and Marston seem to have been only too willing to help finish the job.

That they chose to satirize him as a patronage poet is neither insignificant nor incidental. Much more than has been emphasized, the "poetomachia" was a response to pressures inherent in the patronage system. Earlier scholars stressed its personal nature or its relation to rivalries among the competing theater companies, while the best recent account accentuates its connection to disagreements both aesthetic and intellectual.[4] Each of these factors must have played some role in determining its nature and conduct, but the fact that it was largely (and frequently literally) acted out before audiences significantly composed of the intellectual and social elite—of courtiers and lawyers, of London wits and gentlemen up from the country, of patrons, potential patrons, or the associates of potential patrons—must have deepened its intensity by heightening the participants' sense of the stakes involved. It was one thing to be personally attacked by other writers, another to be satirized on the public stage. What must have mattered most, however, was the threat of being humiliated in front of the influential people on whom one's hopes for future fortune and security depended. The attitudes toward a poet held by fellow writers or by the public at large were surely important. But the opinions that counted most—both practically and in terms of self-esteem—were those of his superiors. It was they who were positioned to determine, through their patronage or neglect, not only how well he lived or ate but whether he would achieve his most important poetic aspirations. It was their opinions that might be prejudiced, either by directly witnessing his humiliation or by hearing reports from those who had.[5]

Satiromastix presents Horace-Jonson not only as a laboriously uninspired poet but as one whose attitude toward his superiors is consciously (if hypocritically) cynical. At one point he refers to his patrons
as rooks and gulls (1.2.163); at another, he is even more blatantly
mercenary (1.2.106–11). Clearly Horace takes pride in his relations with
the powerful, but Dekker depicts him as incapable of the genuine,
ingenuous service the patronage system ideally called for. Jonson is the
play's obvious target, but its satire can also suggest that his patrons were
ultimately the fools. Ostensibly warning them about his selfishness, the
satirists exploit his benefactors' own self-interest. The risk they run in
supporting him is not only of being deceived and betrayed but (in a
society in which perceptions were so important) more damningly of
seeming fatuous "Mecaenasses" (4.2.63). Dekker's strategy is to turn the
standard claim—that associating with a poet could win a patron fame—
into a positive liability for Jonson.

Not all the play's attacks are so obviously connected with patronage.
At one point his days as a bricklayer are mentioned (1.2.137–39), at
another his conversion to Catholicism (4.2.89–91). Three allusions refer
to his conviction for murder (1.2.114–17; 4.1.61–62; 4.3.202–06), and
his physical features and mannerisms are repeatedly mocked. Yet, however remote these hits may seem from the patronage context, all must
have been partly designed to embarrass him with the most significant
part of his audience. It is no accident that Horace's literal untrussing
takes place before the King, or that the act was normally used to dismiss
a dependent from his superior's service, or that the monarch, a few lines
before the end, pronounces himself satisfied with Horace's punishment.
Because he is the play's most important patron (see, for example,
5.2.136; 340), his rejection of Horace is both thematically appropriate
and dramatically effective. It represents the ultimate embarrassment to
which a patronage poet could be subjected.

Although it might seem unusual or even unique, the "poetomachia"
simply carried to an extreme various tendencies crucial to a proper
understanding of Jonson's career. The public rivalry with other authors,
the attempt to embarrass them in front of the influential and their
efforts to retaliate, the attempt to present an attractive image while
simultaneously denigrating others' images and resisting their attempts
at denigration: the poetomachia's sheer complexity epitomizes the complexity of Jonson's social position and its complicated impact on his
writing. Not until near the end of his career did his concern with rivals
once again take such an open and undisguised form, but the lasting
impact of this crucial early rivalry seems difficult to minimize.

The same self-consciousness encouraged by the poetomachia, the
same need to be concerned not only with the impression one made

oneself but with the deliberately or inadvertently threatening impressions made by others, pervades a number of Jonson's shorter satirical poems. These suggest the tremendous value wit enjoyed in his milieu, the powerful advantage it bestowed in the struggle with competitors. Far from expressing relaxed indifference to competition, wit often functioned precisely as a competitive weapon. Jonson's poetic skill—and thus his competitive potency—was revealed not only through artful compliments to patrons but perhaps as importantly through trenchant attacks on rivals. Both kinds of display, by suggesting his reserves of power, might make him more appealing to those seeking to enhance their power by exploiting his.

Several of his satires, however, are interesting for still another reason: they suggest the extent to which he and his contemporaries were acutely conscious of the social context in which poems were written and received. Like the poetomachia itself, they imply an intense awareness of the micropolitical dimensions of literature and thus make clear that reading Jonson's works this way is not an anachronistic imposition but reflects a practice common at the time. Power is an important issue in nearly all his works, but in some of the satires it is also an ex*plicit* issue. "To Fool, or Knave" (*Ep.* 61), for instance, claims that the title figure's "praise, or dispraise is to me alike, / One doth not stroke me, nor the other strike" (1–2). Yet Jonson obviously is not so impervious to such comment that he feels able to ignore it; the poem's very existence expresses the same concern the work openly denies. Similarly, in Epigram 72—"To Court-ling"—the poet faces (on a smaller scale) a predicament much like the one Jonson faced in the larger poetomachia:

> I Grieve not, Courtling, thou are started up
>   A chamber-critick, and dost dine, and sup
> At Madames table, where thou mak'st all wit
>   Goe high, or low, as thou wilt value it.
> 'Tis not thy judgement breeds the prejudice,
>   Thy person only, Courtling, is the vice.
>
>   (1–6)

Jonson's pose of indifference is belied by the poem's existence; obviously Courtling's judgments are important enough to compel a response, and their importance derives precisely from being delivered at "Madames table." By labeling his target "Courtling," Jonson implies his adversary's subservience to patronage concerns and his obsession with self-promotion, while at the same time suggesting that his real significance at court is very small indeed. He plays on Courtling's competitive obsessions even as he ridicules them. In both cases his objective is not only to strike a blow at Courtling's pride but, perhaps more important, to render him far less attractive as a client to "Madame" and her peers. Part of his strategy is to reveal to "Madame" how Courtling exploits their association, as well as to indicate how that association might be made to reflect on her negatively. Jonson's attitude toward the patroness seems deliberately hard to define: the word "Madame" can be read either as a term of contempt, a term of respect, or as a kind of indirect quotation of Courtling's own smug voice and thus as satire on his complacency. The poem allows us to imagine "Madame" either as Courtling's advocate or as his innocent victim. Whether she is his advocate or his dupe, however, the poem makes clear to her and to other potential patrons how the relationship impairs her own image. Jonson's avowed disdain for Courtling—and, by implication, for his self-promotional tactics—disguises the extent to which he necessarily shares Courtling's ambitions and the degree to which such courtlings threaten his own interests. After the brief initial reference, the poet is quick to efface himself from the poem, both to lend his attack greater objectivity (he ostensibly concerns himself with Courtling's judgments of "all wit," not just specifically of his own) and to distance himself from the ambitions that prompt Courtling's behavior.

This same Courtling—or his namesake—appears again in Epigram 52, where the threat to Jonson is made to seem at once more obvious and more subtle:

> Courtling, I rather thou should'st utterly
>   Dispraise my worke, then praise it frostily:
> When I am reade, thou fain'st a weake applause,
>   As if thou wert my friend, but lack'dst a cause.
> This but thy judgement fooles: the other way
>   Would both thy folly, and thy spite betray.
>
> (1–6)

This poem interestingly suggests Jonson's awareness of how competitors could seek to disguise their attempts at impression management, as well as his consciousness of the pressures they were under to do so. Indeed, it is precisely because Jonson is aware of how language can be manipulated that he often seems anxious to make his own motives clear. Courtling employs the same kind of deception— against Jonson and against their common audience—that Jonson himself would later disavow in his great tribute to Shakespeare, where he claims that "crafty Malice, might pretend this praise / And thinke to ruine, where it seem'd to raise" (H&S 8:391). This distinction between thinking and seeming (between true intention and outward appearance) is just as crucial, and just as problematic, in the epigram as it is in the elegy. The epigram's speaker implicitly contrasts his own willingness to address Courtling openly (or "utterly," in the first line's pun) with Courtling's furtive indirection. The weakness that causes Courtling to resort to such a tactic is used as a weapon to render him weaker still; yet Courtling is not so weak that Jonson can afford to ignore his faint praise. His strength derives from the social setting the poem implies, from the fact that he delivers his opinions in front of a courtly audience. His need to make the best impression on them dictates the subtlety Jonson satirizes; yet Jonson's own need to make a good impression dictates the necessity of his attack. Both Courtling and Jonson are caught up in the need to assert power, to perform by pretending not to, and although the poem seems addressed to a specific individual, it is in fact a performance staged for the benefit of a much broader and more significant audience. That audience consisted not only of the superiors who could help determine the poet's status but also of other potential courtlings. Jonson's epigram seems to attack a particular figure, but it also displays his strength, intimidating other would-be courtlings and preempting their own maneuvers.

The concluding couplet raises an interpretive problem that suggests, no matter how one chooses to resolve it, interesting things about the way the poem functions. When Jonson claims that Courtling's deviousness is so transparent that it fools no one but himself, does he assert that the other members of the courtly audience are aware of it? If so—if Courtling's attempted subtlety is so unsubtle that everyone immediately recognizes it for a sham—then his attempts to disguise his spite paradoxically emphasize it. If we interpret the lines this way, then Courtling's efforts are so hopelessly obvious (and therefore ineffective) that there is no reason for the present poem to exist. Clearly, however, Jonson seems to have felt sufficiently threatened by Courtling to retaliate—which suggests that his tactics are neither as unsubtle as Jonson claims nor as ineffective as he might wish. His assertion that those tactics fool no one but Courtling, then, itself functions as a tactic to pressure Courtling's audience into accepting Jonson's interpretation of his performance. Not to do this, the poem implies, would make one an even greater fool than Courtling. The poet thus exposes (and attempts to neutralize) the machinations of his critic while engaging in machinations of his own. The central problem the poem finesses is its own political and rhetorical status. It pretends simply to announce what is already obvious, but its true function is to make a case, to persuade.

Other poems by Jonson deal in more comic fashion with the problems created by the need to manage impressions in a social setting. The intentions of "Groom Ideot" (addressed in *Ep.* 58) seem anything but malign, but he wins the poet's rebuke because, in the process of at-

tempting to enhance his own reputation, he inadvertently threatens
Jonson's:

> Ideot, last night, I pray'd thee but forbeare
>   To reade my verses; now I must to heare:
> For offring, with thy smiles, my wit to grace,
>   Thy ignorance still laughs in the wrong place.
> And so my sharpnesse thou no lesse dis-joynts,
>   Then thou did'st late my sense, loosing my points.
> So have I seene at Christ-masse sports one lost,
>   And, hood-wink'd, for a man, embrace a post.
>
>   (1–8)

If the speaker seems a bit unthankful here for Idiot's efforts, it is because
he recognizes that Idiot's willingness to "grace" his wit is really an
attempt to appropriate it for his own self-serving performance. He cares
and knows little about poetry, yet the need to make a good impression—
to demonstrate his wit—compels him to pretend otherwise, with results
that Jonson claims are ridiculous. But Jonson's concern is less with Idiot
than with the audience for whom they compete, and although Idiot
makes Jonson's verse the centerpiece of his self-display, the epigram
instead turns Idiot into the chief prop of Jonson's own performance. The
final line's heavy use of punctuation ("points") only underscores the
humor. Idiot's labored obviousness and witlessness (even his laughter is
calculated) highlight Jonson's grace and self-assurance; yet Idiot obviously threatened that assurance sufficiently to provoke this response.

Repeatedly Jonson deals with the problems created by literary and
social competition. "On Poet-Ape" (*Ep.* 56) is one of a number of works
that focus on plagiarism and strongly emphasize the idea of literary
property. The poem seems to imply a specific target, but although his
identity cannot be determined today, the problems the work confronts
seem rooted in Jonson's real experience. Indeed, one point of attacking
plagiarism may have been to distance him from the similar charges
often leveled by his own antagonists. Here as in other poems, he assumes an attitude of dismissive contempt, even of pity, toward the
figure he attacks, but once again he is obviously bothered enough to feel
the need to attack him. He is careful, though, to present his attack as a
defensive response to presumptuous thievery. Although the poem ends
by confidently asserting that Poet-Ape's thefts will be noticed and
reprehended by audiences of the future, it implies far less confidence
about the perceptiveness of the present spectators Jonson needed to
attract. Although explicitly the poem attacks the plagiarist, implicitly it
rebukes any auditor foolish enough to fall for his deceptions.

The epigram "To My Meere English Censurer" (*Ep.* 18), although
influenced by several poems by Martial, once again seems directed

against a specific target. Even if the titular figure were Jonson's in-vention, the sense of rivalry the poem communicates would still be strong thanks to its mockery of his real competitors, Sir John Davies and John Weever (4). The "Censurer" to whom Jonson responds is "Meere English" not only in the sense that (like most contemporary readers) he doesn't recognize the foreign literary traditions Jonson exploits, but also in the sense that he knows no other language than his own. (This makes the poem's subtle allusion to Martial all the more clever.) Jonson im-plies that his epigrams, by being both "old" and "true," are also "new" or innovative more deeply and significantly than his critic can appreci-ate (1–2); their novelty derives precisely from their adherence to the ancient traditions his competitors ignore.

Whether or not a particular "Censurer" existed, many of Jonson's satiric epigrams seem to have evolved out of particular biographical events. It is always dangerous, of course, to extrapolate from art to life, but in Renaissance literary London the dividing line between those realms was not sharply defined. Although Jonson was a master of literary tropes and classical conventions, his use of them often suggests a recognition of their tactical value as much as a purely "literary" interest in generic experimentation. Both motives were important in winning the attention and support of patrons: artfully embarrassing a rival was likely to be impressive both aesthetically and socially.[6] Yet we are often prone to dismiss the biographical element as petty or insignifi-cant, or to divorce it from the aesthetic, or to erase it altogether by viewing the poem as purely a conventional exercise. Jonson himself, after all, claimed again and again that he attacked the vice, not the man; and even though many of his contemporaries were skeptical, some recent critics have often seemed eager to embrace such claims. To do so not only enhances our conception of Jonson but makes the poems themselves seem somehow more weighty and important (and also easier to deal with). The poetomachia, however, provides spectacular evidence that Renaissance satire was not always disinterested or sani-tized of personal motives and applications.[7] Several of Jonson's shorter poems can be plausibly related to that feud (see, for example, Epigrams 53 and 68, and the notes in Herford and Simpson), and it seems more than merely accidental that the largest class of his satiric epigrams that include first-person references take unsavory *literary* figures as their targets.[8] Although it cannot be proved that the rivals and rivalries he refers to in those poems really existed, it hardly seems wildly spec-ulative to assume that they did.

In one sense, Jonson's satires on antagonists help assert his indepen-dent power, importance, and judgment; the biting ferocity or disdainful sarcasm they turn against their targets suggest their author's confidence in his autonomous authority. In his satires he seems to stand most separate from the need of others' confirmation; yet all the wit, humor, and self-assurance the poems display are themselves tactics for winning approval, tactics designed to present him as appealingly as possible. Inevitably the poems function partly as advertisements and thus implicitly acknowledge that the source of real power lay outside the poet himself. Jonson's attacks on his rivals demonstrate his dependence precisely by implying his need to persuade: they implicitly concede that his own evaluation—of himself and his antagonists—is less important than the reactions of superiors and peers. Ostensibly displays of strength, such poems partly betray weakness and apprehension. For these reasons, they pose the additional risk of enhancing his vulnerability and heightening his fear. Attacking a rival was inherently ambiguous, since the attempt to weaken him might expose (and thereby promote) the poet's own insecurity.

Any competitor risks losing face, not only because of the threats his rivals pose but also because of his own aggressive response. Every move against his rivals might also tarnish Jonson's public image, forcing him to expose his self-interest even as he attacked the self-interestedness of others. The posture of attack, even if ostensibly defensive, forced him to abandon subtle and unselfconscious self-display, instead forcing him to openly acknowledge explicit self-concern. Personal satire inevitably brings issues of power and competition to the fore and makes the satirist's own ambitions hard to miss. Attacking a rival's maneuvering risks exposing one's own. By causing the satirist to confront and implicitly confess his weakness and fears, the rival can render him unattractive. Any hint of impotence, any sign of jealousy or envy, any indication of essential selfishness could make Jonson seem less appealing as a possible ally, less trustworthy as a potential dependent. Being allied with him might then seem a liability, a negative reflection on a patron's own character and motives.

The envious or jealous person reminds us of the extent to which life *is* political, of the extent to which everyone must compete. He forces us to confront uncomfortable truths about ourselves, others, and our social contexts. His behavior, his concerns, his very existence remind us that politics *is* inescapable and that political struggle produces victims as well as victors. He thus heightens the insecurity of those around him. Yet despite the inevitability of personal politics, the aggressive satirist flies in the face of a natural tendency to deny that fact (a pretense itself partly tactical). The satirist risks seeming petty or preoccupied with the "minor" matters others ostensibly ignore in their pursuit of lofty values or simple pleasures. But his presence is troubling, reminding those others that political security is a main precondition for achieving almost any goals. For all these reasons, the person who feels jealous, envious, or simply threatened has good reasons for disguising or suppressing (perhaps especially from himself) how much his behavior is micropolitically determined. By displaying his vulnerability, he risks increasing it; conversely, by pretending to be stronger than he really feels, he may actually enhance his strength. The public *fiction* of power can help attain the reality.

Rivalry, however, can threaten not only one's public reputation but also one's self-perception. The rival threatens one's sense of security and centeredness, fostering internal agitation and instability. He forces one to admit to oneself—whether or not it is apparent to others—how much one is indeed concerned with competition, with status, with the need for self-display and self-promotion. He challenges not only one's public standing but one's self-image, and even if the rivalry ultimately leaves one's reputation untouched, it can nonetheless cheapen one's sense of character or challenge one's self-respect. Political competition can easily leave one tainted with a sense of immoral self-interest. Partly for this reason, perhaps the best way to think of and depict a rival is as himself (in some way) immoral—not only because this is one of the most effective tactics to use against him, but also because it is one of the best ways to preserve one's own reputation and self-respect. Imagining the struggle in moral terms is potent politically if only because it lends conviction to one's behavior, making it more convincing both to oneself and to others and providing a defense not only against the rival but against anyone who might allege mere self-interest. It makes one the defender not simply of oneself but of higher values, and it generalizes the threat, making the rival seem not simply a personal enemy but a transgressor against hallowed social ideals.

The rival reminds one of one's status as a performer, exacerbating an uncomfortable self-consciousness. No longer can one's behavior seem easy, spontaneous, and wholly unpremeditated: the calculation attributed to the adversary affects and infects oneself; the intense self-awareness imputed to him ironically but inevitably taints one's own self-conception. Although his cunning and guile can only be *assumed* (whereas one's own self-consciousness is certain and inescapable), alleging craftiness against him is an effective tactic. It casts one in the role of self-defender, a role attractive to others and appealing and heartening to oneself. It makes one's interest in politics—and one's self-absorption—seem to result from external constraints and compulsion rather than from inherent, petty self-concern. It helps protect one against charges of jealousy or envy and, perhaps more important, against *feeling* jealous or envious. Traditionally, the envier is one who "eats his own heart out," who sickens himself with his poison for others, but envy could also be self-destructive in a more immediately practical sense. If publicly known or assumed, suspicion of envy would threaten one's reputation and social power. In his essay "Of Envy and Hatred," Plutarch notes that "some there be who confess and take it upon them that they hate many; but no man will be known that he envieth any. . . ." People who envy will allege instead "that they are angry with the man, or stand in fear of him whom indeed they bear envy unto, or that they hate him, colouring and cloaking this passion of envy with the veil of any other whatsoever for to hide and cover it, as if it were the only malady of the soul that would be concealed and dissembled."⁹ Thus the fear of feeling or seeming envious can further heighten self-consciousness.

But while rivalry, in all these ways and for all these reasons, could promote acute self-absorption, it could also paradoxically and simultaneously have the opposite effect, fomenting a peculiarly intense preoccupation with another self. Rivalry, friendship's dark opposite, could often ironically provoke emotions far more deeply felt than most friendships are.¹⁰ Unwillingly but inexorably, one becomes the rival's most interested audience, demonstrating for him a kind of perverse care, a kind of concern and attention rare in most human relations. In loving one's friend, one feels comforted and strengthened by the friend's reciprocal affection; although power might seem and might be the furthest thing from either party's mind, friendship enhances the power of each. But contemplating the rival forces one to contemplate both *his* enmity and one's own, in both cases exacerbating unease. Rivalry is disquieting not only because of the rival's potential effects on one's social standing or material circumstances, but perhaps especially because of his power to dominate and control one's thoughts, to invade the inner sanctum of consciousness and force himself on one's attention. He threatens not only one's public security but one's peace of mind. He helps shape not only one's behavior but one's thinking, and the diminished sense of power that results is perhaps the most painful consequence rivalry entails.

In his extremely important essay on "How a Man May Receive Profit by His Enemies," Plutarch argues that the rival might actually, if inadvertently, improve one's character by providing an incentive to control one's passions and police one's thoughts and behavior. True goodness might result from the rival's threat; inner peace might ultimately follow from anxiety and emotional turmoil. The rival's close attention

compelleth us to live orderly, to look unto our steps that we tread not awry, that we neither do nor say ought inconsiderately or rashly; but always keep our life unblamable, as if we observed a most strict and exquisite diet; and verily, this heedful caution, repressing the violent passions of our mind in this sort, and keeping reason at home within doors, engendereth a certain studious desire, an intention and will to live uprightly and without touch . . .[11]

Plutarch concedes the immense self-consciousness a rival can encourage, but he sees it as potentially beneficial; rivalry can paradoxically work to one's true inner advantage, enhancing one's genuine moral goodness. Of course, the self-conviction of moral worth might seem only a small or partial compensation for the loss of real social power rivalry might cause, but implicit in Plutarch's observation is the idea that right makes might, that the moral attractiveness rivalry sometimes promotes can actually buttress one's pragmatic social standing. The more moral one seems to be, the stronger or less vulnerable one is likely to prove. If nothing else, the inner conviction of morality gives one a determination one might otherwise lack to carry on the struggle. Ideally, of course, virtue is its own reward, but the ideal provides small comfort in the real world of political competition. Plutarch's idea that goodness is the best revenge is loftily appealing; but most competitors would probably also hope that their virtue might be recognized and valued publicly. Contemplating a rival's social successes, especially when his defects of character and morality seemed obvious to oneself, would not encourage much confidence in the inevitable triumph of pure virtue. The more one saw one's rival as morally defective, the more his success would indicate society's ethical myopia. The more he prospered, the less secure one would feel, not only because of his increasing power but because of what it suggested about society's moral indifference. The rival's success would only exacerbate the feeling that performance was at least as important as substance, that the public *image* of virtue was at least as significant as the reality.

Frustrated by the rival's tactics and success and by society's misinterpretation, one might come to feel that the best course of action would be to withdraw, to pull back from the struggle and retreat into Stoic resignation. Yet, to refuse to respond overtly is itself a kind of response, a tactic with its own potential benefits and hazards. Not to heed one's enemies can sometimes seem a sign of strength, partly because it demands an exercise of will and determination, partly because it can convey an impression of confident serenity. By pretending power, one promotes it. Open anger might seem at first a sign of strength but might also be interpreted (and *felt*) as an indication of passionate weakness. Non-response is sometimes the best response, suggesting an indifference to one's public image that might actually help enhance it. Plutarch argues that "in the bearing and putting up of taunts and reproaches, there is observed in it a kind of gravity beseeming the person of Socrates, or rather the magnanimity of Hercules," and he continues: "Neither verily is there a thing of greater gravity, or simply better, than to hear a malicious enemy to revile, and yet not to be moved nor grow into passions therewith."[12] But the appearance of inner calm, of having achieved a "centered self," is often accompanied by internal anxiety and turmoil; outward serenity often only masks churnings within. Ironically, the attempt to *seem* composed can actually intensify unease by emphasizing both the need to perform and the contrasts between appearance and reality. Often the tactics designed to distance oneself from inner conflict may drive it home all the more acutely. Thus, however one chooses to respond publicly to a rival, privately he is difficult to ignore. One way or another, he helps shape one's public behavior, private attitudes, self-conception, sense of security, and social standing.

Jonson's most famous and exasperating rival, of course, was his chief collaborator on the masques for the Stuart court, the architect and designer Inigo Jones. Jonson's attacks on Jones often resonate with odd ironies, with unintended implications for his own situation and status. He mocks Jones for many of the same reasons others mocked him; often, indeed, his assaults vent implicitly his own worst apprehensions, his own fears of how he or his works might be perceived or of what they might become. Thus, it was Jones who was pretentious, Jones who was ambitious, Jones who paraded his erudition, Jones whose works were ephemeral and overblown. Attacking Jones publicly distanced Jonson from all the pitfalls to which his own position exposed him. His satire is at once tactical and purgative, aimed against Jones but also reflexively self-defensive. By impugning his rival's political motives, he de-emphasizes his own; by mocking Jones as merely an adept performer, he downplays the performative aspects of his own works and behavior. Jonson knew where Jones was vulnerable partly because both were products of the same system. Both had to compete in similar ways; both had to present themselves in similar fashions; both exploited similar tactics. Moreover, the parallels between them only made Jonson's attacks all the more inherently risky.

The rancor between them has usually been treated as unfortunate, even embarrassing; the temptation to emphasize the intellectual side of their dispute has been strong. Yet it is striking how many of the same assumptions they shared. Their actual differences in power and influence, moreover—especially in the early years of their acquaintance and especially with regard to the masque—were not very great, a fact that supports the notion that competition is likely to be most intense when the competing parties have least to gain. However much we may wish that the Jonson-Jones feud never happened, however much we may lament, with Herford and the Simpsons, "the melancholy record of the relations between two men of genius, each a true artist in his proper sphere" (H&S 10:692), we cannot ignore the importance of the quarrel to the men involved nor the amount and intensity of the energy they expended on it. Rather than treating the dispute with embarrassed regret or stressing its more palatable intellectual side, it is worth looking at the quarrel as a fascinating example of the importance of personality—of personal differences and personal competition—in the social milieu in which these two men of genius had necessarily to practice their arts and promote themselves as artists.[13]

It is, in fact, Jones's tactics of self-promotion that Jonson emphasizes and lampoons in the two poems from the *Epigrammes* collection probably aimed at his rival. Epigram 115, for instance, portrays Jones as a man who advertises himself as honest, works to win celebrity as a wit, possesses highly developed (although allegedly deceptive) social skills, and is the chief architect of his own fame. Of course, similar charges were frequently leveled against Jonson. His task is to present Jones's self-promotional strategies as morally culpable, yet in a way that distances himself and the present poem from involvement in them. In the opening lines he seems almost to acknowledge syntactically the potential confusion, yet he turns the ambiguity to his own advantage:

On the Townes Honest Man

You wonder, who this is! and, why I name
    Him not, aloud, that boasts so good a fame:
Naming so many, too! But, this is one,
    Suffers no name, but a description:
Being no vitious person, but the vice
    About the towne; and knowne too, at that price.
A subtle thing, that doth affections win
    By speaking well o' the company' it's in.
Talkes loud, and baudy, has a gather'd deale
    Of newes, and noyse, to s[tr]ow out a long meale.
Can come from *Tripoly*, leape stooles, and winke,
    Doe all, that longs to the *anarchy* of drinke,
Except the *duell*. Can sing songs, and catches;
    Give every one his dose of mirth: and watches
Whose name's un-welcome to the present eare,
    And him it layes on; if he be not there.
Tell's of him, all the tales, it selfe then makes;
    But, if it shall be question'd, under-takes,
It will deny all; and forsweare it too:
    Not that it feares, but will not have to doo
With such a one. And therein keepes it's word.
    'Twill see it's sister naked, ere a sword.

> At every meale, where it doth dine, or sup,
>   The cloth's no sooner gone, but it gets up
> And, shifting of it's faces, doth play more
>   Parts, then th'*Italian* could doe, with his dore.
> Acts old *Iniquitie*, and in the fit
>   Of miming, gets th'opinion of a wit.
> Executes men in picture. By defect,
>   From friendship, is it's owne fames architect.
> An inginer, in slanders, of all fashions,
>   That seeming prayses, are, yet accusations.
> Describ'd, it's thus: Defin'd would you it have?
>   Then, *The townes honest Man's* her errant'st knave.
>
> $(1-34)$[14]

Playing on his title and with the reader's curiosity, Jonson calls attention in the first three lines to the act of naming itself—leaving it unclear whether, in referring to one who names "so many," he means himself as poet or his target as boastful name-dropper. By forcing us to puzzle over this problem, he encourages us to recognize and acknowledge a distinction between his own acts of naming and praising the virtuous, and the uses to which names are put by the Townes Honest Man.[15] Jones, he suggests, exploits names purely for self-aggrandizement. Yet both men derived prestige from associating with "names," and many of Jonson's rivals felt that he was just as guilty of name-dropping as anyone. He could hardly hope to convince them otherwise, but the poem might help to persuade the "names" the Man boasts about that their involvement with him damages their own reputations. The poem not only shows how Jones capitalizes on that involvement but also suggests how continued association with him could be self-defeating. As in many of Jonson's satires, the point here is as much to make the target a liability to others as to embarrass the target himself. His satire appeals less to the target's conscience than to others' self-interest, working less through moral reform than through public intimidation. Jonson's refusal to name his target openly is prudent and functions as an added slight, but it also subtly suggests the kind of excommunication Jones would suffer if the poem were widely effective.

By directly addressing us, Jonson betrays that he is less concerned with the Man *per se* than with others' reactions to him. Ostensibly a response to the reader's own "wonder" (to his curiosity as well as to his puzzled astonishment), the poem thereby seems less a purely personal or unprovoked attack. Of course, Jonson does not so much satisfy wonder as foment and feed it; ironically, both he and his rival have strong (if contrasting) motives for creating such interest: while the Man seeks to feed his fame, Jonson seeks to destroy it, recognizing that the Man's power is derivative and dependent. His "fame" is to some extent self-perpetuating: the more he "boasts" it—in the sense of proudly displaying the reality of it—the more famous he is likely to become. His boasting works both to ingratiate and intimidate. By insinuating his popularity, it pressures others to assent: "to boast" can carry the connotation "to threaten." When the Man "boasts" his "good . . . fame," he implicitly challenges the reputation of anyone who refuses to affirm his social eminence. Jonson cleverly equivocates by using the word "good," implicitly distinguishing between a fame that is "good" because it is "prominent" and one that is ethically sound. The distinction cleverly challenges not only the Man himself but also any reader who helps him attain or maintain the first kind of "good" fame without the second.

The poem never clarifies its subject's actual social standing. On the one hand it suggests that his viciousness is well known and makes his hypocrisy seem obvious. On the other hand it credits him with the ability to win affections, acquire the reputation of a wit, and manipulate language to his own advantage. He is at once crude and subtle, ridiculous yet dangerous. The contradiction, if there is one, seems to be partly between Jonson's objective assessment of his rival and a more subjective compulsion to denigrate and weaken him. Yet he is also able to turn these tensions to some account, implying that any reader who grants Jones affection or reputation has been or will be duped. Both the target's character and the reader's perceptiveness are on trial. The poem's emphasis on the Man's hypocrisy is meant to awaken the reader's personal suspicions even while sanctioning the poet's vitriol. The very violence of his indictment—including his taunting references to his rival's physical cowardice—contrasts with Jones's allegedly cunning treachery. Jonson attempts to turn what might otherwise seem an uncouth manifestation of wounded or vulnerable pride into evidence of his own integrity, character, and forthright honesty.

Just as the poem encourages us to peer behind its surface to ascertain the Man's real identity, so it encourages us to reenact its own scrutiny of his character, to probe beneath his appealing image. Yet, of course, in the poem's original context—before it was printed, when Jonson was circulating it among his acquaintances or reading it to them—the identity of its target would have been more immediately and easily known. What could not be safely printed *could* be spoken. Ironically, like the "Honest Man" himself, the poem would achieve much of its power through gossipy colloquies.

Jonson wittily puns by calling his rival the "errant'st knave" (34), since "errant'st" functions not simply to intensify the noun or to suggest his moral waywardness but also to emphasize his literal wanderings, his detached shiftings from place to place and his adoption of different poses wherever he goes. Indeed, Jonson attributes to him all the unattractive theatricality easily associated with his own role, distancing himself not only from his rival but from all the vices of play-acting he personifies. According to Jonson, the Man deceives and betrays his appreciative audiences, making fools of them no less than of himself. He plays on their vanity while exhibiting his own: he fawningly "Executes men in picture" (29) but does not hesitate later to stab them (metaphorically) in the back. Everything he touches he corrupts. Shared meals conventionally symbolize fellowship and communion, but the Man turns them into occasions for slander, deception, and pompous self-display. Yet, for all this, the surest measure of his success is the very fury of the poet's charges.

In a second epigram on Jones (*Ep.* 129, "To Mime"), Jonson's tone is more subdued, his satirical method both more and less direct. Probing questions ostensibly addressed to the target replace the earlier tactic of wholesale public indictment. While the first poem sought to inculcate suspicions in others, this one attempts instead to undermine Jones's confidence in the receptions that greet his performances. Yet some of the same tensions implicit in the earlier work are present here as well:

> That, not a paire of friends each other see,
>   But the first question is, when one saw thee?
> That there's no journey set, or thought upon,
>   To *Braynford, Hackney, Bow*, but thou mak'st one;
> That scarse the Towne designeth any feast
>   To which thou'rt not a weeke, bespoke a guest;
> That still th'art made the suppers flagge, the drum,
>   The very call, to make all others come:
> Think'st thou, Mime, this is great? or, that they strive
>   Whose noyse shall keepe thy miming most alive,
> Whil'st thou dost rayse some Player, from the grave,
>   Out-dance the *Babion*, or out-boast the Brave;
> Or (mounted on a stoole) thy face doth hit
>   On some new gesture, that's imputed wit?
> O, runne not proud of this. Yet, take thy due.
>   Thou dost out-zany Cokely, Pod; nay, Gue:
> And thine owne Coriat too. But (would'st thou see)
>   Men love thee not for this: They laugh at thee.
>
> (1–18)

Jonson's decision to construct the poem out of an ever-lengthening series of unanswered questions was not only technically ingenious but thematically apt. The device builds an enormous tension that the final phrase resolves by exploding it. Yet the tactic is more than a tour de force; its effectiveness derives in part from its special appropriateness to Mime. As his name suggests, Mime has no solid, stable identity. His obsession with others' opinions has left him no core of genuine self-hood worth their respect or his. Hungry for social acceptance, he has ultimately won (or so the poem alleges) only ridicule and disdain, having become an object of public amusement but not in the sense he intends. There is more than simple satiric relish in the poem's final four words; there is a touch of piquancy, too. Mime, from one perspective so absurd, from another seems almost pitiable. Indeed, the ambiguity of the penultimate line's parenthetical phrase—("would'st thou see")—reinforces this complicated sense of the poem's conclusion. Most obviously the phrase is taunting, inquisitional: "would you like to see what people really think about you, instead of how you imagine they think?" But it can also be interpreted more compassionately: "If only you would stop to realize what people really think of you." We needn't speculate about the extent of Jonson's actual pity. The mere appearance of a tinge of pity gives his satire all the more bite by making Jonson himself seem more attractive—partly because more powerful and secure. The phrase's ambiguity communicates superiority, even a touch of disdain, without seeming wholly malicious.

This sense of superiority is more convincingly communicated in the poem's second half than in its first, where some of the same tensions present in the earlier epigram seem once more to lie just below the apparent confidence and self-assurance of the poem's surface. In the opening portion, attention is focused less on Mime than on others' reactions to him and involvements with him. Jonson's purpose, with his series of unresolved dependent clauses, is to keep Mime in suspense—to play on, toy with, and lampoon his consuming interest in others' opinions. Yet even as it manages to emphasize Mime's obsession with his social standing, the opening section also betrays the poet's own uneasiness. After all, the lines do reveal Mime's popularity: immediately inquired about by friends who happen to meet, invited along on journeys outside London, a welcome and prominent guest at feasts and suppers, Jones seems to have enjoyed a social acceptance that Jonson's mocking challenge—"Think'st thou, Mime, this is great?"—cannot entirely dispel. Indeed, there is even a hint of lame and impotent frustration in the question.

The dinners cited are not small or private but are public "feast[s]," paradoxically both open and exclusive. Because they are relatively public, they provide Mime a powerful forum for self-display, but the dinners are themselves part of the competitive display of those who host them. Although feasting is conventionally associated with relaxed communion, Jonson implies that these feasts are used deliberately—by Mime and by those who invite him—to enhance their private power. Indeed, it later emerges that Mime's hosts consciously use the dinners in a blatantly cynical way, that Mime is abused by the very people who seem to value him. He falls victim to motives similar to his own. Ironically, Jonson's readings and circulation of this epigram would also exploit public occasions, both to increase his own standing and to undercut his rival's. He is just as concerned as Mime is with making Mime the center of attention, but their underlying motives are diametrically opposed. Jonson's satire contributes to his own display. Mime's cheap cleverness highlights the poet's true wit; Mime's absurdity underscores the contrasting dignity of the poet.

However, only in the poem's second half, which focuses on Mime's antics, does Jonson succeed in portraying him as clearly ridiculous. Even then, we can ask how far his claim that Mime's audiences laugh derisively is objectively true, and how far it simply voices Jonson's own exasperated desire to see his rival humiliated. The poem seeks not merely to report such laughter but to help create it. Yet this very attempt to increase Jones's insecurity cannot help but betray Jonson's. His attack is part of his effort to prove appealing even while distinguishing his appeal from Mime's. Both men, however, are essentially and inescapably performers, and the poem in which Jonson assaults Mime's performance is part of his own. The fear he plays on at the poem's conclusion—the fear that public approval might be merely superficial, temporary, and self-interested rather than rooted in genuine or lasting affection—was one with which he himself was no doubt familiar. The final lines seek to exploit in Mime a kind of anxiety that would hardly have been unusual. Like many of his satirical works, the epigrams to Jones exhibit Jonson's vulnerability even as they attempt to minimize or overcome it.

Ironically, Jonson's obsession with Mime parallels that of the "friends" he mentions; Mime is just as central to *his* attention as to theirs. If the "friends" seem preoccupied with Mime and if Mime seems preoccupied with feeding their obsession and basking in it, Jonson himself is engrossed by the attention his rival elicits. Of course, he does his best to underplay his absorption, if only to foster an attractive impression of insouciant strength: the epigram's brevity helps make it seem less obsessive than the earlier one. Jonson uses the poem to distance himself not only from Mime's repulsive theatricality but also from those who encourage it. Initially, at least, his satire seems implicitly directed as much at Mime's admirers as at Mime himself, until it later emerges that these people have, if anything, even less genuine respect for him than Jonson does. Although Mime proudly imagines that the attentions paid him enhance his power, and although to that extent he exploits his social relations, Jonson claims that Mime's admirers actually exploit *him* simply for their own amusement. They profit by keeping him around as an entertaining fool or jester; their appreciation is just as self-serving as his buffoonery, and just as calculatedly artificial. What might seem, on both sides, natural and spontaneous behavior is actually (Jonson implies) premeditated, political, and contrived. Although superficially concerned with pleasing other people, Mime ironically falls victim to the same kind of narcissism that determines his own conduct and attitudes. There is an engaging subtlety in the final line, not only because of the appropriately skewed internal echo between "love" and "laugh" but also because of the understated ambiguity of the phrase "for this," which suggests that people laugh at him both "because of" and "in spite of" his efforts.

Yet the dismissive contempt of this attack on Mime cannot wholly disguise the anxiety his popularity fosters in Jonson. Throughout his career, the poet's relations with the architect seem never to have been anything but uneasy. In one of his most famous poems, written a number of years after the epigrams on Mime and the Townes Honest Man, he vents more openly the apprehension that competition with Jones engendered in him. His "Epistle Answering to One that Asked to be Sealed of the Tribe of Ben," written in 1623, comes near the end of a period of seemingly unparalleled success. Even before the folio publication of his *Workes* in 1616, he had achieved a kind of prominence he could only have dreamed of in his younger days. His decision to bring out an elaborate edition of his writings was in one sense the daring act it is often pictured as being. Yet it is unlikely that the folio would ever have been published had not Jonson—and, more to the point, his printer—been sufficiently confident that it would find a market among those who could afford to pay for it. The folio is only the most palpable sign that, by the second decade of James's reign, he had won enviable status in the Jacobean social and literary hierarchy.

In the same year the folio was published, Jonson was granted an annuity of 100 marks by the King, and in the following year he was one of a number of figures listed as possible members of a proposed royal academy. In 1618 he tried to use his influence at court on behalf of his friend John Selden, one of whose books had provoked the anger of powerful clerics. During his famous walking tour of Scotland, he was banqueted and honored by the "Noblemen and Gentlemen" of the north (H&S 1:78), and not long after his return to England he was made honorary Master of Arts by Oxford University. Throughout this whole period, he produced a steady stream of court masques, and his income from these, combined with his annuity and incidental patronage, freed him from any necessity to write for the stage. In the years between 1616 and 1626, no new play of his was performed. One of his masques,

however—*The Gypsies Metamorphos'd*—proved so popular with the
King that it was presented three times during the late summer and early
autumn of 1621. One contemporary report suggested that Jonson's annual pension had been increased from a hundred marks to a hundred
pounds. Although the report was incorrect, the fact that such rumors
about his good fortune were circulating is itself revealing. Another
report claimed that James was planning to bestow a knighthood on the
poet, and in the fall of 1621 he was in fact granted the reversion to the
office of Master of Revels. Thus it may seem surprising to find him,
probably less than two years later, writing a poem as full of insecurity,
bitterness, and grim foreboding about his standing at court as the "Tribe
of Ben" epistle.[16]

Yet the same tensions one finds in that epistle—a concern with his
rivals' influence and machinations; misgivings about the dependability
of superiors and about his own role as poet; a certain cynicism regard-
ing the emphasis on appearance and self-promotion necessitated by the
need to compete—all appear as well in Drummond's notes of his conversations with Jonson during the poet's visit to Scotland in 1618–19.
Their appearance there lends credence to the notion that the exasperation he later expressed in the "Tribe" epistle resulted not simply from a
recent setback or momentary disappointment; it had been building for
years and was not extinguished during the period of his greatest fame
and fortune. Even before visiting Drummond, Jonson suspected the
motives and auspices behind John Taylor, the doggerel-writing "Water
Poet" who had just undertaken a tour similar to his own. Jonson suspected that Taylor had been sent along to Scotland "to scorn him," and
Taylor later felt it necessary to deny in print that he had been "set on by
others, or that I did under go this project, either in malice or mockage of
Maister Beniamin Jonson" (H&S 1:149; 11:382–83). Taylor's denial
sounds sincere enough, and perhaps Jonson accepted it. What is most
intriguing, however, is precisely his suspicion that his enemies were
capable of such a ploy. The episode suggests the self-consciousness and
concern with others' behavior his position encouraged.

Other anecdotes from the conversations confirm this impression that
courtly competition fostered a need to make the right impression—a
need he could disdain but never quite escape. He mocked the flattery
practiced by court preachers (H&S 1:142); he wryly noted Queen Elizabeth's vanity and her underlings' efforts to sustain it (H&S 1:141–42);
and he even alleged that Sir Walter Ralegh, one of his own patrons,
"esteemed more of fame than conscience" (H&S 1:138). His comments
on other writers, moreover, frequently suggest not only mutual dislike
or disapproval but also the recognition that bad feelings could manifest

themselves pragmatically. Thus he reported not merely that he disliked and was disliked by Drayton, but that "Drayton feared him" (H&S 1:136). And he also told Drummond that Sir William Alexander—an influential courtier and office-holder—"was not halfe Kinde unto [Jonson] & neglected him because a friend to Drayton" (H&S 1:137). He considered the poet Gervase Markham "a base fellow" and felt the same way about Day and Middleton (H&S 1:137). In fact, he told Drummond that "Sharpham, Day, Dicker [Dekker] were all Rogues and that Minshew was one" (H&S 1:133). Such extra-literary assessments of fellow writers show him engaging in precisely the kind of gossip of which he himself must often have been a victim.

Probably not long after his return from Scotland, he was attacked in a poem by Jones addressed "To his false friend m^r: Ben Jonson" (H&S 11:385–86). By depicting himself as the aggrieved party, Jones immediately asserts a tactical advantage, while his measured closing assessment of his target—"the best of Poett[s] but the worst of men"—is all the more devastating for being so balanced. What makes the poem especially interesting, however, is how much it resembles Jonson's own assaults on Jones. Like Jonson, Jones accuses his antagonist of being a deceptive, self-serving, hypocritical, and self-conscious social performer. He mocks Jonson's boastful accounts of his trip to Scotland, but he also recognizes how he could exploit that trip to his own advantage. He ridicules his public reading of his poems but recognizes how those readings could enhance Jonson's standing. He attacks Jonson's pride in his social eminence but also seems threatened by that eminence. One purpose of the poem was undoubtedly to undermine that eminence and remind Jonson of Jones's influence and ability to diminish Jonson's standing with superiors (35–36). Jonson may be the poem's specific target, but it is also aimed at a broader, more important audience.

The tensions implicit in Jonson's attacks on Jones, in Jones's attacks on Jonson, and in Jonson's conversations with Drummond seem to have been widespread and inevitable in a literary culture dominated by the need to compete, promote oneself, and heed the self-promotions (even the threatening machinations) of others. Jonson's many years as a court poet could hardly have failed to breed in him an acute sensitivity to the nuances of power relations and of micropolitical status. Certainly the "Tribe" epistle (*Und.* 47) suggests as much. Written in 1623, the poem responds to a very recent and specific disappointment—his failure to be included in a group of courtiers (including Jones and Edward Alleyn, the actor) designated to make official preparations for Prince Charles's anticipated return from Spain. Jonson likens his rejection to a trial that tests his mettle (2–3), yet he knew that the epistle itself was also a kind of trial, a public testing and display of his resilience under pressure. Ostensibly an answer to a young friend's request to be included in the "tribe of Ben," it is also an "answer" to a far more significant matter.[17]

The effect of the poem's title and of its very opening lines is difficult to describe; in them, Jonson concocts an almost unassailable blend of self-assertion and humility, a kind of modest pride. In one sense the title's biblical allusion is seriously meant: Jonson does present himself and his followers as righteous men uncontaminated by the corruption around them. Just as members of the tribe of Benjamin are preserved from the wrath of God in the Book of Revelation, so Jonson suggests that the virtues he and his "sons" adhere to will be ultimately, if not immediately, rewarded. The allusion has the effect not only of enhancing Jonson's moral position but of intimidating his antagonists, indirectly reminding them of one fate that may await them if they continue their vicious practices. Yet this biblical reference, and the ensuing imagery of martyrdom, might seem overweening, overblown, perhaps even blasphemous, if it were not qualified by a hint of self-conscious and humorous irony. In this poem as in others by Jonson, irony is more than simply an aesthetic effect; it is a micropolitical tactic rooted in the poem's status as a self-conscious social performance.

The mere fact that Jonson refers to himself as "Ben" helps undercut any sense of pretension or unlimited pride. Again and again in his later poetry he used the "Ben" persona in this self-mocking fashion—neutralizing potential criticism, turning his foibles and shortcomings to his own advantage, presenting himself as a lovable figure distanced from competitive ambition. Indeed, the "Ben" persona is fundamentally paradoxical. On one level it reflects Jonson's sense of himself as a prominent public figure, as a personality interesting in his own right and not simply because of his writing. In this sense the persona suggests Jonson's recognized social stature and his confident acceptance of it. But in another sense the "Ben" persona reflects the inevitable insecurity of his position; its function is partly defensive. It deflects potential attack, and the good humor it implies and evokes is one tactic for coping with the essential anxiety of Jonson's condition as a courtly poet. The very image of naive ingenuousness the persona conjures up must to some extent have been self-consciously cultivated; in any event, Jonson knew when and how to employ it effectively. In this poem its use, combined with the somewhat self-mocking assertion that he disdains to "speake [himself] out too ambitiously" (6), renders his position nearly impregnable to criticism. Charged with sacrilege, he could reply that his assailant had taken the biblical allusion much more seriously than it had been meant; accused of pride, he could respond that he had himself openly poked fun at this very tendency. The humor of the opening lines is one of the most effective means by which he simultaneously implies, creates, asserts, and defends his social power.

Although Jonson claims to disdain speaking ambitiously because to do so would violate his conscience and compromise his sense of right, he also indicates that to do so would be an act of weakness—one, presumably, that could easily be exploited by his enemies. His modesty here may be adopted not only or even necessarily because he finds it congenial, but also because to assert himself too vigorously might ultimately be ineffective, allowing his antagonists to take advantage of his rhetoric and use it against him. Indeed, throughout his career Jonson exhibits an obsessive concern with controlling his words, with authorizing them and imposing on them a signification that cannot be misconstrued. The dedications, prologues, and inductions to his plays, the marginalia to his masques, the self-conscious voice so common in his poems—all these suggest a need to control and contain the meaning of his words. For all his belief in the power of right language to reform society and move men to virtue (one of his chief justifications for practicing poetry), Jonson also feared words. Or rather, he feared the very ambiguity of language that is often at the heart of his best poetry and that he exploited so effectively to enhance his status. The ambiguity of language was both a source of his power and the potential cause of its loss. For Jonson, language was not an abstract issue: losing control of one's words, especially to rivals, meant losing security. In fact, it is not so much language that he fears as it is the ignorance or malignity of his interpreters. Language itself is neutral, but its meanings can be appropriated, stolen, reassigned, or misinterpreted by others intent on promoting themselves. More than a tool for communication, language becomes a weapon in the struggle for power.

Jonson's expressed need not to seem to speak "too ambitiously" suggests just one of the ways his dependent status encouraged linguistic subtlety and indirection: self-promotion that was too obvious might also be ineffective and vulnerable. Blatant ambition could prove self-defeating. Seeming to seek too desperately the approval of others would make their approval less likely; it would reveal weakness, and weakness would breed weakness by making one less attractive as a friend, dependent, or mentor. Obvious or excessive ambition would make one appear too self-centered to be a reliable ally or trustworthy client. To realize his ambitions, Jonson had partly to disclaim them; to secure his power, he had partly to distance himself from the obvious desire for it. His references to "conscience" and "right" (8) themselves function tactically; by making him appear committed to values higher than the merely political, they advance his political interests. By suggesting his self-respect and self-confidence, they solicit the respect he craved from others. His appeal to internal standards of motive and conduct helps strengthen his external standing, especially in his competition with rivals. His public avowal that he acts not to promote his self-interests but in accordance with his conscience functions, paradoxically, to ensure that those interests are advanced.

Indeed, the distinction the poem attempts to draw between individual values and social ambition is for all practical purposes exceedingly difficult to sustain. However much Jonson may speak of safety and surety as character traits or personal attributes (1–2), their value for him derives precisely from the fact that his social safety and surety have been threatened. Yet Jonson knew that his safeness and sureness could not be defined purely internally, as a reflection of his own personality, but that they inevitably depended to a large extent on the reactions of others. The "Epistle" seeks to shape and guide those reactions—but it does so, ironically, partly by claiming indifference to them. The pose of independence Jonson adopts is itself part of his strategy for winning acceptance, although it functions also as a preemptive tactic for dealing with the possibility of continued rejection. His contempt for "Opinion" (4) cannot disguise his fear of it, and although he claims indifference to insecurity, the "Epistle" in fact attempts to respond to and cope with his unease. Proclaiming his allegiance to safety and surety as personal values is thus a private consolation for social disappointment; at the same time, though, it serves publicly to assert his sense of his own social worth. As he implicitly concedes, the question can only be one of appearing to speak *too* ambitiously (6), not of freeing oneself from ambition completely. Although he claims that he will not compromise his conscience, the whole poem seeks to find a suitable compromise between adherence to personal integrity and the need to make and defend a place for oneself in the world.

Jonson's professed modesty and concern with conscience, his ostensible submission to a higher ideal of right, are meant to stand in clear contrast to the ensuing description of the behavior of those he attacks. In refusing to speak himself out too ambitiously, he had used silence as a means of intimating a worth it would have been boastful to proclaim in detail. His satire aims to point up part of the difference between himself and his unspecified targets precisely by emphasizing their egotistic, self-promotional uses of language. He argues implicitly for the quality of his own words—and word—by accusing his antagonists of vacuous talk, empty protests, hypocritical praise, and self-serving satire. By mocking those "that meerely talke, and never thinke" (9), Jonson implies that his own use of words is closely wedded to reasonable thought, but the phrase also reminds us of other senses in which his language is "thoughtful"—the senses in which it is self-conscious, guarded, and politic. Earlier in the same year this poem was written, he had provoked displeasure precisely by being insufficiently cautious in his use of language: he had exploited the public genre of the court masque for personal satire on the poet George Wither (H&S 10:648). Many of those who first read Jonson's epistle may therefore have glimpsed unintended irony in his attack on others for presuming to "censure all the Towne, and all th'affaires, / And know whose ignorance is more than theirs" (23–24), while anyone who recognized the subtly specific attack on Inigo Jones buried beneath the ostensibly generalized satire of this section may have smiled at Jonson's reference to those who "vent their Libels, and . . . issue rimes" (26).[18]

Clearly, what bothers Jonson about such rivals is not only their abstract moral failings but their success—the fact that, despite short-comings he regards as painfully obvious, they remain menacing competitors for prestige and advancement. At first it might seem that his targets are beneath the need to be attacked; he describes them as apparently inconsequential drunkards and philanderers (9–15). Far more threatening, however, are those "received for the Covey of Witts" (22). Indeed, the threat they pose is the direct result of their reception, their social acceptance and recognition. Their power is no more inde-pendent of society than his, and in fact the real purpose of his satire is less to denigrate them than to influence the perceptions of those who grant them status. Despite all his disdain for "Opinion" (4), his poem is precisely an attempt to shape and direct it. Although reading the "Epis-tle" this way may seem to locate its roots in the poet's "selfishness," from another perspective it helps illustrate how utterly and inescapably *social* his concerns necessarily were.

The "Covey of Witts" Jonson attacks stands directly opposed to the "Tribe of Ben" the poem both celebrates and seeks to augment. In this sense the "Epistle" seems to have grown out of a kind of rivalry and factionalism common in the political and social world of Jonson's day. Like the leader of a political faction, he knew that his appeal inevitably depended partly on his real social power. This is why his failure to be included in the commission must have seemed so variously threaten-ing. Interpreted as a sign of lost stature and influence, it would not only make him more vulnerable to sniping from the sort of "Witts" he attacks here, it would also make him less attractive as the central figure of an alternative group. Excluded from the commission, rejecting and rejected by the rival "Covey," he seems also to have worried about the danger of a more general rejection. Indeed, in an important passage (51–55), he describes this fear almost as if he imagined a chain reaction of renun-ciation.[19]

Perhaps this is one reason the recipient's request "to be Sealed of the

Tribe of Ben" may have seemed so significant, so deserving of an extended and weighty answer. It allowed Jonson to advertise the attraction he still held for some, to show that he could still draw allies in spite of his recent disappointment, and thus to improve his chances of winning others over. In the face of his exclusion from the commission, friendships of the sort celebrated here must have seemed all the more important, not only for the private consolation they offered, not only because they helped shore up his social dignity and self-respect, but because they increased his chances of regaining the power that seemed jeopardized or lost. Although he attacks the "Covey" for issuing "rimes" and for exploiting poetry tactically, his own "Epistle" perfectly exemplifies the tactical use of verse. Generalizing the threat the "Covey" poses (they "censure all the Towne, and all th'affaires" [23]), he plays on his audience's insecurity to enhance his own safety. He wants his readers to feel threatened by the same fear of exclusion and enmity, so that they will join him in excluding the "Covey." However forcefully he rejected the "Covey" personally, he knew that personal rejection was insufficient: only by influencing others could he exert any real effect.

In the second half of the poem, where Jonson presents more explicitly the differences between himself and his satiric targets, the sense of personal threat, as well as its connections with patronage concerns, becomes more pronounced. The distinction he had earlier attempted to draw between his own ostensibly modest use of language and the empty wordiness of his antagonists is reinforced in this section of the poem. Contrasting his plain, steadfast simplicity with their gossipy, self-indulgent speculations, he suggests that while his enemies merely talk about political affairs, he is willing to demonstrate his loyalty to the King through concrete action (39–42). His pose of political indifference is not meant to be read as apathetic but as signaling a more fundamental loyalty; he offers his supposed disinterest in day-to-day political events as a sign of his basic trustworthiness, and in fact the whole poem implies that in spite of his disappointments, he is also "safe and sure" (1) in the larger sense of being politically reliable. In the summer of 1623, when the poem was almost certainly written, such a claim was particularly significant. Indeed, seen in its immediate historical context, Jonson's pose of political indifference could itself have been read as a political—and as a carefully politic—assertion. Many of James's subjects felt at this time that the King's policies toward Spain, toward the recovery of the Palatinate, and toward the promotion of continental Protestantism were too passive. They opposed the marriage negotiations and resisted any move toward greater domestic toleration of Catholics. James himself was even suspected by some of having secret Catholic sympathies, and in general his popularity during this period was not very high. Criticism of government policies from Parliament, from the pulpit, and from other sources had become such a problem that James attempted through various means to constrain and suppress it, annoyed by what he felt was illegitimate meddling with his prerogative and unjustified challenge to his authority.[20]

Seen against this background, Jonson's claimed indifference to day-to-day foreign affairs (31–36) and his protests of fundamental loyalty to the King are particularly intriguing. On the one hand, he seems to behave here as James hoped all his subjects would; he seems to distance himself from the kind of obsessive, intrusive interest in foreign affairs that so many of his contemporaries displayed and that vexed the King so much.[21] Implicitly depicting himself as a model subject, he exhibits his trust in James's judgment, praying rather generally that "high heaven conspire / My Princes safetie, and my Kings desire" (37–38). At the same time, however, his avowed willingness to take up arms in the interests of winning back the Palatinate (39–42) suggests some genuine sympathy with—or at the very least some prudent deference to—those factions at court and in the country at large who favored a more vigorous assertion of English power. Indeed, readers of this persuasion could even have interpreted the poem as subtly endorsing their views, while the King could read it as a straightforward expression of basic loyalty. At the time Jonson probably wrote his poem, it would have been difficult for anyone to predict with confidence how the marriage negotiations would conclude, what policy would eventually be adopted toward the recovery of the Palatinate, or what attitude would finally prevail toward Spain. Jonson's lines on foreign affairs, while professing indifference, can in fact be read as intentionally ambiguous, as deliberately vague, as the cautious expression of a mind highly sensitive to the very fluidity of events he claims to have little interest in. His implicit portrait of himself as a loyal subject and as a forthright, willing patriot can be seen as reflecting an acute political consciousness. His studied indifference to the detailed exercise of state power stands in intriguing contrast to his obsession with the micropolitical maneuvering of his rivals, but it nonetheless plays a significant tactical role in his own efforts at self-promotion.

Aside from any possibly larger political significance, the narrower implications of Jonson's offer to take up his sword in defense of James's interests are complex and far-reaching. On the one hand the offer serves to remind his readers of his past bravery on the battlefield; he seems to have taken pride in his physical prowess—he boasts about it several times to Drummond—and the image of old Ben sallying forth to wage war against the King's enemies is potently attractive. It achieves just the right mixture of appealing vulnerability and indomitable courage; in the same way that Jonson implicitly presents himself as an injured but unvanquished victim of domestic antagonists, so he wins further sympathy for his willingness to risk greater injury in selfless service. The image must have appealed to Jonson especially in its present context because it helps to emphasize, again, the implicit contrast he has been drawing between himself and Inigo Jones specifically. Previous commentators have noted how frequently and precisely Jonson alludes in the first half of this poem to his earlier epigram on "The Townes Honest Man," thus turning his attack on unidentified antagonists into a skillfully direct assault on Jones himself. It does not seem to have been pointed out, however, that Jonson's professed willingness here to "draw the Sword" in the King's service (39) looks back to a line from the earlier poem, where he alleged that the Townes Honest Man would sooner "see it's sister naked, ere a sword" (22). Thus Jonson's avowed readiness to risk his life in his monarch's interest not only testifies to his own exemplary loyalty but also serves to mock Jones's supposed cowardice.

Yet Jonson's purpose may have been more than simply to chide his rival. His declaration of unflagging loyalty and willingness to serve, his forthright prayer on behalf of his King and Prince, stand in suggestive contrast to the neglect or indifference he has suffered in not being "prick'd downe" (47) to participate in the planned reception of Charles and the Infanta. In this as in other ways, Jonson seems to draw subtle attention to James's recent shortcomings as a patron, his failure to live up completely to the ideal of reciprocity that patronage relations should embody—in a sense, his failure fully to merit the devotion that Jonson still selflessly (but publicly) pays him. The poem makes it clear, however, that it is not only the neglect of his superiors that worries Jonson, but what that neglect might portend for his standing and reputation and, more subtly, for his financial security. Since his security to a large extent depended on the protective support and intimidation provided by friendly superiors, any loss of such protection left him immediately more exposed. The language Jonson uses to depict the imagined consequences of such exposure mixes poetic metaphor and blunt realism. He portrays himself as a "fraile Pitcher" that must be kept "from waves, and presse; / Lest it be justled, crack'd, made nought, or lesse" (56–58). The last two verbs seem too abstract to fit the metaphor, but in a sense they confront more directly and concretely than the earlier language Jonson's real fears of loss and humiliation. Although he claims to have "decreed" what to do with himself in order to combat those fears (57), this very word, with its overtones of sovereign power, reminds us of his real dependence on others.

Nowhere does Jonson clearly reproach the King for the neglect he feels he has suffered, but he does offer examples of other associations between superiors and inferiors against which his relationship with James can be measured and evaluated. Thus, after detailing the practical hardships he fears he is likely to endure as a result of having been slighted, he turns to his relation with God for consolation and comfort. That relation is ideally one of purest reciprocity; to the extent that it falls short of the ideal, the fault by definition can only be attributed to the neglect and indifference of the suitor, never to any carelessness on the Patron's part. Jonson has already reminded his readers through his title that God can be relied on to reward his true servants; here he declares his intention to love heaven (and thus merit heaven's love) in part by using "With reverence . . . all the gifts then[ce] given" (62). His relation with God (he implies) gives him a sense of internal security, stability, and well-being that his life at court and relation with his earthly King cannot really provide, and to which it functions in part as an alternative. Yet God's love and concern for his servants also function in the poem as an object lesson for mortal patrons—an ideal they can never, of course, really achieve, but ought nevertheless to aspire toward. The consolation of God's patronage invoked here could, in everyday social terms, be only a partial one for Jonson; he had still to function and survive in a system far from heavenly perfection. Even his introduction of God into the poem can be seen to have tactical implications for promoting Jonson's interests within that system. By invoking the example of his celestial patron he simultaneously comforts himself, intimidates his antagonists, and offers the King a model to emulate.

But God is not the only alternative model Jonson offers. In his own relation with the poetic son who sues for admission into the tribe of Ben, Jonson himself behaves in ways one might expect of an exemplary patron. For while he ostensibly addresses his suitor as a friend, it is clear from the tone of the poem that their relation is not one between exact equals. This is not the sort of poem Jonson would have been likely to address to Camden or Selden or Donne. Perhaps because of a difference of age, there is a tone of good-natured dignity, even a touch of formality, in those portions of the poem where Jonson most clearly addresses its recipient. Indeed, the very last lines ("Now stand, and then, / Sir, you are Sealed of the Tribe of *Ben*") not only pun on the word "stand" to exalt the ideal of ethical stability and moral stasis that (as Richard S. Peterson has emphasized in his book on the poet) is at the heart of so much of Jonson's laudatory verse, but also to call to mind the public act by which a King might create a new knight. Indeed, the double meaning of "stand" suggests, in a nicely paradoxical fashion, a kind of firmness and fixity that is also a kind of ascent. In the same way that God functions as an alternate and in some ways more reliable

patron than James, so Jonson's tribe—supposedly bound in free, cooper-
ative, yet permanent association—ostensibly functions as an alternative
to the world of courtly competition. The ideal of friendship the poem
advocates contradicts the very atmosphere in which, through the King's
neglect or his sudden change of attitude, a loyal servant of the court
need worry about losing all his standing there—not only his favor with
aristocrats but his protection from the machinations of antagonists and
rivals.

The incident that apparently provoked Jonson's poem—his failure to
be included in the arrangements for the Infanta's reception—may seem
slight and his reaction excessive, but that reaction is all the more
intriguing precisely because it is so powerfully and deeply felt. It
suggests that despite his years of unprecedented success—despite his
pension, despite his regular and lucrative employment writing
masques, despite all the other signs of the King's favor—he never really
felt (never really could feel) entirely secure about his status or his
future. Indeed, the more closely associated he became with the court—
the more he sought for, won, and accepted its largess and approval—the
more financially *and psychologically* dependent he became. His pride
in his prominence—as when he boasts that his fame is at least as great
as Jones's (49–50)—coexisted with an ever-present sense that his status
could collapse overnight. The pension could be revoked or left unpaid,
the masque commissions could suddenly halt, old friends and patrons
could lose interest should he—for whatever reason—lose royal favor.
And all these losses would involve more than financial deprivation,
important as that might be to the aging Jonson. They would involve, just
as significantly, loss of prestige and would deny him important forums
in which to achieve a sense of public purposefulness and self-validation. His reaction to the neglect referred to in the epistle, then, is less a
reaction to a single event than a boiling over of anxieties more tena-
ciously rooted. The poem startlingly suggests how vulnerable he felt
even when he seemed to enjoy far more security than at any other time
in his career, certainly far more than other poets of his social background.

It also suggests just how ambivalent his attitude toward the court
was—the contempt he could feel for it yet his inability (even reluctance) to break free. However much the poem satirizes the court and
courtiers, it never entirely rejects them. However often he derided the
court's artificiality and pretense, it was nevertheless the crucial center
of social and psychological *reality* for him during this period; being cut
off from it could produce a profound alienation—a feeling likely to be
all the stronger in someone, like Jonson, who had tasted its appeals.
Thus, although he speaks of withdrawing within the circle of himself

(60), this very poem is part of an attempt to extend and strengthen his circle of influence. Ostensibly written to approve the admission of a petitioner into the "Tribe of Ben," it also constitutes his application for readmission into a larger and more important social grouping. Jonson tells the young man that he approves him "As you have writ your selfe" (77)—a clever phrase that suggests the possibility of inscribing one's character, of re-presenting one's essence on paper, and that thereby implies an ideal that supposedly animates the present poem. In the same way, Jonson seems to hope to be accepted as he presents himself (and his self) in the epistle. One of its functions, indeed, is to reassert his importance in courtly society—by calling the King's "neglect" (54) to his own and to others' attention, by offering an attractive image of the poet, and by embarrassing or attacking actual or potential antagonists. The reference to the "Christmas Clay / And animated *Porc'lane* of the Court" (52–53), for instance, has the effect not only of satirizing the unnamed aristocrats who may already have rejected him, but, perhaps more important, of intimidating those who might. To reject the poet once this satire was circulated might leave one open to the appearance of bearing out Jonson's own assessment of the character and motives of his rejectors, might make it seem that that assessment was personally applicable to oneself. Paradoxically, whatever real social power Jonson's satire possesses derives from his subjects' concerns for their own reputations in a courtly context. Of course, the satire would exert a different kind of power, a different sort of appeal to other courtiers, for other reasons: uncomfortable with the rivalries, anxieties, compromises, and inevitable pretense dictated by their participation at court, they could, by approving the satire, disinfect and distance themselves from a milieu they could never completely reject. Moreover, their approval of Jonson's apparently forthright and principled allegiance to higher values would provide a means of characterizing themselves and of promoting their own images and competitive interests.

The "Tribe" epistle is fascinating precisely because it was written near the height of his career. Reminiscent, in the profound sense of insecurity it conveys, of the epistle to the Countess of Rutland (*For.* 12) composed more than twenty years before, the poem suggests that the competitive tensions Jonson felt then, when he was just beginning as a patronage poet, had neither disappeared nor diminished with time. In this poem as in that one, he is troubled less by a rival's success than by the neglect it suggests on the patron's part. Jonson knew that Jones was no threat unless the King—inadvertently or deliberately—allowed the threat to exist, and while in both poems his frustration is most obviously directed at his rival, there is in both an undercurrent of disappointment with his benefactors. There is an implicit sense of betrayal, as if Jonson feels he deserves better treatment from his superiors than he has received. Paradoxically, while he could infallibly depend on the hostility and ill-will of his rivals, he could be much less reliably certain of his patrons' friendship or encouragement. Any apparent lack of consideration on their parts, however innocent or unintentional, could seem far more worrisome than an antagonist's machinations. Jonson seems to have been less afraid of rivals than of their effects on his standing with patrons. The "Tribe" epistle is addressed to them at least as much as to the unnamed friend its title implies.

Disappointing as his failure to be included in the commission may have been, later in 1623 Jonson suffered what may have seemed an even greater misfortune. His house burned, destroying many of his manuscripts and much of his library. Yet in response he produced one of his best-known and most attractive poems, the "Execration Upon Vulcan" (*Und.* 43), which comically blames the disaster on the god of fire. In attacking Vulcan, Jonson seems to attack no one in particular; the poem largely lacks the edge of defensive personal bitterness that characterizes so much of his other invective. Fun is poked at contemporary tastes in writing and (implicitly) at some contemporary writers, but for the most part the "Execration" can seem less a response to external stimuli than a self-contained tour de force, as if its humor were its chief excuse for being. But when the poem is viewed in context—especially in the context of the difficulties that helped produce the "Tribe of Ben" epistle, which probably preceded it by only a few months—its complexion becomes far more complicated. When that context is broadened still further to include George Chapman's curiously bitter reaction to the poem, it becomes all the more fascinating.

The work begins with a quarrelsome and querulous half-line ("And why to me this" [1]) that might lead the reader to expect a piece of genuine complaint and self-pity, but of course the "Execration" is so masterful precisely because Jonson seems to achieve so easily the opposite effect. The opening actually highlights the success of his achievement by suggesting how whining the tone might have been in someone else's hands. The impression of complaint is immediately checked by an ensuing catalogue of witty questions and humorous insults (1–10), but it is exactly this playfulness that makes the poem so effective as self-promotion and self-display. Ironically, although the threat it confronts might seem far larger and more ominous than the one confronted in the "Tribe" epistle, the tone of the "Execration" seems far more masterful and self-assured. Fire's physical destruction seems to have been easier for Jonson to accept than threats to his standing caused by neglect at court. Indeed, the "Execration" turns the fire to powerful social and political advantage, adopting a stoic response far more convincing and good-humored than the one attempted in the "Tribe" epistle.

The similarities between the two poems are striking, yet they highlight important differences. Both poems rebuke superiors, but since those in the epistle are real rather than imaginary, Jonson cannot afford to be quite as explicit or demeaning in his comments. In the "Execration" nothing is really at risk, so the tone is at once more humorous and more savage; at the same time, the poem to Vulcan lacks the mood of embittered disillusionment that colors its predecessor. The playful tone of the "Execration" makes it in some ways a more powerful political document than the "Tribe" epistle, in which Jonson's concern to promote and protect himself is exceedingly clear. In both poems Jonson feels unfairly victimized, and while in the "Tribe" epistle the idea of being tested by fire had been simply a passing metaphor (3), in the "Execration" that image is implicit throughout. In both poems Jonson is given (or rather, creates) an opportunity to test his mettle in public; each deals, in its own way, with the instability of fortune, with mutability, with loss of power and lack of control. But in the "Execration" Jonson's response can afford to be much more genuinely philosophical, since there the test indeed results from bad luck, whereas the neglect protested in the "Tribe" epistle may have been caused by political scheming or personal hostility. Malevolence is merely a fiction in the "Execration"; despite the poet's exasperated claims, Vulcan did not deliberately single out Jonson for attack. Claiming that he did is part of the poem's humor. But the sense that one could quickly and irrevocably lose everything—or at least almost everything that mattered—is an important one in both works.

The resemblances between the poems are numerous. In both works Jonson's strategy is partly to embarrass his superiors, stressing how his attempts to act responsibly have been greeted by their hostility or neglect. Just as the "Tribe" epistle protested his basic political loyalty, so in the "Execration" he denies having written anything treasonable or heretical (15–18). Just as the "Tribe" poem attacked immorality of all sorts, so in the "Execration" he disclaims having ever written anything "loose, or s[c]urrile" (20). In the earlier poem he assaulted anarchic purveyors of political gossip; in the latter he rejects any desire to "wound the honour of the Crowne" or "taxe the Glories of the Church, and Gowne," any "Itch to defame the State" or "brand the Times" (23–25). He even denies any intent to promote himself in "selfe-boasting Rimes" (26), implying that such a desire would in any case prove counterproductive. This assertion is doubly ironic, not only because Jonson's works of the past year had been so much concerned with self-promotion and self-defense, but also because the "Execration" is one of his most subtly effective instruments of self-display. Read in light of the political and literary events of 1623, this whole string of denials takes on a more specifically combative tone, as if to suggest that many other writers (the "Covey of Witts," for instance) do engage in all the activities Jonson attacks and thus deserve Vulcan's wrath far more than he. Seen in this light, his lines of self-defense perhaps continue the kind of attacks on rivals also present in *Time Vindicated* and the "Tribe" epistle. Once again Jonson calls our—and the King's?—attention to the kind of writer he is, to his reliability. Only this time, by doing it in a less obviously self-interested way, he promotes his interests more effectively.

In both poems Jonson distinguishes not only between true and false art but between true and false artists. By mocking the various kinds of contorted, contrived poetry he does *not* write (29ff.), he calls all the more attention to his skill and success in the "Execration" itself. As in the "Tribe" epistle and *Time Vindicated*, he rebukes popular tastes, and his list of the projects on which he had been working before the fire struck suggests his laureate status and ambitions (89ff.). Despite his earlier claimed disinterest in political gossip, the poem repeatedly alludes to contemporary controversies; read with a knowledge of domestic and foreign events in 1623, it is a much more richly political work than has sometimes been emphasized. Its closing allusion to the bitter warfare in the Netherlands is a good case in point. Jonson instructs Vulcan that there he has a perfect opportunity

> On both sides [to] doe your mischiefes with delight;
> Blow up, and ruine, myne, and countermyne,
>   Make your Petards, and Granats, all your fine
> Engines of Murder, and receive the praise
> Of massacring Man-kind so many wayes.
>
>   (204–8)

The last two lines of this passage typify the syntactical wit for which Jonson has sometimes been given too little credit. All the ambiguity hinges on a single word: "Of" (208). Does the poet mean that Vulcan would be praised *for* massacring mankind or *by* it? In the first case, men are Vulcan's victims; in the second, he is merely the instrument of their own destructive hatred. The passage not only emphasizes one of the larger themes of the poem—sudden, wanton destruction—but also implies that such impulses are loose in the passions of the rival writers and political agitators Jonson had been attacking throughout 1623. The poem ends by endorsing Jacobean pacificism—a hotly contested issue at the time—but the endorsement is hardly extraneous. It is linked to the work's central thematic core.

Even after placing the "Execration" in its biographical and political contexts, George Chapman's savage reaction to it still seems startling and revealing. Far from viewing it as an exercise in good-humored stoicism, Chapman attacked it as a clever, calculated ploy, as a boastful bid for patronage. In a poetic "Invective" attacking Jonson, Chapman unleashed a furious assault on his target's pride and self-promotion, mocking his pretensions to learning, wit, and social greatness (H&S 11:406–11). His indictment implies an acute sensitivity to self-promotional nuances in Jonson's verse, a sensitivity probably lost to modern readers. When Chapman read the "Execration," he saw more than its evident good humor; he saw how it functioned as a competitive instrument, as a poem of patronage.

His examination is in fact an exposé, an attempt to subvert the poem's effectiveness by disclosing its devices and questioning its purpose. One needn't completely accept his analysis to acknowledge its value as evidence that when Renaissance writers read each other's poems, they were as much alive to their social implications as to their more obvious "aesthetic" qualities. Chapman lampoons the stoic pose of the "Execration," charges Jonson with false modesty and disingenuousness, and even implies that the poem's reference to "mastry in the Arts" (88) slyly advertises his honorary Oxford degree. The work's promotion of Jonson as a learned poet seems particularly to have irked Chapman, perhaps because the claim had long proven so effective in winning him "learned admirers" (H&S 11:410). But his most interesting charge is that the poem was less a good-humored, gallant attempt at self-consolation than a crafty device to win the King's attention and financial support (H&S 11:410). It is, of course, impossible to say just how much credence this accusation deserves. Shortly before the fire, Jonson had indeed (in the "Tribe" epistle) expressed an intense preoccupation with continued royal patronage, and Chapman's reference to Jonson's "petulencies" (H&S 11:410) may possibly glance at that poem's attacks on Jones and others. But Chapman's allegation is less important for what it may tell us about Jonson's real or imagined motives than for what it reveals about the social atmosphere in which those motives took shape. The patronage system made competition inevitable, yet it also made blatant self-promotion a distinct liability. Obvious self-promotion risked alienating patrons and providing rivals an easy target. Competition ensured self-interest but made its blunt and open acknowledgment doubly unattractive. In such an atmosphere, hidden agendas, suppressed motives, and the kind of suspicions and charges Chapman vents were bound to flourish.[22]

Jonson seems to have been particularly sensitive (and susceptible) to doubts about his real motives, especially when other writers were concerned. In his famous tribute to Shakespeare, for instance (*U.V.* 26), the long introductory passage disclaims any ambiguous purpose. His praise, he asserts, is prompted neither by "seeliest Ignorance" nor by "blinde Affection" (7; 9). More interesting, however, are his denial that he intends to draw any "envy" on Shakespeare and his acknowledgment that "crafty Malice, might pretend this praise, / And thinke to ruine, where it seem'd to raise" (11–12). Although he dismisses these possibilities, readers have rarely felt entirely comfortable with the work's tone. Dryden, no doubt, went too far in calling it "an insolent, sparing, and invidious panegyric," but certainly Jonson uses the poem—like many of his commendatory works—to reflect as favorably as possible on himself.[23] To say this is not to deny his tribute's beauty or challenge its sincerity; it is only to recognize that few of his poems can be entirely divorced from the competitive context in which they were written. Several lines from the elegy, for instance, implicitly mock another elegy, by William Basse (H&S 11:145); even in honoring a dead colleague, Jonson could not resist derogating a living rival. In this and in other ways, his celebration of Shakespeare is a highly wrought, highly self-conscious *performance*—one that not only promotes his particular interests and aesthetic but calls attention to the ampleness of its own achievement.

The competitive tensions merely implied in the Shakespeare elegy seem far more obvious in the Chapman "Invective," in the "Tribe" epistle, and in Jonson's attacks on Wither earlier in 1623. But a concern with rivals and rivalry, with antagonism and the need for self-assertion and defense, seems always to have been present to one degree or another in his thinking. One might argue, in fact, that in his final decade or so, such concerns became—for good reasons—increasingly important and pronounced. After James's death and Charles's succession in 1625, the lucrative masque commissions suddenly ceased, and did not resume for a number of years. When they began again, Jones's role in preparing the masques was much enhanced, and Jonson even charged him with usurping his own prerogative as "Fabler." During the years when Jonson ceased writing masques, he turned back to the stage. But his success there was at best uneven, and the reception accorded his 1629 play, *The New Inn*, was disastrous. The play's weakness—due in part, no doubt, to a paralytic stroke the year before—gave his antagonists ample ammunition, and his embittered response to their criticisms only enhanced his vulnerability. Thus, Owen Felltham attacked his "saucy way / Of baiting those that pay / Dear for the sight of your declining wit" (H&S 11:339–40), while another writer charged that although his talent was failing, his arrogance had increased (H&S 11:345). Of course, not everyone attacked him; Thomas Carew was one of several who came to his defense. But even Carew, embarrassed by his "itch of prayse," seems to have realized that Jonson's ineffective rebuttals only opened him to further criticism. His own poem defends him while distancing Carew from the unattractive aspects of Jonson's self-defense (H&S 11:335–36).

Jonson and his defenders indirectly suggest one especially significant reason for the old poet's concern: the most vociferous critics of his play seem largely to have been "gentles" of the kind described by Ann Jennalie Cook in her study of "privileged playgoers." The defenses almost routinely refer to his critics as those prosperous enough to trick themselves out in silken clothes and as sufficiently sensitive about their own status to display their wealth and wit. The opinion of such people, the courtly satellites and self-proclaimed intelligentsia, were obviously important to Jonson. Although most were probably not patrons themselves, their assessments of him could help determine whether a patron would win public respect by associating with or supporting him. Jonson could (as his friends urged) choose to ignore criticism by such audiences or by antagonists seeking to puff their own reputations by mocking his. Or he could lash out at it, as in fact he did. But in either case he would be reacting to it, and his reaction would largely be determined by his felt need to redeem his reputation, by his sense of the need to compete. Just how threatened he felt by competition at this time is suggested by his contemptuous references to "Broomes sweepings" (H&S 6:493n), a jab at the literary efforts of his one-time servant, Richard Brome.

In the years following *The New Inn,* Jonson's problems with rivals and antagonists and his concerns with competition hardly subsided. His next play, *The Magnetic Lady,* was also strongly criticized, both in the theater and out. Alexander Gill (who seems to have been as much interested in embarrassing Jonson as in censuring the play) attacked it as "the Childe" of its author's "Bedridden witt" and emphasized its rejection by the privileged audiences Jonson most needed to attract. At a time when Jonson felt increasingly threatened by Jones, Gill also gleefully alluded to the latter's derisive reaction to the play, saying that "Inigo w[i]th laughter ther grew fatt / That thear was nothing worth the Laughing att" (H&S 11:347). Jonson responded with a small masterpiece of invective, yet that he felt compelled to respond at all implies that the attack stung. Other evidence from this period also suggests his sensitivity to hostile criticism. In a poetic petition asking the King to increase his pension, he cited the "envie" his previous annuity had provoked and alluded to various attacks by "the lesse-*Poëtique* boyes" (H&S 8:259). Twice during this period (for two different reasons), he was satirized by John Eliot (H&S 11:406), but the person he felt most threatened by was of course Jones. Their always uneasy partnership finally collapsed during the early 1630s, and Jonson issued perhaps the most thorough-going assault he ever unleashed on his rival's motives and character. But the "Expostulation With Inigo Jones" (U.V. 34) is unusual only for its length and ferocity; otherwise it encapsulates more than twenty years of bad feelings and bitter accusations. It also typifies the anxieties and insecurities, the combative impulses and contentious attitudes, fostered by patronage competition in general. It usually made sense to suppress these, but they could—often at the slightest provocation—come boiling to the surface and explode. In the "Expostulation" and in other works from this period, explode they did. Jonson's purpose was as much to admonish the King about the risks posed to his own reputation by his support of Jones as to attack Jones himself. The attacks, however, proved counterproductive; even Jonson's friends warned him that the King was "not well pleased" with such assaults on his architect, and Jonson "lost some ground at Court" by his intemperance (H&S 11:151–52). It is a sign both of his fury and perhaps of his desperation that he assailed Jones more openly and directly than he ever had before.

After 1631, Jonson was commissioned to write no more masques for Charles's court. One contemporary reported that he had been "for this time discarded, by reason of the predominant power of his Antagonist, Innigo Jones . . ."[24] It is easy to exaggerate the extent of his decline and equally easy to overemphasize Jones's responsibility. After all, Jonson did continue to be patronized by some of the kingdom's most powerful men, and any decline in his court fortunes was probably also due to deteriorating health. Presumably bedridden and thus unable to visit the court very often if at all, he must have felt less and less able to exert much influence there, especially in the face of rivals' maneuvering. His status in these final years must have struck him as annoyingly ambiguous. His generous annuity helped assure him an income most writers would have envied, yet the prestige that came from close association with the court was inevitably subsiding, and he found himself increasingly subject to attack. One of his last poems—a commendatory epigram on a play by Joseph Rutter—implicitly captures some sense of his paradoxical position (U.V. 42). On the one hand, he was obviously respected enough—by Rutter and others—for Rutter to seek his testimony. On the other hand, he spends much of the epigram wondering whether his opinion will "be heard" (3) and fulminating against unnamed figures "Cry'd up of late" as "a new / Office of Wit" (21; 19–20). He had expressed such contempt and exasperation previously (most notably in the 1629 "Ode to Himselfe"), but then he had been able to attain some consolation. In the epigram to Rutter, however, his continued assertion of his standards is largely overshadowed by apprehension that his opinion now no longer counts, that he is not so much disputed as ignored. He apparently felt that many regarded him as a figure from the past not worth heeding. No doubt he exaggerated (the persons he attacks here, for instance, were probably not indifferent to his satire), and perhaps the poem merely expressed a passing mood. Nonetheless it seems revealing. It suggests that after a lifetime of self-assertion and of struggle with rivals, he had come to feel that he was no longer taken seriously enough even to be the target of rivalry. The poem to Rutter responds less to attack than to neglect, to being forgotten and abandoned. As Jonson had known all along, hostile criticism—though obviously bothersome and threatening—was still an implicit tribute to the power of the person criticized.

Yet even after he died in August 1637, Jonson remained controversial. Although his funeral was attended by "all or the greatest part of the nobilitie and gentry then in the town" (H&S 1:115), and although he was buried in Westminster Abbey, the attacks that had agitated him throughout his life and intensified during its final decade apparently continued. Like some of the aristocrats he had earlier lauded, Jonson did not escape posthumous defamation. The elegists who praised him half a year later in the pages of *Jonsonus Virbius* expressed confidence that his fame would prove eternal; nevertheless they felt the need to devote a surprising number of lines to defending him against detractors past and present (H&S 11:429–81). It seems an overstatement to claim that "the passing of Ben was, for the entire English world of letters, the passing of its king" (H&S 1:115). In the period immediately following his death, at any rate, his reputation was far from entirely assured. *Jonsonus Virbius* seems less to celebrate the old writer's greatness than to assert it in the face of opposition. The promotion of the poet had to continue even after his death.

Like many of his own poems, the works of Jonson's elegists embody twin impulses—the need to present a positive image of the poet and the awareness that it was potentially vulnerable to attack. Like the works they praise, the elegies are responsive to the twin pressures of literary competition and concern with status. Written for the most part by aristocrats, courtly satellites, serious literati, and university wits, they promote Jonson's achievement not only as a writer but as a writer worthy to be read by a certain class, thereby affirming and advertising their own membership in it. From one perspective the volume is indeed, as it is usually depicted, a culminating testimony to the success of Jonson's career. Just as importantly, however, it helps remind us why he could never take that success for granted. Presenting him to the world precisely as he would have wanted to be, the volume also implies the tensions and insecurities inherent in the image he had fashioned. It represents not so much the end of his struggle for social validation as a continuation of it. Its affectionate portrait of the dead poet is colored by its contributors' awareness that many disputed their view.

The first writer to come to Jonson's defense did not belong to the privileged group who contributed to *Jonsonus Virbius*—although John Taylor's poem seems to have been written partly with the hope of making an impression on such people. Addressed to "The Right Honourable, Worshipfull and Others, that are understanding Readers and Impartiall Censurers," the Water-Poet's "Funerall Elegie" was published a number of months before the appearance of *Jonsonus Virbius*.[25] It laments not only Jonson's death but the fact that no one else had as yet seen fit to commemorate his passing. Like much of Jonson's own epideictic poetry, the elegy calls implicit attention to the homage it performs, and part of its function seems to have been to associate "the Scullor" (as Jonson once called him) with the more respectable poet he praised. Indeed, many of the elegies on Jonson betray an awareness of the ambiguity of tribute—the fact that in honoring someone, perhaps especially when that person is no longer a living subject for obviously self-interested flattery, one also presents an appealing image of oneself to the world. Many of the young contributors to *Jonsonus Virbius* no doubt shared with Taylor the motive of thus advertising themselves, of presenting attractive self-images even as they sought to exalt and defend the image of Jonson. They disclaim this motive often enough to lend it further credibility, and no matter what their conscious intents, self-advertisement is an inevitable result of their praise.

Various parts of Taylor's "Elegie" suggest that it may have been fashioned partly with an eye toward appealing to the "nobilitie and gentry" who attended Jonson's funeral. In the prefatory verses, for instance, Taylor announces that he speaks to "You that are men of worth,"

> Not to the partial and prejudicate:
> Nor to the ribble rabble sencelesse crue,
> The *Hydra* monster inconsiderate,
> Who scarce know P from G, or blacke from blew,
> I neither doe respect, their love or hate,
> For him deceas'd, and for your loves I pend it,
> And to your good protections I commend it.
>
> (17–24)

These lines leave unclear whether the criticism Taylor anticipated would be motivated more by dislike for his poem or for its subject; perhaps the ambiguity is deliberate, as if he meant to suggest that the same ignorants who once attacked Jonson's verse would now attack his.

This would have the effect, again, of elevating Taylor's social importance: he and Jonson would seem to share the same enemies and thus
the same values and (ideally) the same friends.

Although Taylor begins by claiming that Jonson was *"belov'd"* (8),
much of his poem refutes attacks that had been—and apparently were
still being—leveled against the poet. Many of the issues he confronts
appear again in *Jonsonus Virbius* itself. Taylor mentions the "mis-
chievous detraction" aimed at Jonson's plays (87), referring not only to
the "dotages" but to works from the beginning and middle of his career.
Repeatedly he is forced to qualify his statements about the approval
Jonson won; at one point he refers explicitly to the attacks of rival wits
and writers (60–68). But he also makes clear that even after Jonson's
death, his antagonists did not confine themselves to satire on his works
alone. "A lying rumour up and down doth run," says Taylor,

> Reporting that he was a *Bricklayers* Sonne,
> Which if 'twere true was no disgrace or scorne,
> For famous *Virgil* in a ditch was borne,
> And many men of meane obscure degree,
> Have risen to the height of Soveraignty.
>
> (115–20)

Although this may have been intended partly to reflect on Taylor's
own circumstances, it more importantly suggests just how significant
Jonson's enemies thought his low social origins could be in tarnishing
his public reputation, even after his death and even after a lifetime of
accomplishment. Despite his claims that such a background was
nothing to be ashamed of, Taylor does his best to redeem Jonson's status.
He reports that the poet's father was "A reverend Preacher" (122) who
provided carefully for his son's education, even sending him "up to the
university" (128) to pursue his studies. Only after Jonson's father died,
when Ben at seventeen was already on the verge of manhood, did his
mother marry the bricklayer (135–44). Like most people, this second
husband held "*Learning* in a beggerly esteeme" (146), and he put
Jonson to work at his own trade. But by then Jonson's character had
presumably been firmly shaped by his father's gentlemanly influence
and by his extensive schooling, and the rest is history.

Taylor's tale contradicts not only modern biographers but Jonson's
own statements to Drummond. He told Drummond, for instance, that
his father had died months before Jonson was born, and his mother's
remarriage seems to have taken place within a few years of his birth.
Jonson's stepfather was thus an important influence almost from the
start. This might make the boy's later accomplishments seem all the
more remarkable and praiseworthy, but Taylor was obviously respond-

ing to a very different notion of what constituted social worth than we are used to today. His tale gives Jonson a more respectable, more genteel background and upbringing than he seems in fact to have enjoyed—and thus it paradoxically perhaps helps improve the chances that his works might be read more (if not entirely) on their own merits. The fact that Jonson's critics would resort to such posthumous attacks on his writing, character, and status, and the fact that Taylor felt the need to spend so much time and effort refuting them, both vividly illustrate the kind of social pressures Jonson operated under during his lifetime.

Like several of the writers for *Jonsonus Virbius*, Taylor juxtaposes the attacks made on Jonson with the estimation in which he was held by his patrons. Implicitly appealing to their higher social and intellectual authority, he thereby justifies his own defense of Jonson while intimidating the poet's antagonists. No sooner does he report, for instance, that "Ther's some will prate" about Jonson's alleged slowness as a writer than he illustrates how differently the poet's most important patrons valued his art:

> He serv'd two Kings, with good integrity,
> From whose free grace and liberality,
> He had a Royall pension, and true pay,
> Which still he spent before the quarter day.
> For he was no close fisted usurer,
> No *Mammons man*, no base extortioner,
> He lov'd not gold and silver, and almost,
> It lov'd him so, that still no love was lost.
>
> (205–12)

Taylor's reference to Jonson's lack of avarice specifically supports his earlier, more general statement that Jonson served his patrons "with good integrity." A man for whom money seems to have been so unimportant was unlikely to prostitute his talent for pay or prove an "extortioner" to his patrons. And yet one cannot help wondering whether Taylor, in making this claim about Jonson's integrity, was simply reporting a fact or was responding once more to specific criticisms. Given the defamatory context implied by other parts of Taylor's poem, nearly every statement in it can be seen as in some sense defensive or tacitly apologetic. It seems less a celebration of the common view of Jonson's merits than an attempt to promote such a view.

Much the same seems true of *Jonsonus Virbius*. Issued six months after Jonson died, it opens with its printer's apology for the delay. Taylor himself had earlier called attention to the lack of published praise that followed Jonson's death (thus calling attention to his own fidelity), and had suggested that an absence of "good will" toward the poet might be one cause (14). But the printer claims instead that "*so great an Argument*" required careful deliberation and judgment, that elegies on so commanding a figure could not be lightly dashed off. This claim at once pays tribute to Jonson and implies the potential embarrassment of failing to praise him properly. Many of the writers of the individual elegies return to this theme; they claim the unfitness of their own art in the face of Jonson's achievement and express a sense of intimidation, as if in praising him they will be compared with him—and with the other elegists—and their writing found wanting. At the same time, they disavow any ambition to call attention to themselves by celebrating the dead poet. In both cases they suggest a self-consciousness about their own performances, indeed a consciousness of their works *as* performances. In this respect as in many others, their works resemble those of the man they praise. The fact that many were young writers or intellectuals trying to make names for themselves, and that a number stood in dependent relationships with friends or one-time patrons of Jonson, only enhances the resemblance. *Jonsonus Virbius* is responsive to many of the same pressures and social influences that affected the production and character of Jonson's own works.[26]

One clue to the social function of the volume is suggested by its arrangement. The first and longest of the poems is an "Eglogue" by Lucius Cary, who was celebrated in Jonson's great Cary-Morison ode. This might be reason enough to grant his poem priority, but another reason is implied by the way the poem is signed: "Falkland." It was Cary's social position as much as either his friendship with Jonson *per se* or the objective skill of his praise that seems to have dictated the *placement* of his poem. The first four of the elegies, in fact, are identified as having been written by men of rank, and the author of the first poem in the section devoted to Latin tributes is similarly identified as a "Baronet." In part such placement reflects simple courtesy and conventional deference. But from another perspective it must have had the effect of enhancing Jonson's social respectability, especially in response to the sort of innuendo about his bricklaying background to which Taylor refers.

Like Taylor, Falkland carefully enumerates Jonson's aristocratic patrons, and like Taylor he does so immediately after mentioning Jonson's detractors. The effect, once more, is to refute the poet's critics by citing the better judgments of their social betters. Falkland's poem is itself an instance of this strategy. Moreover, even as it asserts Jonson's prestige by depicting his critics as socially ridiculous, it also distinguishes Falkland and the other men of his status who appreciated Jonson from the vulgar, ignorant rich who did not. The fact that Jonson was not universally admired may, indeed, have helped make him to some an attractive subject of praise. By praising him they asserted their membership in an elect circle of people virtuous and intelligent enough to value his genius. Championing Jonson in the face of "ignorant" opposition provided a means of asserting one's own social worth. It permitted one to align oneself publicly with the kings and queens, noble men and noble ladies, learned scholars and influential courtiers who, by acknowledging and rewarding Jonson's talents, had given them important social sanction.

The attacks against which Jonson's elegists defend him are painfully familiar. In some cases the elegists allude to the more recent criticism of his "dotages," but in general the charges they confute are the same ones that had bedeviled him throughout his career. And repeatedly the contributors indicate that the attacks did not end when he died. His eulogists were not able to look back on his early critics and smile serenely at their foolish impercipience: the same aspersions were still being cast. Much more than has been recognized, *Jonsonus Virbius* is an embattled, contentious book, which simply continues Jonson's own enterprise of self-assertion and self-defense. It defends him, for instance, against the familiar charges that he was slow and that he plagiarized, that he lacked genius and depended too much on outside resources. It upholds his works' chasteness and insistently absolves him of accusations that he filled his writing with personal invective, that he used his talents to vent his gall and exercise personal revenge. His critics, it suggests, included Puritan "Zelots" and partisans of Shakespeare, political renegades and ignorant courtiers (H&S 11:472). And, in the best Jonsonian tradition, there is at least one swipe at Jones (H&S 11:468). Often Jonson's maligners are identified as men of "plush and velvet"—the gentlemen or pretenders to gentility who frequented the theaters and the court. Even when his detractors are associated with the masses, it is not clear whether this is objective information or simply a means of degrading his critics, of subverting their affectations to social importance. What *is* clear is that many of the tactics Jonson's eulogists exploit in defending him had already been perfected by Jonson himself. In its matter and its manner, *Jonsonus Virbius* epitomizes some of the same pressures, tensions, and the responses to both that characterized his own art and career. In his life, and at least immediately after his death, neither his social nor his literary status was ever quite assured. By defending one, his eulogists sought to uphold the other.

For Jonson, intimately caught up in a world of dependency and power relations, complete assurance could never be achieved. Even at the height of his success in the mid-Jacobean period, he realized that his success was largely *given*, that its continuance depended on the continuing favor and support of the powerful. The attacks and tactics of his rivals, the uncertain encouragement of his patrons, the subordinate role society assigned him, along with his own assertive personality and steadfast belief in the value of art—all these factors and more combined to make his position exceedingly ambiguous. Constantly renegotiated, his role (like the poems that grew out of it) was complex and entangled, equivocal. The voice that speaks in his poems is a self-conscious voice, but more importantly it is a voice aware of other voices, to which it expectantly responds and adjusts itself. And the same seems true of his sons, or at least of the voices we hear in the poems they wrote to lament his passing. These works echo his own awareness of the knotted connections between poetry and power. This consciousness is one of his most fascinating legacies to his heirs.

6
Poems on Friends and Friendship

Jonson's poems to friends are among his most appealing works. Unlike his satires or the poems on rivals and patrons, the poems to friends may at first seem remote from competitive anxieties or ambitions. The poems to patrons, despite his best intentions, can never completely free themselves from suspicions of flattery, while the poems aimed at rivals often reveal an aggressive rancor, even an apparent pettiness, that has sometimes seemed unbefitting a major poet. The poems on Jones, for instance, have more often provoked embarrassment than admiration, and even the more general satires, for all their wit and vitality, may strike some readers as arrogantly self-assured. The very poems that seem most concerned to promote Jonson are the ones that may seem least attractive, while, ironically, those in which he seems least openly concerned with power are often the most powerfully effective. Few works, for example, are more immediately appealing than "Inviting a Friend to Supper" (*Ep.* 101), which cultivates his image while (but also by) claiming not to do so. The poems to friends, precisely because they so often seem apolitical, are among the most politically potent; they advance his interests more subtly and persuasively than other works that seem more obviously self-interested. But this is hardly the only paradox connected with them.[1]

Writing, circulating, and publishing a poem to a friend are themselves ambiguous acts. Paying open tribute to him and showing that one values him enough to value him publicly, they stand as the outward signs of inward communion. As such they express faith in the friendship's permanence while pragmatically helping assure it. But they also exploit the friendship, using it to advertise the praiser even if—perhaps especially if—all his praise is truly "sincere." The poem to a friend points outward from the friendship (often a refuge from the pressures of the wider world) and addresses that world: it is both a celebration of private relationship and a micropolitical performance that inevitably affects one's broader social standing. Every poem Jonson wrote and circulated is political in this sense; every poem would have some impact on his status. This is no less true of the poems on friends than of the poems on rivals or patrons.

So Jonson's poems to friends are inseparable from his experience as a poet seeking patronage. By demonstrating his capacity for genuinely reciprocal relations, such poems advertise his dependability as a client. By displaying his alliances and publicizing his appeal to others, they enhance his attractiveness to patrons, exhibiting his social power in a way that actually makes him a more valuable dependent. While friendship might relieve the stress of competing for patronage, it was also a competitive asset. Inevitably one's friendships affected one's reputation and thus one's standing with superiors.

Voluntary by definition, friendships affirmed one's sense of independent power. This gave them enormous resonance in a culture founded on obligatory relations between superiors and dependents. Yet the freedom that made choosing friends so satisfying could also arouse anxiety: the right to reject meant the threat of rejection. This possibility was all the more important since friendships, although in one sense freely chosen, in another sense were unavoidably necessary. Lacking friends meant lacking both the feeling and the reality of power. One projected influence not only *on* friends but *through* them; to lack friends was not to be taken completely seriously. Just as a patron's power could be measured by the number of his "friends" and followers, so could anyone's. But numbers alone were not enough: one was also judged by the quality and influence of one's friends. To feel truly confirmed by a friend, his support had to seem worth possessing. Being surrounded by the impotent or attracting only the unattractive would actually diminish one's subjective and objective sense of strength. The whole issue of friendship, then, was deeply implicated in issues of status and power.[2]

Friendships with people of varying rank could create varying benefits but also varying ambiguities. Friendship with inferiors allowed one to experience and exercise power in a particularly satisfying way. The respect of men like Jonson's "sons" could only increase his self-respect; it confirmed the value of his past accomplishments and implied the survival of his influence. Yet the rewards of their friendship were more psychological than immediately pragmatic. Since inferiors could not offer benefits equal to those they received, benefiting them validated one's power but might also foster a sense of unequal obligation. Moreover, friendship with inferiors might also involve uncertainty about the nature of their respect. Their friendship affirmed one's status but might also prove unsettling if status seemed too important to them, if one suspected that their regard would diminish if one's power did. Jonson's poems often raise the discomforting possibility that friendship might be rooted in a desire for profit, and the more his own power grew, the more he must have realized that part of his attraction for inferiors might lie less in his intrinsic worth than in the profitability of association with him. Paradoxically, in relations with both superiors *and* inferiors, one risked being valued more for one's usefulness than for oneself.

A superior's friendship might affirm one's status, but one could never forget the gap between his power and one's own. Although the benefits he conferred might signify his favor, they also signified his greater authority and control, ratifying while at the same time qualifying a client's security. His friendship might lend prestige, but "lend" is the crucial word, since the power was never wholly possessed. To be gratified by such a friendship was also to fear its loss. Moreover, a superior's friendship might provoke the disdain of his rivals and the envy of one's peers. In all these ways such friendships were caught up in questions of power. So, too, were friendships with equals. The very fact that they might *seem* relatively untainted by power was, paradoxically, one of the ways power inevitably impinged on them, affecting their psychological coloring. Such friendships were defined not only by what they were but by what they were not. One had to be careful, for instance, not to overwhelm an equal with benefits and thus upset the relationship's careful balance. Skillfully done, exchanging benefits with an equal could ratify the power of both parties. Because one risked less in dealing with an equal than with a superior, the relationship might prove more satisfying and less anxious. Self-interests were inevitably engaged, but of the three kinds of possible relationships, that with an equal might provide the greatest sense of being valued for oneself.[3]

Classical commentators usually insisted that the chief prerequisite of genuine friendship was virtue. Aristotle and Cicero both endorse the idea, seeming to imply that true and uncomplicated friendships might exist between individuals of any status as long as virtue was a trait the parties shared.[4] But the ideals posited by the great commentators on friendship are just that—ideals. Their treatises, less descriptive than argumentative, seem designed to champion views not universally shared, let alone universally practiced. They readily concede that ideal friendships are unusual because perfect virtue is rare: Aristotle writes that virtuous friendships are as infrequent as virtuous men, and that although most people "wish for what is noble, [they] choose what is advantageous." Cicero writes at length about how difficult it is to find true and steadfast friends, concluding that they are not only "exceedingly rare" but "almost divine." In the first half of the sixteenth century Sir Thomas Elyot echoed this view, while a few decades later, Walter Dorke lamented that "you may sooner by definition declare what [a true friend] is, than by demonstration shew where he is."[5]

The idealism of traditional theories thus may be seen as partly a reaction to (and partly an attempt to manage) the real complexities of practical friendships. Few real friendships could possibly have lived up to the lofty classical ideals. The very writings that exalted friendship also implied the risks and disappointments most friendships might involve; the very ideals that made friendship seem so attractive must have made most real friendships seem somewhat compromised and incomplete, less than wholly fulfilling. The ideals provided a standard by which the friendships of everyday life could be judged but also one by which they could be found wanting. Theories designed to codify friendship helped expose its dilemmas (even while inadvertently disclosing their own).

The very idea of friendship implies a world in which all people cannot be friends, in which intimacy and trust are rare, in which only some relations are not tacitly competitive or indifferently neutral. Certainly this is true in "Inviting a Friend," where the amiable gathering is set against a background of distrust and insecurity: the supper offers a welcome (but brief and unstable) refuge from outside threats. By its very nature, friendship involves both excluding and being excluded. Supposedly free of jealousy, envy, and the other anxieties competition can foster, it nonetheless involves competition of its own: the friend inevitably competes with other present or potential friends who might prove more attractive or satisfying.[6] Even the common notion of a "best friend" implies not only competition but also the possibility that one's other friends might not be so satisfactory or reliable.

In contrast, the amiable competition Cicero exalts in *De Amicitia*, a competition in which friends compete in doing good, must have exerted strong appeal in a culture rooted in patronage.[7] Robbed of any sense of threat or moral compromise, such rivalry benefited one's friend, oneself, and society at large. Ideal competition of this sort contrasted starkly with the competitive pursuit of patronage, which implied loss, self-interest, and conscious calculation. By offering relief from the intense self-consciousness such factors bred, friendship might paradoxically allow one to be and to feel more truly oneself. This is because self-consciousness involves not so much consciousness of a "true" or autonomous self as of an image of the self created for others to observe. It involves not so much literal self-preoccupation as preoccupation with others and others' power. Friendship could thus seem, in many ways, an alternative to relations rooted in fear.[8]

Yet even friendship could never be wholly untainted by anxiety and self-consciousness. The very qualities prized in friendship—the freedom to relax, to drop all pretenses and share concerns and vulnerability—gave the friend extraordinary power and made choosing

one an act of great moment.[9] The truest friend could become the
greatest threat if he abused his trust and exploited the intimacy he had
shared.[10] Intimacy made one *psychologically* vulnerable if it were for
any reason violated. Intense attachment might trigger equally intense
dislike if the friendship failed—perhaps because of the extra harm a
former friend could work.[11] For these reasons, friendship for Jonson
apparently did not imply complete relaxation; indeed, many of his
poems to friends seem intensely self-conscious. In some cases almost
contractual in nature, they scrupulously define what it means to be a
friend even as they advertise the qualities of the poet's friendship. In
part this self-consciousness reflects his determination to teach the
truths of friendship to his readers. But it is also rooted in the complexities of friendship itself—complexities of which he was acutely
aware.[12]

To get a feel for these matters, one need only turn to Plutarch's essay
"How to Tell a Flatterer from a Friend"—an essay on which Jonson drew
in composing two of his most interesting poems. Plutarch stresses the
difficulties of distinguishing true friends from false, emphasizing the
formidable subtlety of flatterers: "flattery which blends itself with every
emotion, every movement, need, and habit, is hard to separate from
friendship," he writes.[13] Flatterers often imitate the earnestness and
frank speech typical of friends. Many of the qualities associated with
true friendship—as well as many of those associated with Jonson's own
self-presentation—might easily be mimicked. Besides frankness (which
Plutarch repeatedly stresses), these include gravity, diligence, emulat-
ing a good man's behavior, claiming to base opinions on judgment
rather than emotion, deferring to another's superiority, respecting another's wisdom, and hatred of iniquity.[14] Plutarch does offer advice for
separating flatterers from friends, but before discussing it, it is worth
remarking how his well-known treatise might ironically serve as a
handbook to make flattery even more subtle and sophisticated.

Plutarch himself distinguishes between the obvious flatterers who are
simple to spot and the craftier ones his treatise is designed to uncover.[15]
It would not require an especially clever flatterer, however, to realize
that Plutarch offers a kind of guide to those who wished to escape
detection. Thus Jonson, or anyone who for any reason sought to avoid
appearing a flatterer, could infer from Plutarch's essay that he should
not seem too self-deprecating, nor too easily agreeable, nor too interested in pleasure, nor inclined to praise men rather than their actions,
nor prone to talk behind others' backs, nor overly harsh, nor humorless,
nor concerned with trifling misdeeds, nor given to irrational or emotional appeals, nor oversolicitous, nor pleased to point out another's
faults, nor jealous, scurrilous, arrogant, or smug.[16] If, as Plutarch con-

cedes, a flatterer might disguise his vice by feigning frankness, presumably he might also escape discovery by feigning the attractive opposites of these other unattractive traits. Thus, even while offering a method for distinguishing appearance from reality, Plutarch's essay inadvertently suggests numerous ways in which flatterers might more effectively masquerade as friends.[17]

One shortcoming of the treatise, moreover, may be that Plutarch assumes that a flatterer always acts consciously, that his flattery involves deliberate and willful choice. But there are great incentives sincerely to think of oneself as *not* a flatterer, to conceive of one's behavior and motives more positively. In this sense, recognizing flattery *as* flattery might be especially difficult for someone whom others considered a flatterer. Plutarch insists from the start that distinguishing flattery from true friendship will not be easy, but one finishes his essay with perhaps an even greater sense than he intended of the difficulties involved.[18] Here, as so often in traditional theorizing about friendship, the theory exposes more contradictions than it puts to rest.

How *does* one pierce below appearance to the reality beneath? Paradoxically, Plutarch suggests that one method is to manipulate appearances oneself: "The changes of the flatterer, which are like those of a cuttle-fish, may be most easily detected if a man pretends that he is very changeable himself and disapproves the mode of life which he previously approved, and suddenly shows a liking for actions, conduct, or language which used to offend him." Likewise, "dissimulated praise, which calls for a more cunning sort of precaution, is to be brought to light by deliberately formulating absurd advice and suggestions, and by making senseless corrections." Thus, to combat superficiality, one becomes superficial; to free oneself from pretense, one pretends. To escape from political maneuvering, one maneuvers politically. To defeat the flatterer, one must imitate his techniques.[19]

But distinguishing flattery from friendship involves self-conscious concern with appearance in other ways as well. It is not enough to avoid *being* a flatterer; one must also avoid *appearing* to be one, an effort complicated by the ability of flatterers so astutely to manipulate appearances.[20] A poet like Jonson might feel sincerely convinced (to his own satisfaction) that he was not motivated by flattery; but this would be insufficient. He would also need to convince friends and patrons, which would require the use of the tactics, strategies, and behavior needed to confirm his image as a person free from flattery.[21] Ironically, many of these same tactics might be adopted by a willful flatterer interested in disguising his true intentions. Or they might be adopted by someone who did not think of himself as a flatterer but whom others so regarded. The whole issue of distinguishing true friendship from false thus is profoundly problematic and ambiguous; separating "appearance" from "reality" is difficult, but bringing appearance into convincing conformance with reality involves still further complications.

The problem of distinguishing between true and false friends is the subject of Jonson's "Epistle to Master Arth: Squib" (*Und.* 45), a work influenced by Plutarch's essay. In the epistle, Jonson's confidence that false friendship is self-defeating is offset by an acute sense of its pervasiveness, profitability, and hardy resilience. On the one hand it is depicted as a badly knit garment that must inevitably unravel, on the other as an effectively deceptive counterfeit coin demanding the most careful scrutiny:

> What I am not, and what I faine would be,
>> Whilst I informe my selfe, I would teach thee,
> My gentle *Arthur*; that it might be said
>> One lesson we have both learn'd, and well read;
> I neither am, nor art thou one of those
>> That hearkens to a Jacks-pulse, when it goes.
> Nor ever trusted to that friendship yet,
>> Was issue of the Taverne, or the Spit:
> Much lesse a name would we bring up, or nurse,
>> That could but claime a kindred from the purse.
> Those are poore Ties, depend on those false ends,
>> 'Tis vertue alone, or nothing, that knits friends:
> And as within your Office, you doe take
>> No piece of money, but you know, or make
> Inquirie of the worth: So must we doe,
>> First weigh a friend, then touch, and trie him too:
> For there are many slips, and Counterfeits.
>> Deceit is fruitfull. Men have Masques and nets,
> But these with wearing will themselves unfold:
>> They cannot last. No lie grew ever old.
> Turne him, and see his Threds: looke, if he be
>> Friend to himselfe, that would be friend to thee.
> For that is first requir'd, A man be his owne.
>> But he that's too-much that, is friend of none.
> Then rest, and a friends value understand,
>> It is a richer Purchase then of land.
>
> (1–26)

Here as in many of his works, humility and self-assertion are effectively intertwined. Jonson presents himself both as superior and equal, as teacher and student. His poem enacts the poet's self-education (suggested by the richly equivocal phrase "informe my selfe" [2]) even as it educates its reader(s). At once meditative, personal, and public, it defines friendship against a background of necessary suspicion and inevitable distrust. "Deceit is fruitfull" (18) in the double sense of being both abundant and advantageous.

Jonson lends subtle irony to his description of false friends, alluding to kinship and nursing (9–10) to suggest relationships rooted in genuine love. Similarly, he paradoxically implies that friendships based on desire for wealth are in fact "poore Ties" (11). Later he takes up the language of money even more openly, using it cleverly to describe how ideal friendship transcends mercenary interests (13–17; 25–26). Following Plutarch, he suggests that friends must be examined as closely as coins; implying that he has already performed this procedure on Squib, he tacitly invites Squib to reciprocate. The poem itself tests Squib: his reaction will indicate his own reliability. The metaphor of testing a coin is apt, since strong friendships provided social credit and power in much the same way money did.

The poem's avowed certainty that social deceptions "with wearing will themselves unfold" (19) offers little immediate comfort. The short, emphatic phrases in line 20 proclaim confidence and assurance so insistently that they suggest more doubts than they settle. Jonson plays with the classical idea that the most intelligently self-interested man is the one truly committed to goodness, since good is the source of all true profit.[22] Thus he suggests that although false friendships are rooted in self-interest, they ultimately prove self-defeating. The false friends who deceive others end by deceiving themselves. Yet for all his vaunted confidence that flatterers cannot prevail, he seems genuinely worried about their real and immediate power. Intense vigilance is essential, yet such watchfulness can be both a "wearing" (19) and wearying experience, after which "rest" (25) is both a requirement and a reward.

As the epistle winds to its own rest with a calmly conclusive aphorism, the reader recognizes that both the "value" of friendship and one's understanding of it have been enhanced by a discrimination simultaneously described and enacted. Urging himself and Squib to appreciate the worth of friends, Jonson subtly implies how he implements his own advice: the epistle publicly testifies to his regard for Squib, to Squib's worth, to Jonson's worthiness in recognizing Squib, and thus to Jonson's intrinsic value as a friend as well as to the practical benefits of a poet's friendship. More than generalized commentary, the poem is a complex micropolitical performance.

The epigram to Squib suggests Jonson's need to distinguish not only flatterers from friends but also himself from flatterers; in this sense, all his poems on friendship are exercises in public self-definition. In one of his most fascinating poems, which again alludes to Plutarch, Jonson wrestles with these and related problems. Titled an "Epigram. To a

Friend, and Sonne," it precedes the famous Cary-Morison ode in
Under-wood (69). This placement has led to speculation that it may in
fact have been addressed to Lucius Cary, a "son" of Jonson who was also
his social superior and patron (see H&S 11:94). There is no way to know
for sure whether Cary was the addressee, although some of the poem's
language suggests that this "Sonne" was prominent and wealthy. More
interesting are the techniques Jonson uses to distance himself from the
flatterers he attacks. Simply calling the friend his "Sonne" is one of
them; it implies an especially close and trusting relationship, rooted in
particular affection. It suggests a kind of superiority but therefore an
absence of competition. A "friend" might prove a flatterer but rarely
would a father, who by definition has his son's best interests at heart.
Jonson opens the poem, moreover, by suggesting that he has tested the
"Sonne"; only afterward did he grant him the privilege of friendship.
The self-respect and aloofness this implies suggest Jonson's difference
from fawning flatterers. By forthrightly confronting the issue of flattery,
moreover, he conveys his confidence in his own sincerity, while his
comic disdain suggests that the very idea of flattery is beneath him. His
humor implies a moral superiority and detachment that make flattery
for him both unnecessary and impossible. Finally, the closing lines
implicitly challenge the reader's own conscience in a way that makes
Jonson seem principled and frank. From start to finish, the epigram is
not only an assault on flatterers but a skillful, crafted performance
designed to assert Jonson's own freedom from falseness:

> Sonne, and my Friend, I had not call'd you so
>   To mee; or beene the same to you; if show,
> Profit, or Chance had made us: But I know
>   What, by that name, wee each to other owe,
> Freedome, and Truth; with love from those begot:
>   Wise-crafts, on which the flatterer ventures not.
> His is more safe commoditie, or none:
>   Nor dares he come in the comparison.
> But as the wretched Painter, who so ill
>   Painted a Dog, that now his subtler skill
> Was, t'have a Boy stand with a Club, and fright
>   All live dogs from the lane, and his shops sight,
> Till he had sold his Piece, drawne so unlike:
>   So doth the flatt'rer with faire cunning strike
> At a Friends freedome, proves all circling meanes
>   To keepe him off; and how-so-e're he gleanes
> Some of his formes, he lets him not come neere
>   Where he would fixe, for the distinctions feare.
> For as at distance, few have facultie
>   To judge; So all men comming neere can spie.

Though now of flattery, as of picture, are
    More subtle workes, and finer pieces farre,
Then knew the former ages: yet to life,
    All is but web, and painting; be the strife
Never so great to get them: and the ends,
    Rather to boast rich hangings, than rare friends.

(1–26)

That the word "Sonne" implies both intimacy and subordination makes the possibility that this "Sonne" may have been Jonson's superior all the more interesting to contemplate, since he would then have enjoyed practical power greater than his father's. The immediate shift to "Friend" suggests that Jonson grants his son a kind of equality, that he recognizes and respects his *moral* equivalence, whatever their relative social positions were. Jonson equivocates when he mentions having "call'd" the son: the word refers both to past occasions when he termed him a friend and to the poem's so terming him now, but it also suggests summoning and selection, as if the poet deigns to bestow the honor of his friendship. Jonson dismisses the possibility that "show, / Profit, or Chance" might motivate their relationship (2–3), although the poet does "show" himself to a wider public (his second audience) as well as to the friend he addresses. "Freedome, and Truth," he says with a subtle sense of paradox, are the qualities true friends "each to other owe" (4–5); friendship, then, involves both liberty *and* obligation. "Freedome" implies honesty as well as freedom from the fear of being honest, but it also suggests a more general absence of artificial inhibition. True friendship creates both public and private obligations; what Jonson "owes" to his friend he "owes" (or acknowledges) publicly through the poem.

Significantly, Jonson makes "love" the *consequence* of freedom and truth: it does not precede or promote them, nor does it arise spontaneously; instead, it results from the conscious testing they allow. (Similarly, love, once born, presumably encourages even greater truth and freedom.) Although all three qualities might seem spontaneous or unpremeditated, Jonson punningly calls them "Wise-crafts" (6), both to distinguish them from the crafty but ultimately self-defeating tactics of flatterers and to suggest the determined effort required to build a trusting friendship. Throughout, the poem exhibits both an acute awareness of the false motives that might prompt apparent friendship as well as a striking self-consciousness. Jonson betrays a penetrating awareness of what his poem is doing, of its potential impact. His "plain" language is the achievement of a highly skilled artist. No gesture, no word or combination of phrasing, is wholly uncalculated; yet Jonson implicitly distinguishes his own calculations from the crafty artificiality of flatterers. He calls attention to his motives (1–4), both to guide our reactions and to guarantee the probity of his behavior: all his own calculations are, ostensibly, above board and publicly displayed.

Although the poem's second half argues that deceptions disintegrate when set beside the traits of genuine friends, it also credits flatterers with the skill to delay, even prevent, such comparison. Jonson's ridicule of flatterers coexists with an uneasy acknowledgment of their real social power. Ridicule helps counteract his fears as he counterattacks their source. Flatterers "strike / At a Friends freedome" (14–15) in several ways: by preventing his free access, by assailing his honesty, and by mimicking his frankness. The comic simile about the painter and the dog, which simplifies the problem of distinguishing truth and falsity, eventually gives way to a more sober assessment of the dangers and difficulties flattery creates. Thus the poem provides no clear or simple criterion for distinguishing true friends from false; instead it vacillates between dismissive humor and genuine apprehension. (The vacillation may be only apparent, however, if the humor is seen as a tactic for coping with, and thus as a manifestation of, the fear.) The "subtler skill" Jonson first mentions (10) is plainly unsubtle and ludicrous, but the apparently synonymous "faire cunning" of line 14 cannot be so lightly dismissed. Although the poem emphasizes flatterers' fears, it also accentuates three different kinds of apprehension they might provoke: fear of being mistaken for a false friend, fear of being deceived by one, and fear of competing with one for a third party's attention. This last fear gains added point if the epigram was indeed addressed to a patron. The poem would then function not only as personal warning and self-defense but also as a tactical maneuver in the poet's struggle to achieve and maintain security.

However worrisome flatterers might prove, the poem's last lines raise an even more troubling concern. Once again Jonson's confidence that flatterers can be detected collides with fear that they might not be. But while earlier this possibility was attributed to their "faire cunning" (14), now it is ascribed partly to the collusion of their victims, who actively seek out and display false friends just as wealthy aristocrats might display acquired paintings. Such ironic mutuality parodies the opening emphasis on reciprocal love between Jonson and his "Sonne," thus giving the work a kind of skewed symmetry. Whereas their love ostensibly renounced narrow self-interest, the relationships implied at the conclusion represent an unstable marriage of such designs, relationships in which either party is most concerned to profit himself. The flatterers' frantic efforts to ward off competition, which Jonson earlier ridiculed, now find their ironic counterpart in the "strife" of those who compete for flatterers' attentions (24). By warning his friend away from those who seek to promote their particular interests, Jonson inevitably promotes his own. The epigram's chief purpose, however, is less cautionary than celebratory: to "boast" (26) and thereby more firmly cement the friendship it extols, "rare" in the double sense of being both valuable and uncommon.

Jonson's epigram implicitly appeals for the poet to be valued correctly even as it advertises how much he values his "Sonne." Plutarch had written that one of the best ways to combat flattery is to examine one's conscience, to become aware of the personal weaknesses a flatterer might exploit.[23] Jonson's poem appeals to its reader's conscience and moral values, but it also appeals to his necessary self-interest, using the son's concern with reputation to enhance the poet's own standing. Jonson implies that the flatterer, although apparently willing to conform completely to another's will, actually serves only himself. Seeming to confirm his victim's power, he potentially undermines it, exploiting his friend's or patron's ambitions to promote his own. But eschewing flattery hardly means abandoning ambitions; rather, it is a sensible way to protect and advance them. The epigram effectively demonstrates how choosing a flatterer for a friend actually makes one vulnerable to ridicule. Its own tactics suggest that the best way to promote self-interest is precisely to avoid appearing selfish. For all its disdain of mere appearance, the epigram demonstrates how important appearances are.

But it also demonstrates the difficulties of separating appearance and reality. Another's praise might or might not be flattery; his frankness might or might not be sincere.[24] The epigram suggests that friendship, at least in its early stages, may involve even more scrutiny and suspicion than common relationships, precisely because it is so rare and important. Although classical commentators implied that goodness was inherently attractive and formed the best basis for true friendship,[25] in everyday life goodness was often a matter of interpretation. Several passages from Jonson's *Discoveries* suggest his realization that moral worth is not always immediately recognized, and that, even if it were, it might not always prove attractive or be rewarded. At one point he notes that

> *Some* Actions be they never so beautifull, and generous, are often obscur'd by base, and vile mis-constructions; either out of envy, or ill nature, that judgeth of others, as of it selfe. Nay, the times are so wholly growne, to be either partiall, or malitious; that, if hee be a friend, all sits well about him; his very vices shall be vertues: if an enemy, or of the contrary *faction*; nothing is good, or tolerable in him: insomuch, that wee care not to discredit, and shame our judgements, to sooth our passions. (H&S 8:579)

Elsewhere he notes that "the man that is once hated, both his *good*, and his *evill* deeds oppresse him: Hee is not easily *emergent*" (H&S 8:563–64; see also 572). A person like Jonson, who seems to have believed he was a good man, was not always so regarded by others, nor could he simply rest content with his self-perception. To advance his self-interest or, more altruistically, to make his goodness known and efficacious, inevitably he had to display and advertise it, to make it socially attractive and guide others to share his private evaluation of himself. The problem of who determines "goodness" is as much a pragmatic political issue as a clear question of morality.

By emphasizing the complexities of separating appearance from reality, Jonson's epigram points to a problem inherent in all his works but especially acute in the poems to friends or patrons. It involves whether or not or to what extent language *can* function mimetically, whether it can ever really be used or wholly trusted to represent the reality of another's self or even of one's own. Leaving aside the extent to which selves may in turn be constituted by language, the extent to which independent selfhood may be illusory, Jonson's poetry reveals a radical uncertainty about the possibility of ever using words to make assured and certain contact with others. Moreover, it insistently (if sometimes obliquely) raises the problem of ever being able to represent oneself adequately or convincingly through discourse. Although words ideally foster communication, they sometimes seem to Jonson opaque or impenetrable. Beneath the apparent assurance of his works lies a persistent dread that language may always be only appearance, that one can never use it *surely* to make certain contact with another or to represent one's self unambiguously. The insecurity at the heart of so many of his poems to patrons and friends is due mainly to his dependency, but it is also due to a discomfort with the fundamental inscrutability of words. It is an insecurity at once social, epistemological, and semantic.

"*Language*," Jonson wrote in his *Discoveries*, "most shewes a man: speake that I may see thee" (H&S 8:625). Almost by definition, a friend is a person whose language can be trusted. Because, ostensibly, his words reveal him, the political anxieties of discourse ideally become unimportant. Even between friends, however, discourse is inescapably political, especially when it is also public, as in a poem. Conscious of his own power to promote himself through words, Jonson would have been all the more conscious that others could do the same. His poems on friendship embody political complexities while asserting distance from them. In many of his poems on friendship, he is forced to confront the possibility that his friends might have their own self-interests chiefly in mind, that the ideal of reciprocity that should characterize a true friendship might be illusory. Yet in celebrating that ideal, he inevitably promotes his own particular interests.

Friendship and self-promotion are important themes in "Inviting a Friend to Supper" (*Ep.* 101), one of Jonson's best-known and most appealing works. Influenced by a number of epigrams by Martial, the poem is nevertheless more than an exercise in literary emulation. While Jonson no doubt intended readers to notice his debt to his classical predecessor, "Inviting a Friend to Supper" is so convincingly English in substance and tone that the reader has little trouble assuming, along with the Oxford editors, that the party and guests he describes are more than fictional (H&S 11:20). The poem seems to have grown out of—and to have helped shape—an actual social occasion.

Yet, as in a number of his satiric epigrams, Jonson demonstrates in this poem an awareness of how social gatherings can be exploited to individual advantage. In "To Censorious Courtling" (*Ep.* 52), for instance, he exposed the ways a rival, posing as a friend, used frosty praise and "weake applause" to attack his verse while pretending to commend it. In "To Courtling" (*Ep.* 72), he betrayed sensitivity to the power his rival enjoyed as a "chamber-critick . . . / At Madames table" (3), while the epigram "To Groom Ideot" (*Ep.* 58) attacks him for using his reactions to Jonson's poetry to call attention to himself. The gathering proposed in "Inviting a Friend" derives much of its charm and significance from its apparent contrast with these more competitive social encounters. Yet Jonson's own power would inevitably be affected both by the success of his performance at dinners like this and by the opportunities they offered to make and cement profitable connections. In fact, the opening lines evince an explicit concern with "esteeme," at the same time minimizing any obvious or threatening sense of egocentric self-interest partly by gracious deference to the guest and partly by the subtle good humor with which the issue is raised. The concern for "esteeme" expressed here is ostensibly different from what one finds in those works in which Jonson feels his own public or self-esteem threatened. In "Inviting a Friend to Supper" the unnamed friend is offered the chance to advertise his own worth; the event to which Jonson invites him will afford an opportunity for self-display, but that display will not menace Jonson. His feast, he claims, will be dignified by the guest's presence, so that the guest's acceptance of his invitation will produce mutual social profit. The importance of the poet's dinner—and thus the importance of the poet—will be enhanced, even as the guest's sense of his own social status is confirmed. The very invitation not only pays tribute to the guest's virtues and power but implies the poet's. The gravity and graciousness he ascribes to the guest are displayed in his poem, with its balanced tone of composed merriment, its well-mannered intimacy. Absent is the note of arrogant self-regard that many contemporary and later readers found so unattractive in so many of Jonson's other writings. In its place is a good-humored gravity that insinuates self-assurance, suggests social strength, and thus implicitly denies any desperate need for the very kinds of social connections the poem solicits. Implying confident self-regard and reserves of social power, the poem thereby presents Jonson to his best advantage as an attractive potential ally or friend.

Although the poem pays open tribute to the friend's character and status, it implicitly—if mildly—challenges both, reminding him that "It is the faire acceptance, Sir, creates / The entertaynment perfect: not the cates" (7–8). Although these lines seem merely to compliment the guest, suggesting that his presence is more important to the event's success than the food itself, they also pose a subtle threat: to refuse the invitation will not only ruin the entertainment but reflect negatively on the guest's character. Jonson's gracious invitation affords the guest an opportunity to reciprocate graciously—or else to reveal himself incapable of a truly "faire" acceptance. Even now the couplet's resonance is unexhausted, for the lines also suggest that a "faire acceptance" will be one in which the guest shows as much disinterest in the fare provided as the host is anxious to ensure its bountiful provision. "Faire acceptance" involves not only a formally gracious response but one that is rightly motivated, one in which the simplest and most symbolic expression of self-interest—personal appetite—is firmly subordinated to the desire to share a friend's company. Fair acceptance "creates" the perfect entertainment both because it helps beget the festivities and because the motives that prompt a "faire acceptance" are needed if the right spirit is to be sustained.

Jonson leaves deliberately vague the actual status of the banquet he promises. Again and again he describes it in conditional terms: "a short-leg'd hen, / If we can get her . . . wood-cock, of which some / May yet be there; and godwit, if we can" (11–12; 18–19). In the central qualifying line, of course, he comically admits, "Ile tell you of more, and lye, so you will come" (17). But there is more than humor in this admission, and the line does more, too, than simply emphasize his limited finances. More significantly, it raises again the question of the guest's motives. By playfully suggesting that the guest can be bribed to accept the invitation, Jonson credits him with more honorable intentions. The line is funny precisely because taking it seriously would undermine both the proposed entertainment and the poem's mood. If the guest could be bribed—if the delicacies Jonson inventories were in fact important to his friend—then the character of their relationship would be wholly different from what the poem suggests. Paradoxically, Jonson's lavish catalogue of culinary attractions is, if he has correctly assessed his friend's mettle, in the strict sense superfluous—except insofar as it illustrates the speaker's intended generosity and desire to please. His admission that the menu is at least partly fictitious is, therefore, both a testament to his friend's character and a means of subtly testing it.

"Inviting a Friend" celebrates a relationship free from motives of selfish exploitation, yet a persistent awareness of the possibility of such motives informs the celebration, lending it internal tension as well as power and appeal. The "entertaynment" Jonson proposes is defined not only in opposition to the external threats referred to at the poem's conclusion, but also by contrast with a potential for internal instability. The spies Jonson mentions—and he mentions specific names—make the external threat seem plausible and authentic. Much more than Martial's poems, "Inviting a Friend" conveys a sense of the supper as a refuge from a world of power games and political intrigue.[26] Yet the spies only objectify, only externalize, a danger already inherent in the supper itself. The spies are, after all, men who operate with hidden agendas, with secret motives. They enter into relationships only to exploit others; they corrode social relations by fomenting profound distrust and self-consciousness. They monitor the words and behavior of others as carefully as they conceal and control their own. In short, they carry to extremes the kind of calculating, tactical behavior the courtly system of Jonson's day encouraged. Thus the poem suggests that while the supper offers relief from such behavior, it provides a possible forum for it. The mere absence of spies cannot guarantee absolute freedom from mistrust and wariness.

The occasion Jonson celebrates is one in which host and guests may ideally "speake [their] minds" (23)—one in which they not only need not fear the repercussions their words might have with outside agents, but also one in which language is used for real communication and communion, in which the need for constant posturing, pretense, and performance is eliminated. To speak one's mind implies a harmony between thought and word, an absence of self-censorship and intellectual inhibition, that must have been rare in a society in which being on guard was often an inescapable necessity. Jonson creates an appealing vision of a supper at which the mind is nourished as well as the body, of a feast that satisfies flesh and intellect, of friends sharing ideas as well as food as they commune freely with one another and with the disembodied minds of the classical past. The poem communicates and exemplifies a strong sense of art firmly rooted in real social relations, and it presents a striking blend of lofty ideals and concrete (but imagined) quotidian detail. Praising sack and good-naturedly mocking the legend-ary "*Thespian* spring" (33), Jonson presents a relaxed and appealing image of himself as poet, as a man speaking to men. Inevitably, however, the very absence of calculation and lack of self-consciousness that the poem seems to exhibit work to the poet's micropolitical advantage.

"Inviting a Friend to Supper" exalts a world—small, protected, and self-enclosed—in which the gap between intention and expression has been abolished, and in which the freedom to be oneself encourages rather than constrains the freedom of others. Jonson is careful to dis-tinguish this freedom of self-expression from self-indulgence, just as he later implicitly distinguishes "libertie" from license: he will not, he professes, use the dinner as an occasion to promote himself as a poet, or even as a reader of poems. His announcement that "[his] man" will read to the guests from the Roman authors not only asserts the relative dignity of his social position—nicely balancing earlier references to his financial limitations—but also de-emphasizes Jonson himself as a per-former at the supper (20). To announce that he himself would read would make the dinner seem simply an occasion for pompous self-display.[27] In one of the more intriguing passages of the poem, Jonson indicates, while mocking, how byzantine the expressions of this need for self-aggrandizement could become. After disavowing any intention to read his own poetry, he continues: "To this, if ought appeare, which I not know of, / That will the pastrie, not my paper, show of" (25–26). The lines seem to suggest an elaborate ruse. Ian Donaldson's helpful gloss illuminates part of the statement's meaning. "[T]he cook may produce a pastry surprise," his note reads, "but Jonson will not produce a surprise reading."[28] What needs further clarifying, however, is the element of pretense to which the lines allude. Jonson imagines a situation in which a host not only surprises his guests with the unexpected circula-tion of his verse, but in which he pretends to be surprised himself. The lines suggest a situation in which the host goes to elaborate lengths in order not to appear to promote himself, that being his intention all the while.

Whatever his conscious intentions concerning the present poem, the fact remains that by forswearing any such self-promotional designs, Jonson promotes a very attractive image. He has no need to perform openly at the supper, since his poetic invitation—and the entire supper as well—are themselves consummate performances. Through the poem he implicitly offers his own behavior as an ideal for his guests to emulate; as he repudiates self-aggrandizement, so, ideally, should they. In one sense a modest invitation, the poem is, in another, a fully developed social contract, its terms set out—and their fulfillment ex-emplified—by the poet himself. Despite its celebration of an evening free from the need for self-promotion; despite its apparent embodiment of the spirit of such an occasion; although the epigram itself seems an instance of the ideal it exalts, an example of the poet freely "speaking his mind"—in spite of all this, the poem can never really achieve or participate in the innocence it extols. Inevitably it is more self-conscious, artful, and fashioned than the supper it proposes. Although Jonson disavows any intention of using the supper as a springboard to promote himself, his poetic evocation of it inescapably does just that. Indeed, since the poem so obviously invites comparison with earlier works by Martial, part of its effect must be to draw attention to Jonson's own skill and accomplishment. This effect would be all the more obvious if the poem were simply a literary exercise, and not a real invitation to a real supper after all. If one is willing to assume, however, that both invitation and supper were authentic, then the poem illustrates how inextricably self-promotion entered even into a situation ostensibly defined by its absence.

"Inviting a Friend" celebrates a world from which the two sources of threat facing any patronage poet—the competitive egoism of others and anxiety about superior authority—are supposedly eliminated. Yet a pervasive awareness of both threats colors the whole poem. The first threat is confronted in the beginning with the lines on "faire acceptance." The second is alluded to at the end, with the reference to spies. No spies, the poem states, will be present, yet neither will they be necessary. The poem not only paints an attractive portrait of Jonson as a friend but depicts him and his companions as politically trustworthy and socially reliable. Their cups will make no "guiltie men" (37), because the friends will be guilty of no embarrassing or excessive behavior, and because not even drink can compromise their fundamental innocence. Yet to think of the poem simply as constructing (or embodying) an uncomplicated and harmonious ideal of social relations is to fail to give adequate emphasis to tensions within the work, to the awareness the poem betrays of the tenuousness and instability of such harmony. It is also to fail to appreciate how the poem functions not only to promote that harmony but as a weapon in the poet's personal struggle. In "Inviting a Friend to Supper," friendship offers a satisfying but only a temporary refuge from social competition; the last word—"to night"—emphasizes the respite's fleeting fragility. But the poem that celebrates the supper itself becomes another means of competing. The social ideal Jonson imagines in such works is complicated because his presentation of the ideal must speak to the social reality of his time. Beneath the carefully-poised balance that the poem exalts—the balance between the interests of guests and host, between self-assertion and deference, between mundane facts and lofty ideals, between freedom and restraint—runs an unsettling but inexorable sense of tension and threat.

Thus, even such a poem as "Inviting a Friend to Supper" is on one level an exercise in power. Both the poem and the supper it celebrates are designed to enhance the poet's reputation and public "esteeme." Both, for all their seeming naturalness and spontaneity, actually are carefully managed, carefully calculated, with Jonson skillfully attempting to shape and control reactions to both. His modesty about the supper anticipates and defuses criticism, putting the meal in a context that confirms its value to anyone who might doubt it. The same modest tone also protects the poem from unfriendly attack. Jonson's comic catalogue of lavish food has the serious effect of reminding us of real, genuinely lavish banquets of the sort that were increasingly common in the Jacobean period. Such banquets were intended precisely to advertise the power of those who sponsored them; their purpose was not so much fellowship as self-assertion. Unable to compete on these terms, Jonson uses his poem to define new terms that, although they seem to reject competition, actually strengthen his competitive stance. As in his great poem "To Penshurst," his celebration of an ideal situation free from self-promotional designs and tensions makes his work exceptionally effective as self-promotion. The epigram's disinterest in and disdain for power makes it a more powerful work—more appealing to allies and patrons, more threatening to antagonists and competitors.

"Inviting a Friend to Supper" is typical of Jonson's numerous poems to or about friends: few of them can be separated completely from the circumstances and challenges he faced as a poet of patronage. However sincere his feelings for particular individuals, his public expression of them—in poems circulated among an audience that included his superiors and rivals—must have been informed by an intense self-consciousness. Few of the friendship poems are simply private, yet neither are they didactically impersonal. Nearly all are affected by Jonson's need to fashion an attractive (and defensible) self-image.

Partly because of this concern with self-presentation, Jonson's poems on friendship are inevitably reflexive, sometimes obviously so (as in the famous tribute to Shakespeare), sometimes more subtly (as in the Cary-Morison ode). Sometimes his concern with patronage is explicit (as in his poem on Donne's satires, written to the Countess of Bedford); more often it is merely implied. Sometimes he uses poems to commend friends or their works (as in his epistle to John Selden); always he betrays immense self-consciousness about the risks and rewards such praise entails. Indeed, his poems on friendship are often shot through with self-awareness and with an acute sensitivity to micropolitical circumstances (as in his poem to Michael Drayton). Sometimes cleverly modest (as in one of the epigrams to Sir Henry Goodyere), at other times they test and even intimidate their recipients (as in the "Epistle" to an unnamed friend with which this chapter closes). In Jonson's poetry, tactical sophistication is inseparable from artistic subtlety, yet sophistication and subtlety often cannot disguise or entirely control the deeper tensions the poems reveal. These problems, rooted in the inherent limitations of his medium, involve ambiguities of interpretation and intent. How can the poet prove his sincerity with words? How can he surely discern the sincerity of others by the words they use? Such questions, basic to any social use of language, become especially acute in the poems on friendship, partly because they are the last place one might expect such questions to arise.

The difficulties of using language to convey sincerity and communicate friendly intentions are strikingly posed in a poem Jonson once wrote on behalf of his old nemesis, Michael Drayton (*U.V.* 30). He begins by disputing a charge that he is incapable of genuine amity. The poem's first lines leave little doubt that he is responding to authentic accusations, while the concluding couplet ("I call the world, that envies me, to see / If I can be a Friend, and Friend to thee") ironically suggests that the work was prompted as much by the need to defend himself as by any regard for the person and writings he commends. In fact, so effusive is his tribute that some critics have doubted its sincerity (see H&S 11:147–49). Although arguments can be made on either side, the interpretive difficulties the poem poses are precisely what make it so intriguing. Although it goes on for ninety-four lines and makes perfect grammatical and syntactical sense, its deeper meaning remains finally impenetrable. This indeterminacy is less the result of time having passed than of the impasse inherent in the interpretation of all human language and behavior. Even Jonson's contemporaries interpreted his behavior differently than he did; his poem, apparently intended to correct mistaken impressions of his motives, has only fueled the uncertainty.

The poem's stunning opening has not received the attention it deserves: Jonson admits to having been accused of incapacity for genuine friendship with *anyone.*[29] This was hardly the first time he was charged with essential selfishness, but for precisely that reason the poem raises a problem crucial to his career and central to his poems to friends and patrons: how could he *demonstrate* his sincerity? How could he prove through language the reality of friendly motives? The poem to Drayton confronts this issue by implying that his critics view friendship superficially; they demand visual evidence before crediting a man's sincerity. Jonson argues, to the contrary, that true friendship is more weighty, its substance proved by its freedom from any need of substantive demonstration. To publicly flaunt friendship, he suggests, is unnecessary when true friendship truly exists. Yet, even as he mocks the belief that friendship must be displayed, he displays his for Drayton; even while satirizing concern for public reputation, he nonetheless betrays such concern. The poem is a concession (perhaps ironic and sarcastic) to the very pressures it disdains.

Some of the issues raised by the poem to Drayton reappear in the well-known eulogy to Shakespeare (*U.V.* 26). There Jonson denies that his praise intends to draw any "envy" on Shakespeare's name, although he acknowledges that sometimes "crafty Malice, might pretend this praise, / And thinke to ruine, where it seem'd to raise" (11–12). Although praising the dead might seem free of ambiguity, just for that reason it might be especially effective as self-promotion. Ironically, if Jonson's eulogy has discomforted some readers, it is less because he promotes himself than because he does so with insufficient subtlety. Clearly the Shakespeare Jonson values is the one his poem constructs, a writer who imperfectly approaches its author's own ideals of the true artist. The parenthetical phrases and afterthoughts inserted into the section extolling careful revision (58–64) reveal Jonson practicing the virtues his poem preaches, and in every sense his elegy is a highly wrought, self-conscious performance. His precisely calibrated praise, meant to reflect his careful judgment, also suggests the persistence of competitive feelings.[30] The opening lines suggest that Shakespeare had already achieved the kind of posthumous fame Jonson hoped for. The elegy enhances Shakespeare's renown but also qualifies and exploits it. In many ways, then, the work is deeply implicated in issues of power.

This may be true of the poems to Drayton and Shakespeare, men who were in some senses Jonson's rivals. But do power and self-promotion figure in the poems addressed to those more clearly and unambiguously his friends? As has already been suggested, inevitably the answer is "yes," less because of any special self-interest they exhibit than because any praise involves self-display. Jonson's poems take seriously the axiom that friends provide opportunities to communicate about oneself; his praise is inherently and often subtly reflexive. In the famous Cary-Morison ode, for instance, analogies between moral and poetic achievement form one of the poem's central motifs (*Und.* 70). The inevitable effect is to remind the reader of the poem he is reading and the poet who wrote it. But Jonson brings himself into the work, of course, in a far more spectacular and notorious manner. Morison, he declares,

> . . . leap'd the present age,
> Possest with holy rage,

To see that bright eternall Day:
Of which we *Priests*, and *Pöets* say
Such truths, as we expect for happy men,
And there he lives with memorie; and *Ben*

Jonson, who sung this of him, e're he went
Himselfe to rest,
Or taste a part of that full joy he meant
To have exprest,
In this bright *Asterisme* . . .

(79–89)

The almost comic audacity of this self-interjection—with Jonson leaping the gap between stanzas as Morison leapt the confines of time—is immediately tempered by the poet's reference to his own mortality. Indeed, the momentary indulgence of authorial pride renders Jonson's anticipation of his own death all the more poignant, just as his admission that his poem cannot fully express his joyful intentions nicely balances his lofty equation of poet and priest. Jonson's artistry makes his own intrusion seem something other than arrogant; not only inoffensive, it actually contributes to the work's larger meaning. Paradoxically, at the moment when he might seem most vulnerable to charges of indecorous self-promotion, he achieves some of the poem's most delicate (and personally attractive) effects.

Delicacy of a different kind—though with similar results—can be glimpsed in the ode's concluding stanza. There, praising once more the perfect friendship of Morison and Cary, Jonson observes that

. . . such a force the faire example had,
As they that saw
The good, and durst not practise it, were glad
That such a Law
Was left yet to Man-kind;
Where they might read, and find
Friendship, in deed, was written, not in words:
And with the heart, not pen,
Of two so early men,
Whose lines her rowles were, and records.
Who, e're the first downe bloomed on the chin,
Had sow'd these fruits, and got the harvest in.

(117–28)

In this passage all the earlier correspondences between good writing and good living find both their culmination and their apparent reversal. Jonson seems to assert, as Ian Donaldson has remarked,

the superiority of deeds to words, of hearts to pens. . . . a good poem
(Jonson implies) is of less value than a good life . . . Reversing a
familiar poetic commonplace, Jonson implies that it is the friendship
itself, not the poem commemorating the friendship, which will
achieve immortality.[31]

Yet while the passage *does* seem to undermine the importance Renaissance poets frequently claimed for their work, more obliquely it
ratifies that claim. By contrasting friendship "in deed" (123) with a
friendship of words, Jonson invites us to notice how his ode resolves
the conflict, expressing his own regard for Cary and Morison in an order
of words that is also very much a public deed, in a poem written with a
"pen" but also from the "heart" (124). More important, the poem implies its own crucial role in preserving "the faire example" of friendship
the two men set (117), even as it becomes itself a "faire example" of the
poet's value as a friend. Jonson speaks of Cary and Morison's friendship
in the past tense, subtly reminding his audience (especially Cary) that
with Morison's death, the *presence* of their friendship's example can
manifest itself only in Jonson's ode.

Claiming the superiority of deeds to words, the poem nonetheless
implies its own importance in preserving the deeds it celebrates. Praising Cary and Morison as men "Whose lines" were the "rowles . . . and
records" of friendship (126), it indirectly suggests their incapacity to
live up to the terms of such praise. Mortality ensures that their "faire
example" will someday no longer be "read"—except as it is preserved
in Jonson's ode (117; 122). At precisely the moment when he seems
most deferential, Jonson's tacit assertion of his poem's importance is
most striking. Just as he earlier tempered his self-assertiveness, so here
his modesty is more complicated than it first appears. This blending of
humility and self-assertion, although a recurrent feature of his poetry, is
particularly appropriate in a work addressed to a man much younger
than he, a man who was at once his friend, his "son," and his patron.

Jonson's ability to advertise himself in poems celebrating his friends
is widely evident. Thus a poem to Sir Henry Goodyere (*Ep.* 85) that
focuses on hawking compares the hawk's flight to the pursuit of truth
("She doth instruct men by her gallant flight / That they to knowledge so
should toure upright, / And never stoupe, but to strike ignorance" [5–
7]). Although at first Jonson presents himself as merely a witness to
Goodyere's sport, the rest of the poem tacitly magnifies his role: no mere
observer, he creates and imposes on events the significance he describes. His initial pose of attentive student subtly calls attention to his
role as teacher, as he draws out the didactic import of the behavior he
has "discerned" (11)—a word that finely epitomizes his ambiguous

role, since it suggests both passive recognition and analytical discrimination.

In another poem, to John Donne (*Ep.* 96), Jonson submits himself for analysis: "Who shall doubt, Donne, where I a *Poet* bee, / When I dare send my *Epigrammes* to thee?" (1–2). The first line seems boldly assertive, but then the next immediately qualifies this apparent pride. The poem clearly suggests a friend's value as ratifier of one's reputation, especially in a culture rooted in patronage. Not only Donne will know Jonson's quality, but also the unnamed others influenced by Donne's opinion and by Jonson's public willingness to submit himself to judgment. Such submission implies strength and exhibits self-confidence. The word "dare" suggests some slight anxiety but also countervailing courage; when Jonson concludes that "A man should seeke great glorie, and not broad" (12), he implies his own manfulness. His modest pride is inherently more attractive than either unvarnished arrogance or utter self-abnegation. According to one classical axiom, the best friends are those who least *need* friends, [32] and this attitude undoubtedly contributed to the tone of self-respect he adopts in so many of his works on friendship. Ironically, advertising power and self-sufficiency made one a more attractive ally; demonstrating strength would likely increase it, as long as it did not seem excessive or threatening. The poem to Donne carefully balances self-assertion and humility; in fact, the humility it displays is self-assertion of a different kind.[33]

In an even more famous poem, the epistle to John Selden (*Und.* 14), Jonson stands as judge over a friend's writing. His commendatory poems often demonstrate the very qualities they praise in others even as they advertise the poet's public status, either by attaching themselves to another's fame or by suggesting their author's own importance. However, the Selden epistle deals largely with the dangers of praise. As it emphasizes the risks of moral compromise posed by engaging in what Jonson splendidly calls "vitious Humanitie" (12), it also insinuates how obligatory praise can threaten one's power and damage one's reputation:

> I know to whom I write. Here, I am sure,
> Though I am short, I cannot be obscure:
> Lesse shall I for the Art or dressing care,
> Truth, and the Graces best, when naked are.
> Your booke, my *Selden*, I have read, and much
> Was trusted, that you thought my judgement such
> To aske it: though in most of workes it be
> A pennance, where a man may not be free,
> Rather than Office, when it doth or may
> Chance that the Friends affection proves Allay
> Unto the Censure. Yours all need doth flie

Of this so vitious Humanitie.
Then which there is not unto Studie'a more
Pernitious enemie; we see, before
A many'of bookes, even good judgements wound
Themselves through favouring what is there not found:
But I on yours farre otherwise shall doe,
Not flie the Crime, but the Suspition too:
Though I confesse (as every Muse hath err'd,
And mine not least) I have too oft preferr'd
Men past their termes, and prais'd some names too much,
But 'twas with purpose to have made them such.
Since, being deceiv'd, I turne a sharper eye
Upon my selfe, and aske to whom? and why?
And what I write? and vexe it many dayes
Before men get a verse: much lesse a Praise;
So that my Reader is assur'd, I now
Meane what I speake: and still will keep that Vow.

(1–28)

Although the poem opens by focusing on the relation between Jonson and Selden, although indeed it idealizes that relation and marks it as special, the epistle is addressed not only to Selden but of course also to readers of his *Titles of Honour*, which it prefaces. Jonson's emphasis on his special relation with Selden helps lend the poem its public interest and contributes to his public self-display. In a narrow sense Jonson does know to whom he writes, but in a broader sense he cannot know; he cannot be sure who may read the poem when it appears in Selden's book. He must present an attractive aspect to the world not only for his own sake but for his friend's; in this work, the poet's self-advertisement serves both Jonson's interests and Selden's. His self-concern also implies concern for his friend.

Jonson's opening claim that he knows to whom he writes gives the poem a tone of attractive self-assurance that also functions tactically. It helps manage the insecurity of not knowing who besides Selden will read the poem. The claimed indifference to the larger audience is a means of dealing with and appealing to them, and although Jonson asserts his unconcern for artistic contrivance (3–4), clearly the epistle is quite self-conscious in its craftsmanship. Even the abrupt opening lines subvert their apparent plainness by toying with the sounds of "sure," "short," and "obscure," while the clever formulation about the naked "Truth, and . . . Graces" (4) clothes them in the attractive dressing of Jonson's wit. Similarly, the claim that "much / Was trusted" when Selden chose to submit his book to Jonson's judgment (5–6) is equivocal in its effect. At first the words might suggest that Selden took a risk in submitting the book to Jonson, but then it becomes clear that his doing so reflected his trust in the poet's good sense and perceptiveness. The compliment to Selden is reflexive, and here and throughout the poem, Jonson seems quite conscious of the epistle as a public performance, one that will affect both his friend's reputation and his own. He feels compelled to explain his motives not only to Selden but to their common audience.

Although Jonson adopts the role of disinterested critic of his friend's work, this very role promotes his interests. Thus he seems particularly anxious to claim it and to distance himself from any charge of praising undeservedly. He realized that "good judgements wound / Themselves" not only in the lofty, abstract sense of falling short of their own principles and standards (15–16) but in a very practical social sense as well. Being asked to perform as public judge of another's work paid tribute to one's social power, but it also exposed that power, opening it to public judgment. Jonson's conspicuous confession that he has occasionally "prais'd some names too much" (21) is complex in its implications. He uses the confession to enhance his standing: what might have diminished his reputation actually helps rescue it. What might have humbled him gives his present voice an added worth. While the confession seems to imply his security and his willingness to expose past foibles to public view, in another sense it implies his insecurity, his need to defend himself, to guide his readers' response, to correct or preempt possible misinterpretations of his motives. Jonson is not content to let the confession speak for itself, to admit past mistakes and then simply promise not to repeat them. Instead he feels the need to reinterpret his past actions. The "sharper eye" he now turns on himself (23) becomes a way of appropriating, preempting, and deflecting scrutiny by others. He will beat potential critics at their own game, examining himself more intently than they could ever hope to do. His claim that he now "vexe[s] it many dayes / Before men get a verse: much lesse a Praise" (25–26) implies not only a concern with the morality and craft of his writing but an extreme social self-consciousness. Such anxious vexation makes for a striking contrast with the tone of firm self-assurance with which the poem began.

By this point in the poem, however, self-assurance is of less concern to Jonson than assuring the reader of his true intentions. Here as so often elsewhere he runs up against a problem at the heart of his poetic enterprise, perhaps at the heart of all language: the problem of how (or whether) words can ever be used to certify motives unambiguously. The most Jonson can do in the Selden epistle is to beg the question by assuring his readers that they *are* assured ("So that my Reader is assur'd, I now / Meane what I speake" [27–28]). In the strict sense, this is true: Jonson does perform the act of assurance. But in a deeper and more important sense this act is fundamentally ambiguous: we can never be completely assured, even by another's open assurances about his motives. Jonson attempts to dissolve the distinction between how words can be interpreted by others and how the speaker intends or wants them to be interpreted. In line 28, he tries (almost physically, on the page) to abolish the distance between meaning and speaking. Philosophically the attempt may be doomed to failure, but as a social *tactic* it is not a waste of time. By telling the reader that he *is* assured, Jonson pressures him to accept that assurance; he seeks to intimidate the reader, challenging him to take his words at face value. To suspect his motives after he has so candidly confessed past sins and laid his cards so openly on the table would risk a loss of face on the reader's part. To challenge the speaker's veracity after such elaborate assurances would be bad manners if nothing else. In the Selden poem as in Jonson's writing generally, the philosophical slipperiness of language does not prevent it from being used tactically, as an instrument of social power.

Although the rest of the poem seems to focus less on Jonson than on Selden, the "Object" of his praise (29), still that praise inevitably reflects back on himself. The stability attributed to Selden in line 31 looks back to similar phrasing about Jonson in line 28. The praise of Selden for observing "men [and] manners" (33), for his "skill" (35), for his desire to teach (37), and for numerous other qualities—all this helps illuminate Jonson's own general character and the specific characteristics of this poem. When we are told that Selden has "vext" fables (39), we cannot help but think of Jonson's earlier vexed determination to tell the truth (25). When Jonson exclaims, after a long and powerful catalogue of Selden's virtues, that "the matter of your praise / Flowes in upon me, and I cannot raise / A banke against it" (61–63), the poet may at first seem simply an empty reservoir into which ideas are poured. On reflection, however, the phrasing magnifies the fecundity of his own imagination. The catalogue, after all, did not simply happen; Jonson invented it. Despite his self-consciously modest metaphor, the poet is not a barren beach on which ideas wash up like driftwood; he is a conscious, creative discoverer who forms and orders the elements of praise.

The closing section of the epistle displays Jonson's poetic (and therefore his social) ingenuity at its best. When he congratulates Selden for "offering this thy worke to no great Name, / That would, perhaps, have prais'd, and thank'd the same, / But nought beyond" (69–71), we can be forgiven for assuming that he intends to contrast such a reaction with his own. But no sooner does the poem invite this interpretation than it ostensibly averts it: the fit audience to whom Selden has presented the book is not (only) Jonson but "Thy learned Chamber-fellow," Edward Hayward, who "knowes to doe / It true respects" (72–73). Of course, Jonson's generous and attractive praise of Hayward reflects back on himself. His friendly tribute to his two friends paradoxically uses language associated with the counting-house to underscore the immaterial spirit of their fellowship (79–81; 84). The famously abrupt closing line ("You both are modest. So am I. Farewell" [86]) brings the poem full circle by recalling its abrupt beginning. But it also functions tactically, as a nicely nuanced joke. By asserting his modesty in this half-mocking way, Jonson preempts and defuses any criticism of the poem for lacking modesty, for implicit self-praise. By making the praise of himself so explicit at the very end (but in a funny way that denies such self-praise any seriousness), Jonson deflects attention from the more subtle and ingenious means by which the poem serves to praise him earlier and throughout. Ending the poem with a joke helps exemplify the fellowship and good feeling the three men share. The clever denial of self-praise contributes to the poem's effectiveness as self-promotion.

Although the Selden epistle suggests some of the ways in which determining or communicating the truth of friendship can be ambiguous and uncertain undertakings, it also suggests that the pragmatic political dimensions of friendship are less open to doubt. In poem after poem, Jonson addresses the subject in ways that subtly but clearly advance his own interests and reputation. His epigram "To Lucy, Countesse of Bedford, With Mr. Donne's Satyres" (*Ep.* 94) praises the Countess's freedom from vice in a way that draws attention to Jonson's freedom from envy or jealousy of Donne. The poem thus exemplifies the "rare" friendship it commends in the Countess (6). Similarly, an epistle addressed to an unnamed friend (*Und.* 37) offers thanks for a gift in a way that displays the deliberateness and value of Jonson's own gratitude:

> Sir, I am thankfull, first, to heaven, for you;
> Next to your selfe, for making your love true:
> Then to your love, and gift. And all's but due.
>
> (1–3)

Seeming to devalue the gift, Jonson shows his ability to value it properly. Similarly, although he says that his thanks are "but due" and thereby minimizes their unique importance, the preceding lines demonstrate his skill at making what is merely "due" seem something special. Only in the second stanza do we learn that the gift was a book—a present at once material and spiritual, uniting matter and mind in a fashion appropriate to the combined realism and idealism of the friendship. Jonson speaks of their relationship as having been born from "letters, that mixe spirits" (12)—a phrase that calls attention to one function of his own poem.

Throughout, the epistle displays a profound self-consciousness and alertness to the minute implications of social acts. Its second half, for instance, raises the serious question of how frankly true friends can afford to deal with one another. Accused of having been "too severe, / Rigid, and harsh" (16–17), Jonson seizes the rhetoric of moderation to characterize his ideals. He rejects both severe reproval and complete indulgence. In some ways the most natural of relations, friendship must also be "practiz'd" (26), in several senses of that word. Balancing disagreement and praise, contentiousness and modesty, the epistle exemplifies the moderation it exalts. As an act of both self-assertion and self-defense, it exhibits considerable tactical sophistication.

Jonson's tactical sureness in addressing friends is nowhere better illustrated than in *Und.* 17, a poem that confronts two of the chief sources of his insecurity: possible betrayal by superiors and uncertainty about the real motives of the friends who provided one of the limited alternatives to total dependence on "the great." In this "Epistle to a Friend," Jonson quickly makes his failure to pay a debt seem less important than his friend's response. Although he fully exploits his own sense of victimization, at no point does he ever really seem on the defensive:

> They are not, Sir, worst Owers, that doe pay
>   Debts when they can: good men may breake their day,
> And yet the noble Nature never grudge;
>   'Tis then a crime, when the Usurer is Judge.
> And he is not in friendship. Nothing there
>   Is done for gaine: If't be, 'tis not sincere.
> Nor should I at this time protested be,
>   But that some greater names have broke with me,
> And their words too; where I but breake my Band.
>   I adde that (but) because I understand
> That as the lesser breach: for he that takes
>   Simply my Band, his trust in me forsakes,
> And lookes unto the forfeit. If you be
>   Now so much friend, as you would trust in me,
> Venter a longer time, and willingly:
>   All is not barren land, doth fallow lie.
> Some grounds are made the richer, for the Rest;
>   And I will bring a Crop, if not the best.

(1–18)

The epistle becomes less an apology than a challenge to the friend's character. It gives him the chance to manifest his "noble Nature" (3) by consenting to the delay in repayment. Next to the betrayal Jonson has suffered, the friend's inconvenience is minor. To insist on repayment would be an even more callous breach of trust than that committed by the "greater names" (8). Thus while the epistle works to embarrass the superiors (carefully unspecified in the text but undoubtedly known to the poem's first circle of readers), another potential effect is to embarrass Jonson's friend. An expression of confidence in his character, the poem is also a subtle exercise in intimidation. The friend is offered the choice of enacting either an exemplary contrast to the bad behavior of Jonson's patrons or an even worse reflection of it. Much more than money is put at issue: the poem raises problems crucial to Jonson's social experience. The potential instability of support from patrons is magnified because the trust betrayed was a sworn commitment. Even (or perhaps especially) when a superior's pledge was most formal and contractual, then, it might be disavowed. Yet the poem confronts not only the reality of abandonment by patrons but the threat of abandonment by friends. It raises the specter of the poet as an isolated self—alienated, forsaken, cut off from all hope of dependable support.

This mysterious and little-remarked epistle—addressed to a friend whose name we do not know, critical of "greater names" its author dared not specify in print—emphasizes again the complex impact power exerted on Jonson's poems to friends and, implicitly, on his friendships in general. Although it claims that "in friendship . . . [n]othing . . . / Is done for gaine: If't be, 'tis not sincere" (5–6), the epistle suggests that the issue of friendship is necessarily less simple. However sincere Jonson's motives, no poem could be relied on to give them certain and unambiguous expression. Yet the epistle obviously serves his practical interests in several respects; even the passage on sincerity contributes to its tactical effectiveness.

All Jonson's poems are implicated in issues of power and self-promotion. But perhaps this is especially true of the poems on friendship, in part because such issues initially seem so distant from them. Appealing partly because they seem to promise an escape from competition and politics, they make the ideal of true friendship—otherwise so often elusive—seem both possible and real. They suggest certainty and assurance in a world of instability and flux. They imply that language is an instrument of communion, not a manipulative tool or an isolating prison. They exalt relationships that are permanent, virtuous, beneficent, and benign. They seem to resolve tensions between self-interest and the interests of others. Inevitably, though, they are tinged by the same concerns and uncertainties, the same ambitions, ambiguities, and tensions they reject—a fact that contributes to their poignancy, complexity, and continuing fascination.

7
The Masques and Entertainments

Even in his own day, the audience for Jonson's masques was relatively small and select, and the intervening centuries have done little to change that. Ironically, however, Jonson's present audience may be better-positioned to appreciate the subtleties of his masques than were most of his own contemporaries. They, of course, could see the masques performed in all their splendor, whereas modern readers can only imagine the performances by consulting the printed texts and a few surviving sketches. But, thanks to recent scholarship, Jonson's modern audience may have a clearer insight into the masques' aims and aesthetic designs than did most of the original spectators, who often misunderstood what he was up to. Stephen Orgel has shown that the masques were sometimes disliked precisely for challenging their audiences in unexpected ways, presenting them with artistic innovations they were unprepared to grasp. Orgel's work, like the scholarship it synthesized and inspired, has helped make Jonson's modern readers truer "understanders" of his masques. This increased understanding has promoted increased admiration for the artistic skills they display.[1]

Emphasizing the masques' artistic and philosophical seriousness helps refute any view of them as merely elaborate flattery. Jonson's effusive celebrations of James and Charles seem more palatable when seen in the light of generic conventions, Renaissance mores, and the ethical ideal of instruction through praise. Often his own elaborate annotations suggest how he wished the masques to be regarded: as works of artful beauty but also of deliberate and careful thought. Designed to express the highest ideals of Renaissance moral philosophy, they exemplify the Horatian dictum of teaching by pleasing. But they are also political works, often caught up in the specifics of Jacobean and Caroline domestic policies or foreign diplomacy. The recent writings of Leah S. Marcus, in particular, have shown how fully they responded to their "present occasions" and to contemporary political concerns.[2] And, as Orgel himself has so well demonstrated, the masques served more generally to display and enhance the power of the English monarch and his court. Their purpose was never simply aesthetic nor recreative; they were designed to celebrate (and thus to help create) the glory and magnificence of British power.

My concern, however, is less with these larger issues than with how the masques and entertainments also helped enhance, display, and create the power of the poet. Aside from advertising Britain's might, they also offered the poet a splendid opportunity to promote his own interests. Surprisingly little has been written about this aspect of the masques, perhaps because too much attention to the self-interests they embody might threaten our sense of their artistic worth and intellectual seriousness. It might seem to raise again the specter of flattery and make the masques seem less lofty or transcendent. Rather than addressing timeless moral concerns or achieving an ageless beauty, they might seem instead mere vehicles for the poet's personal ambitions. Rather than confronting the important political questions of a significant historical era, they might appear instead to be rooted in their author's limited desires and designs. An approach that emphasized the masques as vehicles for Jonson's self-advertisement might seem crudely reductive; it might seem to cheapen their aesthetic value by highlighting how their every aspect could contribute to the poet's individual power.

Yet there is no denying the role they played in helping to create and cement Jonson's prestige and prominence. The masques provided him an unprecedented opportunity to display himself and his talents before an audience of "courtly Pearles," as he called them in his very first aristocratic entertainment (H&S 7:129). Although he sometimes mocked the pompous self-display the masques encouraged—once referring to the "short braverie" of masquing (H&S 8:96) and at another time sneering at the "animated *Porc'lane* of the Court" (H&S 8:219)—even these attacks were part of his self-presentation. They suggested implicitly (as he indicated more explicitly elsewhere) that he took the masques far more seriously than did many of their participants. His occasional attacks on masquing suggest not his contempt for the form but precisely his sense of its importance and his determination to fashion masques according to his own purposes and values. Writing them was not only far more lucrative than writing for the stage and thus an important source of his income, it was also a far more effective way of displaying himself and his abilities before the most influential audience possible.

Ingeniously and variously, Jonson exploited the numerous opportunities the masques provided to enhance his personal power. By peopling his works with attractive stand-ins for himself; by also presenting unattractive foils; by celebrating or more subtly insinuating his own talents; by using the masques to allude to his other works, to champion his aesthetic ideals, to reflect on the artfulness of his writing or on his own *sprezzatura;* by displaying his range, inventiveness, and generic creativity; by exploiting courtly interest in love as a subject and by sometimes cleverly playing with a humorously familiar tone; by carefully shaping his texts and by using marginal notes to comment on them and on his own circumstances and concerns; by situating himself and his art in a long tradition of previous works and authors; by engaging in limited courtly satire; by exploiting the masques to defend himself, to attack his rivals, to vindicate the form, to guide interpretation, to distance himself from flattery, and to advance specific political positions; by using the masques to teach, maneuver, and solicit his patrons and to play on their insecurities—in these and other ways, his masque writing had implications not only for his own power and authority but also for the intricate artfulness of the works themselves. Reading them with an eye toward their micropolitical dimensions is neither reductive nor demeaning: instead, it offers one more way of coming to grips with their full and intriguing complexity.

Preparing the masques allowed Jonson to enjoy far more intimate and continuous contact with leading aristocrats than he could hope for at the theater; working on them gave him an invaluable entree into the complicated and overlapping networks of aristocratic patronage. Thanks to the decorum demanded at court, a masque performance was in some respects less risky than the theatrical staging of a play: although his dramas were always subject (and were often subjected) to open ridicule and derision in the playhouse, the only recorded disruption of any of his masques was committed by James himself (H&S 10:583). Yet although, for this reason, masque writing involved less anxiety than writing for the stage, there were other, far greater risks: Jonson hazarded his reputation with the most important of all patrons each time his works were performed. As long as he satisfied the King, he was likely to win the increasing support and encouragement of other aristocrats; but loss of royal favor could entirely ruin his appeal to the socially powerful. Although criticism of the masques could not occur openly during performance, sniping at them afterward was not uncommon. One of the most remarkable negative comments was provoked in 1618 by the unsuccessful *Pleasure Reconciled to Virtue;* of it, Nathaniel Brent wrote that "The maske on 12th night was not coṁended of any   yᵉ poet is growen so dul yᵗ his devise is not worthy yᵉ relating, much lesse yᵉ copiing out. divers thinke fit he should retourne to his ould trade of bricke laying againe" (H&S 10:576). This hit at Jonson's background, coming after almost fifteen years of prominent and devoted service as a masque writer and after almost two decades of effort to establish his credentials as a serious and respectable poet, suggests how fragile his status could be, how astonishingly persistent were the class biases by which his value was partly measured. The comment startlingly emphasizes that the performance of his masques reflected not only on them but on himself, that more was at risk in a masque's failure than Jonson's artistic reputation. Without question, the masques gave Jonson both a far wider audience than he could achieve by circulating a single poem, and an audience far more influential than he could achieve by the single performance of a play. But for precisely these reasons, the risks were at least as great as the opportunities.

Throughout the masques and entertainments, Jonson indicates his clear awareness of the personal stakes involved in their success or failure and betrays an acute awareness of the influence of his aristocratic audience. In the notes to *Hymenaei*, he carefully disclaims any intention of flattering the noble participants (H&S 7:229). In the 1603 *Entertainment at Althrope*, his first such work, one character directly addresses the assembled "Queene, Prince, Duke, Earles, / [and] Countesses" (H&S 7:129). This was heady company for a former bricklayer, and Jonson undoubtedly realized the social opportunity the work presented. Introducing a morris dance by some country clowns, one character remarks that they have "come to see, and to be seene" (H&S 7:129)—words that apply equally well to Jonson and the assembled aristocrats. The entertainment is partly *about* self-presentation but also an exercise in it, and the same is true of all the masques. Griffith, a comic Welshman in the 1618 masque *For the Honour of Wales*, remarks that it " 'Is not a small matter to offer your selfe into the presence of a king, and aull his Court" (H&S 7:497); Jonson surely felt the personal implication of these words. It was precisely the ill success of *Pleasure Reconciled to Virtue* less than two months earlier that prompted him to write the latter work. The Welsh masque was thus a response to Jonson's need to prove appealing, to reclaim some of the credit he had lost with the relative failure of his earlier effort. The danger of appearing as a laughing-stock before the King and court is one that worried not only Griffith but Jonson, too. Part of the work's cleverness is that those characters who worry about discrediting themselves do so in such a comically appealing way that they bring credit to their creator, even as they highlight the distinctions between themselves and him.

Indeed, the Welsh masque provides particularly clear and effective examples of the tactics Jonson used to promote and defend his own interests through his courtly entertainments. Thus Jenkins's comic obeisance and exaggerated praise of King James (H&S 7:498) emphasizes Jonson's more dignified praise and distances him from the buffoonery of excessive deference. Jonson realized that superiors might scorn an impotent dependent (see, for instance, H&S 4:263), and the tone of sturdy self-reliance he so often adopts testifies less to his true autonomy than to his need to seem attractive. In fact, the Welsh masque's tone of good-natured, good-humored familiarity contributed to its success: one contemporary singled out for praise its "pleasant merry speeches made to the kinge, by such as Counterfeyted wels men, & wisht the kinges Comynge into Wales" (H&S 10:577). In this work, Jonson has it both ways: his characters' comic indiscretions reflect equally on his creativity and on his own dignity and decorum.

But Jonson uses humor in other ways as well. When Jenkins complains that the "Prince of *Wales*, the first time he ever play Dance, [was] pit up in a Mountaine (got knowes where) by a palterly *Poet*" (H&S 7:498), Jonson alludes to earlier criticism directed at *Pleasure Reconciled to Virtue*. That work, intended to display Prince Charles, was attacked by some for not displaying him to best advantage. Jenkins's comment simultaneously allows Jonson to answer his critics, to caricature them, and to concede implicitly yet attractively some justice to their objections. The allusion's humorous tone enhances his power without quite erasing the threat; the reference to the "palterly poet" is appealingly self-deprecatory but also calls attention to the real talent the masque exhibits. Similarly ambiguous—and similarly effective—is Jenkins's self-satisfied question to the King concerning whether he has ever heard better singing than the comic doggerel just concluded (H&S 7:507). The question can be variously answered. On the one hand, since the songs are comically bad, the answer might be "yes," and Jonson's own lovely songs in earlier masques would provide an effective contrast. Yet since the Welshmen's songs are *meant* to be poor, the answer might just as well be "no," and Jonson would, through the question, call attention to his facility in fashioning them. Moments like this—and they are numerous—allow him to advertise his art without being too obvious. Similarly adroit is the way he alludes in this masque to two of his earlier successes. The whole manner of the Welsh masque—with its heavy dependence on farce and comic dialects— recalls *The Irish Masque* of four years earlier, which was apparently quite popular (see H&S 10:541). And the reference in the Welsh masque to awaking Merlin (H&S 7:509) may have been meant to recall the wonderful moment in *The Speeches at Prince Henry's Barriers* when the old magician is reborn (H&S 7:327). Such an allusion would be especially appropriate, since it would remind Jonson's audience of his successful previous efforts in promoting and celebrating Prince Henry, the earlier heir. Both allusions recollect and quietly emphasize his loyal and long-standing service, and thus help defend him against his critics.

Although masques and entertainments seem to exist almost entirely to celebrate others, Jonson repeatedly uses them to promote himself.

Again and again he uses them to draw attention to his as well as their own accomplishments, and the variety of tactics he employs is considerable. In the *Entertainment at Highgate*, performed in 1604, King James and Queen Anne are offered an apology for the "vaine / And empty passe-times" they have witnessed so far and are promised better things in the future (H&S 7:139–41). But the apology, and the lovely description of the imagined future celebrations, are so beautifully crafted that they paradoxically accentuate and contribute to the success of the work they disparage. At the end, when Pan bids the audience to "Thanke Hermes, my father, if ought have delighted" (H&S 7:144), he implicitly emphasizes Jonson's own role as creator, both of the entertainment and of the appealing Pan himself. In the 1603 *Entertainment at Althrope*, commissioned by Robert Spencer to amuse Queen Anne during her visit to his estate, one character explicitly raises the possibility that Spencer might be considered "a sorry entertayner" (H&S 7:126)—a comment that helps call attention precisely to the care and success of Jonson's work and thus reflects well both on him and on his patron. Jonson uses the work to enhance Spencer's standing with the Queen and his own standing with her, with Spencer, and with Spencer's peers and competitors. Thus Jonson serves Spencer's interests but also advertises his skills and availability to all the others present.

Indeed, Anne's witnessing of this work may later have led her to commission Jonson's first masques for the court. In those works, too, he demonstrated his talents for subtle self-promotion. His printed notes to the *Masque of Blacknesse*, for instance, emphasize that the Queen herself wanted to appear with her ladies in black-face, and that Jonson met this demand by making the characters "*Black-mores*" (H&S 7:169). The note advertises his powers of invention and close cooperation with the Queen while also defending him against murmuring that such disguises were undignified (see H&S 10:449). Later, in the masque itself, the character Niger mocks "Poore brain-sicke men, stil'd *Poets*" who have "sung / The painted *Beauties* [of] other *Empires*" (H&S 7:174)—lines that reflect well on Jonson's present undertaking, emphasizing his poetic powers and sense of humor. In the subsequent *Maske of Queenes* (1609), the self-celebration becomes even more explicit (H&S 7:302–03), and, generally, the further his career proceeded, the more explicit his own role and contribution became. In *Love Restored* (1612), he jokes openly about poets not being paid (H&S 7:377); in *Newes from the New World* (1620), he alludes to himself and his recent trip to Scotland in a modest and self-mocking way that actually promotes his interests and calls attention to the masque's facility and success (H&S 7:518). Keenly aware of himself as a public figure, he alludes to criticism of his recent non-productivity precisely to direct attention to the present masque's achievement (H&S 7:518). (In fact, much of the impetus for his self-promotion was his felt need to defend and define himself in the face of competition and hostile criticism.) In *The Gypsies Metamorphos'd* (1621), "Good Ben" is mentioned for the first time by name (H&S 7:615), and in general the later masques use Jonson's fame itself to help cement and extend his reputation. The masques not only acknowledged his fame but were one of the best means of advancing and protecting it. His increasingly open self-allusions are only partly self-congratulatory; they also serve specific tactical purposes. While affirming his power, they imply his uncertainty and continuing need to compete.

Not all Jonson's techniques of self-promotion are so open; often the reader is merely pointed in the right direction. Thus *The Gypsies Metamorphos'd* opens with a speech about the difficulty of finding appropriate words of greeting—a tactic that in fact helps emphasize Jonson's eloquence here and throughout the work. Everything the masque's opening deals with, claims the prologue's speaker, can be reduced to the single word "*Wellcome*" (H&S 7:565). Yet the prologue expands on and explicates that word's significance at such length and with such power that we cannot help but notice the copious fecundity of Jonson's rhetoric. When the speaker claims that the host who should welcome the King is silent not out of rudeness but because he is unsure how to show his gratitude, we are implicitly invited (with the patron) to notice how well the masque solves this problem (H&S 7:565). Similarly, in the *King's Entertainment at Welbeck* (1633), the poet credits the "Welcome *of our great, and good* King" to "*the general voyce*," but since this assurance is in some respects merely an attractive pretense, it emphasizes the specialness of Jonson's role (H&S 7:792). The very title of *Pleasure Reconciled to Virtue* is full of comparable implication, since it refers not only to the masque's subject matter and action but also to a central purpose of the whole genre (as Jonson conceived it) and to the poet's own role as the active and creative *reconciler* of seemingly opposed values.

This is a role implied in any number of the masques. Their very structure is often built around a conflict between forces of enormous energy, appealing because of their liveliness but also disruptive and potentially destructive, and forces representing stable dignity and control.[3] The plots usually set these forces in opposition, and the masque structures usually emphasize the cleavage between them. But Jonson as poet resolves the conflict, since he creates and manipulates *both*. Both the energy and the decorum represent aspects of his own creativity and public character. He incorporates into the masques the very disorder they attack; they absorb its energy and vitality in ways that prevent them from being static or staid. Jonson *as poet* implicitly exemplifies the possibility of disciplining tremendous energy and channeling it into useful and serviceable directions. *Lovers Made Men* (1617) reconciles love and wisdom by celebrating love without condoning its excesses. The final three words—"love with wit" (H&S 7:460)—epitomize the harmony the masque both extols and embodies. Similarly, *Christmas His Masque* (1616) stretches the boundaries of the courtly genre by incorporating the energies and characteristics of city comedy (H&S 7:442–43).

In *Mercury Vindicated* (1616), Jonson himself, unlike the corrupt alchemists he satirizes, is implicitly depicted as an artist who cooperates with Mercury (knowledge); he overcomes in himself and through his works the opposition between art and nature on which the masque so often dwells (H&S 7:413). At the end, Nature commands the masquers to "shew" their "artes" (of dancing), suggesting that true art and nature are in harmony (H&S 7:415). In *Newes from the New World* (1620), the implied conflict is between ephemerality and permanence; Jonson lampoons contemporary newsmongers, who deal with the insubstantial and unimportant. Although similar charges might be (and often were) leveled against masquing, Jonson implies repeatedly that his masques deal with the essential and true. While contemporary "newes" reports are fundamentally amoral and pander to base curiosity, his masques are didactic and elevating. Yet Jonson makes his masque morally serious while also making it lively, engaging, and apparently spontaneous. It thus possesses many of the very qualities that gave "newes" items their appeal. But whereas "newes" chroniclers fill up books by the ream, thinking that bulk guarantees worth (H&S 7:514), Jonson boils essentials down into a small and finely shaped form. The Chronicler's claim that he loves "to give light to posteritie in the truth of things" (H&S 7:514) merely reveals his mundane interest in quotidian detail. Jonson, to the contrary, demonstrates a concern for higher and more essential truths, yet he does so engagingly, in a form that allows for the inclusion of such realistic elements as the pompous Chronicler himself. He makes the newsmongers' "newes" part of his own masque; although his and the Chronicler's roles are implicitly but insistently contrasted, he nonetheless preempts and exploits the Chronicler's more appealing aspects. He himself becomes a kind of Chronicler, yet he resolves the tension between that function and his higher calling. This emphasis on resolution is also evident in such a work as *The Irish Masque at Court* (1613–14), in which, after some comic Irishmen speak in farcical dialect and dance to *"rude musique,"* a *"civill gentleman of the nation"* steps forth to introduce (in dignified and stately English) an Irish bard to celebrate the King (H&S 7:403–05). The masque effectively juxtaposes comedy and dignity, and Jonson as author incorporates the prosy vitality of the fools, the measured urbanity of the gentleman, and the lyric deftness of the bard.

The bard's presence in the *Irish Masque* suggests still another means by which Jonson promotes his own interests through these works: often he includes figures who act as stand-ins, figures who reflect favorably on his own role and motives. In the *Entertainment at Highgate* (1604), Mercury performs this function, especially when he announces that his presence tempers the behavior of the boisterous Pan, which might otherwise "turne to be gall, and bitternesse" (H&S 7:142). Conventionally, both Mercury and Pan are associated with poetry, and Jonson employs them almost as two extremes on a scale that precisely calibrates and advertises his own aesthetic decorum. In *Hymenaei* (1606), Reason is the poet's spokesman; by having Reason detail the significance and symbolism of the costumes, Jonson insinuates the inability of such physical splendors to speak for themselves, to make their own meaning unambiguously clear (H&S 7:217–18). He thus demonstrates the importance of his own contribution to the work's collaborative success. In the *Haddington Masque* (1608), Hymen reports, in words that emphasize Jonson's present labors, that Vulcan is forging "Some strange, and curious peece, t[o]'adorne the night, / And give these graced *Nuptials* greater light" (H&S 7:257), and Pyrcamon's later praise of Vulcan as "Our *great artificer*" just as clearly reflects upon Jonson's own accomplishment (H&S 7:260). Merlin and the Knight Meliadus, in the *Speeches at Princes Henry's Barriers* (1610), implicitly match the pairing of Jonson and the young prince he celebrates, just as the work itself explicitly claims that "letters reare / The deeds of honor high, and make them live," that indeed "armes and arts sustaine each others right" (H&S 7:326). The powerful and intriguing moment when Merlin and Meliadus are magically summoned and suddenly appear (H&S 7:326–27) is a dynamic, enacted analogy to Jonson's favorite claim that kings and poets are equally rare. In *Oberon* (1611), Silenus is the figure with whom the poet seems to identify most closely, while in *Love Restored* (1612), a closing reference to Love's "next showes" (H&S 7:385) suggests the spirit in which Jonson's masque was offered. In *The Vision of Delight* (1617), the character Peace mentions "The many pleasures that I bring / . . . of youth, of heate, of life, and spring / . . . prepard to warme your blood" (H&S 7:467)—lines that invite us to note the similarities between the roles of Peace and poet. *Pleasure Reconciled* (1618) presents a number of figures—Hercules, Mercury, and Daedalus—who are variously associated with their creator. And in *Neptune's Triumph* (written in 1623 but never actually performed), a genuine Poet appears, closely modeled on Jonson and paired off with a comic Cook. When the Cook concedes that the Poet's art is more serious than his but asks the Poet not to disparage him (H&S 7:692), he only calls attention to the fact that Jonson combines the art of both.

The value of that art is often highlighted in the masques by allusions to the art of Jonson's predecessors. Often the poet invokes or even presents his precursors, not only to suggest his place in the long tradition of European literary culture but sometimes to imply his transcendence of those who came before him. Reminding his audience of famous predecessors also reminds them that poets have been capable of winning lasting renown for themselves and their patrons. The "Shades of the olde *Poets*" in *The Masque of Beautie* (1608) magnify Jonson's own role (H&S 7:189), and the numerous allusions throughout his early masques to such forerunners as Homer and Virgil enhance his works' dignity and importance. In *The Golden Age Restored* (1615), after the vices have been defeated and Astraea has returned, the old poets— "*Chaucer, Gower, Lidgate* [and] *Spencer*"—are summoned to help sustain the new state of affairs (H&S 7:425). Jonson thus honors his English predecessors, situates himself in a tradition of native poetry, and calls attention to the ancient dignity of his role. He also subtly emphasizes that these poets are his own creation, that they are incapable of doing the work he assigns them, that they cannot help restore the golden age (although their surviving writings may play some part). It is Jonson, the living artist, whose powers must be exerted (and in this masque are *being* exerted) to help restore past greatness—as, indeed, his figurative restoration of the old poets symbolizes. Jonson's invocation of his precursors highlights his own significance. Thus, in *The Masque of Owls* (1624), a ridiculous but historically-based character named Captain Cox mentions that he once helped entertain Queen Elizabeth (H&S 7:782)— a comment that calls attention to Jonson's present function while also insinuating the important transformations he has devised in aristocratic entertainments since the old-fashioned days of the Tudors. Similarly, references in *The Fortunate Isles* (1625) to the old poets Skelton and Scogan allow him to poke fun at his profession and public image while placing his efforts in a context that emphasizes his real quality and distinction (H&S 7:716–17). By exploiting the Skeltonic verse form (H&S 7:719–21), he subtly reminds his audience how far English poetry has come in the last century and how much he himself is responsible for that progress. And by reminding them of how highly valued such poets as Scogan and Skelton were in their days, he advertises his own prominence (like Skelton, he too had become a kind of "worshipfull *Poet* Laureat" [H&S 7:717]) even as he insinuates his dissatisfaction with contemporary attitudes toward poets and his worries about recent threats to his own security (Scogan "was paid . . . , / Regarded, and rewarded: which few *Poets* / Are now adaies" [H&S 7:717]). Here and elsewhere, his allusions to predecessors often prove multivalent and contribute powerfully to his works' rich resonance.

As the examples of Scogan (who wrote in "fine tinckling rime! and flowand verse! / With now & then some sense!" [H&S 7:717]) and of Captain Cox imply, Jonson was often able to characterize his own motives and accomplishments not only by presenting attractive alter egos but also by depicting unattractive or ridiculous opposites. The Chronicler in *Newes from the New World*, already mentioned, in some respects falls into this category, as do the alchemists in *Mercury Vindicated*. Comus, in *Pleasure Reconciled to Virtue* (1618), seems almost a comic parody of his creator, while in *The Masque of Owls*, Cox enters mounted on a "Hoby-horse" identified as "the *Pegasus* . . . [of the] *Warwick* Muses" (H&S 7:781). But the classic instance is Chronomastix in *Time Vindicated to Himselfe, and to his Honours* (1623). Based on George Wither, Chronomastix is a whipper of the times whom Jonson proceeds to flog unmercifully. He defines and asserts his own legitimacy by attacking this perversion of what a true poet should be. The fact that Wither was well-regarded in some influential circles seems only to have fed Jonson's fury. To him, Wither seems to have been more than a bogus pretender; he was a genuine threat. Ironically, Chronomastix is the closest Jonson came to using a poet as a major character before he concocted the attractive Poet in *Neptune's Triumph*, a work never actually performed. More ironic still, many of the charges he levels against Wither/Chronomastix were similar to charges often leveled against himself: that he attacked others' faults while ignoring his own, that he was hungry for fame, that he craved social status, and that he was sycophantic in his dealings with superiors. Like Jonson, Wither saw himself as an upright and resolute defender of virtue; like Jonson— whom, in earlier years, he had praised (H&S 10:651)—Wither carefully cultivated his image as the moral conscience of his time. It may have been Wither's appropriation of so many of Jonson's own tactics, claims, and personae that especially bothered the older writer. His need to distinguish himself from Wither would have been partly fueled by Wither's studied adoption of a Jonsonian public stance.

Jonson's attack on Wither was hardly the only time he used a masque to engage in personal politics; as we have seen, every aspect of the masques is political in the sense that their every detail affected his power and public reputation. But the masques also are often political in a more obvious and narrow sense: often he uses them quite clearly to defend himself, to attack his antagonists, to embarrass his rivals or rebuke his critics. Although from a distance they may seem simply celebratory and lightly joyous, viewed more closely they take on a darker hue. They are often tinged with self-conscious anxiety, for Jonson realized that each new work was a gamble, a precisely calculated risk. At stake in its failure or success was his enviable status as the court's chief masque writer—a literary position of unrivaled prominence and prosperity. Especially in the masques written near the beginning and end of James's reign, when Jonson's position was less secure, his works reflect his felt need to compete, to assert and defend himself. Sometimes this need is reflected in textual annotations; sometimes it affects the narrative itself. And sometimes intriguing connections link the plots and the notes published to explain them.

Often the notes are anything but extraneous; instead, they respond to real problems similar to those addressed more remotely or fancifully in the masque itself. Frequently they bring the masques' symbolism down to earth and show how the masques' themes are relevant to the immediate practical concerns of courtly existence. Sometimes the notes analogize the poet to the heroes the masques extol; often they relate directly to Jonson's micropolitical problems or aesthetic positions. Thus Niger, in *The Masque of Blacknesse* (1605), asserts that "the immortall soules of creatures mortall, / Mixe with their bodies, yet reserve for ever / A power of separation" (H&S 7:173)—words that parallel Jonson's distinction in an introductory note between the "*carkasses*" and "*spirits*" of masques themselves—a distinction central to his running quarrel with Inigo Jones. A note in *Love Freed from Ignorance and Folly* (1610–11) comments that "*Ignorance* . . . is alwaies the enemie of *Love, & Beauty,* and lyes still in wait to entrap them" (H&S 7:359)—sentiments whose meaning for Jonson was more than merely abstract. Similarly, the textual references to envy incorporated in *The Masque of Queenes* (e.g., H&S 7:288) resonate effectively with Jonson's attempt in the notes to put down the envy of his critics and competitors.

But the best example of this kind of resonance occurs in *Hymenaei* (1606), where the annotations once more take up the quarrel with Jones to emphasize the preeminence of the masque's written "soul" over its physical "body." In a long introductory note, Jonson stresses the perishability of sense and the durability of understanding, and—in a passage probably intended as much to persuade as to describe—he credits his patrons with an interest in the masque's "soul" at least equal to their interest in its splendor. He insists that the "*inventions*" of the "inward parts" of a masque should be "grounded upon *antiquitie, and solide learnings*" (H&S 7:209), metaphorically ascribing solidity to something immaterial even while insisting that literal materiality is subject to disintegration and decay. He satirizes those who attack excessive learning in masques, and the bitterness of his attack suggests that he may have been responding to actual criticism of his own works (H&S 7:209–10). Just as the masque's opening song bids "all profane away," the notes that immediately precede it serve the same function. Just as Reason confronts ignorance in the masque, so Jonson opposes ignorance in the running battle he conducts through his annotations.

Although some of the notes might have seemed to confirm antagonists' charges that his work was derivative, they also served to display his harmonizing powers, his ability to assimilate and coordinate a vast body of information in an apparently effortless way. The notes exemplify how a masque can suggest, symbolize, and allude to far more than it explicitly states; they memorably display the power of the word. Moreover, they sometimes provide a somewhat intimidating model for the reader, since they show Jonson enacting the process of deciphering his own works. Yet while they thus seem to express his literal and figurative authority, his secure self-confidence, they also imply his insecurity, his self-consciousness, his attempt to affirm his power partly by appealing to political or literary authorities outside and above his own texts.

Jonson thus uses the notes to promote his interests in a variety of ways, all intimately connected with micropolitics, with his need to compete. The annotations display his learning and support his insistence on the form's fundamental seriousness. And they also imply his ready familiarity with classical texts, buttressing his claim that his wide reading was at his immediate command. A long note in *Oberon* praises Virgil as the most learned of poets even as it demonstrates Jonson's own erudition (H&S 7:343). The same note speaks of the "gravitie, and profound knowledge" of the "*Silenes*"—qualities also displayed by Jonson's annotations. In a dedication to Prince Henry prepared for *The Masque of Queenes*, the poet apologetically mentions that tracking down all the sources of his masque (in order to prepare the printed notes) has not been easy, since many of the allusions were drawn out of the "fullnesse, and memory of [his] former readings" (H&S 7:281). He thus subtly advertises how much his scholarship was second nature, implicitly defending himself against charges that he paraded his learning ostentatiously. By ascribing to Henry an interest in the annotations, he makes his inclusion of them seem less pretentious and, more important, less susceptible to criticism. The supposed frivolity of the masque form would have made Jonson's learning seem all the more impressive, advertising his authority and highlighting his powers as an innovator. Moreover, the notes' constant interruption of the texts would have emphasized, among those who had already witnessed the masque, the smooth *sprezzatura* of the actual performance and accentuated the deceptive artlessness of the text itself. But juxtaposing the notes with the texts could also prove striking for other reasons: in *The Masque of Queenes*, for instance, the witches' crazed disorder and perverted rituals are framed by Jonson's scholarly thoroughness and rationality: their unruly passion highlights his devotion to learning and reason (H&S 7:301).

Jonson often uses the notes, and the masques as a whole, to distinguish himself not only from fictional figures but from the real contemporaries, his rivals and antagonists, who genuinely threatened his security. Another note in *The Masque of Queenes*, for example, explains that ignorance begets (through a long chain of intermediary vices) slander, execration, fury, and mischief. The note exists primarily to explain the behavior of certain "Hagges" in the masque who seek "w[i]th spight, / To overthrow the glory of this night" (H&S 7:287). As elsewhere, the plot relates to Jonson's own circumstances: such vices were particularly bothersome to him at the time he wrote. Thus the note is juxtaposed with a textual defense of his dramatic methods and an elaborate attack on his critics (H&S 7:286–87). Jonson's editors see this defense, moreover, as an oblique slap at the alternative methods of Samuel Daniel, one of his masque-writing competitors (H&S 10:501). His purpose, then, is not only to defend himself but to discredit implicitly the work of a particular rival. When Jonson insists in a subsequent note that a poet's work requires "so much exactnesse, as indifferency is not tolerable" (H&S 7:288), he not only defends his own procedures (including the use of notes) but sets up a standard by which his competitors may be assessed and dismissed.

The most obvious instance of Jonson's use of the masque to discredit antagonists is his assault on Wither in *Time Vindicated*. But there are numerous other examples. *For the Honour of Wales* lampoons his critics by putting their arguments into the mouths of comic Welshmen, while *Newes from the New World* distinguishes him not only from newsmongers but from a contemporary rival: one passage probably mocks an idea recently broached in a masque by Thomas Middleton (H&S 10:601). In the *Haddington Masque* (1608), Jonson quotes lines by Martial on plagiarists who claim credit for others' work, lines that both warn such co-workers as Inigo Jones and defend Jonson against the often-leveled charge that his work was derivative (H&S 7:260). Jones, of course, was at once Jonson's chief collaborator and his chief rival; almost from the start there is evidence of tension between them, especially in Jonson's repeated insistence on the greater importance of the "spirit" of the works as opposed to their physical "bodies." The anxiety of working on the masques must have been heightened by the fact that they *were* collaborations: success or failure depended not only on himself but on others. The same was true of the public theater, of course, but at court the stakes were greater. Opportunities for tension abounded, and the fact that Jones and Jonson shared so many aesthetic presumptions only makes their conflict seem even more obviously rooted in personal politics.[4]

Jonson often effectively uses the masques' printed texts to score points in his conflict with Jones. His arguments for the greater durability of the masques' "spiritual" aspects are reinforced by the mere existence of the surviving texts, often printed before or shortly after the performance and distributed both to the aristocratic participants and to members of the courtly audience. By their very nature the printed texts emphasized Jonson's contribution at the expense of his collaborators; they made his labors difficult to forget or ignore. Yet they preserved the memory not only of *his* accomplishments but of those of the aristocrats and audience as well: the text was their common surviving link to an exalted occasion. Ironically, even Jones's elaborate sets and costumes survived in memory almost solely through Jonson's written descriptions, although, paradoxically, the more elaborate these descriptions were, the more they implicitly emphasized the perishability and impermanence of the things described: the more detailed they were, the more they highlighted the poet's greater power to combat the corrosive effects of time. From the start, Jonson thought of such works in their printed form as coherent texts rather than as simple transcripts of real performances: the text for *The Entertainment at Althrope* prints two speeches not actually heard or delivered when the work was performed (H&S 7:128–31), while the text for the *Haddington Masque* prints as a single poem an epithalamium actually "*sung in pieces, betweene the daunces*" on the day of performance, so that originally it "*shew'd to be so many severall* songs" (H&S 7:260). Although a closing song in *Love Freed from Ignorance* insists that the masque's beauty will escape the ravages of time, the printed version only emphasizes how much of that beauty has been lost except through the poet's preservation of it (H&S 7:370). Such insinuations do not so much *stress* his power as help create it. Jonson's claims to imaginative potency are tactics that increase his real social prominence, and the two kinds of power—artistic and social—are intimately bound up together, each an essential precondition for the full and forceful exercise of the other.

While the masques create Jonson's power by illustrating it, they also enhance his security by playing on the insecurities of his patrons and audience. Although the masques, as entertainments or amusements, might seem to have offered the participants and witnesses an escape from the perils of courtly existence, they often exploited those uncertainties in ways that promoted the poet's interests. The masques were celebrations, performed at times of festivity and holiday cheer; they were communal, participatory; they offered appealing images and embodiments of actual and figurative harmony. For a brief time, for a shining moment, the pettiness and competition and narrow self-concerns of court life could be forgotten, and all those who took part or watched could be united in an almost mystic ritual of hierarchic concord. But such a view is too simple and naive: although this notion of the masque no doubt accounted in part for its appeal, it was hardly the whole story, and Jonson knew it. Although the masque might in some ways offer a momentary escape from political struggle, this very aspect of its charm enhanced the poet's political standing. By implicitly presenting himself as a figure capable of creating and celebrating harmony, of dispersing for a time the court's deepest anxieties, he inevitably advanced his own individual interests.

But the micropolitical nature of Jonson's masques and entertainments is more complex still. Often they openly allude to competitive tensions and take advantage of others' insecurities in ways that highlight the poet's usefulness and benefit his public standing. Right from the start one can see Jonson exploiting concerns with courtly *realpolitik* in ways that promoted his own power. *The Entertainment at Althrope* (1603), for instance, was written during the crucial early days of James's reign, when courtiers were jockeying with one another even more vigorously than they usually did to improve or maintain their standings. The *Entertainment* as a whole was part of Robert Spencer's bid to secure his status under the new regime; indeed, he and Jonson were in that respect similarly situated. The work constituted an elaborate advertisement for them both. Near the mid-point of the entertainment, Queen Mab presents a jewel to Queen Anne on behalf of Spencer, although she carefully insists that he had nothing to do with arranging the gift. The disclaimer, of course, calls all the more attention to his careful arrangement of the welcoming, magnifying the value of the gift precisely by denying his connection to it (H&S 7:125). But Mab's next denial is even more interesting: she disclaims any "cheape intent / In particular to feed / Any hope that should succeed, / Or our glorie by the deed" (H&S 7:125). Suddenly, in the midst of a lively and fantastical romp, Jonson glances at the real anxieties such courtship involved, exploiting his patron's concern about the misinterpretation of his motives and especially his anxiety about appearing too ambitious. Just as the lines plant the idea of reward in the Queen's mind, they explicitly deny that seeking reward is Spencer's chief ambition, preempting any criticism of his motives. Yet all the preceding and attractive playfulness of Mab and her cohorts, all their vitality and good humor, may in fact be seen as tactical preparations for this highly-charged moment of gift-giving: the humor, by suppressing and disguising the political aspects of the situation, effectively serves the political interests of both poet and patron. Subsequent speeches distancing Spencer from the arts of flattery and self-promotion are themselves, of course, artfully designed to promote his interests (H&S 7:126–28), while a passing reference to "Envy" would remind him of the dangerous competition he faced (H&S 7:127). The closing image of the sun cheering even "objects farre remov'd" plays on any courtier's discomfort in being too distant from the court, from the source of all power and social energy (H&S 7:130), while the concluding attack on the *"Envie"* and *"Flatterie"* that potentially threaten even the royal family's security highlights the ostensibly opposite virtues of both Jonson and his patron (H&S 7:131). In the *Entertainment at Althrope*, Jonson hardly pretends that political struggle does not exist; instead, he plays on his patron's awareness of it so as to emphasize—to the patron and, ironically, to the patron's competitors and superiors—the usefulness of a poet's allegiance.

Jonson exploited courtly insecurities to enhance his own power in various ways throughout his career. His *Entertainment of the King and Queen at Theobalds* (1607), written to commemorate the transfer to King James of Robert Cecil's family home, defends the Principal Secretary against charges that his generosity was motivated by ambition (H&S 7:156), and it also plays on Cecil's sense of his own mortality in a way that adroitly emphasizes his ostensibly selfless devotion to the King (H&S 7:154; 157). *Hymenaei* (1606), written to celebrate a marriage through which Cecil hoped to secure his family's status, also responds to the stringent criticism of James's plan to unite Scotland and England; in both ways the masque aids powerful figures who nevertheless felt embattled. Its closing reference to *"treason"* is nicely ambiguous: it plays on one of James's most deep-seated worries while counseling him that commitment to "Truth" and good rule can help make treason less likely (H&S 7:241). Many of James's fears in this regard went back to the so-called "Gowrie conspiracy," an incident in Scotland in which his life had once been threatened. Jonson alludes to the conspiracy several times in the masques (H&S 7:256; 608), and, in the *Speeches at Prince Henry's Barriers* (1610), his reference to potential assassination concludes by warning that "great chiefes" must "keepe their traynes / About 'hem still, and not, to privacie, / Admit a hand that may use treacherie" (H&S 7:330). Later he claims that James's virtue has "fixed fast / The wheele of *chance*, about which Kings are hurl'd" (H&S 7:334), but, as so often elsewhere, the very extravagance of his rhetoric works to his advantage in ways not immediately obvious. By ascribing more power to the King than the King really possessed, the poet might paradoxically undermine the monarch's sense of security and thus highlight his dependence on such faithful (and useful) subjects as the poet. In *Pan's Anniversary* (1620), the celebrations end with a curious warning against the deceptions wrought by "hirelings" (H&S 7:538), a group from which the poet of course excludes himself.

The occasional excesses of Jonson's praise have struck some readers as the baldest sort of flattery; others have defended it by pointing to Renaissance notions of ideal kingship or of teaching through commendation.[5] But not much has been made of the possibility that his praise sometimes deliberately undercuts itself, that it is its own best antidote, that it not only exalts the King's power but subtly questions it, and that it might thereby promote the poet's power. James knew, perhaps more clearly than anyone else, that his power was not and could never be entirely secure. Divine right propaganda was simply that: a tactical device to increase and defend his prerogative. Jonson's praise insinuates not only his loyalty but his usefulness, and its occasional excess helps make his allegiance more valuable by reminding the King of the real limits to his autonomy. Nowhere is this clearer than in *Neptune's Triumph for the Returne of Albion* (1623–24), written to celebrate the return of Prince Charles from his ill-fated trip to win the hand of the Spanish Infanta. Although the masque extols the authority and glory of Neptune (identified with James), the King's real position at this time was hardly as exalted as the masque pretends. Old, his health failing, his pacifist foreign policy criticized as weak and indecisive, his commitment to his Protestant allies seen as wavering, his domestic policies subject to increasing challenge, and his real power slipping out of his hands and into the hands of Buckingham and the Prince, James must have felt far less "mightie" than Jonson credits him with being (H&S 7:686).[6] The poet makes James seem the moving force behind the Spanish trip, when in fact it was sprung on him by Buckingham and Charles; in this and other ways he credits the King with more control over events, and with less anxiety about their outcome, than was actually the case. But if Jonson implicitly comes to the King's defense, he even more openly defends the favorite, who was widely criticized by many for his part in engineering the scheme. Although Jonson dismisses such "envie," the masque implies its own role in helping to combat it; it advertises the poet's usefulness in reviving a reputation that supposedly needed no aid (H&S 7:686). The work plays on Buckingham's concern with his public standing even while helping enhance it. Years later, when Charles was King and was facing more severe public criticism than even his father had provoked, Jonson praised him in *The King's Entertainment at Welbeck* (1633) as "the Rule unto his Subjects"—praise that could only remind him of how many subjects objected to his rule (H&S 7:802). But the *Entertainment* closes by referring ominously to an even more essential kind of insecurity, reminding the King of his inevitable appointment with death (H&S 7:803). References such as this place the poet's usefulness in a perspective even larger than the simply political.

Although the occasional extravagance of Jonson's rhetoric could subtly question the power it seemed to uphold, it also ran the risk of seeming sycophantic. Of course, the decorum of the masque practically prescribed exuberant praise, and since the poet was largely fulfilling a public role, the masque's voices were partly distanced from his own. Yet he was ultimately responsible for them, and the more Jonson used the masques to make himself a public figure, the more personally responsible he became. Even in his earliest entertainment, he ends by attacking "Flatterie," in part defending himself against any such charge (H&S 7:131), while one text of Hymenaei asserts that he flatters neither his collaborators nor "Great ones" (H&S 7:232). Often, though, Jonson could turn the problem to good account: in the Speeches at Prince Henry's Barriers, Merlin refrains from elaborating on James's virtues for fear of flattering him (H&S 7:335), thus paying him the more subtle and valuable tribute of assuming that excessive praise would offend him; similarly, in The Masque of Queenes, Jonson expresses concern that he not over-praise Queen Anne, thereby complimenting her virtuous modesty (H&S 7:312). Although flattery might seem one of the most obvious means by which a poet could promote his interests at court, Jonson realized that obvious flattery could easily undermine his hopes. An obvious flatterer was of no use to an aristocrat in competition with his peers, so obvious flattery put the sycophant at a clear disadvantage in his own competition with other writers.

Sometimes Jonson distances himself from flattery by satirizing court practices in the masques. He thereby not only suggests his moral independence but also (paradoxically) makes himself a more valuable, credible, and attractive spokesman for courtly ideals. His satire elevates the seriousness of the form, making it something more than self-indulgent spectacle and thus distinguishing it from the courtly vices it upbraids. Jonson's satire is sometimes a foil to set off his patrons—as when in the Entertainment at Althrope he distances Robert Spencer from flattery and bribery as instruments of self-promotion (H&S 7:126–27), or when he compliments (and maneuvers) Queen Anne by suggesting that these old practices will no longer be tolerated under the new regime (H&S 7:127). But inevitably and primarily, his satire characterizes himself, inviting the audience to identify—and to identify him—with the virtues to which he gives voice. The glancing reference to "beg'd monopolies" in Hymenaei (H&S 7:236); the mocking allusions to courtly ambition and competition in Love Restored and Mercury

Vindicated (H&S 7:384; 411–12); the explicit pronouncement, at the conclusion of *Pleasure Reconciled to Virtue*, that only virtue can make one great, *"though place, here, make you knowne"* (H&S 7:491); and the extended mockery of courtly ostentation and duplicity in *Newes from the New World* (H&S 7:520–22): all these instances ·and others allow Jonson and the individual members of his audience to participate in the court without thinking of themselves as being infected by its corruptions, as being "courtiers" in the compromised and pejorative sense. Just as the plots of the masques typically involve a kind of purging and purification of their own elements, so the masque as ritual probably performed a comparable psychic purification for individual courtiers, allowing them to identify with ideals inevitably compromised in the day-to-day struggle to achieve and maintain courtly power. The masques offered their audiences the same kind of optimism often found in contemporary treatises on court life, which often proclaimed—despite all the evidence they present to the contrary—that vice would inevitably founder and goodness finally prevail.[7] The masques celebrate a vision in which right and might are eventually united, in which virtue and power coalesce (in the court and in the poet), in which chaos and instability give way to smoothly functioning concord, and in which individual interests are at last subordinated to the good of the whole. Their inclusion of satire only makes their final harmony—and its author—all the more powerful and attractive. The masque writer is implicitly presented as co-creator, with the King and the masque participants, of the court's mystical energy and aura; it is he who helps lift what is already a sacred center of social reality to an even higher plane. It is he who helps the court ratify and reaffirm its magnificence, not only for such outside observers as foreign ambassadors but, perhaps even more importantly, for the hundreds who daily and regularly participated in its mundane and routine functionings. The reaffirmation of the court's significance involved a reaffirmation of the courtiers' own self-worth.

Through a combination of satire and celebration, then, Jonson reasserted the higher values of court life, thereby implying and demonstrating his own importance. But the masques' seriousness, whether satiric or encomiastic, should not overshadow another effective technique the poet used to promote his power. That technique—the tone of licensed familiarity he so often employs—contributed significantly to the appeal of these works. *For the Honour of Wales*, for instance, was more popular than *Pleasure Reconciled to Virtue* because of its "pleasant merry speeches made to the kinge" (H&S 10:577), while *The Gypsies Metamorphos'd*, one of his more intimate masques, was also among his most successful. Whether teasing about penises or about the King's love of hunting and indifference to smocks in the *Entertainment at Highgate* (H&S 7:142–43), or whether speculating about the love-making of a newly-married court couple in *A Challenge at Tilt* (H&S 7:390–91), or whether filling the *Entertainment at the Blackfriars* with sexual innuendo and joking allusions to members of the audience, Jonson repeatedly exploited the opportunities these works provided to violate the normal decorums operative in a rigidly hierarchical society. Ironically, the relaxed tone the masques so often display was necessarily the product of careful calculation: the poet had to know how far he could go, how far was too far. But as long as he kept his teasing within limits, it could greatly enhance his image and appeal. His tone of familiarity sometimes permitted him to confront his superiors (if only momentarily and indirectly) on more equal terms than usual. And he could benefit from the jocular indiscretions of his boisterous characters while distancing himself from them, using them to define by contrast his own greater sense of dignity.

The intimacy the masques sometimes exhibited had paradoxical effects. It obliquely ratified the authority of those who were its objects by temporarily pushing close to that authority's limits, challenging their power but only in the most playful and non-threatening way. The masques' humorous familiarity could suggest a temporary relaxation of power distinctions, a relaxation as appealing to superiors as to dependents. For superiors the appeal lay in being treated simply as human beings rather than as sources of power to be courted and exploited; they knew, better than most, that the obeisance normally offered them was inevitably rooted as much in self-interest as in genuine respect. Jonson's superiors must often have felt the desire to be honored in simpler terms, to be valued more for their true nobility than for the influence they could exert, to be treated with authentic regard rather than regarded as potential conquests. Excessive deference might suggest more concern for the power they wielded than for them, and one of the most appealing aspects of Jonson's masques is the balance they often achieve between too much and too little deference. Yet while his familiarity seems to involve a relaxation of concern with power, for that reason it was one of his most effective means of enhancing his own influence. Thus his good-natured teasing of the court ladies in various masques not only allows him to assume the role of gentleman courtier (temporarily making common cause with other men, including his superiors, in the sexual game-playing popular at court); it also suggests his recognition of the real power women exercised in such a milieu. By teasing the ladies he appealed both to them and to their male counterparts. And because his teasing seemed to distance him from flattery or from displaying suspiciously excessive deference, it actually promoted his interests and image effectively. Such familiarity (especially when combined with the self-mockery sometimes found in the later masques) implied his own security, his sense of inner strength, and thus made him more attractive to his superiors, his equals, and his inferiors. His teasing advertised his courtly grace and urbanity as well as his easy relations with some of the most powerful figures in the kingdom.

It also helped display the range of tone he was capable of achieving. In the *Entertainment at Highgate* he juxtaposes boisterous humor and delicate stateliness, while in the *Entertainment at the Blackfriars*, dignified prophecy follows hard upon farcical debate (H&S 7:776). Despite their broad generic similarities, individual masques and entertainments often exhibit a surprising degree of variation and uniqueness, and even when Jonson repeats significant themes or techniques (as when *For the Honour of Wales* echoes aspects of *The Irish Masque*, or when *The Masque of Augures* repeats motifs from *Mercury Vindicated*), the echoes recall the poet's earlier successes, emphasize his subtle innovations, and in both ways enhance his power. The inventiveness Jonson displayed simply in his frequent use of Love as a theme and character could only magnify his audience's sense of his imaginative potency, especially after he took the trouble to deny any ability to treat the subject successfully.[8] The more creative resourcefulness he exhibited, the more likely he was to win real influence: literary power was his surest key to social prominence. For that reason, however, his status was fundamentally less secure than that of others who served the court in more mundane capacities. Any hint of imaginative failing, any indication that his muse had deserted him, any suggestion that his work was becoming stale or predictable could seriously affect his social standing.

Perhaps partly for that reason, Jonson did not always rely simply on a present work's success to cement his reputation; often he alludes to past services or anticipates and advertises future plans. A passing reference in the *Entertainment at Althrope* recalls his fame as a writer of humour plays (H&S 7:126), while the close of the *Masque of Blacknesse* anticipates its sequel, the *Masque of Beautie* (H&S 7:180). Textual notes in *The Haddington Masque* recall two earlier works (H&S 7:251; 255), while references in *Oberon* (1611) would have reminded Prince Henry of the *Speeches* Jonson had composed on his behalf the year before (H&S 7:351–52). And *Mercury Vindicated*, of course, could not help but recall the author's great stage comedy about alchemists. Through such allusions Jonson fosters confidence in his enduring talent, partly by displaying such confidence himself. By alluding to his past works, he suggests that his whole output is part of a larger *oeuvre*, that all his works in some sense fit together, and that his artistic and social worthiness must be judged by a lifetime of accomplishments and not simply by his latest contribution. In one sense an expression of pride, the allusions also are a means of self-defense.

But the surest way for Jonson to advertise his talent and promote his power was to exploit the opportunities his present works provided to accentuate their own qualities and achievements. The masques and entertainments are often highly reflexive, and, by calling attention to themselves, they indirectly call attention to their maker; by emphasizing their own success, they promote his. Throughout his career, Jonson used a variety of tactics to underscore his works' attractive features. Thus the text of the *Althrope* entertainment reprints "*a speech sodainly thought on, to induce a morrise of the clownes*" (H&S 7:129). Mentioning its spontaneity makes whatever triumph the speech achieves seem all the more impressive, while the fact that Jonson was asked to compose this spur-of-the-moment addition implies the success of his immediately preceding efforts. He thus guides the reaction of readers by implying the reaction of his patrons, even as he advertises his *sprezzatura*, the easy naturalness of his talent. The point was especially worth making because Jonson was so often accused of lacking ease. These charges went to the heart of his status as a poet, implying that he was essentially a pretender, an ungifted hack whose repute derived mainly from uninspired study and plodding determination. Such attacks were direct challenges to his poetic power.

Taken as a whole, the masques and entertainments—with their comic vitality, their lyric delicacy, and their penchant for clever innovation— seem almost deliberately designed to refute such charges, but at the level of specific detail Jonson's methods can also be quite effective. *Love Restored*, for instance, opens abruptly with a long, exuberant speech by Masquerado apologizing for the ensuing masque's lack of professional polish. The speech itself, for all its apparent spontaneity, only highlights Jonson's engaging artfulness, not to mention his wit (which "costs him nothing") in conceiving of such a figure and of such an amusing gambit (H&S 7:377). Indeed, the whole first part of *Love Restored* is a kind of self-conscious joke by means of which Jonson advertises his artistry while ostensibly postponing it. The antimasque is given over to attacks on masquing by Plutus, and to Robin Goodfellow's excited expectations of the masque and his eager attempts to witness it. The joke, of course, is that all the while, he is a conspicuous and entertaining *part* of the masque he anticipates. Plutus's attacks, meanwhile, serve several purposes: they mockingly reflect on contemporary critics of masquing yet imply that there may have been some justice to their criticisms. By so doing, the attacks accentuate how far Jonson's own works surpass the "superfluous excesses" Plutus disdains (H&S

7 : 381).[9] In various ways, then, *Love Restored* is a prime example of how Jonson could adroitly use his art to indicate his artistry, of how he could call attention to his success even while achieving it.

Artistic success was surely the prime and over-arching means by which he used the masques to promote and solidify his power. Each time his works were well-received, his status grew that much more secure. Each well-regarded performance helped shape his audience's artistic expectations according to his own aesthetic ideals and thus helped ensure the continuity of his influence. Certainly it would be a mistake to regard his masques simply as self-conscious tactical ploys for personal advancement, as if he were only concerned with narrow self-interests. But it would be equally a mistake to overlook their very real and intricate tactical dimensions, the minute and insistent ways they work to his advantage. In the masques as in nearly all his writings, there can be no easy or absolute separation of the aesthetic from the tactical: whatever was artistically attractive promoted his power, and (as *Love Restored* exemplifies) whatever best promoted his power was also most aesthetically appealing. The various self-promotional techniques he exploited cannot be considered apart from their contribution to his works' total effect. Ostensibly designed to enhance the image and celebrate the authority of the King, the court, and the nation, the masques more immediately and undeniably affected the image of their creator. Jonson knew this, and he took every advantage of the opportunities they provided. The results, inscribed indelibly in the rich texture of his works, continue to affect his status and power to this day.

8
The Plays

Patronage was obviously an important influence on Jonson's poems and masques, but its impact on his drama is less immediately clear. Many of his poems are addressed explicitly to patrons, while his masques were sponsored by the court and were performed for its recreation. The plays, however—especially the great comedies on which his reputation depends—seem more distanced from any open concern with patronage. The fact that they *are* plays is partly responsible: in them Jonson speaks less clearly in his own voice, and the audience he addresses seems broader than the single patrons of the poems or the select groups privileged to witness the masques. Some of the early plays, in which his motives of self-promotion seem most distinct, can seem somewhat tiresome and stale. They too obviously advertise their author. But Jonson never ceased using his plays for self-promotion; he simply learned to use them more subtly and effectively. The influence of patronage on his drama is not confined to such early plays as *Cynthia's Revels* or *Poetaster*. In various intriguing and complicated ways, it extends throughout his career.[1]

The society in which Jonson wrote and sought advancement was relatively closed and constricted. London, although huge for its day, was no larger than a medium-sized modern city, and the circle of those who exercised real power there was smaller still. A phrase in the "Dedication" to *The New Inn* implies that printed texts of plays made it possible for the dramatist to advertise himself among "rusticke" audiences who could not depend on seeing stage performances regularly (H&S 6:397). Even so, a writer with Jonson's ambitions had few real alternatives: his career, especially as a dramatist, would either prosper or fail in the capital. And whether it prospered—particularly in the ways he wanted it to—depended less on the public at large than on that segment of his audience whose opinions counted most.[2]

This "privileged" group included nobles, gentry, courtiers, legal and ecclesiastic officials, intellectuals, wealthier merchants, recognized "gentles," and aspirants to gentility. In short, it included those who exercised patronage or whose power depended on the patronage of others.[3] This is the group in which Jonson implicitly claimed membership when he signed himself a "gentleman," and these were the people he seems to have had most clearly in mind when he wrote his plays. They make up a large part of his *dramatis personae* and comprise the portion of his audience he seems to have been most conscious of and concerned about. Their influence on his drama was less simply economic than profoundly psychological. Whenever one of his plays was staged, he knew that he was presenting an implicit image of himself to members of this powerful group for validation or attack. Although he often satirizes characters drawn from this segment of society, his attacks suggest not indifference to its power but precisely the opposite. They imply recognition of its importance and suggest his determination to wield power himself by directly influencing those who wielded it. His power to influence them derived less from their fear of him than from their dread of being embarrassed before their peers. His satire on "privileged" characters is thus tactical in several senses: by attacking their foolishness, he helps determine the behavior acceptable for the "privileged" outside the play; he implicitly invites them to increase their power by behaving differently from his fools; and he stakes his own claims to be taken seriously by serious superiors. The impact of patronage on his plays was less a matter of pounds and shillings than of how the *psychology of patronage*—the habits of mind engendered by a culture rooted in hierarchy and in the competition for status—shaped his conceptions of himself, his role, and his works. His plays reflect the challenges and tensions, the motives, behavior, and concerns conditioned by the social system in which he lived and worked.

Clearly the drama offered Jonson a splendid platform for self-advertisement, a public forum in which to display his poetic gifts and otherwise enhance his social power. Ironically, some of his weakest plays—works that seem to have left him feeling most vulnerable and exposed—were those in which his self-advertisement was too blatant and direct. The irony is all the greater since those plays often satirize characters who promote themselves blatantly and therefore ineptly. One recalls the description, in *Every Man Out of His Humour*, of Delirio "apishly imitat[ing] / The gallant'st courtiers, kissing ladies' pumps . . . fearful to be seen / With any man, though he be ne're so worthy, / That's not in grace with some, that are the greatest" (4.2.33–39). Delirio's hapless efforts actually undermine his prospects; his blatant attempts to advertise power emphasize his weakness. His problem is not that he seeks status while others do not but that he seeks it too clumsily and thus opens himself to his competitors' mockery and his targets' disdain. His interest in tactics is hardly unique; his tactics are simply too transparent. If he were more clever he would be less contemptible. He is as scheming as Volpone but much less adept.

Jonson's characteristic stance of independent self-regard was no doubt meant to distance him from the Delirios of his day, thus paradoxically improving his own chances of social acceptance. Yet if Delirio aroused disdain because of his obvious self-abasement, Jonson might equally provoke hostility by self-promotion of a different sort, the sort that smacked of arrogance. *Every Man Out, Cynthia's Revels,* and *Poetaster,* with characters who were obvious stand-ins for Jonson (or could easily be mistaken for such), inadvertently supplied his antagonists with dangerous ammunition, and in *Satiromastix,* for instance, Thomas Dekker used it with deadly effect. Stung by such attacks and by the reception that greeted *Poetaster,* Jonson temporarily abandoned comedy and produced one of his two surviving tragedies, *Sejanus.* In that play and in the great works that followed it during the next decade, he was far more circumspect about making himself the center of dramatic attention. Partly because his own status was becoming more secure, he may now have felt less need to confront the patronage issue quite so openly or to promote himself quite so blatantly. When his status became less certain after James's death, such plays as *The New Inn, The Magnetic Lady,* and *A Tale of a Tub* once again addressed concerns about patronage in ways reminiscent of his early works. Yet all his plays seek to promote his interests and image with the audience that counted most. The great plays simply do so more subtly than the others, in the same way that Volpone is more subtle than Delirio.

Often the dramas deal explicitly with relations between patrons and dependents: Volpone's with Mosca are the most noteworthy, but many other plays also deal with such connections. By focusing on the corruption of these contacts—whether the abuse of an inferior by his superior or the deception of a patron by his client—Jonson implies his own commitment to the underlying ideal of reciprocal service and trust. Again and again he focuses on ambiguous hierarchical relations, including those between Lorenzo Senior and Musco in *Every Man In His Humour,* Carlo Buffone and Fastidius Brisk in *Every Man Out,* Sejanus and Tiberius in *Sejanus,* Face and Lovewit (or the knaves and their customers) in *The Alchemist,* and Waspe and Cokes in *Bartholomew Fair.* Sometimes he depicts ideal patronage relations, such as those between Crites and Arete in *Cynthia's Revels* or between Horace and Maecenas in *Poetaster;* doing so allows him to shape perceptions of what constitutes an exemplary patron. He thus asserts power indirectly by molding the ideals that influence how power is exercised by others. By fashioning ideal patrons in his plays, he helps fashion the behavior and self-perceptions of his own superiors.

Moreover, a play like *Poetaster* allows him to see enacted his own fantasies of attaining a secure social position and, obversely, of ensuring the irreparable humiliation of his antagonists. In *Poetaster* the merit of Jonson's alter ego, Horace, is immediately recognized and appreciated by his superiors and by the best of his peers; unlike Jonson, he needn't advertise himself or proclaim his own worthiness. The dramas gave Jonson a power he lacked in real life to control behavior and determine outcomes, and part of his attraction to playwriting may have been rooted in this sense of mastery. Yet this illusion of power could only be momentary and fleeting; especially in the playhouse, his control could never be complete. It was complicated and qualified by the vagaries of audience response and by the constraints of social expectations he could not ignore.[4] The last act of *Poetaster* ends with Horace triumphing over his foes and receiving Caesar's praise, but the printed text ends with Jonson's ambivalent "Apologetical Dialogue," in which his frustrated claims of indifference to attacks on the play only emphasize how much they bothered him.[5] His plays imply his real-life subordination precisely because of his need to make them—and himself—appealing. But they also gave him a kind of authority he missed in real life.

Although Jonson sometimes presents ideal patronage relations, he more often focuses on the ambiguities and ambivalences they invite, on their potential for mutual exploitation. Often he focuses on problems superiors and dependents have in deciphering each others' true motives: Sejanus and Tiberius are the classic instance. Neither can be sure about the other, nor can the other characters be sure of these two. Both dissemble their power to increase it; both pretend to serve larger interests while seeking to advance their own. Attempting to manipulate Tiberius by exploiting his unease, Sejanus unwittingly arouses the emperor's suspicions and provokes his counter-plot. The dependent's effort to increase his strength by exploiting another's weakness ends by subverting his own ambitions. But where Sejanus fails, Jonson largely succeeds. Like Sejanus, he plays on the uncertainties of his audience, exploiting (both in superiors and inferiors) many of the same insecurities with which his characters are obsessed. Jonson implies that when money and personal power supplant love and mutual respect as the bases for social relations, the security of both inferiors *and* superiors is at risk. Although most of his plays treat the self-interested pursuit of power comically and depict its eventual defeat, by emphasizing such problems he at once increases the insecurity of his audience, enhances the relevance of his plays, and thereby promotes his own power.

Jonson uses his dramas to exploit the insecurities of superiors in various ways. In the otherwise flattering "Epilogue" to *Every Man Out*, he nonetheless reminds the aging Elizabeth of her inevitable death, subtly underscoring his role in preserving her memory from the "envie" implicitly threatening her (H&S 3:600). Similarly, in *Cynthia's Revels* he alludes to the severe criticism provoked by her treatment of Essex and attempts to defend her against it (5.11.1–45). *Catiline* refers in passing to the contempt inferiors feel for their masters (3.1.611), and frequently Jonson insinuates the servant's ability to exploit a superior's shortcomings and trust. Although Sejanus serves a master whose apparent weakness masks his strength, Mosca serves one whose strength is largely rooted in self-deception.[6] Jonson implies that the servant's very dependency often gives him a kind of power, and he emphasizes the many ways in which superiors grow dependent on their own dependents. Volpone reasserts power over Mosca only at the cost of social impotence, while the fascination of *The Alchemist* derives partly from our final uncertainty about who has really triumphed, Face or Lovewit. In his plays as in his poems, Jonson undermines the confidence of the powerful by demonstrating and thus exploiting their vulnerabilities. By playing on their insecurities and by implicitly presenting himself as reliably committed to virtue and fair dealing, he enhances his own strength and attractiveness.

Unlike many of the self-serving dependents his plays depict, Jonson presents himself as committed to higher values than mere egotism. If his fools lack a secure sense of their own power and need others to ratify their identities, his knaves refuse to submit to anyone. Jonson uses the plays to depict himself implicitly as a strong personality (unlike the fools), yet as one committed to higher values (unlike the knaves). His ideal figures are generally secure persons capable of true attachments to like-minded others.[7] Often Jonson implies his own freedom from excessive concern with patronage by mocking characters thus preoccupied. Yet his mockery is tactical, presenting an attractive image precisely by lampooning those obsessed with self-presentation. His shows of strength thus silently signify his relative social weakness.[8] The ambivalence of his own position is apparent in his depiction of Crites, the moral center of *Cynthia's Revels*. Crites represents balanced sanity in a world brimming with excess and affectation; indeed, his self-assurance seems almost boring in the context of the lively idiocy that surrounds him. Yet near the end of the play, calling himself "a creature . . . despisde, and poore" (5.1.27), he worries that his satire on corrupt courtiers may bring punishment down on him. Obviously this was a worry Jonson himself confronted—that satire aimed only at the perverse might cause indiscriminate offense. When Mercury reassures Crites that "The better race in court, / That have the true nobilitie, call'd vertue, . . . [will] approve / The fit rebuke of so ridiculous heads, / Who with their apish customes, and forc'd garbes, / Would bring the name of courtier in contempt" (5.1.30–36), his comment signifies less Jonson's assurance than his insecurity. It is less an objective observation than a tactic for controlling audience response. Mercury's confidence is not Jonson's. Indeed, the playwright's comic heroes often demonstrate a calm assurance and restraint Jonson could rarely achieve. The self-mastery he admired could never be completely his. Crites's concerns suggest the real worries of an author intimately familiar with the ways power was exercised in the patronage system.

Yet even when patronage is not an obvious issue, Jonson's plays nearly always imply the more fundamental problems created by a culture *rooted* in patronage. They examine these issues, but they also exploit them to promote his advantage. Every aspect of his plays contributes (successfully or otherwise) to his own self-presentation; every detail implies something about him and serves either to increase, ratify, or diminish his social standing. Attacks on sycophants suggest his forthrightness; satires on deception imply his honest dependability. Indictments of corrupt artists reflect his commitment to art's proper use; attacks on manipulative language distance his words from similar suspicions. By satirizing self-promotion, he promotes himself; by mocking excess ambition, he helps realize his own goals. For all his satire, he seeks to distance himself from satirical extremes, to distinguish himself from the intemperate railers who populate his plays. That the distinction is not always clear to his critics can hardly be denied, although imagining the railers' physical presence can help: their limitations would be even more apparent on the stage than on the page. Despite his hostility toward the theater, the ironic fact remains that Jonson's drama depends much more fully than Shakespeare's on the talents of competent actors, since his are mainly dramas of characterization rather than of plot.[9]

Jonson had many good reasons not to want to be confused with his railers, but most lead back to one: such characters are weak. Their fury signals their impotence; their insistent sarcasm indicates their powerlessness. As Judd Arnold persuasively argues, Jonson implicitly identifies not with the railers but with the "gallants"—with the self-possessed, self-controlled young men who are less threatened than amused by the fools around them.[10] These are the characters with whom Jonson identifies most closely—not, however, because he shares their calm self-possession, but precisely because he does not. The power they bear so lightly yet confidently was a power he lacked; identifying with them was less a means of displaying strength than of striving to achieve it. Jonson distances himself from the railers because their weakness is *obvious*, and its obviousness intensifies it and makes it self-perpetuating. His ability to stand back and mock them helps assert his own judgment and discrimination. Yet his need to identify with the gallants also signals a kind of weakness, less apparent but no less real. It is a weakness born of his need to be concerned with others' perceptions. Thus Mosca may have represented his worst fears of how his own position could cause him to be perceived. As a parasitical subordinate driven by desire for power his place denies him, who lives by his wits, and who takes pride in his ability to design plots, manipulate behavior, and exploit the resources of language, Mosca is all that Jonson might have seemed. But Jonson uses their potential similarities to help establish their differences. All his characters variously illuminate their creator.

The vices Jonson attacks are usually individual rather than systemic. Or, if the system is at fault, it is more often because of degeneracy than inherent corruption. Generally, he seems more interested in micro- than in macro-politics, more concerned with how power is used and abused by individuals than with larger questions of ideology or institutional hegemony. He de-emphasizes the possibility that the "vices" he attacks might be endemic to patronage relations; such a position, literally revolutionary in its implications, would not only conflict with his generally conservative social stance; it would also call into question his participation in the system and undermine his ability to win a place for himself in it. Jonson sometimes complains about his society's emphasis on blood and birth rather than on virtue,[11] but he generally attributes evil to the collective perversity of individuals rather than to a determining, systemic corruption. Thus, Silius explains that the tyranny of Tiberius and Sejanus grew first from the tyrannous domination of men's souls by their own passions, "To which betraying first our liberties, / We since became the slaves to one mans lusts; / And now to many" (1.1.62–64). Although undoubtedly influenced by Christian notions of original sin, Jonson's emphasis on individual vice was also tactically serviceable and strategically prudent.

Jonson hardly considers the possibility that the "vices" he attacks are inherent in *any* political system, indeed, that they are inevitable concomitants of all political behavior. By tainting all politics (or rather, by making all behavior seem fundamentally political, fundamentally concerned with power and domination), such a position would undercut his authority and undermine his claims to be a reformer, making them seem essentially tactical or self-serving. By eroding his own and others' confidence in his objectivity, it would compromise both the conviction and the effectiveness of his self-presentation. His rejection of such thorough-going skepticism was no doubt wholly sincere, born of an implicit but deeply-felt recognition of its potentially destructive social consequences; his plays repeatedly indicate his revulsion at the thought of a society in which each individual nakedly and doggedly pursues his own self-interests merely. Yet his very revulsion inevitably serves his own interest: rejecting micropolitics is itself politically effective. His satire on rampant egotism distances him from an unappealing self-conception and social image even as it de-emphasizes cynical, unpleasant, or anxious thoughts about the nature of social existence.

Jonson's drama not only implies positive images of the poet by contrasting him with unsavory characters; it is also an indirect defense against antagonists' charges that he displayed the same vices he assaults, from hypocrisy to greed, from pomposity to excessive ambition, from plagiarism to envy, flattery, and misanthropy. Perhaps his satire was meant to acknowledge his own fallibility; but even if this were so, any public exhibition of humble self-criticism would serve to promote his power.[12] Indeed, his ability to poke fun at himself—as in the "Induction" to *Bartholomew Fair*, or when he presents a comically exasperated Horace in act 3 of *Poetaster*—was one of his most effective tactics, and even here part of the effect was defensive, implicitly refuting charges of essential arrogance. In fact, his plays—or at least the great plays of his middle period—often provided more effective means of self-defense and self-promotion than his poems, precisely because they were further distanced from his own voice. His personal interests were less obtrusive, less obviously engaged, and therefore less threatening and more likely to be realized.

Volpone, for instance, advances his interests far more effectively than the "Expostulation with Inigo Jones" (*U.V.* 34), because the play contrasts Jonson implicitly with a fictional bogus artist, while the obvious jealousy the poem expresses subverts his pose of moral aloofness. If the play appeals partly because of its imaginative strength, the poem betrays an unattractive impotence. For all its fury and cynicism, *Volpone* indirectly affirms an optimistic belief in transcendent moral values; the "Expostulation," however, reminds us of the extent to which even the greatest minds are inevitably caught up in micropolitical squabbling. Perhaps the poem is unattractive partly because it reveals the limits not only of Jonson's power but of our own.

Volpone suggests how specifically Jonson's plays sometimes confront the issues raised by patronage relations. Mosca's betrayal of *his* patron is prefigured by Volpone's betrayal of God. Jonson seems to imply (here and elsewhere) that once man neglects his obligation to the supreme patron, his relations with other superiors and with inferiors are bound to suffer. Volpone's surprise when Mosca betrays him is itself surprising in view of his own earlier blasphemy and sacrilege: he fails to see how *his* treachery prefigured Mosca's. Volpone's apostasy helps insinuate the playwright's Christian allegiance, an allegiance probably attractive to earthly patrons both because of the dependability it suggested and because of the advantages of publicly supporting exemplary dependents. Although Jonson's characters may abuse their God-given gifts of intellect and although they may trivialize the powers of art, the poet himself, by creating such characters, displays a proper use of his gifts and a commitment to serious artistic purposes.

In various ways, Jonson turns the abuses of art to good advantage by incorporating them, often with great irony and wit, into his own socially useful writing. His imagination, ostensibly driven by a larger moral purpose, contrasts implicitly with the aimless and empty cleverness of a character like Musco in *Every Man In*. In that play, as in *Epicoene*, *Bartholomew Fair*, and other works, he demonstrates his own poetic excellence by creating characters who write poems so inept, affected, and shallow that they highlight by contrast the easy grace of Jonson's talent as well as the social power his skills imply. Like the attractive wits in *Epicoene*, Jonson's own writing resolves the tension between naturalness and art debated in that play's much-debated opening scene; and indeed, making that point seems part of the scene's effect. In Jonson's plays, bad writing is not only aesthetically offensive; it also goes hand-in-hand with social weakness. Jonson's artistic talent was also his passport to power. This link between artistic and social ineptness is wonderfully illustrated by the extreme artificiality of Puntarvolo in *Every Man Out*, who courts his own wife as if she were a character from the romances he reads (2.2.1ff.). Puntarvolo's comic stiffness and affectation highlight the natural ease of Jonson's own art, increasing our sense of the poet's power. We ascribe to the playwright the *sprezzatura* his character so obviously lacks. Whereas Puntarvolo mentally inhabits a fictional world he tries to impose upon reality, Jonson ostensibly uses his art both to expose reality for what it is, and also to imply values that transcend the merely "real."

Repeatedly, Jonson's corrupt characters are trapped in their own narcissistic fictions, but often they attempt to impose their personal control and limited visions upon the social world by manipulating others. Certainly Sejanus does this, as do Volpone and Mosca, Face and Subtle, Morose, Catiline, and Zeal-of-the-Land Busy. Mosca plays on Volpone's passions no less than on the passions of his other "patrons." Subtle and Face similarly use their artfulness, their imagination, and especially their great rhetorical gifts to increase their own power through deception. But although his dramas often deal with smug and manipulative plotters, they and their schemes are themselves exploited by Jonson's plotting.[13] He promotes his own interests by ostensibly using his art not to disguise reality but to reveal it, not to deceive his patrons but to

enlighten them, not to manipulate his audience's passions but to warn
them against the dangers of excessive passion. Yet, like the characters
who so plainly fascinated him, he too manipulates his audience and
uses fictions to enhance his prestige. What his plays repeatedly display
(and thus assert and enhance) is the imaginative *power* of the playwright. Like Cicero in *Catiline,* Jonson combines rhetorical skill with
pragmatic political intuition.

Unlike Volpone or Mosca, Jonson is implicitly both a responsible
artist and a responsible servant.[14] Unlike Mosca or Face or Subtle, he
claims not to flatter his audience but to confront them with truths that
can enhance their social power. If Jonson's knaves play upon the fools'
desires to increase their power and status, Jonson himself plays with his
audience's desires to maintain their status and reputations. If Jonson's
knaves exploit the greed of the fools, Jonson himself exploits the insecurities of his audience. Potent though it is, his knaves' rhetoric is still
his creation, and the connection only emphasizes how different his
intentions are from theirs. The irony so characteristic of his works not
only undercuts the power of the knaves and fools but also silently
illustrates and emphasizes Jonson's. Thus Volpone's comments about
contemporary social abuses (1.1.35–40) inadvertently highlight his own
crimes, while his attempted seduction of Celia reminds us of all the
moral standards he violates. Sir Epicure Mammon's flights of rhetorical
fancy emphasize Jonson's imagination and inventiveness even as they
make Mammon seem increasingly ridiculous and repulsive.

Although Jonson's virtuous characters seem impotent compared with
the vicious, the true opponent of someone like Volpone or Sejanus is
not Bonario or Arruntius. The true opponent is Jonson himself. Arruntius's words are far more effective and literally powerful as speeches in
Jonson's play than as speeches at Tiberius's court; Celia's indictment of
Volpone is not half so potent as the withering irony Jonson builds into
Volpone's own words. If the "moral" characters often seem rather limited, the moral lessons the dramas teach nonetheless are powerfully
effective. Again and again the plays implicitly call attention to Jonson's
own ethical and social function. Sometimes they do so obviously, but
often they work less directly. Tiberius's long speech disclaiming pride
and ambition and stressing his mortality (1.1.439ff.) is ironic not only
because it is insincere, but because it boomerangs: Tiberius *is* only
mortal, and he *should* fear seeming to challenge the gods. The very
standards he hypocritically invokes help convict him, while his hopes
for future fame are part of a play that unrelentingly indicts him. Similarly, Sejanus's smug dismissal of the historian Cordus as a mere
"writing fellow" (1.1.304) insinuates Jonson's status as heir to Cordus's
role and virtue, while the later persecution of Cordus inadvertently

calls attention to Jonson's punishment of Sejanus. Yet that punishment is both belated and limited. Here as elsewhere, Jonson's power seems ambiguous and confined, and the fact that he was hauled before the Privy Council on account of this play heightens our sense of the limits he faced. In a real sense he himself shared some of the impotence and vulnerability that often paralyzed his moral characters.

Besides irony, Jonson uses other means to reflect favorably on his own role as artist. Sometimes, as in The Devil is an Ass, he draws on traditional plot elements to emphasize his own skill in using and updating them; sometimes, as in the early "comical satyres," he advertises his talents for innovation. The subtitle of The Magnetic Lady, one of his last plays, is Humors Reconciled, thus recalling the triumphs of his youth, while praise of Lovell's poetry in The New Inn underscores his own skills as a love poet (3.2.269–70). Occasionally he uses the plays to advertise his talents in other genres (as when Horace composes odes in Poetaster [3.1.1] or when, in The Magnetic Lady, Jonson displays his skills for writing epigrams, blank verse, and character studies [1.2.33–37]), and at least once (in Cynthia's Revels) he seems to use a play to bid openly for patronage as a masque writer (5.5.39–55). Sometimes his plays recall earlier dramatic forms or particular works by other playwrights (such as The Spanish Tragedy); by means of these allusions Jonson distinguishes his work from the (inferior) productions of his predecessors. At other times, however, he advertises his connections to the great traditions and precursors of his art. The very self-consciousness of his artfulness helps display it, but he can also be less direct. Thus, submerged allusions in Epicoene to Sidney's Apology invite us to notice how well Jonson's work lives up to Sidney's standards (2.3.109–18), while contrasts between ephemeral news and eternal verities in The Staple of News underscore his clever use of a timely topic to deal with important larger issues. A matter-of-fact reference in that play to Zeal-of-the-Land Busy (a character from Bartholomew Fair, composed ten years earlier) suggests the continuing relevance of Jonson's writing, in contrast to the fleeting "news" his comedy mocks (H&S 6:345). Often he uses his plays to assert distinctions between himself and other contemporary playwrights, and occasionally he even uses them to mock the writing, character, or physical mannerisms of his play-writing rivals or other antagonists. The Staple of News is crammed with jokes at Nathaniel Butter's expense, while A Tale of a Tub satirizes the masque-writing abilities of Inigo Jones, implying that any patron who employs him does so at the risk of looking ridiculous. Although clearest in his early and late plays, Jonson's need to promote himself through his works was grounded in his need to make a place for himself in the contemporary social hierarchy. For him as for his audience, "literature" and "society" could never be wholly separate or distinct.

Self-promotion in Jonson's plays is inseparable from the numerous themes in his dramas directly relevant to the psychology of patronage, to the experience of living in a competitive, hierarchical society. Certainly this connection with real life holds true of the theme of distinguishing appearance from reality, so prominent in so many works of Renaissance literature. In Jonson's culture, properly interpreting others' motives was vitally important to one's security, and concern with the appearance one projected was often tied to a concern with the reactions of superiors and rivals. In *Cynthia's Revels* Amorphus even contends that faces themselves must be patterned to prove appealing (2.3.11–50). His speech carries to a parodic extreme the emphasis on appearance in Jonson's culture. Similarly, in *Sejanus* we watch the corrupt physician Eudemus as he helps the adultress, Livia, apply her cosmetics (2.1.53ff.). Yet while Eudemus pretends to serve Livia, he covertly serves Sejanus—but ultimately serves himself. Both he and Livia put on appearances—she literally, he figuratively. Eudemus's confidence that subsequent ages will admire Livia's adultery calls attention to Jonson's own role in highlighting her moral ugliness (2.1.90–94) and thus implies Jonson's contrast with Eudemus. Jonson is the true physician. While Eudemus works to disguise Livia's blemishes, Jonson works to expose her true nature for all to see. He strips away any illusions about her beauty in the very act of having Eudemus apply the cosmetics. If Eudemus perverts the ideals of his profession, Jonson ennobles the role of playwright, using his talents to expose deformities, not disguise them.

One irony of this whole scene, of course, is that while Livia thinks she is deceiving her husband, she is actually being deceived both by Eudemus and by Sejanus. But this irony relates to the larger irony of the play, which is that while Sejanus thinks he is manipulating Tiberius, he is the victim of the emperor's stratagems. Indeed, *Sejanus* (along with *Volpone*) is one of Jonson's most searching examinations of the problem of distinguishing between appearance and reality. It repeatedly emphasizes the difficulties of separating the merely apparent from the truly real, as well as the constant need to manage appearances. Right from the start it communicates a strong sense of what it is like to live in a court culture in which one's every move is observed and scrutinized by those who will not hesitate to exploit any sign of weakness. Repeatedly Jonson suggests that desiring and possessing power in such a culture go hand in hand with deep insecurity. The insecurity feeds the hunger for power, but the kind of power achieved creates, in turn, further unease. Such power is inherently unstable because, as the product of competition, it can as easily be lost.[15]

Again and again (most obviously in *Volpone*), Jonson scrutinizes the use of disguise as a means of social deception and as a tactic for gratifying selfish ambition. Throughout his career he shows a keen interest in how people can mask their true motives in order to promote personal power, but he also sometimes suggests that such disguising can lead to self-deception, to the disguiser's own eventual inability to separate the apparent from the real. This confusion can lead in turn, as it does for Volpone and Sejanus, to an exaggerated and ultimately disastrous self-confidence. Deceiving others by manipulating appearances can create a smug blindness to others' manipulations. Sejanus no more expects betrayal from Tiberius than Volpone expects it from Mosca, yet both deceivers are deceived; the virus with which they poison healthy relations eventually undoes them both. The deceit central to their power is also the key to their weakness. By implicitly attacking such characters, Jonson insinuates his own integrity and disdain for manipulation. Although a dramatist, he tacitly repudiates drama's potential for deception. Instead he uses the theater to attack the whole notion of social play-acting; he focuses on characters obsessed with self-promotion, simultaneously distancing himself from their motives while promoting his own image and interests. Parallel trial scenes in both *Sejanus* and *Volpone* highlight his use of theater to attack deceptive theatricality. In the performance Tiberius and Sejanus stage before the assembled Senate in act 3, Jonson mocks their perverse play-acting, while in *Volpone* the trial that should serve to reveal and affirm truth actually serves to disguise it. Both works communicate a strong sense of the trial as play, as performance; in both trials, certain characters assume roles but by doing so unwittingly reveal significant aspects of their true selves (as when Voltore pretends to be fundamentally irrational [5.12.21–28]). In both cases, then, the trial-as-play becomes part of Jonson's larger play-as-trial, his use of the theater to delve into the truth and publicly expose it. Both scenes further undermine our respect for the corrupt characters even as they enhance our respect for the playwright's power.[16]

If Jonson's plays work to promote his own security, they also play on his audience's need to feel secure. Although his characters are often easily deceived, he usually makes it relatively simple for us, as audience, to separate the apparent from the real—at least while watching his plays. Mammon and Drugger may fall for the deceptions of Face and Subtle, but *we* are not so foolish. While witnessing Jonson's plays, we possess the kind of satisfying insight usually denied us in the world of everyday social relations. We can scrutinize the motives of his characters in a way impossible in "real life"; we can know their true intentions as we can never know the motives and intentions of our own peers, rivals, and superiors. In the theater, we are in the privileged position of spectators, watching as some characters craft performances while others succumb to them; yet all the while, we are remote from the immediate threat such deception poses. In the comedies, we can laugh at others' gullibility because our own interests are not directly threatened; indeed, the comedies temporarily heighten our sense of personal power by allowing us to observe the drama of deceit and manipulation without being immediately implicated in it or intimidated by it. The playwright thus enhances his power partly by enhancing ours, allowing us to share in a superior vision, a secure insight into others' motives not often available outside the theater. Both in his comedies and in his tragedies, Jonson implicitly serves as our interpreter of social reality, our guide to what is (or is not) real and legitimate. He implicitly affirms that there *is* a reality to be known and discovered, that appearance is not all there is, that objective truth exists, and that he possesses insight into it. The confidence his works exude strengthens his own position, and indeed, the more sincerely confident he seemed, the stronger his own appeal was likely to be.

But Jonson does not always or completely make interpretation easy; often his plays leave us in the midst of motivational tangles and interpretive blind alleys. To us, at least, Face and Subtle are obvious charlatans, but what about Lovewit? What do we make of the judges in *Volpone* or of Quarlous and Winwife in *Bartholomew Fair?* Tiberius in *Sejanus* is almost as difficult for us to figure out as for the characters on stage; we never quite know what his real feelings are or what he might do next. By making him so difficult to comprehend, Jonson makes us *feel* the interpretive uncertainty, even the paranoia, so central to the play's themes and mood. Here and in his other dramas, he plays on the anxiety inherent in all social interpretation, distancing us from it partly but not entirely. His works exploit our desire for sure and certain readings of others' motives, and for the most part they offer more surety and certainty than is ever possible in everyday life. But even in the early plays ambiguities remain. Lorenzo Senior in *Every Man In*, Asper in *Every Man Out*, Ovid in *Poetaster*: these are just a few of the characters Jonson makes it difficult for us to interpret easily. Such ambiguity contributes to the complexity and interest of his plays, adding tension to works whose narrative thrust is often weaker than their emphasis on character exposition. The unstable union between Doll, Face, and Subtle in *The Alchemist*—prominently emphasized in the play's opening scene—lends the play a tension it would otherwise lack, for while we watch the cheaters bilk the fools, we are constantly aware that they may turn on one another. The actions of Face and Subtle can always be interpreted not only as devices in a plot to deceive the visiting gulls but also as tactics in their own struggles for *personal* dominance. Sometimes it seems as difficult for us as for their allies to discern their real motives.[17]

Much the same is true of *Volpone:* almost immediately Jonson begins insinuating the independence Mosca eventually displays; almost from the start we sense that Volpone is less potent than he imagines, that Mosca is more crafty than he lets on, and that Mosca has a shrewder— and more powerful—understanding of Volpone's vulnerabilities than Volpone does of others'. And yet our inability (for much of the play) to decipher Mosca's motives contributes not only to our sense of the irony of his relations with his patron but also to the total complexity of the play. The ambiguity at the heart of so much of Jonson's drama undermines any exaggerated confidence we might otherwise have in ourselves as interpreters. Some uncertainty seems almost always part of our experience of his plays, reminding us of the even greater difficulties of interpreting persons and situations in "real life" and thus heightening our insecurity. Such uncertainty enhances the value and power of the poet who claims to grasp—and provide a guide to—the complexities of social experience.

For the most part, Jonson makes it easy for us to discern who are the vicious and who are the fools, who is sincere and who is not. That he doesn't always do so indicates not the failure of his art but its success, not the limits of his authority but the tactical sophistication with which he promotes it. For instance, any misgivings we may feel about the gallant heroes at the end of *Epicoene,* or any uncertainty we may have about Lovewit's moral stature in *The Alchemist,* or any discomfort we may feel with Quarlous, Grace, or Winwife in *Bartholomew Fair* reflect back positively on Jonson himself. His ability to make us scrutinize the real motives and true worth even of characters who might otherwise seem conventionally admirable reflects positively on his own powers of moral discrimination and on his ability to help us share in those powers. The more subtle his characters' shortcomings are, the more they insinuate their creator's ethical acuity. His ambiguous characters challenge us most forcefully to develop our own powers of discrimination. The skills he encourages his audience to hone would have been relevant to their actual social experience; the uncertainty he plays on would have been rooted in the similar uncertainties of their everyday lives. Given the importance of dependency in his culture, issues of interpretation were less a matter of philosophical musing than of pragmatic social survival. Jonson's interest in deception and distrust may have grown out of his own experiences with the challenges his culture posed; certainly it must have resonated with his audience, especially with that most important segment whose lives were most directly affected by the need to manage appearances and distinguish the bogus from the sincere.

The very need to be concerned with separating appearance from reality is linked to the extent to which the self in Jonson's culture was conditioned and defined by the individual's role as a social *performer*. The ability to manipulate appearances was grounded in a fundamental *need* to do so, and that need reflected one's ultimate lack of independent security. An extreme example is Kastril, in *The Alchemist*. At first glance, he seems anything but dependent. Angry and abusive, he seems positively *anti*-social, an extreme egotist who viciously threatens his own sister and demonstrates even less concern for others. He epitomizes and carries to parodic excess the egocentric combativeness latent in most of the play's other characters (including Face and Subtle). But the parodox of Kastril's behavior is that he acts this way partly to win acceptance. Although anger might seem one of the most spontaneous emotions, his is carefully constructed with an eye toward its *effect*. Because he thinks combativeness is the current fashion (and in a sense the play proves him right), Kastril's passion is partly affected: he uses it to attract attention, to carve out a recognized social niche. His hostility reflects not his independence but his driving need to be accepted; it reflects not an excess of power but deep-seated feelings of powerlessness. But it also helps him deny to himself and others just how dependent he is. La Foole, in *Epicoene*, seems fundamentally Kastril's opposite. If Kastril is bitterly abusive, La Foole is almost hypersociable. But his good humor is a thin veneer overlying an essential egotism and self-concern. He too depends on others to affirm and ratify his power. For all their obvious differences, both characters share a fundamental hunger for acceptance by those for whom they lack any genuine concern. Their self-absorption is intimately connected to their essential insecurity.

Many of Jonson's fools exhibit this same lack of integrity and independence; indeed, it is this trait that makes them so easy to manipulate and deceive. Stephano in *Every Man In*, Fungoso in *Every Man Out*, Asotus in *Cynthia's Revels*, Cokes in *Bartholomew Fair*, and numerous other characters in other plays all betray a fundamental insecurity that leaves them with no central core of stable selfhood. Explicitly, Jonson contrasts such characters with the knaves who exploit them, but implicitly he contrasts them with himself. His fierce satire on their empty pliability asserts his own firmness and strength of character. But he asserts this security precisely to help create it; his claims to inner fortitude are designed to promote his power by making him more publicly attractive. Although he attacks characters for whom perform-ing is everything, these very attacks are part of his own performance. Gripped by many of the same pressures that weigh on his fools (such as the desire to be accepted as a gentleman), Jonson mocks them so as to distance himself from them. By mocking others' bogus aspirations he signifies the naturalness and legitimacy of his own. Emphasizing their ineptness helps intimate *his* social and artistic decorum. Although the plays imply his fundamental indifference to the pressures his fools buckle under, the plays themselves constitute intriguingly complex responses to similar challenges and expectations.

This is why social ostracism and ridicule—partly represented within the plays and partly incited by them—are so often the punishment the fools receive; to them, nothing is more devastating than rejection. Yet the same derisive laughter Jonson both depicts in the plays and provokes in the audience destroys the fools' power while signifying and affirming his own. Such laughter exhibits his ability to control others' reactions, to direct and focus their contempt where he will. Laughter allows members of the audience to distance themselves, in public, from the depicted foolishness; ostensibly spontaneous and automatic, it be-comes part of their own social display. Shared laughter signifies each spectator's membership in a larger community. The general relaxation it allows, creates, and publicly manifests signifies a temporary, partial cessation of competition, a brief escape from the insecurity and uncer-tainty of normal interaction. It thus affirms the audience's sense of its own power, individually and collectively. And the same laughter that signals rejection of Jonson's fools signals acceptance of their creator; it stands as public affirmation that he possesses the very skills his fools lack. Of course, Jonson could hardly predict how audiences would respond; their failure to laugh could (and sometimes did) put him in the same position as his fools. Absence of laughter could mean public humiliation, exhibiting his lack of literary and social power and thus further undermining his security. Spectators would then affirm their own collective and individual strength by making common cause against the poet rather than against his characters; they would subject *him* to the same ostracism his fools feared—ostracism his plays were designed to control and direct. Jonson often attempts to protect himself against this possibility by implying his essential unconcern with au-dience reaction, his essential confidence in the objective worth of himself and his works. But such a stance is itself strategic, designed to appeal to the audience by implying the poet's forthright self-respect. The danger, of course, is that it risks seeming arrogant, so that by attempting to affirm one's power one seems to challenge and rebuke the audience. A strategy devised to shield one from criticism might inadvertently provoke even more virulent contempt.

Jonson's plays are thus theatrical in ways that transcend the obvious. They are part of his own performance, as he himself clearly recognized. How else account for their extreme self-consciousness, for the pervasive sense they communicate explicitly (through dedications, inductions, choric figures, epilogues, and other devices) and implicitly (through themes, plot emphases, and character portrayals) that the audience has come to judge not only the work but also the author? The exercise of individual power is both the central subject and one of the fundamental objects of his plays. A concern with micropolitics is built into their very devices and structures. Jonson shows relatively little interest in larger, macropolitical problems; his drama is not designed primarily to comment on great ideological issues.[18] Even when it does comment on them, it generally does so in ways that promote his own interests. Mostly, though, his drama is concerned with how power is used and abused, accumulated and lost, in the everyday lives of particular people. Even the two tragedies emphasize micropolitics: Sejanus and Catiline struggle not for impersonal principles (not even perverted ones) but simply to advance their own ambitions. Jonson seems less concerned with the impact of large transcendent forces (whether economic, ideological, or religious) than with the ways individuals exercise and respond to personal power. In a culture such as his, this emphasis is hardly surprising.

Jonson seems to have realized that the theater itself could be a potent arena for micropolitical struggle. Because it brought together large numbers of influential people, it offered an obvious platform for the playwright to promote himself. He did so, however, not only implicitly and explicitly through his plays, but sometimes also personally, through his behavior at the playhouse. Jonson's rivals sometimes mocked the way he courted superiors at the theater (H&S 11:369), but their mockery testifies to the threat they felt. His own ridicule of ambitious sycophants seems partly designed to distance him from the suspicions they provoked. The plays repeatedly imply his recognition that naked ambition is counterproductive. As the derisive reaction to some of his early and late plays suggests, however, he was not always the best judge of his own subtlety and tact. In *The Magnetic Lady*, one character even concedes that Jonson's efforts to shape audience response often boomeranged, but the admission itself is part of yet another attempt to guide reaction (H&S 6:511).

Every element of Jonson's plays has some micropolitical aspect and effect. This seems especially true when one remembers the social composition of his audience, the fact that its most important and influential members were also the most powerful members of society. Throughout his career, his plays suggest an acute sensitivity to his spectators' rank and standing. His many contemptuous references to "gentles" and "gallants" hardly refute the point and in fact confirm it. Such references indicate his special need to control and contain their reactions; his satire on the "plush and velvet" crowd who criticized or upstaged his works serves to distinguish such "*fastidious*" and "impertinent" pretenders from the *true* gentles he hoped to impress (H&S 6:397, 493). By caricaturing and ridiculing the behavior of *some* privileged spectators, he attempts to impose his own definition of what counts as acceptable behavior for the privileged at large. His attacks on "gentile ignorance" (H&S 6:511) are aimed primarily at malefactors, but they also seek to influence the majority of gentles to share his views and to ostracize those who threaten him. His satire on some of the privileged only indicates how generally important to him that group was.

At the theater, Jonson could mingle with notables from all spheres, and they in turn could profit from being seen in his company. One play alludes to the practice of banqueting the playwright; doing so advertised his hosts' generosity while allowing them to bask in his fame (H&S 6:270). But the playhouse itself provided a forum for the audience. Some of the wealthier spectators used performances as an opportunity to exhibit their patronage, buying blocks of tickets for their "friends" and thus creating a kind of personal *faction* within the broader audience (H&S 6:15). Many spectators attended the theater as much to display themselves as to witness plays; Jonson's works are full of frustrated references to theatergoers who sought to appropriate his plays for their own performances. By sitting on stage, by commenting too loudly, or by dressing in the latest fashions, they hoped to advertise themselves before their superiors, competitors, and influential equals in an important public forum. Micropolitics, then, was not simply a recurring theme of the plays, not simply a concern of the playwright or his characters. It was a driving force behind the real-life drama the audience enacted before, after, and even during the regular performance. The same ambitions, tensions, and ambiguities of behavior and motive that Jonson explores in his plays were very much present in the playhouse itself.

At the very least, Jonson must have hoped that the audience's performances would not conflict with his own; ideally, theirs would ratify his or be guided by it. His various attempts to control their reactions only make his drama political in yet another sense. The issue was not only who would have power over the interpretation of his *texts* but who would control an important opportunity for public self-display. Like many of his poems to patrons, Jonson's dramas seek to manipulate and guide response, to set the terms (explicitly, in the Induction to *Bartholomew Fair*) of the interaction between playwright and spectators. All dramatists, of course, manipulate their audiences; ironically, though, sometimes the very obviousness of Jonson's efforts destroys their effectiveness. His heavy-handed self-assertion often undermines the authority it seeks to uphold. The very aspects of his plays that seem to advertise his power and self-regard—the inductions, the prologues and epilogues, the choric commentary, the characters clearly modeled on the poet—all testify as well to his anxious vulnerability. Although he frequently claimed indifference to public reaction, such claims underscore his real concern even as they seek to shape, blunt, or at least preempt audience response. But the devices he used to assert power over his texts often provided his antagonists with potent weapons to use against him. His studied fearlessness, far from increasing strength by displaying strength, could make him seem pompous and arrogant. In a sense, his tactical blunders evince the competitive pressures he labored under; his mistakes more often result from desperation than from unconcern.

The theater's public nature raised the stakes of the poet's failure or success there; humiliating ineptness, either on or off the stage, would not pass unnoticed or unremarked. Much more was at risk when a writer presented himself through a play than when he showed a single poem to a particular patron, and the risks were intensified by the very size and composition of the audience. Moreover, the fact that in writing for the stage the dramatist depended on sometimes unreliable intermediaries—the actors—could only increase his cause for concern. It was particularly in connection with his plays that Jonson felt the full force of his dependency; most of his legal troubles resulted from suspicions concerning his dramas, and many of his surviving letters to superiors solicit help in dealing with such problems (H&S 1:190–202). It is easy to exaggerate the independence the plays exhibit; their satire on courtiers, gallants, and lawyers, for instance, bespeaks not so much an indifference to those groups as precisely a recognition of their social importance and an attempt to shape the behavior and attitudes acceptable among them. Thus, in mocking sycophantic courtiers Jonson not only defines himself by contrast with them but also makes common cause with the vast body of courtiers—almost all of them, no doubt—who did not regard themselves as sycophants. Generally his satire takes aim at the artificial, the insincere, and the egotistical, and it could be expected to appeal to anyone who fancied himself free from such traits. His satire could increase his power by inviting others to embrace and endorse the self-image it presented.

Within limits, a reputation for independence could hardly hurt Jonson in the competition for patronage. Horace in *Poetaster* remarks on the poet's need to avoid appearing a flatterer (3.5.33–36), and elsewhere in that play Jonson implies the dangers of seeming too dependent upon superiors (4.7.8–11). Chloe, the social-climbing jeweler's wife, is advised to treat her superiors "impudently," since "they will count them fooles" who treat them with excessive deference (4.1.31–39). The effect of this passage is complex: Jonson mocks the speaker, the noblewoman Cytheris, who gives Chloe such devious advice about how to act naturally. Jonson's mockery insinuates his own greater respect for legitimate social distinctions, but the passage also implies his recognition that superiors had little use for obvious flatterers, because flatterers diminished their public power and were unreliable clients. Caesar at one point in *Poetaster* thanks Horace for answering him with "free, and holesome sharpnesse: / Which pleaseth Caesar more than servile fawnes. / A flatterd prince soon turnes the prince of fooles" (5.1.94–96). Once again, the effect is complicated: Jonson offers his own superiors a model to emulate, a model few could match. At the same time, Caesar's comment is sensibly pragmatic: only when inferiors are honest can a superior's power be secure.

Jonson uses his plays to proffer himself as a forthright and dependable counselor, but he was never unaware of the risks involved in writing for the theater. At least twice he withdrew in disgust, and during the period of his greatest economic security, no new play of his was performed. Competition in the theater could be fiercer and more open than in other spheres, and attacking an enemy through a play heightened the consequences for both parties involved. The early poetomachia or "war of the theaters" was fueled by an intense psychic energy born of the participants' sense of how much was at stake. Their own livelihoods, their own standing with peers and superiors and with the public at large—all this was potentially imperiled. The quarrel must have fascinated theater-goers partly for this reason; for them it was a kind of blood sport: it offered the spectacle of real defeat and real triumph and involved genuine pain, humiliation, exaltation, and assorted other passions, all deeply felt. Although presented on stage by actors playing parts, this was no fiction, and the audience knew it.

But their interest may have been piqued for still another reason: the poetomachia had all the allure of the familiar. Such quarrels were hardly unusual in Jonson's day; similar motives and passions prompted much of the infighting and jealousy common at court, itself a forum not unlike the playhouse. In both places, personal ambitions were acted out before an audience of highly significant others whose reactions and assessments might determine one's public standing. The poetomachia was fueled by competitive, micropolitical motives of the sort Jonson explores more widely in his drama—motives which his audience could hardly fail to recognize or take some personal interest in. His plays allowed him to explore and examine—for himself and for others—some of the central issues raised and crucial challenges posed by participation in a culture rooted in dependent power relations.

In the broadest sense, the problems Jonson deals with in his dramas were problems immediately relevant to the lives of a great many members of his audience. The patronage concerns that color so many of his other works inevitably affected the plays as well. Whether addressing patrons, rivals, or friends, whether writing masques for the court, dramas for the theater, or single poems for private circulation, Jonson was always conscious of the social context in which his works were performed. Saying this, however, by no means reduces them to simple historical or biographical documents, interesting only for the light they shed on the poet's personality or on their particular moments in political or cultural history. Rather, it suggests how a patronage perspective can enrich and complicate our understanding of Jonson's works *as* works of art. The intricate, potentially ambiguous relations between the poet and his audience are reflected in the formal, artistic intricacies of his works themselves.

Written for an audience of superiors who could reward, punish, or damagingly ignore their author, for rivals who might attack him, for allies and friends who might offer assistance or consolation, or for a broader public itself implicated in hierarchical social relations, Jonson's works (simply as pieces of rhetoric) were bound to have been multilayered and entangled. Even a poem of "plain" statement came inevitably to be more than that, for the statement it made concerned not only its own meaning or "message" but its author's image of himself and his attempt to project that image into the social world. Poems of so-called direct address are in some ways among the most indirect and complicated of all, for in them the poet most clearly confronts another ego, and in them his image is most obviously exposed to potential criticism or rejection.

Studying Jonson's writings, including his dramas, as patronage poems involves not simply understanding their economic or social "background" but appreciating the often immense and intricate impact the patronage situation could have on the minute details of particular works. It suggests new ways of reading such works with close and fruitful attention. But, at the same time, it is capable of drawing strength and sustenance from most other approaches to Renaissance literature. Since nearly every other approach implies something about the poet's presentation of himself to an audience, there would seem to be little difficulty in relating most other ways of reading Renaissance literature to a patronage perspective. Indeed, such an endeavor, by complicating and deepening our understanding of how a patronage poet like Jonson interacted with his audience, could only further enrich our understanding of his works themselves.

Notes

Chapter 1. Introduction: Poets and the Psychology of Patronage

1. A strong sense of the pervasiveness of patronage relations in Renaissance culture is communicated, for instance, in the interdisciplinary collection of essays *Patronage in the Renaissance*, ed. Guy Fitch Lytle and Stephen Orgel (Princeton: Princeton University Press, 1981). Equally comprehensive, although less detailed, is the collection *The Courts of Europe: Politics, Patronage and Royalty: 1400–1800*, ed. A. G. Dickens (New York: McGraw-Hill, 1977). On political patronage one of the best short treatments remains the article by Wallace T. MacCaffrey, "Place and Patronage in Elizabethan Politics," in *Elizabethan Government and Society: Essays Presented to Sir John Neale*, ed. S. T. Bindoff, et al. (London: University of London, Athlone Press, 1961), 95–126. See also Linda Levy Peck, *Northampton: Patronage and Policy at the Court of James I* (London: George Allen and Unwin, 1982); and, in particular, the first chapter of Conrad Russell's *Parliaments and English Politics, 1621–1629* (Oxford: Clarendon Press, 1979). A fine sense of the comprehensiveness of artistic patronage is communicated by James Neil O'Neill, "Queen Elizabeth I as Patron of the Arts" (Ph.D. diss., University of Virginia, 1966). On music see, for example, David C. Price, *Patrons and Musicians of the English Renaissance* (Cambridge: Cambridge University Press, 1981); on painting, William Gaunt, *Court Painting in England from Tudor to Victorian Times* (London: Constable, 1980). One of the best treatments of church patronage remains Christopher Hill's *Economic Problems of the Church* (Oxford: Clarendon Press, 1956).

For a sophisticated discussion of many of the larger issues touched on in this chapter, see Linda Levy Peck, " 'For a King not to be bountiful were a fault': Perspectives on Court Patronage in Early Stuart England," *Journal of British Studies* 25 (1986): 31–61.

2. On connections between patronage, patriarchy, and the broader world view, see for instance Peter Laslett's *The World We Have Lost*, 2d ed. (New York: Scribner's, 1971), especially the first chapter. See also Gordon J. Schochet, *Patriarchialism in Political Thought: The Authoritarian Family and Political Speculation and Attitudes Especially in Seventeenth Century England* (New York: Basic Books, 1975), esp. 54–84. Ann Jennalie Cook usefully summarizes a great deal of pertinent sociological information in her study, *The Privileged Playgoers of Shakespeare's London, 1576–1642* (Princeton: Princeton University Press, 1981).

On more general issues of power and literature in the Renaissance, see for instance Stephen Greenblatt, *Renaissance Self-Fashioning* (Chicago: University of Chicago Press, 1980); Jonathan Goldberg, *James I and the Politics of Literature* (Baltimore: Johns Hopkins University Press, 1983); Jonathan Dollimore,

Radical Tragedy: Religion, Ideology and Power in the Drama of Shakespeare and His Contemporaries (Chicago: University of Chicago Press, 1984); Jonathan Dollimore and Alan Sinfield, eds., Political Shakespeare: New Essays in Cultural Materialism (Ithaca, N.Y., and London: Cornell University Press, 1985); and Eckhard Auberlen, The Commonwealth of Wit: The Writer's Image and His Strategies of Self-Representation in Elizabethan Literature (Tübingen: Gunter Narr Verlag, 1984). Although my approach to some of the issues dealt with in these books often differs from the approaches taken by the authors, all have proved stimulating in various ways. For further discussion of these general questions, see, for instance, various recent essays and books by Louis Adrian Montrose, Annabel Patterson, Frank Whigham, Arthur Marotti, Leonard Tennenhouse, and others, some of which are listed in my bibliography. See also a number of essays published in recent issues of the journal Representations, several of the essays included in the Spring 1983 issue of New Literary History, the Winter 1986 special issue of English Literary Renaissance, and the collection of essays edited by Stephen Greenblatt, The Power of Forms in the Renaissance (Norman, Okla.: Pilgrim Books, 1982). For helpful surveys of some of the best recent scholarship and of the issues it raises, see Jonathan Goldberg, "The Politics of Renaissance Literature: A Review Essay," ELH 49 (1982): 514–42; Annabel Patterson, "Talking About Power," John Donne Journal 2 (1983): 91–106; Jean E. Howard, "The New Historicism in Renaissance Studies," English Literary Renaissance 16 (1986): 13–43; and Kevin Sharpe, "The Politics of Literature in Renaissance England," History 71 (1986): 235–47.

An exceptionally provocative discussion of the place of the poet in the English Renaissance is offered by Richard Helgerson in his book Self-Crowned Laureates: Spenser, Jonson, Milton, and the Literary System (Berkeley: University of California Press, 1983). Leah S. Marcus's recent book, The Politics of Mirth: Jonson, Herrick, Milton, Marvell, and the Defense of Old Holiday Pastimes (Chicago: University of Chicago Press, 1986), appeared as my book was being prepared for the press. Like her previous work, this new study makes a major contribution to our understanding of the period and especially to our sense of the detailed complexities of Jonson's writing. Although it focuses on the France of Louis XIV, Norbert Elias's The Court Society (trans. Edmund Jephcott [New York: Pantheon, 1983]) is an immensely suggestive sociological study, especially intriguing for its discussion of competitive anxiety at court. And, of course, anyone who writes about power today must perforce acknowledge the stimulating influence of Michel Foucault; see, for instance, Power/Knowledge: Selected Interviews and Other Writings 1972–1977, ed. Colin Gordon (New York: Pantheon, 1980) or the appendix to The Archeology of Knowledge and the Discourse on Language, trans. A. M. Sheridan Smith (New York: Pantheon, 1972).

3. On traditions of patriarchy and their connection with larger social and political assumptions see, in addition to Laslett and Schochet, Michael Walzer's The Revolution of the Saints (New York: Atheneum, 1973), 183–93. On patronage in the classical period see, for instance, Literary and Artistic Patronage in Ancient Rome, ed. Barbara K. Gold (Austin: University of Texas Press, 1982).

4. This point has been argued very forcefully and persuasively, for instance, by Conrad Russell, in his Parliaments and English Politics, 1621–1629. See also Kevin Sharpe, "Introduction: Parliamentary History 1603–1629: In or Out of Perspective?" in Faction and Parliament, ed. Kevin Sharpe (Oxford: Clarendon Press, 1978), 1–42. Both Sharpe and Russell argue that the division of early Stuart political life into "court" and "country" parties seriously simplifies a

very complex reality. No "country" politician could stand wholly separate from the court, since it was chiefly at or through the court that his own hopes for advancement could be fulfilled and since it was from the court that benefits for his constituency would be derived. Although some of the more extreme versions of the "revisionist" view of early Stuart history have come under strong attack, even many opponents of the revisionists concede that their emphasis on micropolitics and patronage has proven a helpful corrective to an over-emphasis on ideological disputes and conflicts of principle. For typical statements of the anti-revisionist position, see, for instance, three articles published in the August 1981 issue of *Past and Present* (no. 92): Theodore K. Rabb, "The Role of the Commons" (55–78); Derek Hirst, "The Place of Principle" (79–99); and Christopher Hill, "Parliament and People in Seventeenth–Century England" (100–24). The first two articles are published under the general title, "Revisionism Revised: Two Perspectives on Early Stuart Parliamentary History."

5. For an excellent consideration of some of the issues raised here, see Margot Heinemann, *Puritanism and Theatre: Thomas Middleton and Opposition Drama Under the Early Stuarts* (Cambridge: Cambridge University Press, 1980).

6. For discussion of these facts and developments, see (in addition to Laslett, Walzer, and Schochet) Lawrence Stone, *The Family, Sex and Marriage in England 1500–1800*, abridged ed. (New York: Harper and Row, 1979), 69–180.

7. One of the most intriguing specimens of this kind of writing is *Sir William Wentworth's advice to his son* in *Wentworth Papers, 1597–1628*, ed. J. P. Cooper, *Camden Society Publications*, 4th ser., vol. 12 (London: Royal Historical Society, 1973), 9–24. Stone, in fact, singles out Wentworth's advice for particular discussion, remarking that the "thoroughly cynical view of the human condition and social relationships" presented in the volume "can be duplicated in many other examples of this genre of 'Advices', even if the somewhat paranoid overtones are peculiar to William Wentworth" (*The Family, Sex and Marriage*, 79).

For tamer examples of the "advice" genre, see *Advice to a Son: Precepts of Lord Burghley, Sir Walter Raleigh, and Francis Osborne*, ed. Louis B. Wright (Ithaca, N.Y.: Cornell University Press, 1962). In interpreting such precepts, it is always worth asking whether the writer intended his advice to be circulated among a broader audience, or whether the advice was strictly intended only for his son's eyes and consideration. The latter very definitely seems to have been the case with Wentworth's precepts.

8. On the centrality of the court see, for instance, G. R. Elton, "Tudor Government: The Points of Contact," in his *Studies in Tudor and Stuart Politics and Government*, 3 vols. (Cambridge: Cambridge University Press, 1983), 3:3–57. See also Lawrence Stone, *The Crisis of the Aristocracy, 1558–1641* (Oxford: Clarendon Press, 1965), esp. 385–504. See also Perez Zagorin, *The Court and the Country: The Beginning of the English Revolution* (New York: Atheneum, 1971), esp. 40–73, and J. E. Neale, "The Elizabethan Political Scene," in *Essays in Elizabethan History* (London: Jonathan Cape, 1958), 59–84. One of the most penetrating analyses of court psychology is Frank Whigham's "The Rhetoric of Elizabethan Suitors' Letters," *PMLA* 96 (1981): 864–82. Whigham stresses the anxiety of being present at (but especially of being absent from) the competitive atmosphere at court. He also shows how many of the rhetorical tactics that I discuss in this book in connection with literary texts also pervade the pragmatic, "non-literary" correspondence of the period. For an even fuller discus-

sion of the interpenetration of the artful and the pragmatic in this era, see his book *Ambition and Privilege: The Social Tropes of Elizabethan Courtesy Theory* (Berkeley: University of California Press, 1984). For a valuable discussion of the continental background to courtesy theory, see Wayne Rebhorn, *Courtly Performances: Masking and Festivity in Castiglione's "Book of the Courtier"* (Detroit, Mich.: Wayne State University Press, 1978).

9. An early but still useful study of English Renaissance literary patronage is Phoebe Sheavyn, *The Literary Profession in the Elizabethan Age*, 2d ed. (New York: Barnes and Noble, 1967). Some of Sheavyn's arguments—especially about the system's decline—have been challenged, and her book should be supplemented by later discussions. See, for instance, the chapter on patronage in Edwin Haviland Miller, *The Professional Writer in England: A Study of Non-dramatic Literature* (Cambridge, Mass.: Harvard University Press, 1959). See also Patricia Thomson, "The Literature of Patronage, 1580–1630," *Essays in Criticism* 2 (1952): 267–84; H. S. Bennett, *English Books and Readers 1558 to 1603* (Cambridge: Cambridge University Press, 1965); Eleanor Rosenberg, *Leicester: Patron of Letters* (New York: Columbia University Press, 1955); J. W. Saunders, *The Profession of English Letters* (London: Routledge and Kegan Paul, 1964), and his article "The Stigma of Print: A Note on the Social Bases of Tudor Poetry," *Essays in Criticism* 1 (1951): 139–64; Daniel Javitch, *Poetry and Courtliness in Renaissance England* (Princeton: Princeton University Press, 1978); R. W. Short, "The Patronage of Poetry Under James First" (Ph.D. diss., Cornell University, 1936); James Neil O'Neill, "Queen Elizabeth I as Patron of the Arts"; and Graham Parry, *Seventeenth-Century Poetry: The Social Context* (London: Hutchinson, 1985).

10. One of the best and briefest discussions of the distinctions between different kinds and classes of Renaissance writers is provided in the first chapter of John Danby's *Poets on Fortune's Hill* (London: Faber and Faber, 1952). For an overview of the "literary system" during this period, see the first chapter of Helgerson's *Self-Crowned Laureates*.

For a highly suggestive discussion of some of the ways in which the psychology of courtiership could affect the works of a nonprofessional poet, see Arthur F. Marotti, *John Donne: Coterie Poet* (Madison: University of Wisconsin Press, 1986).

11. Whether the conditions of medieval writers were really better than those of Renaissance writers seems less important than the latters' frequent assumption that conditions had deteriorated. Their satisfaction or dissatisfaction with their own situations was often tied to their view of how well patronage had functioned in the past, whether in the time of Chaucer or (more often) in the days of the Roman patrons Maecenas and Augustus.

Chapter 2. Jonson and the Poetics of Patronage

1. The quotations are from Jonson's *Conversations* with William Drummond of Hawthornden, printed in *Ben Jonson*, ed. C. H. Herford, Percy and Evelyn Simpson, 11 vols. (Oxford: Clarendon Press, 1925–52), 1:139. References to this edition will cite the abbreviation "H&S" and volume and page numbers. The various collections of Jonson's poetry will be abbreviated as follows: *Ep. (Epigrammes); For. (The Forrest); Und. (Under-wood); U.V. (Ungathered Verse)*. In quotations from Renaissance documents, *i, j, u*, and *v* have been regularized.

2. Ironically enough, had Jonson been born a gentleman or an aristocrat, he might not have felt the need to acquire so assiduously the immense learning

and highly developed skills he eventually used to pull himself up from his low status. Again and again throughout his career both he and his rivals recognized the added social potency his learning gave him.

3. On Jonson's early life, see H&S 1:1–17; Marchette Chute, *Ben Jonson of Westminster* (New York: Dutton, 1953), 17–60; and Rosalind Miles, *Ben Jonson: His Life and Work* (London and New York: Routledge and Kegan Paul, 1986), 1–48. David Riggs's forthcoming biography of Jonson makes many interesting suggestions about the possible connections between the poet's childhood and his later behavior and attitudes.

4. The distinction between writing for the theater and writing for the court may not have been nearly as clear-cut as is sometimes assumed. Ann Jennalie Cook, for instance, has recently argued that the audiences for Elizabethan and Jacobean plays may have been far less "popular" than we have become accustomed to imagining, that they were probably composed to a very large extent of the wealthy, the aristocratic, and the relatively well-educated—the same classes of people from whom Jonson's potential patrons and rivals would be drawn. See her study, *The Privileged Playgoers of Shakespeare's London, 1576–1642.* Failure in the theater could thus also mean a higher chance of failure in the courtly world from which the most influential segment of the theater's audience was largely drawn. The participants in the so-called "poetomachia," for instance, may have been motivated to a great extent by a desire to embarrass their rivals in front of this influential audience; for further discussion of this point, see chapter 5 below. It is also important to remember that plays were frequently performed before the court itself. Even when writing for the stage, then, Jonson could never entirely ignore the pressures of patronage competition. For discussion of a recent challenge to Cook's argument, see chapter 5, note 5, below.

5. For Gifford's defense of Jonson, see *The Works of Ben Jonson*, ed. Francis Cunningham, 3 vols. (London: Chatto and Windus, 1897–1903). For Parfitt's attack on views of Jonson as a poetic prostitute, see "History and Ambiguity: Jonson's 'A Speech according to Horace,'" *Studies in English Literature* 19 (1979): 92n.

Some of the best recent Jonson criticism discusses the kinds of tensions inherent in Jonson's verse; see, for instance, George Parfitt's *Ben Jonson: Public Poet and Private Man* (London: Dent, 1976), or the section on Jonson in Isabel Rivers, *The Poetry of Conservatism, 1600–1745: A Study of Poets and Public Affairs from Jonson to Pope* (Cambridge: Rivers Press, 1973), and also by the articles by William E. Cain ("The Place of the Poet in Jonson's 'To Penshurst' and 'To My Muse,'" *Criticism* 21 [1979]: 34–48), and by Don E. Wayne ("Poetry and Power in Ben Jonson's *Epigrammes*: The Naming of 'Facts' or the Figuring of Social Relations," *Renaissance and Modern Studies* 23 [1979]: 79–103). None of these studies, however, approaches Jonson from quite the perspective of patronage and self-presentation adopted here. Richard Helgerson's *Self-Crowned Laureates* does discuss poetic self-presentation, although not in quite the same terms or with the same emphases used here. More recently, Eckhard Auberlen has discussed Jonson and patronage in his book *The Commonwealth of Wit*; his discussion nicely sums up Jonson's views, whereas my own emphasis is on the ambivalences and ambiguities of his situation and their impact on his texts. Douglas M. Lanier has recently shown how "Patriarchy provided Jonson with one means of understanding and controlling the relations that mark literary authority. Jonson sought to represent his poetic autonomy in two ways: a struggle against discursive fathers, and a fathering of his own [poetic] sons." See his suggestive article, "Brainchildren: Self-representation and Patriarchy in Ben Jonson's Early Works," *Renaissance Papers* (1986): 53–68, esp. 67.

In one of the most richly provocative of recent articles on Jonson's poetry ("Authors-Readers: Jonson's Community of the Same," *Representations* 7 [1984]: 26–58), Stanley Fish explores the strategies by which Jonson attempts to "assert his freedom and dignity in the face of everything that would seem to preclude them" (27). Yet after exploring these strategies in exciting detail, Fish feels compelled to conclude that "There is every visible sign that Jonson is constrained by all the ties . . . that he proceeds to reject" (56). Although he chooses not to pursue the implications of this concession, it is precisely the effects of such constraints on the texture of Jonson's works that I have chosen to emphasize. Perhaps no one has described Jonson's conception of himself and his aesthetic better than Fish has done. My own effort, however, has been to explore the ambivalences embedded in that conception and the tensions between it and the social reality Jonson could not really exclude or ignore. For this reason I depart from Fish's contention that Jonson's poetry "is not designed to be *persuasive*" (56), that "so far is he from courting public recognition that he flees it, and is reluctant even to venture out in speech" (55). Instead, I argue that every aspect of Jonson's writing was inexorably rhetorical, self-consciously public, and inherently performative and representative. Jonson may have been "opposed to [a] vision of a theatrical life" (55), but that very opposition was part of his public display (which is not, however, to imply that it was insincere). Fish, of course, knows this (as the final paragraph of his article implies), but he is interested in pursuing other aspects of Jonson's art, and he does so with great effectiveness.

For discussion of Jonson from a macropolitical perspective, see Joseph John Kelly, "Ben Jonson's Politics," *Renaissance and Reformation*, n.s., 7 (1983): 192–215, and David Norbrook, *Poetry and Politics in the English Renaissance* (London: Routledge and Kegan Paul, 1984). Some suggestive general discussions of Jonson's poetry include: Thomas M. Greene, "Ben Jonson and the Centered Self," *Studies in English Literature* 10 (1970): 325–48; Arthur F. Marotti, "All About Jonson's Poetry," *ELH* 39 (1972): 208–37; Jonathan Z. Kamholtz, "Ben Jonson's *Epigrammes* and Poetic Occasions," *Studies in English Literature* 23 (1983): 77–94; and W. H. Herendeen, "Like a Circle Bounded in Itself: Jonson, Camden, and the Strategies of Praise," *Journal of Medieval and Renaissance Studies* 11, no. 2 (1981): 137–67. H. Jennifer Brady discusses Jonson's power in the sense of his strategies for intimidating readers in " 'Beware the Poet': Authority and Judgment in Jonson's *Epigrammes*," *Studies in English Literature* 23 (1983): 95–112.

6. Whether the charges lodged against Jonson by his detractors were true or not, he still had to be conscious of avoiding the appearance of confirming them. This self-consciousness must have pervasively affected the verse he wrote. His satirical poems, for instance, may have been as much defensive as offensive— not only in the sense that they may have been designed to respond to attacks, but in the sense that the image of Jonson they presented made him in various ways less vulnerable to criticism.

7. The most suggestive and influential account of these relations has, of course, been offered by Harold Bloom in *The Anxiety of Influence: A Theory of Poetry* (New York: Oxford University Press, 1973). Bloom focuses most of his attention on the Romantic and post-Romantic poets; and indeed, despite its emphasis on the pressures poets are under when they write, Bloom's theory

seems to presuppose a view of the poet as a fundamentally autonomous ego. The view of poetic anxiety offered here is one anchored in the pressures of the Renaissance poet's actual social position: the sources of that anxiety are not only the poet's "fathers" (literally: his patrons) but also the poet's siblings (his rivals for the patrons' attentions).

8. More broadly, Hugh Dalziel Duncan argues that *all* communication is a plea, an act of persuasion, and that whatever the content of our pleas may be, the forms through which such pleas will be made are affected by status considerations. See his book *Language and Literature in Society* (Chicago: University of Chicago Press, 1953), 121–22.

9. Similarly, those not directly threatened by the self-promotional tactics of their equals may actually have an incentive to suppress conscious awareness of them as tactics *per se*, since such awareness might be perceived as a threat by the other and thus contradict one's own self-interest.

10. My thinking about some of the theoretical issues touched on here has been influenced by a number of writers. See, for instance, several works by Erving Goffman: *The Presentation of Self in Everyday Life* (Garden City, N.Y.: Anchor Books, 1959); *Interaction Ritual: Essays on Face-to-Face Behavior* (Garden City, N.Y.: Anchor Books, 1967); and *Strategic Interaction* (Philadelphia: University of Pennsylvania Press, 1969). As the subtitle to *Interaction Ritual* suggests, Goffman's concern is primarily with the ways people interact with one another in actual daily meetings. I look at poems as, in one sense, "frozen" maneuvers from such personal interactions.

Other writers whose ideas have proved variously stimulating in my thinking about the problems this study raises include: Peter L. Berger and Thomas Luckmann, *The Social Construction of Reality: A Treatise in the Sociology of Knowledge* (Garden City, N.Y.: Anchor Books, 1967); Peter M. Blau, *Exchange and Power in Social Life* (New York: Wiley, 1964); Hugh Dalziel Duncan, *Symbols in Society* (New York: Oxford University Press, 1968); Edward E. Jones, *Ingratiation: A Social Psychological Analysis* (New York: Irvington, 1975); Mauk Mulder, *The Daily Power Game* (Leiden: Martinus Nijhoff Social Sciences Division, 1977); James T. Tedeschi, et al., *Conflict, Power, and Games: The Experimental Study of Interpersonal Relations* (Chicago: Aldine, 1973); and James T. Tedeschi, et al., "The Exercise of Power and Influence: The Source of Influence," in *The Social Influence Processes*, ed. James T. Tedeschi (Chicago: Aldine; New York: Atherton, 1972), 287–345. For some recent attempts to use these kinds of ideas to analyze Renaissance society, see *Persons in Groups: Social Behavior as Identity Formation in Medieval and Renaissance Europe*, ed. Richard C. Trexler (Binghampton, N.Y.: Medieval and Renaissance Texts and Studies, 1985); see particularly the essays by Peter Marsh and Ronald F. E. Weissman.

11. Claude J. Summers and Ted-Larry Pebworth, in their excellent Twayne series study *Ben Jonson* (Boston: Twayne, 1979), summarize the views of many critics when they assert that "It is a central fact of Jonson's personality and of his integrity as a poet that he is impressed by virtue and achievement rather than by title or position. . . . Jonson's integrity functions in many ways throughout all of his poems, but it is especially important in the complimentary epigrams, where it insulates him from any suspicion of sycophancy" (141). The Summers-Pebworth study is valuable not only in its own right, but also because its format helps make it a convenient reflection of the central tendencies of the best recent Jonson criticism.

12. Michael Korda, in his best-selling modern-day conduct book, *Power!*

How to Get It, How to Use It! (New York: Ballantine Books, 1975), points out that power "is perhaps the most personal desire we have, since even the intimacy of sex is usually shared with someone else. Power, by contrast, is a *private* passion, the winning and losing are internal, only we can know whether or not we've won our game" (64–65).

In his study of *Ingratiation*, the psychologist Edward E. Jones notes that "the omnipresence and importance of ingratiation are quite dramatically confirmed by observing what happens when the topics of flattery, manipulation, and deceptive social tactics are introduced into casual conversation. A common reaction to the intrusion of such topics is an almost palpable discomfort or at least ambivalence. There is often considerable interest in pursuing the theme, and it readily captures conversational attention; at the same time, however, there is an undercurrent of uneasiness which becomes more and more pronounced as the conversation continues. There seems to be ultimately something disruptive about making the arts and strategies of impression management salient and putting them on public display—even when everyone is obviously trying to be 'detached and objective' " (15).

However one chooses to regard the *desire* for power, participation in society seems to make it inevitable that one will be implicated in the processes by which power is won, lost, or maintained. As Tedeschi argues, "The presence of interdependent outcomes, whether admitted by the parties or concealed by social norms, gives one a rational motive to attempt to influence and maximize long-term gains. Even the person who wants nothing from others and desires to stay above the fray is not likely to succeed. As long as one stays in society, one must vie for power in order to counter the attempts of others to gain what one has or may be expected to maintain. The exercise of influence, offensively or defensively, is not so much a matter of morality as it is of necessity." See Tedeschi et al., "The Exercise of Power and Influence," in *The Social Influence Processes*, 324. It is the very inevitability of power relations that makes them potentially fruitful subjects of study, whether in sociology, psychology, or in social-psychologically oriented criticism.

13. In his provocative study, *The Birth and Death of Meaning*, 2d ed. (New York: Free Press, 1971), Ernest Becker observes that the main thing that gives conviction to a social performance is the self-conviction of the actor, since the self is largely an attitude of self-regard (108). Edward Jones argues that "ethical constraints do not prevent ingratiation, but often set the stage for self-deceptive cognitive work" (*Ingratiation*, 105)—which seems to mean that the actor has an incentive to regard even behavior (or perhaps especially behavior) whose practical effect is ingratiatory as virtuous behavior. Sheldon L. Messinger, et al., warn against confusing the analyst's perspective on a subject's behavior with the subject's own conscious awareness. They caution that one should not confound the perceptions of the first with the self-perceptions of the second. See Sheldon L. Messinger, with Harold Sampson and Robert D. Towne, "Life as Theater: Some Notes on the Dramaturgic Approach to Social Reality," in *Drama in Life: The Uses of Communication in Society*, edited by James E. Combs and Michael W. Mansfield (New York: Hastings House, 1976), 81–82. This anthology comprises one of the most comprehensive guides available to the dramatistic approach to human behavior.

Tedeschi argues that it is probably no accident that most of the influence modes available to (relatively) weak individuals are considered immoral, that it is easy to be virtuous when one is powerful (see *Conflict, Power, and Games*, 109). Ironically, because Jonson was in a position that made him more likely to be suspected of having self-conscious ingratiatory motives, he had all the more incentive to disguise them from others or to deny them in himself.

14. For an examination of the importance of this period, see W. David Kay, "The Shaping of Ben Jonson's Career: A Reexamination of Facts and Problems," *Modern Philology* 67 (1970): 224–37.

15. The life of Roger Manners is outlined in the *Dictionary of National Biography* (hereafter referred to as *DNB*); a more detailed account (especially of his finances) is provided by Lawrence Stone in his *Family and Fortune: Studies in Aristocratic Finance in the Sixteenth and Seventeenth Centuries* (Oxford: Clarendon Press, 1973), 176–84. In his forthcoming biography of Jonson, David Riggs argues that at the time the "Epistle" was written, the faction associated with the Earl of Essex, with which Manners was allied, was threatened with a diminishment of its power. This presumably would have made Jonson's celebration of the Countess's character and status all the more welcome in her eyes.

16. Stone, *Family and Fortune*, 180.

17. In quoting from any of Jonson's works, I use the text given in the Herford and Simpson edition. Other editions of Jonson's poetry, consulted because of the helpfulness of their commentary and notes, include: *The Works of Ben Jonson*, ed. Francis Cunningham (see note 5 above); *The Poems of Ben Jonson*, ed. Bernard H. Newdigate (Oxford: Basil Blackwell, 1936); *The Complete Poetry of Ben Jonson*, ed. William B. Hunter, Jr. (New York: Norton, 1963); *Ben Jonson*, ed. Ian Donaldson (New York: Oxford University Press, 1985); and *Ben Jonson: The Complete Poems*, ed. George Parfitt (New Haven: Yale University Press, 1982).

18. For a representative comment on the poem's opening passage see the analysis in the Twayne *Ben Jonson*, 163–64. A number of other reactions to the poem are summarized by James D. Garrison in his article, "Time and Value in Jonson's 'Epistle to Elizabeth Countesse of Rutland,'" *Concerning Poetry* 8 (1975): 53–58. For a sensitive discussion of the syntax of the opening passage, see Richard C. Newton's comments in his "'Ben./Jonson': The Poet in the Poems," in *Two Renaissance Mythmakers: Christopher Marlowe and Ben Jonson*, ed. Alvin Kernan (Baltimore: Johns Hopkins University Press, 1977), 165–95, esp. 171–74.

19. Ernest Becker, in *The Birth and Death of Meaning*, offers an interesting discussion of the attractiveness of the socially powerful individual, noting in particular that "To present an unfallible self is to present one that has an unshakeable control over words. . . . The proper word or phrase, properly delivered, is the highest attainment of human interpersonal power. The easy handling of the verbal context of action gives the only possibility of direct exercise of control over others" (93–94). These observations are especially interesting in light of the conclusion of Jonson's poem, where a faltering of the epistle's tone coincides with Jonson's sense of a possible threat to his status.

20. Becker notes that "Words are the only tools we have for confident manipulation of the interpersonal situation. By verbally setting the tone for action by the proper ceremonial formula, we permit complementary action by our interlocutor—*compel* it, if he is to sustain his face" (*The Birth and Death of Meaning*, 95).

21. Jones, *Ingratiation*, 32.

22. Percy Simpson makes the case for Daniel as the unnamed rival here; see "Jonson's Sanguine Rival," *Review of English Studies* 15 (1939): 464–65. In an earlier article with the same title, Raymond W. Short had argued that Daniel could not have been the poet referred to; see *Review of English Studies* 15

(1939): 315–17. The relationship between "Drayton and the Countess of Bedford" is discussed at length by Dick Taylor, Jr.; see *Studies in Philology* 49 (1952): 214–28. Jonson's relationship with Lucy is discussed in detail by Jennifer Reynolds Taylor in "Lucy Countess of Bedford, Jonson, and Donne" (Ph.D. diss., McMaster University, 1979).

23. Jackson I. Cope, in "Jonson's Reading of Spenser: The Genesis of a Poem" (*English Miscellany* 10 [1959]: 61–66), suggests that Jonson may be alluding in this epistle to some of the language of Spenser's *Ruines of Time*, in which Spenser had celebrated the Bedfords and the Sidneys together (63). By reminding the Countess of Bedford of her family's patronage of one of England's greatest recent poets, Jonson may once more be implicitly criticizing her own patronage of a mere "verser."

24. Hugh Duncan makes a similar point: "We fear indifference more than hate, because we can't address those who are indifferent to us, and we cannot be sure that if we do address them they will respond. Those who hate us *attend* to us, and we to them. . . . Individual disorganization originates in the *indifference* of those whose responses are necessary to our definition of our self. Hate, as much as love, organizes our social energies"; see his *Symbols in Society*, 102; 104.

25. My thinking about the problem of envy in general and about the particular theme of envy in Renaissance literature has been stimulated by Helmut Schoeck's masterful study *Envy: A Theory of Social Behavior*, trans. Michael Glenny and Betty Ross (New York: Irvington, 1966) and Ronald Bruce Bond's "A Study of *Invidia* in Medieval and Renaissance English Literature" (Ph.D. diss., University of Toronto, 1972).

26. Goffmann, *The Presentation of Self*, 36. Peter Berger, in his suggestive study *The Sacred Canopy: Elements of a Sociological Theory of Religion*, points out that "the subjective reality of the world hangs on the thin thread . . . of our conversation with significant others" (Garden City, N.Y.: Anchor Books, 1969 [17]). For Jonson the *most* significant others were the aristocrats who controlled his society, and whose patronage he sought throughout his career. It is always worth stressing that in his dealings with these people, far more than money was at stake.

27. For Drummond's reference to the poem, see H&S 1:135. Drummond later reports that Jonson's "censure of my verses was that they were all good, especiallie my Epitaph of the Prince save that they smelled too much of [the] schooles and were not after the Fancie of [the] tyme, for a child sayes he may writte after the fashion of [the] Greeks & latine verses in running. yett that he wished to please the King, that piece of Forth-Feasting had been his owne" (ibid.).

28. For further discussion of this issue, see chapters 3 and 5.
On non-print publication of poetry in the Renaissance, see J. W. Saunders, "From Manuscript to Print: A Note on the Circulation of Poetic MSS in the Sixteenth Century," *Proceedings of the Leeds Philosophical and Literary Society* 6, pt. 8 (1965): 507–28.

29. Tedeschi, et al., *The Exercise of Power and Influence*, 326.

30. On the complimentary poems as "inert," see E. Pearlman, "Ben Jonson: An Anatomy," *English Literary Renaissance* 9 (1979): 378. For Tedeschi's point, see *The Social Influence Processes*, 19.

31. William E. Cain makes a somewhat similar point in "The Place of the Poet," 41.

32. On Lodge's claim and the social motives behind it, see Catherine Constantine Koppell, " 'Of Poets and Poesy': The English Verse Epistle, 1595–1640"

(Ph.D. diss., University of Rochester, 1978). In a valuable article ("Mediation and Contestation: English Classicism from Sidney to Jonson," *Criticism* 25 [1983]: 211–37), Don E. Wayne argues that "Jonson's classicism was motivated in part by a calculated strategy of self-assertion" (217). In a book published just as mine was going to press, Sara J. van den Berg also comments thoughtfully on the motives and effects of Jonson's classicism. See *The Action of Ben Jonson's Poetry* (Newark: University of Delaware Press, 1987), 118.

One of the most suggestive discussions of Jonson's adaptation and assimilation of the classics is the chapter on him in Thomas M. Greene's *The Light in Troy: Imitation and Discovery in Renaissance Poetry* (New Haven and London: Yale University Press, 1982).

33. Stone, *Family and Fortune* (179), mentions Rutland's purchase of a copy of Sidney's *Arcadia* in 1599; he remarks, however, that Rutland's generally "very limited expenditure on books," coupled with other evidence, "suggests a young man of some natural intelligence but who had failed to master the classics and whose main interests lay elsewhere."

34. Jonson told Drummond that "Beamont wrot that Elegie on the death of the Countess of Rutland, and in effect her husband wanted the half of his. in his travells" (H&S 1:138). The elegy to which Jonson refers includes the following lines:

> As soone as thou couldst apprehend a griefe
> There were enough to meet thee, and the chief
> Blessing of women: marriage was to thee
> Nought but a sacrament of Misery:
> For whom thou hadst, if we may trust to Fame,
> Could nothing change about thee, but thy name.
> A name which who (that were again to do't)
> Would change without a thousand joyes to boot
> In all things else, thou rather leadst a life
> Like a betrothed Virgin than a Wife.

See *The "Conceited Newes" of Sir Thomas Overbury and his Friends*, ed. James E. Savage (Gainesville, Fla.: Scholars' Facsimiles and Reprints, 1968), 40. At around the time of the Countess's death (Rutland himself had already died), Beaumont became financially secure by marrying an heiress; his retirement from the theater also dates from this period. These circumstances may have made him less concerned with discretion than he might otherwise have been. Even so, when the poem was published it was published anonymously, and Drummond's question indicates that even a number of years after its composition the identity of its author was still unknown to some, but also that the poem had achieved a certain notoriety. (Beaumont himself was dead by the time Jonson's *Conversations* took place.) Anthony Miller's discussion of a possible alternative reading of one word of the conclusion does not affect the substance of my discussion; see his article, "Ben Jonson's 'Epistle to Elizabeth Countesse of Rutland': A Recovered MS Reading and Its Critical Implications," *Philological Quarterly* 62 (1983): 525–30.

Lawrence Stone, incidentally, raises the possibility that it may in fact have been Elizabeth who was sterile (see *Family and Fortune*, 196).

35. H&S 1:142.

36. Goffman, *Presentation of Self*, 11.

37. It made some difference, of course, *whom* an epitaph commemorated. Celebrating a child actor was one thing; celebrating the scion of an aristocratic

family was another. For further discussion and illustration of the impact of power on such poems, see my note "Jonson's Epitaph on the Countess of Shrewsbury," *The Explicator* 44, no. 3 (1986): 15–17. See also the discussion of the epitaph on Cecilia Bulstrode in chapter 3 of this book and of the eulogy on Shakespeare in chapter 6. Important recent discussions of the epitaphs include Jack D. Winner, "The Public and Private Dimensions of Jonson's Epitaphs," in *Classic and Cavalier: Essays on Jonson and the Sons of Ben*, ed. Claude J. Summers and Ted-Larry Pebworth (Pittsburgh: University of Pittsburgh Press, 1982), 107–19; and G. W. Pigman III, "Suppressed Grief in Jonson's Funeral Poetry," *English Literary Renaissance* 13 (1983): 203–20.

38. I briefly discuss Jonson's love poetry elsewhere in this book. See, for instance, chapters 3, 4, and 7. See also my article on "Ben Jonson's Chaucer," forthcoming in *English Literary Renaissance*.

39. For one more example, see my note on "Jonson's *Epigrammes* 1–3," *The Explicator* 45, no. 2 (1987): 7–10. In an insightful article, Jack D. Winner shows how Jonson distinguished his collection of epigrams from similar poems written by contemporary competitors; see "Ben Jonson's *Epigrammes* and the Conventions of Formal Verse Satire," *Studies in English Literature* 23 (1983): 61–76.

Chapter 3. Issues of Flattery and Freedom

1. See Elizabeth Hamilton, *Henrietta Maria* (New York: Coward, McCann and Geoghegan, 1976), 100–01. See also H&S 11:93.

2. This wordplay has also been noted by Stanley Fish in the course of his careful examination of the poem; see "Authors-Readers," 45–46.

3. See, for instance, Alice-Lyle Scoufos, *Shakespeare's Typological Satire: A Study of the Falstaff–Oldcastle Problem* (Athens: University of Ohio Press, 1979), 246–62 and passim; and Charles Nicholl, *A Cup of News: The Life of Thomas Nashe* (London: Routledge and Kegan Paul, 1984), 242–56.

4. Philip J. Ayres, "Jonson, Northampton, and the 'Treason' in *Sejanus*," *Modern Philology* 80 (1983): 362–63.

5. Ibid., 359.

6. Annabel Patterson, *Censorship and Interpretation: The Conditions of Writing and Reading in Early Modern England* (Madison: University of Wisconsin Press, 1984), 50.

7. For the circumstances surrounding the *Eastward Ho* controversy, see R. W. Van Fossen's edition of the play (Baltimore: Johns Hopkins University Press, 1979), 1–11. An appendix reprints the relevant letters of Jonson and Chapman; for the passage quoted, see 218–19. In his forthcoming biography of Jonson, David Riggs interestingly discusses the play in the context of contemporary infighting between factions at court.

8. For the comment on Jonson's "magnanimous gesture," see Summers and Pebworth, *Ben Jonson*, 28. As Van Fossen notes, "Nothing in any of the letters . . . substantiates Jonson's statement to Drummond that he had given himself up voluntarily; probably it is a case of Jonson's recounting the events in such a way as to cast himself in a better light" (5). On this point, see also Pearlman, "Ben Jonson: An Anatomy," 373–74.

A number of commentators have suggested that Chapman and Jonson tried to blame Marston for the offending passages, but the relevant evidence is open to other interpretations. The account of the *Eastward Ho* incident in the biography of Jonson in the Herford and Simpson edition is misleadingly phrased, suggesting a more deliberate satirical intent on Jonson's part than the evidence indicates (H&S 1:38).

9. Wright won fame as a Catholic who was loyal to the English cause. See Theodore A. Stroud, "Father Thomas Wright: A Test Case for Toleration," *Recusant History* 1 (1951): 189–219. By 1605, Wright's loyalty was so well trusted that he was deputized by the government to interrogate Guy Fawkes; see Thomas O. Sloan's introduction to his edition of Wright's book, *The Passions of the Minde in Generall* (Urbana: University of Illinois Press, 1971), xxii. Jonson's relationship with Wright, as well as the impact of his Catholicism on his social fortunes, are discussed by Stroud in "Ben Jonson and Father Thomas Wright," *ELH* 14 (1947): 274–82.

10. G. E. Bentley, *The Jacobean and Caroline Stage*, 7 vols. (Oxford: Clarendon Press, 1941–68), 4:619.

11. See *The "Conceited Newes" of Sir Thomas Overbury and His Friends*, ed. James E. Savage, xiii–lxxix, for a full discussion of the game's contexts and participants. For further details on Bulstrode, see R. C. Bald, *John Donne: A Life* (New York: Oxford University Press, 1970), 177–79; and, for a more speculative discussion, Barbara N. De Luna, *Jonson's Romish Plot: A Study of Catiline and its Historical Context* (Oxford: Clarendon Press, 1967), 156–70. Jongsook Lee reviews much of the biographical information (but does not mention Savage's data) in "Who Is Cecilia, What Was She: Cecilia Bulstrode and Jonson's Epideictics," *Journal of English and Germanic Philology* 85 (1986): 20–34. Whereas Lee de-emphasizes the biographical problems connected with Jonson's poems on Bulstrode, I argue that they are central to a proper understanding of those poems and also highly suggestive about our ways of reading Jonson's works in general.

12. But for this one valuable piece of historical information, it would today be possible to claim that Jonson had daringly and openly challenged the friend of one of his most important patrons. Or, without Drummond's double confirmation of the Pucell's identity, it would be possible to claim that the poem was merely a conventional satiric exercise with no particular target. The "Gentleman" who stole the poem from Jonson's pocket presumably knew it was there only after Jonson had made its existence known to him, perhaps by reading it to him. It would be interesting to know the gentleman's own motives in showing the poem to its target.

13. Isaac Walton, in notes he sent to John Aubrey for a biographical sketch of Jonson, claimed that some of the money Jonson received from superiors was "well pay'd for love or fere of his raling in verse, or prose, or boeth" (H&S 1:181). This raises the intriguing possibility that some of Jonson's contemporaries were so intimidated by his satirical talents that they sought to buy him off. Unfortunately, Walton does not elaborate, and the truth—if any—of his claim cannot be proven; still, the fact that he could even suggest such a possibility is significant.

14. On the possibility of a pun on the name of John Cocke, a participant in the wit combats, see Savage, *The "Conceited News*," lvi–lxii.

15. See Jennifer Taylor, "Lucy Countess of Bedford, Jonson, and Donne," 185–86.

16. For Hunter's comment, see *The Complete Poetry of Ben Jonson*, 53n. See also Ian Donaldson, *Ben Jonson*, 663. For Partridge's comments, see "Jonson's *Epigrammes*: The Named and the Nameless," *Studies in the Literary Imagination* 6, no. 1 (1973): 153–98, esp. 184–85. Similarly, Auberlen mentions Jonson's "courage in publishing the poem" (*The Commonwealth of Wit*, 125). See also

Rosalind Miles, *Ben Jonson: His Life and Work*, 173. I discuss the poetic strategies and historical context of the poem to Neville much more fully in an essay forthcoming in *The Muses Common-weale: Poetry and Politics in the Earlier Seventeenth Century*, edited by Claude J. Summers and Ted-Larry Pebworth.

17. For details of Neville's life, see Owen Duncan, "The Political Career of Sir Henry Neville: An Elizabethan Gentleman at the Court of James I" (Ph.D. diss., Ohio State University, 1974); see also the *DNB* and the important article by Clayton Roberts and Owen Duncan, "The Parliamentary Undertaking of 1614," in *English Historical Review* 93 (1978): 481–98; and the first chapter of Clayton Roberts, *Schemes and Undertakings: A Study of English Politics in the Seventeenth Century* (Columbus: Ohio State University Press, 1985). For the details of his career just mentioned and for the particular assessment of his position in the Jacobean hierarchy just cited, see esp. 494 in the article by Roberts and Duncan. The diarist John Manningham wrote in February 1602 that "When Sir Ed[ward] Hoby heard of Sir H[enry] Nevils disaster with the E[arl] of Essex, he said that his cosen Nevil was ambling towards his preferment, and would needs gallop in all the hast, and soe stumbled and fell" (see *The Diary of John Manningham of the Middle Temple, 1602–03*, ed. Robert Parker Sorlien [Hanover, N.H.: University Press of New England, 1976], 193). If this were a common assessment of Neville's motives, then Jonson's poem praising him for being unconcerned with "private gaine" could be seen as functioning almost as a defense of Neville's character. For discussion of Neville's later hopes of preferment, see the following note.

18. For brief discussions of Neville's initially auspicious but eventually unsuccessful candidacy for the secretaryship, see Samuel R. Gardiner, *History of England from the Accession of James I to the Outbreak of Civil War*, 10 vols. (London: Longmans, Green, 1883–84), 2:147–48; David Harris Willson, *The Privy Councillors in the House of Commons, 1604–1629* (Minneapolis: University of Minnesota Press, 1970), 136–37; Owen Duncan's dissertation; the article by Clayton Roberts and Owen Duncan; and the chapter on Neville in the book by Clayton Roberts. Far more interesting than secondary accounts of the campaign, however, are the many references to it recorded in John Chamberlain's letters, which give a powerful sense of the hoping and waiting, the frustrations, expectations, and delays Neville encountered for the almost two years (from 1612 to 1614) during which he pursued the office (see *The Letters of John Chamberlain*, ed. Norman Egbert McClure, 2 vols. [Philadelphia: American Philosophical Society, 1939], 1:338–511, passim).

Neville's candidacy was strongly supported by men who were also supporters of Jonson. T. L. Moir (*The Addled Parliament of 1614* [Oxford: Clarendon Press, 1958]) calls the Earl of Pembroke "Neville's chief backer in the privy council" (106); Linda Levy Peck (in *Northampton*) calls him "Pembroke's candidate" (31). Lord Chancellor Ellesmere, another of Jonson's patrons, was a member of Pembroke's group (Peck, *Northampton*, 25). Neville's hopes were doomed when Rochester, the favorite, married into the Howard family, leaders of a faction strongly opposed to Pembroke's. Northampton, Jonson's "mortall enimie" (H&S 1:141) was one of Neville's fiercest opponents. For contemporary readers, Jonson's praise of Neville must have taken on a richer resonance in the context of this factional clash.

Despite the support of such powerful men as the Earl of Pembroke (Jonson's patron), Rochester (the royal favorite), Sir Thomas Overbury (the favorite's favorite), and the Earl of Southampton, James never did appoint Neville—partly, it seems, because he resented the extent of the solicitation on Neville's behalf, and perhaps also because he recognized that Neville could be of more use to him as long as he was kept in a constant state of expectation. Francis Bacon, in fact, in a memo to the King dated 1613, expressed the opinion that James had effectively neutralized any potential opposition from such men as Neville by "having kept a princely temper towards them," meaning that he had chosen "not to persecute or disgrace them, nor yet to use or advance them." Bacon felt that, for the time being, the King had little reason to expect much opposition from Neville, because "Nevell hath his hopes" (see *The Works of Francis Bacon*, ed. James Spedding et al., 14 vols. [London: Longmans, Green, 1862–1901], 11:365).

It would be useful to know when exactly Jonson's poem was written, what immediate context it might have grown out of, how it was circulated, etc.—but unfortunately, these are precisely the kinds of facts lost to us in the cases of most of Jonson's poems. It seems unlikely that we will ever know when precisely or under what circumstances Jonson's poem was written. It does seem safe to say, however, that praising Neville was not quite so audacious an undertaking as has sometimes been suggested.

Neville seems to have been one of a group of London wits and intellectuals with whom Jonson enjoyed regular contact and companionship. For details, see Baird W. Whitlock, *John Hoskyns, Serjeant-at-Law* (Washington, D.C.: University Press of America, 1982), esp. chapter 12, "The Company of Wits," 381–426.

19. For a provocative discussion of strategies of indirection in Jonson's writing, see Annabel Patterson's *Censorship and Interpretation*.

20. Edward Partridge sees the poem in loftier terms: "That Jonson may be getting even with a courtier who actually condescended to him as a mere 'poet' is not the point here—indeed, by the way he handles the poem the incident is lifted above"—a significant phrase—"the level of gamesmanship and personal spite. With superb ease he demonstrates how a poet who has been treated shamefully can use his poetic skill in a socially acceptable and therefore unanswerable way to give an arrogant lord a new and more appropriate name at the same time that his real name is 'killed.' The revenge, then, is in precisely the same coin as the shame was—a name, but a typifying and demeaning name." See "Jonson's *Epigrammes*," 191. Peter Womack has recently commented that Jonson's "revenge pays for its completeness by its ineffectiveness, since no one—least of all, perhaps, the ignorant addressee—knows who the poet has in mind." This is true only if the poem is abstracted from its immediate personal context and regarded purely as text—a practice Womack eloquently warns against elsewhere. Although his book appeared too late for me to make much use of it, and although it focuses chiefly on the plays, I agree with much of what he says about Jonson's social insecurity and the instability of his poetic language. See *Ben Jonson* (London: Basil Blackwell, 1986), esp. 24–25 and 81–87; for the quoted passage, see 83.

21. Of Sir Robert Wroth, the subject of one of his most famous commendatory poems, Jonson said to Drummond that "My Lord Lisles daughter my Lady wroth is unworthily maried on a Jealous husband" (H&S 1:142). Immediately following this anecdote is one concerning the Earl of Rutland's anger at his wife for keeping "table to poets, of which she wrott a letter to him [Jonson] which he answered My Lord intercepted the letter, but never chalenged him" (H&S 1:142).

22. For an extended discussion of this poem, see Barbara Hutchison, "Ben Jonson's 'Let Me Be What I Am': An Apology in Disguise," *English Language Notes* 2 (1965): 185–90.

23. In *The Sociology of Art*, trans. Kenneth J. Northcott (Chicago: University of Chicago Press, 1982), 52. Leah S. Marcus explores some of the ambiguities of Jonson's status and attitudes in *The Politics of Mirth*; see, for instance, 6–9.

24. In her book *Censorship and Interpretation* and in a recent article ("Jonson, Marvell, and Miscellaneity?" in *Poems in Their Place: The Intertextuality and Order of Poetic Collections*, ed. Neil Fraistat [Chapel Hill and London: University of North Carolina Press, 1987], 95–118), Annabel Patterson argues that Jonson used the ordering of poems in his *Under-wood* collection as a way of retrospectively commenting on and coping with the kinds of tensions, ambiguities, and compromises with which this chapter has been concerned. In her article, she asserts that "The evidence as presented in 1640 argues that [Jonson's] idealism was not empty, his venality and servility not unselfconscious, his stand, finally, not without courage" (106). Although my focus in this chapter and throughout this book is on the more immediate, inescapable contexts of individual works, Patterson's arguments are very suggestive about the kinds of limited, retroactive strategies a writer could employ in attempting to assert some measure of control over the interpretation of his past writings.

Chapter 4. Poems for Patrons

1. On the contexts of Jonson's poem see James D. Garrison, *Dryden and the Tradition of Panegyric* (Berkeley and Los Angeles: University of California Press, 1975). Jonson's first readers must have seen the poem as at least in part an attempt to rival Daniel's recent "Panegyrike" to the King. Jonathan Goldberg discusses Jonson's poem in *James I and the Politics of Literature*, 120–24. H. Jennifer Brady discusses Jonson's attitudes toward James, and several of his poems to the King, in "Jonson's 'To King James': Plain Speaking in the *Epigrammes* and the *Conversations*," *Studies in Philology* 82 (1985): 380–98. See also Rhodes Dunlap, "Honest Ben and Royal James: The Poetics of Patronage," *Iowa State Journal of Research* 57 (1982): 143–51.

2. Unfortunately, P. M. Handover's biography, *The Second Cecil: The Rise to Power, 1563–1604, of Sir Robert Cecil, Later First Earl of Salisbury* (London: Eyre and Spottiswoode, 1959), ends with 1604. For brief treatments of his whole career, see Joel Hurstfield, "Robert Cecil, Earl of Salisbury, Minister of Elizabeth and James I," *History Today* 7 (1957): 279–89; and David Cecil, *The Cecils of Hatfield House: An English Ruling Family* (Boston: Houghton Mifflin, 1973), 99–162. See also G. P. V. Akrigg, *Jacobean Pageant: or The Court of King James I* (Cambridge, Mass.: Harvard University Press, 1962), 105–12.

3. Lawrence Stone reports that Cecil's huge income—eventually one-twelfth the annual income of the whole state—derived almost entirely from political offices whose continuance only the monarch could ensure; see "The Fruits of Office: The Case of Robert Cecil, First Earl of Salisbury, 1596–1612," in *Essays in the Economic and Social History of Tudor and Stuart England*, ed. F. J. Fisher (Cambridge: Cambridge University Press, 1961), 89–116; see also Thomas M. Coakley, "Robert Cecil in Power: Elizabethan Politics in Two Reigns," in *Early Stuart Studies: Essays in Honor of David Harris Willson*, ed. Howard S. Reinmuth, Jr. (Minneapolis: University of Minnesota Press, 1970), 64–94. Paradoxically, the spending designed to display and solidify his status left him with persistently gigantic debts; see Lawrence Stone, *Family and*

Fortune, 28. Fed in part by insecurity, Cecil's attempts to bolster his power thus also helped generate further insecurity.

4. See Scott McMillin, "Jonson's Early Entertainments: New Information from Hatfield House," *Renaissance Drama*, n.s., 1 (1968): 153–66.

5. Jonson's comment to Drummond helps emphasize that neither poets nor patrons could be entirely confident of each other's motives. Yet his expressed admiration for Salisbury was not necessarily cynical: Edward Jones notes that dependents typically become attracted to those they depend on, as if to justify dependency (see *Ingratiation*, 102).

Another of Drummond's notes is often used to suggest that Jonson may have once openly voiced resentment: "being at ye end of my Lord Salisburie's table with Inigo Jones," Drummond reports, "& demanded by my Lord, why he was not glad My Lord said he yow promised I should dine with yow, bot I doe not, for he had none of his meate, he esteamed only yt his meate which was of his owne dish" (H&S 1:141). In interpreting this, much depends on what one assumes about its tone and manner of delivery; that it wittily alludes to a poem by Martial should not be forgotten (H&S 1:166). Still, it implies at least an undercurrent of hostility and aggression, perhaps also present in the poems.

It has often been suggested that the "worthlesse lord" Jonson attacks in the epigram "To My Muse" may have been Cecil. (James A. Riddell has recently supported this contention by discussing several significant differences between the printed text and a surviving holograph copy; see his article "The Arrangement of Ben Jonson's *Epigrammes*," *Studies in English Literature* 27 [1987]: 53–70, esp. 55–56). By the time Jonson came to assemble his book of epigrams for the printer, he may have felt that it was safe—even advantageous—to make his misgivings about Cecil more widely apparent. The *Epigrammes* volume was entered in the Stationers' Register on 15 May 1612, and although no copies of this possible printing survive (suggesting that the poems may not actually have been issued until four years later, as part of the folio edition), there is some evidence to suggest that the quarto may in fact have been issued (see H&S 8:16; 11:356). If one *is* willing to assume that the poem was printed in 1612 and in the place it now occupies, one can find many reasons, corroborating those offered in the poem, for thinking that Jonson may have wished to dissociate himself from Cecil at this time. For more than a year the Earl had been losing favor with the King, influence in Parliament, and standing at court, and by the end of 1611 he had also become seriously ill. By February 1612 it had become clear to many that his power at court must soon be relinquished, if for no other reason than his poor health. He died on 24 May—less than a week after Jonson's book had been entered in the Register—and he was (according to D. H. Willson) "grossly maligned after his death" (see *King James VI and I* [New York: Oxford University Press, 1956], 267–70; for the quotation, see 269). Samuel Gardiner reports that "The news of the Treasurer's death was received in London with satisfaction" (*The History of England*, 2:143). Chamberlain's *Letters* are full of evidence to support this claim (see 1:350ff.).

Thus Jonson, in setting the poem to his muse alongside the poems to Cecil for publication in the *Epigrammes* volume of 1612—if, indeed, that is what he did and when he did it—may arguably have had more considerations in mind than the prompting of his conscience alone. If B. N. De Luna's analysis (in *Jonson's Romish Plot*) of Jonson's long association with Cecil is correct, Jonson may have felt all the more strongly the need to dissociate himself publicly from the man with whom he was, according to De Luna, so strongly linked in the public mind. It was only in the year before Cecil's death, after all, that Jonson's alleged play-length defense of Cecil, *Catiline*, had been publicly acted. (This fact itself might help us to date the epigram to the worthless lord: would Jonson have written it before 1611, when he was championing Cecil and accepting his patronage? If he did, what would that suggest about his honesty in his relations with his patrons? If De Luna is right, there would seem to be good reason for supposing that the satirical epigram was composed at some point *after* the performances of *Catiline*—i.e., during the period when Cecil's health and influence were in decline, or perhaps even after his death.)

Byzantine as this argument may seem, it may also help to explain why Jonson, if he truly felt that Cecil was a worthless lord, bothered to print his poems in praise of Cecil in the *Epigrammes* collection. If the poems were as widely known as Jonson's general relationship with Cecil seems to have been, perhaps he felt that he had little choice but to print them—that trying to pretend he had not written them would prove fruitless and embarrassing. Instead he prints them but juxtaposes them with a satirical poem that explains his betrayal to and deception by the worthless lord and, in so doing, partly exculpates himself.

6. The introduction and annotations to the text of *Hymenaei* imply tensions of another sort—competitive tensions that must have been more personally important to Jonson than any he dealt with in the masque itself.

7. See B. N. De Luna's discussion (in *Jonson's Romish Plot*, 42–50) of Cecil's 1606 *Answere to Certain Scandalous Papers*. She builds an intriguing circumstantial argument that Jonson's *Catiline* was in large part written to vindicate Cecil's role in the Gunpowder Plot. Whether or not this assertion is true, her book amasses much evidence concerning threats to Cecil's reputation and security.

In his *An Answere to Certaine Scandalous Papers, scattered abroad under colour of a Catholicke Admonition* (London, 1606), Cecil reports that he has been "bitterly calumniated" (sig. Br) and worries "lest any of those clouds which are unjustly cast upon mee, might darken the brightnesse" of the King's regard (sig. Bv). Claiming to be "onely great in the eyes of Envy" (sig. D2v), he seeks to preserve his "poore reputation from these cruell aspersions" (sig. E4v). Although he indicates several times that he is "in such an absolute possession over my owne soule in patience, as it is not in the power of any calumniator to disturbe the peace of a quiet minde" (sig. B2r), his *Answere* provides ample evidence that such attacks troubled him.

Francis Osborne (in his memoirs reprinted in *The Secret History of the Court of James the First*, 2 vols. [Edinburgh: John Ballantyne and Co., 1811]) suggested that Cecil himself might have fabricated the attack to which he responds in the *Answere* in order to magnify his service to religion and to the state and in order to overcome his unpopularity with admirers of the executed Earl of Essex (1:180–181). Osborne (no admirer of Cecil) stresses Cecil's insecurity (see 1:112; 162) and emphasizes how disliked he was in his final years (1:235). Sir Anthony Weldon, in his unflattering account of the Jacobean Court (also reprinted in *The Secret History*), likewise depicts Cecil as insecure and unpopular (1:322–23; 343–44) and emphasizes the precariousness of his status immediately before his death (1:325–27). The author of *Aulicus Coquinariae* (also reprinted in *The Secret History*) attempts a general refutation of Weldon and specifically disputes his depiction of Cecil's motives, actions, and standing (2:146–57). Bishop Godfrey Goodman, also responding to Weldon's memoirs (in *The Court and Times of King James the First*, ed. John S. Brewer, 2 vols.

[London: Richard Bentley, 1839]), nonetheless emphasizes the insecurity of the Earl's final years (1:42–45), his decreasing influence with James (1:40; 44), his effort to cultivate friendships with the courtiers James brought with him from Scotland (1:51–52), and even his attempts to play up and exploit James's own sense of danger and unease (1:44). Eric N. Lundquist (in "The Last Years of the First Earl of Salisbury, 1610–1612," *Albion* 18 [1986]: 23–41) argues that Salisbury's position was not in fact as insecure as it seemed to some, maintaining that "Salisbury fell certainly only when he died" (37). While in retrospect this may be true, neither Salisbury nor his contemporaries could foresee the outcome of the events in which they were involved. This inability naturally made for greater uncertainty, anticipation, and anxiety on their parts; Lundquist perhaps both underestimates the importance of their perceptions and overemphasizes the importance of settled "facts" seen (and interpreted) from a distance of several centuries. The final sentence of his article exemplifies this distinction between contemporary perceptions and retrospective assessment: "Although at the time, under the strain of defeat, Salisbury himself may have feared the worst, the failure of the Great Contract was not the great crisis of his career" (41).

John Harington's *Nugae Antiquae* (ed. Thomas Park, 2 vols. [London: Vernor and Hood, 1804]) contains a 1603 letter from Cecil describing the dissatisfactions and insecurities of life at court (1:344–46). "I am pushed from the shore of comforte," he writes, "and know not where the wyndes and waves of a court will bear me" (345). Richard Johnson's *Remembrance of the Honours Due to the Life and Death of Robert Earle of Salisbury* (London, 1612; reprint, Newcastle: S. Hodgson, 1818) speaks not only of the posthumous "envy, ingratitude and unkindnesse" aimed at Cecil (ix) but of earlier "biting malice" (4) and of "the devouring teeth of envy, which upon sundry suppositions, was (even then) [during the late Elizabethan period] whetted to make havock of all his fortunes, here was his wisdom tride upon the tutch, the world and time grew unconstant, began to pick quarrels, misdeemd honest actions, and invented false informations, *yet was his cares so watchfull*, that he saved himselfe from the subtilest snare of secret envy" (4–5; emphasis mine). Cyril Tourneur's *Character of Robert Earle of Salisburye* (in *The Works of Cyril Tourneur*, ed. Allardyce Nicholl [London: Franfrolico Press, 1929], 259–63) speaks of the "publique daungere, or privat Threatnings . . . w[hi]ch weare manye, and bould uppon him" (260).

Even as death drew near, Cecil was reportedly preoccupied with threats to his power. John Chamberlain, describing the journey toward London during which Cecil died, wrote that "[some] thincke he hastened the faster homeward, to countermine his underminers, and (as he termed yt) to cast dust in their eyes: as the case stands it was the best that he gave over the world, for they say his friends fell from him apace, and some neere about him; and howsoever he had fared with his health it is verelye thought, he wold never have been himself again in power and credit"; see *The Letters of John Chamberlain*, 1:350–51.

8. Robert Cecil, "The State and Dignity of a Secretary of State's Place, with the Care and Peril Thereof," in vol. 5 of *Harleian Miscellany* (London: R. Dutton, 1808–11), 5:166–68.

9. Moreover, if a poet felt he had gone out of his way to attract a patron's response, that response (however much sought after at first) might then come to seem less valuable once granted. On this point, see Jones, *Ingratiation*, 49. See also Jonson's "Epistle to Sir Edward Sacvile," lines 22–24: "Gifts stinke from

some, / They are so long a comming, and so hard; / Where any Deed is forc't, the Grace is mard." For a discussion of the scatological pun in these lines, see my note, "Jonson's 'Epistle to Sir Edward Sacvile,' " *The Explicator* 43, no. 3 (1985): 7.

10. See Anthony Esler, *The Aspiring Mind of the Elizabethan Younger Generation* (Durham, N.C.: Duke University Press, 1966), 135.

11. For these reasons I have trouble accepting Stanley Fish's suggestion that the poem's questions are not "*seriously* entertained"; see "Authors-Readers: Jonson's Community of the Same," 41. This article, which makes many fine points about the poems to Cecil during a stimulating larger discussion, perhaps underemphasizes their micropolitical aspects.

12. *Family and Fortune*, 38.

13. See Roger Wilbraham, *The Journal of Sir Roger Wilbraham*, ed. Harold Spencer. The Camden Miscellany 10 (London: Royal Historical Society, 1902), 99–100.

14. On Pembroke as a courtier and as a patron of Jonson and others, see two articles by Dick Taylor, Jr.: "The Masque and the Lance: The Third Earl of Pembroke in Jacobean Court Entertainments," *Tulane Studies in English* 8 (1958): 21–53, and "The Third Earl of Pembroke as a Patron of Poetry," *Tulane Studies in English* 5 (1955): 41–67. See also Brian O'Farrell, "Politician, Patron, Poet: William Herbert, Third Earl of Pembroke, 1580–1630" (Ph.D. diss., University of California, Los Angeles, 1966), and Margot Heinemann, "Middleton's *A Game at Chess*: Parliamentary-Puritans and Opposition Drama," *English Literary Renaissance* 5 (1975): 232–50. In "The Masque and the Lance" Taylor is especially suggestive about Jonson's rivalries with Daniel and Jones and about the role Pembroke played in each; O'Farrell is most helpful in explicating Pembroke's political involvements. In his forthcoming biography of Jonson, David Riggs emphasizes the importance of the poet's connections with the Pembroke faction.

15. On Drummond's relationship with Pembroke, see O'Farrell, 209ff.

16. On Pembroke's connections at court and political status in general, see O'Farrell. There is plenty of evidence that Pembroke took his status very seriously. In 1610, in a dispute over seating arrangements with the Scottish Earl of Argyle, Pembroke threatened to run Argyle through with his rapier if he provoked him in the future; see Great Britain, Historical Manuscripts Commission, *Report on the Manuscripts of the Marquess of Downshire*, 4 vols. (London, 1924–40), 2 : 216. In 1608 Pembroke did come to blows, and almost engaged in a duel, with Sir George Wharton in a dispute over card playing and over Wharton's right to strike one of Pembroke's pages (see Edmund Lodge, *Illustrations of British History, Biography, and Manners*, 2d ed. [London: John Chidley, 1838], 3 : 242–45). In 1609 the Venetian Ambassador thought it significant enough to report to his superiors that Sir Anthony Ashley, "Secretary to the Council of State, a few days ago came to disagreement with the Earl of Pembroke, on account of certain confiscation brought by the secretary to the infringement of the Earl's office. Pembroke was supported by Salisbury [Robert Cecil] and the Secretary would not give way. [He] was suspended and is in danger of absolute ruin, for his enemies have taken the opportunity to declare certain errors committed by him." See Great Britain, Public Record Office, *Calendar of State Papers, Venetian* (London, 1864–1947), 11 : 362. The year before, the Ambassador had reported that "The Prince of Wales, who has been staying in the country some distance from the King, his father, complained to his Majesty of this distance and was told that he might make what arrangements he liked. He

sent to tell the Earls of Southampton and Pembroke to move their households and their horses as he desired to occupy their lodging. They refused and the Prince had them removed by his people to the indignation of these gentlemen, who are of very high rank" (11:206). All these anecdotes suggest that Pembroke was quite conscious of his power and not reluctant to assert it.

For Clarendon's comment, see David Nichol Smith, *Characters from the Histories and Memoirs of the Seventeenth Century* (Oxford: Clarendon Press, 1918), 32.

17. Pembroke's appointment to the Privy Council evoked differing reactions. Robert Sidney, Viscount Lisle and one of Jonson's best-known patrons (his estate is celebrated in "To Penshurst"), wrote to his wife expressing great pleasure at the elevation, confident that the Council would now contain another friend willing and able to promote his interests. See Great Britain, Historical Manuscripts Commission, *Report on the Manuscripts of Lord De L'isle and Dudley* (London, 1925–66), 4:289. On the other hand, Chamberlain, in his *Letters*, reported that "Upon the earle of Pembrokes preferment to that place, the earle of Southampton retired himself into the countrie, but his spirit hath walked very busilie about the court ever since" (1:352). Sidney's reaction is interesting for its frank calculation of personal advantage; Southampton's is intriguing because he is sometimes mentioned as one of Pembroke's allies at court. Both reactions provide some insight into the micropolitical dynamics of Jacobean court life—dynamics also at play in Jonson's poem.

18. On Northampton's career, see Linda Levy Peck, *Northampton*. On the rivalry between Pembroke and Northampton in 1605, see O'Farrell (68), who also quotes from the later letter describing Pembroke as a "Welsh juggler" (74). For Northampton's maneuverings against Pembroke, see Great Britain, Public Record Office, *Calendar of State Papers Domestic, James I, 1611–18*, ed. Mary Anne Everett Green (London: Longman, 1858), 133, 140, 144. Peck offers additional evidence of Northampton's tactics against Pembroke (34; 37). She quotes from a manuscript letter from Northampton to Carr concerning Pembroke, Southampton, and Lisle: "There is no better way to pare their nails . . . than by some withdrawing of your favourable countenance which I do assure you is a groundyard to their boldness and a discharge of many watchful ears and eyes that, setting your countenance aside, would attend them more narrowly" (36). Shortly before his death in June 1614, Northampton requested of Carr "that the earle of Pembroke and the Lord Lile shold not have any of his offices, because accounting them his ennemies he wold not they shold triumphe over him when he was gon" (Chamberlain's *Letters*, 1:542). Peck quotes from the manuscript letter in which Northampton explained his reasons for seeking to thwart Pembroke and Lisle: "for as they hated me, *so they will plague my people and those whom I loved*" (62; Peck's emphasis). Northampton thus sought to protect his dependents even from beyond the grave. Although he is admittedly a biased witness, his comment nonetheless suggests a more complicated view of Pembroke's motives than is implied in Jonson's poem.

19. On the "talismanic" quality of Jonson's naming, see Partridge's important "Jonson's *Epigrammes*."

20. On this point see Joel Hurstfield, *Freedom, Corruption, and Government in Elizabethan England* (Cambridge, Mass.: Harvard University Press, 1973), 193. As a matter of fact, O'Farrell points out that at the time Pembroke served as Lord Chamberlain his income from the office amounted to 4,682 pounds per year, one of the highest incomes of any government official, although the official salary of his post was just 100 pounds per annum (90).

21. Partridge, "Jonson's *Epigrammes*," 192. See also Martin Elsky, "Words, Things, and Names: Jonson's Poetry and Philosophical Grammar," in *Classic and Cavalier: Essays on Jonson and the Sons of Ben*, ed. Claude J. Summers and Ted-Larry Pebworth (Pittsburgh, Pa.: University of Pittsburgh Press, 1982), 91–106. Don E. Wayne, in his fine article "Poetry and Power in Ben Jonson's *Epigrammes*," also considers their factuality and questions Partridge's assumptions in ways that partly anticipate some of my own concerns (85–86).

22. Almost nothing is known about the particulars of Jonson's relations with Wroth, although Lady Wroth (daughter of Sir Robert Sidney) seems to have been an important patron. Several years after Wroth's death, Jonson told Drummond that Lady Wroth had been "unworthily maried on a Jealous husband" (H&S 1:142).

23. "Jonson, Lord Lisle, and Penshurst," *English Literary Renaissance* 1 (1971): 250–60; for the quotation cited, see 255. Nearly every book on Jonson's poetry includes some discussion of "To Penshurst"; for a comprehensive and immensely suggestive approach, see Don E. Wayne, *Penshurst: The Semiotics of Place and the Poetics of History* (Madison: University of Wisconsin Press, 1984). Two of the most provocative recent articles on the poem are by William E. Cain ("The Place of the Poet in Jonson's 'To Penshurst' and 'To My Muse,'") and Alastair Fowler ("The 'Better Marks' of Jonson's *To Penshurst*," *Review of English Studies*, n.s., 24 [1973]: 266–82). Fowler's article helps specify the ways in which Penshurst was in *symbolic* competition with other country houses. Much of the best recent thinking about "To Penshurst" has profited from the insights offered by Raymond Williams in *The Country and the City* (London: Chatto and Windus, 1969). See also, for instance, the passing references to the poem in James Turner, *The Politics of Landscape: Rural Scenery and Society in English Poetry 1630–1660* (Cambridge, Mass.: Harvard University Press, 1979) and in Anthony Low, *The Georgic Revolution* (Princeton: Princeton University Press, 1985).

24. William A. McClung, in *The Country House in English Renaissance Poetry* (Berkeley and Los Angeles: University of California Press, 1977), 51. McClung has suggested that Robert Cecil may have been the target of some of Jonson's satire in this poem (2). Cecil had constructed one of the largest and most expensive houses ever undertaken during James's reign. Moreover, Herford and the Simpsons, along with Ian Donaldson, note in their editions the similarities between lines 65–66 of the poem (about placement at "great mens tables") and Jonson's self-described comment to Cecil on the same subject. If Jonson did intend specific satire on Cecil, would this not be an example of his poetic daring? Perhaps not, for Rathmell offers evidence suggesting that the poem was written sometime after May 1612 but before September of that same year (252–53)—i.e., in the period immediately following Cecil's death, when his reputation was being generally traduced, and when Jonson may have been trying to distance himself from the man with whom he had once been so closely connected (on this point, see note 5 above).

John Nichols's *Progresses, Processions, and Magnificent Festivities of King James the First*, 4 vols. (London: J. B. Nichols, 1828) makes no mention of a royal visit to Penshurst during this period, but neither does it make any mention of a visit to the estate before or after 1612. The visit could not have taken place later than 1612, when Prince Henry died. James and Henry did participate in an extensive progress during the summer of 1612, but their itinerary seems mainly to have taken them north of Westminster, whereas Penshurst lies to the south (see Nichols, *Progresses* 2:451ff). Nichols himself asserts that Jonson's poem provides the only record of the visit (1:xvi), and Rathmell, who has examined the records of the estate, mentions no specific date. In his forthcoming biography of Jonson, David Riggs suggests that James was in fact spending time in the general vicinity of Penshurst in the late spring and early summer of 1612.

Whenever the visit itself may have occurred, Rathmell's suggestion that the poem was written sometime in the late spring or summer of 1612 is intriguing in its own right. Jonson's panegyric, undertaken shortly before or perhaps during the King's progress north, may have been intended to cheer the Sidneys at a time when the King was visiting far more lavish houses; or to remind the court of the attractions of Penshurst at a time when they were admiring the splendors of the other estates; or to remind the King and others of his own expressed admiration for the house; or perhaps to do all these things.

25. Rathmell, 251. In the fall of 1612, Jonson accompanied Sir Walter Ralegh's son on a lengthy tour of the Continent. Serving as a tutor to a patron's child was one of the most common functions that writers fulfilled in Jonson's age.

26. On the details of William Sidney's life, see Lisle Cecil John, "Ben Jonson's 'To Sir William Sidney, On His Birthday,'" *Modern Language Review* 52 (1957): 168–72.

27. Summers and Pebworth, *Ben Jonson*, 170–71.

28. Drummond's report helps remind us that not only the poems Jonson explicitly addressed to patrons may have been directly influenced by the patronage context. It is worth wondering how many other of the poems he apparently wrote for their own sakes grew out of the kind of situation described here. In any case, it is possible to argue that *all* his poetry was influenced to some degree or another by his consciousness that it would be read by his social superiors.

29. In 1622 James "invited" Jonson to prepare an English translation of one of the King's favorite books, a Latin romance by John Barclay; in 1623 the translation was entered in the Stationers' Register, but the famous fire in Jonson's house soon afterward apparently destroyed the manuscript (11:73; 78).

30. It is interesting to note how many of the "love" poems considered by Anne Ferry in her study of seventeenth-century love poetry, *All in War with Time* (Cambridge, Mass.: Harvard University Press, 1975), are addressed to patrons or deal with patronage as a theme (127–82).

Pembroke's own poetry has been reprinted in *Poems Written by the Right Honourable William Earl of Pembroke*, ed. Gaby E. Onderwyzer (Los Angeles: Clark Memorial Library, 1959). Onderwyzer writes that the subject of love is so prevalent in Pembroke's poetry that "one almost feels tempted to apply it as a negative determinant of Pembroke's authorship of particular poems." In fact, he states categorically that all of Pembroke's known poems "deal with aspects of love" (iv).

31. For a discussion of the few known facts of her relationship with Jonson and of her own poetry, see Graham Parry, "Lady Wroth's *Urania*," *Proceedings of the Leeds Philosophical and Literary Society* 16, no. 4 (1975): 51–60; and the introduction to *The Poems of Lady Mary Wroth*, ed. Josephine A. Roberts (Baton Rouge: Louisiana State University Press, 1983).

32. Since Egerton was Donne's most important early patron and continued to aid him even after he dismissed him from his service, Bald's biography is an important source of information about Egerton during the Elizabethan period; see esp. 93–142. W. J. Jones considers Egerton's later career in "Ellesmere and

Politics, 1603–17," in *Early Stuart Studies: Essays in Honor of David Harris Willson*, ed. Howard S. Reinmuth, Jr. (Minneapolis: University of Minnesota Press, 1970), 11–63. The most comprehensive treatment, from which many of the details of this section have been drawn, is Susan Miller Laffitte's "The Literary Connections of Sir Thomas Egerton: A Study of the Influence of Thomas Egerton Upon Major Writers of Renaissance Literature" (Ph.D. diss., Florida State University, 1971). See also *DNB* and the section on Egerton by Knafla in French R. Fogle and Louis A. Knafla, *Patronage in Late Renaissance England* (Los Angeles: William Andrews Clark Memorial Library, 1983).

33. Bald, *John Donne*, 110.

34. Herford and the Simpsons print the text of a letter by Jonson to Thomas Bond, Egerton's secretary, in which he requests Bond's "help to the furdering this Gentleman's suite, the bearers, with my lords favor" (H&S 1:201). Whether this letter relates to the same case referred to in the epigram cannot be said; it is interesting, however, as evidence of Jonson's ability (or at least his attempt) to use his connections with powerful court figures to the advantage of third parties. Another letter, perhaps to John Leech, Pembroke's secretary, asks him "to be careful of this Gents: necessitie, and succoure it willingly, and in tyme, you shall make me ever beholden to you" (H&S 1:200). Whether this is the same man mentioned in the letter to Bond is, again, unknown, as is the date of each letter. Jonson's connections with powerful figures at court enhanced his own power as an intermediary. For discussion of his assistance to John Selden and to others, see H&S 1:86–87. Jonson's ability to perform such favors derived from his status but also helped display it.

35. Chamberlain noted that although Egerton left a great estate, yet "withall he left but an indifferent name beeing accounted too sowre, severe, and implacable, a great enemie to parlements and the common law, only to maintain his greatnes, and the exorbitant jurisdiction of his court of chauncerie. He gave order in his will to have no solemne funerall, no monument, but to be buried in oblivion . . . One thing is much noted in his will that he gave nothing to the poore or to any charitable use, nor to any of his servants, nor very little to his grandchildren but left all to his sonne" (see *Letters*, 2:65).

Apparently it was not unusual in Jonson's society for powerful figures to be derogated after their deaths—perhaps because it was no longer necessary to show them any deference. Commenting on Cecil's death a few years earlier, the Earl of Dorset more generally observed that "When great men die, such is either their desert or the malice of the people, or both together, that they are ill-spoken of." See Nichols, *Progresses*, 2:445n. Jones ("Ellesmere and Politics") reports that a few years after Egerton's death it was quipped that he had "died on conceit, fearing to be displaced" (11). This comment and Chamberlain's letter support the suggestions made in Jonson's poems that Egerton did have detractors, some of whom apparently regarded him as no less ambitious and concerned with status than other courtiers.

If powerful figures like Egerton knew that their reputations would very likely be besmirched after they died, this knowledge might make the solicitations of poets like Jonson—who could promise a certain kind of immortality—more pragmatically attractive. In fact such praise has indeed played a part in subsequent assessments of historical figures. Dick Taylor, Jr., for instance, pits the favorable testimony of Jonson and other poets concerning William Herbert against the less flattering testimony of the seventeenth-century historian Edward Hyde in "Clarendon and Ben Jonson as Witnesses for the Earl of Pembroke's Character," in *Studies in the English Renaissance*, ed. Josephine

Bennett (New York: New York University Press, 1959), 322–44. O'Farrell, in "Politician, Patron, and Poet," similarly finds the "bluntly honest writings of Jonson" a more reliable guide to Pembroke's character than Clarendon (22). In her study of Egerton, Laffitte draws heavily on the positive poetic testimony of Donne and Jonson (94–95).

36. Jonson's verbal ambiguity seems even more apt when one remembers, as Laffitte points out, that Egerton's court was the highest court of appeals and depended on the conscience of the Chancellor, who in his judgments was more responsible to the King than to written statute and precedent (93–94).

37. See "Francis Bacon and His Father," *Huntington Library Quarterly* 21 (1957): 133–58; for the quotations cited in this paragraph, see 139 and 147.

No examination of Bacon's life is possible without consulting Spedding's edition of *The Letters and the Life of Francis Bacon*, which constitute the last seven volumes of *The Works*. An extremely valuable book on Bacon, especially for an understanding of his role in the patronage system of his day and of how he used his writings to promote himself within that system, is Jonathan Marwill's *The Trials of Counsel: Francis Bacon in 1621* (Detroit, Mich.: Wayne State University Press, 1976). A useful book is Joel Epstein's *Francis Bacon: A Political Biography* (Athens: Ohio University Press, 1977). Catherine Drinker Bowen's *Francis Bacon: The Temper of a Man* (Boston: Little, Brown, 1963) is a solid but undocumented companion study to her impressive earlier book *The Lion and the Throne: The Life and Times of Sir Edward Coke* (Boston: Little, Brown, 1956), which is full of information about Bacon, Coke's nemesis.

38. See Spedding, *The Works*, 11:33–34. In 1608 Bacon prepared a private book of memoranda to remind himself of actions he planned to undertake. One entry reads as follows: "To make him ['my L. of S.'] think how he should be reverenced by a L. Chr yf I were; Princelike" (11:93). Spedding supposes that the "L. of S." referred to in the immediately preceding note is Suffolk, the Lord Chamberlain; but Bowen suggests that it is Salisbury (*Francis Bacon*, 122). Of the two, Salisbury enjoyed the greatest power, and for that reason might seem the more likely target.

Bacon's memoranda reveal, in various other entries, his awareness of a courtier's need to make the right impression, to manage carefully his self-presentation. Witness, for instance, his intention "To have particular occasions, fitt and gratefull and contynuall, to mainteyn pryvate speach wth every ye great persons and sometymes drawing more than one of them together Ex Imitatione Att. This specially in publike places and wthout care of affectation" (11:93).

39. For an account of these events, see Bowen, *The Lion and the Throne*, 336–41; for an excellent recent overview of Coke's career, see the first chapter of Stephen D. White's *Sir Edward Coke and "The Grievances of the Commonwealth," 1621–1625* (Chapel Hill: University of North Carolina Press, 1979). James's distrust of Coke should not be exaggerated; apparently he hoped that by removing Coke from his troublesome position while at the same time elevating his status in other ways, Coke could be made more pliable. At the same time that Coke became Justice of the King's Bench, for instance, he was also made a Privy Councillor—"which honor" (Chamberlain reported) "no man envies him yf he keepe on his right course, and turne not to be atturny again" (*Letters*, 1:485). A short time later he was considered by some to be in the running for the Treasurership (ibid. 1:493), and as late as February 1615/16 Bacon considered Coke a serious enough potential rival to succeed Egerton as Lord Chancellor that he wrote a memorandum to the King listing possible objections to Coke and proposing instead his own candidacy ("For myselfe, I can only present your

Majesty with *gloria in obsequio* . . ."). See Spedding, *The Works*, 12:241–44. Bowen writes that "[f]or the first years" after his elevation to the Chief Justiceship, Coke did seem to become more compliant; she mentions his role in advising James to call a parliament in 1614: "Bacon, Coke, Winwood advised that with proper management, the Commons would give down milk"; see *The Lion and the Throne*, 342; 348.

These data are important because of Jonson's epigram to Coke, written *"when he was Lord chiefe Iustice of* England" (*Und.* 46). In the poem Jonson praises Coke as one of the most virtuous of "all rais'd servants of the Crowne" (line 2) and commends him for having "Stood up thy Nations fame, her Crownes defence" (line 14). Jonson seems careful in the poem to steer clear of any hint that he might be praising Coke as the judge who once opposed extension of the King's prerogative, and the facts just presented suggest that for much of Coke's tenure as Chief Justice, it would have been perfectly safe to praise him. It was not until the spring of 1616 that he was clearly out of favor, and later that year he was dismissed. It seems likely, both from the title of the epigram and from its opening and closing refrains (concerned with Coke's elevation) that the poem was written around the time of his actual and prospective promotions in the winter of 1613/14. As the newest Privy Councillor he would have been a likely recipient of one of Jonson's poems.

I discuss the poetic strategies and historical context of the epigram to Coke much more extensively in an essay forthcoming in *The Muses Common-weale: Poetry and Politics in the Earlier Seventeenth Century*, ed. Claude J. Summers and Ted-Larry Pebworth.

40. For these events, see Bowen, *The Lion and the Throne*, 393–411, and Spedding, *The Works*, 13:223–58.

41. See Bowen, *Francis Bacon*, 160; see also Chamberlain's *Letters*, 1:492.

42. See Marwill, *The Trials of Counsel*, 67–70; 80–81; 101–02.

43. See Eric Linklater, *Ben Jonson and King James* (London: Jonathan Cape, 1931), 98, 105. On Bacon's connections with Jonson's friends, Sir Robert Cotton and William Camden, see Kocher, 148. For further evidence of Jonson's relations with Bacon, see H&S 1:141.

44. Auberlen also juxtaposes the poems to Bacon and Sidney in *The Commonwealth of Wit* (109–11). Although my discussion was written before I discovered Auberlen's, and although my treatment of the poem to Bacon stresses its biographical aspects, we both explore Jonson's strategies of self-distinction in that work.

45. Whalley long ago noted the harshness of the poem's verse; see Cunningham, *Works*, 3:330n.

46. For the figures, see Bowen, *The Lion and the Throne*, 433. Gifford claims with some exaggeration that "When Jonson wrote this poem, Lord Bacon was in the full tide of prosperity; the year after, misfortune overtook him; and he continued in poverty, neglect, and disgrace till his death, which took place in 1627. Yet the poet did not change his language; nor allow himself to be checked by the unpopularity of the ex-Chancellor's name, or the dread of displeasing his sovereign and patron, from bearing that generous testimony to his talents and virtues which is inserted in his *Discoveries*" (see Cunningham, *Works*, 3:330n).

Bowen notes that after Bacon's death "a flood of eulogy poured out—from friends and strangers, from playwrights, historians, political pamphleteers," including a tribute from George Herbert (*Francis Bacon*, 227).

47. See B. Dew Roberts, *Mitre and Musket: John Williams, Lord Keeper, Archbishop of York, 1582–1650* (London: Oxford University Press, 1938), 18.

Roberts's biography, like almost everything else written about Williams, depends very heavily on John Hacket's *Scrinia Reserata: A Memorial Offer'd to the Great Deservings of John Williams, D.D.* (London: Samuel Lowndes, 1692). Hacket was for many years Williams's protégé; his biography is designed in part to vindicate Williams's reputation. A less flattering but necessarily sketchy picture is presented by Akrigg, *Jacobean Pageant*, 316–19.

48. The editions by Herford and the Simpsons, Newdigate, Hunter, and Donaldson all suggest that Williams lost his office three years later, in 1628. Only Cunningham gives the correct date of 1625. I shall argue later why the date of the poem's composition may be important.

I discuss this poem more fully in an essay forthcoming in *The Muses Common-weale: Poetry and Politics in the Earlier Seventeenth Century*, ed. Claude J. Summers and Ted-Larry Pebworth.

49. Roberts, *Mitre and Musket*, 108–9.
50. Roberts, *Mitre and Musket*, 109.
51. Roberts, *Mitre and Musket*, 106.

Chapter 5. Poems on Rivals and Rivalry

1. Roscoe Small, in his account of *The Stage Quarrel Between Ben Jonson and the So-Called Poetasters* (New York: AMS Press, 1966), surmises that the play was written around August or September, 1601 (119). Cyrus Hoy more cautiously says only that it was written "sometime prior to 11 November 1601 (when it was entered in the Stationers' Register)." See his *Introductions, Notes, and Commentaries to Texts in 'The Dramatic Works of Thomas Dekker'* (Cambridge: Cambridge University Press, 1981), 1:180. I discuss the structural and thematic unities of this play much more fully in my article, "Jonson, Satiromastix, and the Poetomachia: A Patronage Perspective," *Iowa State Journal of Research* 60 (1986): 369–83.

The best discussion of this period in Jonson's life is W. David Kay's "The Shaping of Ben Jonson's Career: A Reexamination of Facts and Problems."

All references to *Satiromastix* are to the text printed in the first volume of *The Dramatic Works of Thomas Dekker*, ed. Fredson Bowers, 4 vols. (Cambridge: Cambridge University Press, 1953).

2. See Hoy's commentary, 1:207–08. Summers and Pebworth remark that the fact that Jonson is pictured "laboring over a love lyric may indicate begrudging recognition of the poet's aspiration in this genre"; see *Ben Jonson*, 158. But this comment may underemphasize the patronage context indicated in the play; the point seems less to comment on Jonson's aspirations as a love poet than to burlesque his ambitions as a patronage poet.

3. See Small, 2.

4. The fullest account of the conflict is given by Small; it is discussed briefly by Robert Boies Sharpe in *The Real Wars of the Theaters* (Boston: D. C. Heath, 1935). W. David Kay, in his "Ben Jonson, Horace, and the Poetomachia: The Development of an Elizabethan Playwright's Public Image" (Ph.D. diss., Princeton University, 1968), discusses the social background in his first two chapters; for the most part, though, he stresses the differences and similarities between the artistic and critical assumptions of Jonson and Marston. Like some recent writers on the conflict between Jonson and Inigo Jones, Kay argues that the aesthetic disagreements between Jonson and Marston were actually quite small—an assertion which, if accepted, only enhances the importance of a

micropolitical explanation of their conflict. That Jonson and his opponents so often held ideas and basic assumptions in common would have made their competition all the keener.

Although Dekker was primarily responsible for *Satiromastix*, it has usually been assumed (in Small's words) that "Marston was at Dekker's elbow during the composition" (122). I refer to the play as a collaborative effort only to indicate that it presents a defense of both men against Jonson's earlier attack (in *Poetaster*).

The poetomachia is one of the most confusing episodes in Elizabethan literary history. Attempts by earlier scholars such as F. G. Fleay to find traces of it nearly everywhere produced an inevitable reaction. Small attempts to limit the scope of the quarrel by disputing many of Fleay's more questionable identifications, but later writers have gone even further. Ralph W. Berringer, in "Jonson's *Cynthia's Revels* and the War of the Theaters" (*Philological Quarterly* 22 [1943]: 1–22), argues against seeing that play as an attack on Marston and Dekker, and contends that the quarrel probably involved only *Poetaster*, *Satiromastix*, and Marston's *What You Will*. Kay also attempts to limit the dispute to a few plays, believing with Berringer that many of the characters identified by subsequent commentators with Elizabethan literary personalities were actually mere character types. I have chosen to limit the following discussion of the poetomachia to one of the two plays indisputably involved, not because I am entirely convinced by such arguments, but simply to indicate that the case can be made using the most conservative approach to the evidence possible.

Despite the excesses of Fleay, two arguments by R. W. Ingram are worth repeating:

> When a type of a particular individual was satirized, only one or two personal traits needed to be displayed by the stage character, and those did not need to be presented consistently for the likeness to be pointed. If, on occasion, the reaction to Hedon [in *Cynthia's Revels*] is, 'That sounds like Marston,' or 'That reminds one of Marston,' the job has been done. An audience could notice such touches without being perturbed that no total identity exists between the stage character and the living person he recalls.
>
> The second point to be borne in mind is that, even if close examination of the text produces nothing to support Dekker's charge, the denial is being made by a later reader of the play and not by a witness of its performance. The theater is particularly suited to satirize a person without necessarily giving any clear indication of it in the text of the play. On the stage, a physical mannerism, a trick of gait, a gesture with the hand, a manner of talking, an unusual inflection or pronunciation can be quite enough to direct attention to a comparison with a living person (*John Marston* [Boston: Twayne, 1978], 45–46).

5. Ann Cook's important argument, in *The Privileged Playgoers of Shakespeare's London*, that the audiences for Elizabethan plays included a far higher proportion of "privileged" members than was earlier assumed has recently been faulted by Martin Butler (*Theatre and Crisis, 1632–42* [Cambridge: Cambridge University Press, 1984]), although he criticizes her more for the alleged imbalance of her account than for the inaccuracy of her evidence. Even if Cook overestimates the number of the privileged in the audiences of Elizabethan playhouses, she is probably correct in assuming that they would make up the most influential, most determining part of the audience—the part the dramatist

would be most concerned to impress. Certainly Dekker suggests in *Satiromastix* that Jonson was interested in impressing them. In act 5, Vaughan accuses Horace of "[sitting] in a Gallery, when your Comedies and Enterludes have entred their Actions, and there [making] vile and bad faces at everie lyne, to make Sentlemen have an eye to you, and to make Players afraide to take your part" (5.2.298–301). Later he is charged with "[venturing] on the stage, when your Play is ended, and [exchanging] curtezies, and complements with Gallants in the Lordes rooms, to make all the house rize up in Armes, and to cry that's *Horace*, that's he, that's he, that's he, that pennes and purges Humours and diseases" (5.2.303–07). A little earlier he had been accused of "skru[ing] and wriggl[ing] himself into great Mens famyliarity, (impudentlie)" and of "wear[ing] the Badge of Gentlemens company" (5.2.255–57). Horace himself at one point threatens to bring "a prepar'd troop of gallants" with him to the theater, "who for my sake shal distaste every unsalted line" in the "fly-blowne Comedies" of his rivals (1.2.143–44).

6. Goffman makes the relevant comment that in aggressive interchanges the winner not only succeeds in introducing information favorable to himself and unfavorable to others, but also demonstrates that he can handle himself better than his adversaries. Evidence of this capacity, he points out, is often more important than all the other information the person conveys in the interchange. See *Interaction Ritual*, 25. Many of Goffman's remarks about aggressive interactions are applicable to Jonson's satiric verse.

7. For further discussion of how Jonson used many of his satirical poems to expose the self-promotional techniques of rivals, see the discussion of his attacks on Inigo Jones, below. In the dedication to the *Epigrammes*, Jonson claimed to have "avoyded all particulars" as well as specific names in his satirical poems (H&S 8:26). This is not quite the same thing as claiming that no specific targets were intended, and in fact at least two of the poems (115 and 129) seem to have been written pretty clearly with Jones in mind. The dedication itself provides interesting evidence of Jonson's assumption that many of his contemporary readers, at least, would take his protestations of generality less than completely seriously.

E. Pearlman offers a relevant warning against the tendency to read medieval and Renaissance literature as if it were strictly conventional—as if social, theatrical, and literary traditions created literature, rather than literature being created by people responsive to these pressures and to others; see "Ben Jonson: An Anatomy," 394n.

It is worth remembering, too, that conventional tropes—satirical and otherwise—could be very useful tactically precisely because they enjoyed the sanction of time. A poet who attacked his personal rivals by reverting to common satirical themes could thus defend himself by claiming that his real interest was in making some larger point. Here, as elsewhere, conventions could be used to distance or objectify motives. Frequently one has to place oneself in the position of one of Jonson's competitors to appreciate the full resonance of a poem. Lines which might seem merely conventional to us could take on real and threatening meaning in a given contemporary setting. While we tend to look on literary conventions as merely literary, contemporaries must frequently have seen them as extensions of practical social tactics.

For discussion of a remarkable instance of the possible disparity between our own reaction to Jonson's poetry and the reaction of at least some of Jonson's contemporaries, see the remarks, later in this chapter, on George Chapman's attack on the "Execration upon Vulcan."

8. See Judith Kegan Gardiner, *Craftsmanship in Context: The Development of Ben Jonson's Poetry* (The Hague: Mouton, 1975), 42.

9. Plutarch, *Moralia*, trans. Philemon Holland (New York: Dutton, n.d.), 324.

10. See Plutarch's essay "How a Man May Receive Profit by His Enemies," in the *Moralia*, trans. Philemon Holland, 331.

11. Ibid., 331.

12. Ibid., 338–39.

13. See D. J. Gordon, "Poet and Architect: The Intellectual Setting of the Quarrel between Ben Jonson and Inigo Jones," in *The Renaissance Imagination: Essays and Lectures by D. J. Gordon*, ed. Stephen Orgel (Berkeley and Los Angeles: University of California Press, 1975), 77–101. Gordon points out that Jonson and Jones shared many of the very same theoretical assumptions—a fact that tended, paradoxically, to make their quarrels all the more personal in nature (96). Although it is perhaps a modern academic tendency to find personal attacks less interesting than intellectual disputes, obviously the former must have seemed most important (because most threatening) to the parties involved.

Patronage competition itself no doubt provided one incentive for rivals to elaborate their arts theoretically and to enhance the claims they made for them. However sincere these claims may have been, they could also prove to be effective competitive tactics. Yet because the patron functioned as a common arbiter, and because the claims were made in a competitive context, theoretical or practical artistic elaboration could not afford to be purely idiosyncratic, dictated simply by the artist's own impulses and attitudes. Innovation could never be wholly personal or eccentric, since the audience—comprised of those one hoped would approve or feared might attack—had always to be kept in mind. Orgel cautions that Jonson was a great theorizer after the fact, and that it is dangerous to accept indiscriminately his own word for what he was doing. See his study *The Jonsonian Masque* (Cambridge, Mass.: Harvard University Press, 1965), 61.

The collaboration and quarrel are also discussed by James Lees-Milne in *The Age of Inigo Jones* (London: B. T. Batsford, 1953), 19–52. According to Lees-Milne, "The fact was that Jonson took the intellectual content of his masques more seriously than anyone else did" (45). See also *Inigo Jones* by J. Alfred Gotch (London: Methuen, 1928), esp. 136–51. Graham Parry, in *The Golden Age Restor'd: The Culture of the Stuart Court, 1603–42* (Manchester: Manchester University Press, 1981) offers a brief overview of Jones's life, emphasizing mainly his architectural contributions (146–64).

For a synopsis of the evidence of Jonson's attacks on Jones, see H&S 10:689–92. Gordon, however, makes the valuable point that "If Jonson appears the more quarrelsome that is partly because we have in print what he said about Jones. We do not know what Jones was saying about Jonson—or doing to him—through these years" ("Poet and Architect," 78). Later in this chapter, I do discuss one of Jones's surviving written attacks on Jonson.

While in Scotland, Jonson claimed to William Drummond of Hawthornden that he had once "said to Prince Charles of Inigo Jones, that when he wanted words to express [the] greatest Villaine in the world he would call him ane Inigo" (H&S 1:145). This attempt by Jonson to influence the attitude of his future chief patron toward his chief rival is especially interesting in light of Jones's subsequent influence at Charles's court. Either Jonson was grossly exaggerating when he called Jones "[the] greatest Villaine in the world," or he felt far more threatened by Jones than we can easily conceive.

14. Coincidentally, Drummond reports of Jonson himself that "of all stiles he loved most to be named honest, and hath of that ane hundredth letters so naming him" (H&S 1:150).

15. On Jonson's general habits of naming see Edward Partridge, "Jonson's *Epigrammes*: The Named and the Nameless," 153–98. Jonson does not mention Jones by name in the text of the poem itself, although in social readings and when the manuscript was circulated the name of the target was undoubtedly made clear to the audience. Too open condemnation of one's opponents was often frowned on at court, and thus could be tactically disadvantageous. Jonson discovered this when he attacked the poet George Wither in one of his masques (for details see Marchette Chute, *Ben Jonson of Westminster*, 281), and of course later, during Charles's reign, when he openly assaulted Jones (see H&S 11:151–52). Jonson's open attacks on Jones during the Caroline period may, in fact, have been one sign of his growing desperation concerning his status.

16. On this period in Jonson's career, see H&S 1:86–88. On the report (by John Chamberlain) that Jonson's pension had been increased to 100 pounds see H&S 10:614. The figure mentioned in McClure's edition of Chamberlain's letters is in fact 200 pounds (*The Letters*, 2:404), and the same figure is cited in the *DNB*. The *DNB* reports the figure as a matter of fact; but stronger evidence suggests that Jonson's pension was not increased from 100 marks until 1630 (H&S 1:96; 245–48). Still, the fact that such rumors were circulating about Jonson's good fortune is itself revealing. Jonson does seem to have been paid the generous sum of 100 pounds by Buckingham for *The Gypsies Metamorphos'd* (H&S 10:612–13). In his forthcoming biography of Jonson, David Riggs mentions this latter fact among various other reasons for questioning the suggestion that the masque may have been intended to satirize Buckingham. For this argument, see Dale B. J. Randall, *Jonson's Gypsies Unmasked: Background and Theme of* The Gypsies Metamorphos'd (Durham, N.C.: Duke University Press, 1975).

John Aubrey's notes on Jonson record a story concerning Jonson's exercise of a different kind of influence at court than he was able to exercise in Selden's case. "B. Jonson had 50 [pounds per] annu[m] for . . . yeares together to keepe off Sr W. Wiseman of Essex from being Sheriff; at last K. James prickt him, & Ben: came to his Ma[jesty] & told him he had prickt him to the heart. & then explayned himselfe, innuendo Sr W.W. being prickt Sheriff: & gott him struck off" (H&S 1:181).

17. The fullest discussion of the poem is offered by Richard S. Peterson in *Imitation and Praise in the Poems of Ben Jonson* (New Haven: Yale University Press, 1981), 112–57. See also William E. Cain, "Self and Others in Two Poems by Ben Jonson," *Studies in Philology* 80 (1983): 163–82. Peterson's emphasis on the intellectual and literary traditions behind the poem differs from the approach taken here, which stresses instead the poem as a response to specific contemporary pressures and insecurities. The poem is also valuably discussed by Sara J. van den Berg in *The Action of Ben Jonson's Poetry* (143–46; 160–69) and by Stanley Fish throughout his article "Authors-Readers: Jonson's Community of the Same." At one point Fish remarks that "Jonson manages (at least in his poetry) the considerable feat of asserting and demonstrating his independence of the 'poore ties' that supposedly constrain and define him. In short, Jonson establishes in these poems an *alternate* world of patronage and declares

it (by an act of poetic fiat) more real than the world in which he is apparently embedded" (38). I would argue, of course, that it was impossible for Jonson to establish such an alternate world, even in or through his poetry, that he realized this, and that his poems are therefore designed tactically to help him cope with a social world he could not ignore or abolish.

Hugh Maclean writes that in this poem, "Jonson draws his view of friendship between individuals together with a statement on the obligation of friends to the body politic. The poem suggests that Jonson regarded the Tribe, his own band of brothers, not at all as an association 'formed for pleasure's sake . . . or merely company,' but as a dependable nucleus of virtuous companions, secure in self-knowledge and the wit to eschew triviality, upon whom the state might rely in all honorable causes." See "Ben Jonson's Poems: Notes on the Ordered Society" in William R. Keast, ed., Seventeenth Century English Poetry: Modern Essays in Criticism, revised ed. (London: Oxford University Press, 1971), 180. The approach taken here emphasizes instead the tensions and anxieties the poem embodies, the implicit recognition it suggests that the ideal friendships it praises are insufficient to guarantee one's status and importance in society, that however dependable and virtuous one might prove and however willing and ready to serve, the state—acting through the individual patrons who control it—might by chance or design turn its back.

18. For the tissue of allusions in this poem to Jonson's earlier satire on Jones, Ep. 115 ("On the Townes Honest Man"), see Ian Donaldson's note in his edition, Ben Jonson, 664–65.

19. Did Jonson have in mind any particular group when he attacked this "Covey of Witts"? It is possible—although this possibility cannot and need not be explored fully here—that his satire was aimed at George Wither and his circle of admirers and favorers, whom Jonson had attacked extensively only a few months earlier in the masque Time Vindicated to Himselfe and to His Honours in terms strikingly similar to those employed in the "Tribe" epistle.

20. For a good brief summary of the political unrest at this time and of James's attempts to deal with it, see Heinemann, Puritanism and Theatre, 153–55.

21. In the masque Time Vindicated, performed on 19 January 1623, Jonson explicitly reprehends unbridled, licentious political commentary and concludes with an endorsement of Jacobean pacificism.

22. Robert Boies Sharpe, in "Jonson's 'Execration' and Chapman's 'Invective': Their Place in Their Authors' Rivalry" (Studies in Philology 42 [1945]: 555–63), suggests that Chapman probably never circulated his poem (and may not even have completed it) in part because he realized that the image Jonson had presented of himself in the "Execration" was unassailable, and that his own poem would appear to be "an outrageous attack on one who was taking a misfortune bravely" (560). Although Chapman seems to have felt that Jonson's poem was designed largely to promote its author's own self-interests, he may also have felt that he could not openly express this opinion without himself risking a possible loss of face. Sharpe's comment on this particular point suggests the likelihood that there existed many more satirical poems or other defamatory written comments on Jonson than we now possess, if only because open and direct attack (especially on a man as prone to defend himself as Jonson was) carried dangers of retaliation and loss of face, while praise was itself commendable and more likely to be preserved. Nonetheless, Herford and the Simpsons also print "another unpleasant poem on Jonson" by Chapman (H&S 11:411–12).

23. John Dryden, *Of Dramatic Poesy and Other Critical Essays*, ed. G. Watson, 2 vols. (London and New York: Dent, 1962), 2:75. For a discussion of the passage, its context, and the reaction of other writers to it, see "Ben Jonson on his beloved, The Author Mr. William Shakespeare," by T. J. B. Spencer, in *The Elizabethan Theatre 4*, ed. G. R. Hibbard (Hamden, Conn.: Archon Books, 1974), 29–30. Spencer speculates interestingly about Jonson's involvement in and attitude toward the publication of the Shakespeare folio his poem prefaces. Roger B. Rollin discusses the psychological ambivalences he finds in Jonson's presentation of Shakespeare; see "The Anxiety of Identification: Jonson and the Rival Poets," in *Classic and Cavalier: Essays on Jonson and the Sons of Ben*, ed. Claude J. Summers and Ted-Larry Pebworth, 139–56; see esp. 139–42. Sara van den Berg finds Jonson's poem a more successful, less ambiguous work than Rollin does, but like him she also shows how Jonson uses the work to justify his own aesthetic. See " 'The Paths I Meant unto Thy Praise': Jonson's Poem for Shakespeare," *Shakespeare Survey* 11 (1978): 207–18. The substance of this article is incorporated into van den Berg's recent book, *The Action of Ben Jonson's Poetry*, where the poem to Shakespeare is thoughtfully juxtaposed with the "Tribe of Ben" epistle and with the "Execration Upon Vulcan" (143–69).

24. G. E. Bentley, *The Jacobean and Caroline Stage*, 5:1228.

25. For the full text, see H&S 11:421–28.

26. Very little can be said for sure about the precise relations among the various contributors to the volume. The editor of the collection, Brian Duppa, was a cleric who held a deanship at Oxford (among other posts), which may help to account for the heavy representation of students from that university among the elegists. Duppa himself had once served as a chaplain to the Earl of Dorset, whom Jonson once praised as a generous patron. Dorset's son, in turn, contributed to the memorial volume. Duppa was a patron to William Cartwright and to Thomas Mayne, who both contributed poems. Cartwright had lately won some recognition as a playwright, although he seems not to have thought of himself as a professional writer. In 1637 he was seeking the assistance of Archibishop William Laud (who patronized Duppa) in winning a position for himself at Oxford. Mayne, in the same year that *Jonsonus Virbius* was issued, began translating a work by Lucian for the Earl of Newcastle, Jonson's old patron.

As even these brief remarks suggest, the relations among the contributors are likely to have been very complex, grounded partly in dependency and partly in more simple friendship. These connections would be worth exploring much more fully, although the information available seems frustratingly limited. As G. B. Evans says at the start of his commendably sober biographical remarks on William Cartwright, the main outlines of his life and of the lives of his contemporaries are well known, but for the details "we search very nearly in vain" (see *The Plays and Poems of William Cartwright* [Madison: University of Wisconsin Press, 1951], 3). Most attempts to discuss the biographical relations among the "Sons of Ben" have therefore been disappointingly skimpy (Mina Kerr, *Influence of Ben Jonson on English Comedy 1598–1642* [New York: Phaedon, 1967]; Joe Lee Davis, *The Sons of Ben* [Detroit, Mich.: Wayne State University Press, 1967]; Kathryn McEuen, *Classical Influence Upon the Tribe of Ben* [New York: Octagon Books, 1968]) or a bit cloying in their impressionism (Kurt Weber, *Lucius Cary: Second Viscount Falkland* [New York: Columbia University Press, 1940]).

For previous discussions of *Jonsonus Virbius*, see Earl Miner, *The Cavalier*

Mode from Jonson to Cotton (Princeton: Princeton University Press, 1971), *passim;* George Parfitt, *Ben Jonson,* 124–29; and H. Jennifer Brady, " 'Beware the Poet'," esp. 95–99.

Chapter 6. Poems on Friends and Friendship

1. Negative modern reactions to Jonson's works still often seem rooted in negative reactions to his *persona.* Previous discussions of Jonson's views on friendship include those by Earl Miner in *The Cavalier Mode,* 250–75; Katherine Eisaman Maus in *Ben Jonson and the Roman Frame of Mind* (Princeton: Princeton University Press, 1984), 115–26; and Richard Finkelstein, "Ben Jonson's Ciceronian Rhetoric of Friendship," *Journal of Medieval and Renaissance Studies* 16 (1986): 103–24. In her recent book, Sara J. van den Berg insightfully notes that as a "man without father or brothers, making his way in London with only wit and talent to help him, Jonson turned to friendship not as a moral platitude or a solace but as a necessity. In the anonymous city, each person had to create a community of friends, chosen because of shared interests, values, personal affinity, or at least temporary usefulness. Jonson made a virtue of that necessity and recognized in the occasion of need the reason for the ideals he espoused. His poems of friendship, therefore, anchor his Humanist ideals in harsh reality and in the actual experience of friendship that helped make that harshness bearable." See *The Action of Ben Jonson's Poetry,* 51–52. Her discussion of his poems on friendship makes many significant observations, particularly on "Inviting a Friend to Supper."

S. N. Eisenstadt and L. Roniger offer a good modern overview (from a sociological perspective) of some of the issues raised in this chapter, including a comprehensive survey of secondary literature, in *Patrons, Clients, and Friends: Interpersonal Relations and the Structure of Trust in Society* (Cambridge: Cambridge University Press, 1984).

2. Even the word "friend" during Jonson's time had wider connotations than today; it could refer both to a patron and to his dependent. In the first sentence of his written advice to his son, Sir Walter Ralegh warns that "There is nothing more becoming a wise man than to make choice of friends, for by them thou shalt be judged what thou are. Let them, therefore, be wise and virtuous and none of those that follow thee for gain." The next sentence shifts the emphasis from the moral to the pragmatic: "But make election rather of thy betters than thy inferiors, shunning always such as are poor and needy, for if thou givest twenty gifts and refuse to do the like but once, all that thou hast done will be lost and such men will become thy mortal enemies"; see Louis B. Wright, *Advice to a Son,* 19. Not being friendly with a particular person might jeopardize one's relations with others; Jonson told William Drummond that "Sir W. Alexander was not half Kinde unto him & neglected him because a friend to Drayton" (H&S 1:137).

3. On the elaborate protocol associated with the exchange of benefits, see Seneca, *De Beneficiis,* in *Moral Essays,* trans. John W. Basore, Loeb Classical Library (1958), 3:287–98, where he confronts and attempts to deal positively with the competitiveness implicit in gift-giving.

4. On the importance of virtue in friendship, and on traditional ideals of friendship generally, see Laurens J. Mills, *One Soul in Bodies Twain: Friendship in Tudor Literature and Stuart Drama* (Bloomington, Ind.: Principia Press, 1937), esp. 7. See also Aristotle, *Ethica Nicomachea,* trans. W. D. Ross, in *The Works of Aristotle* (Oxford: Clarendon Press, 1908–52), 9:1156b. 6–8, and

Cicero, *De Senectute. De Amicitia. De Divinatione*, trans. William Armistead Falconer, Loeb Classical Library (1923), 127.

5. See Aristotle, 1156b. 24–25 and 1162b. 35–36 and Cicero, 173–75 (see also 187–89). See also Sir Thomas Elyot, *The Governour*, Everyman's Library 227 (1907), 162, and [Walter Dorke], *A Tipe or Figure of Friendship* (London: 1589), sig. A4ᵛ.

6. Elyot speaks of how common it is for a friend whose power increases to abandon or distrust his old acquaintances and take up with new ones (188–89).

7. Cicero, 194.

8. It is interesting how many of the stylistic principles Jonson endorses in his *Discoveries* seem rooted in a self-conscious fear of exposing oneself to disgrace and ridicule; see, for instance, H&S 8:628–29.

9. The idea that a friend is a person with whom one can be completely open may seem anachronistically modern and romantically sentimental. Certainly Aristotle had written that although the very sight of a friend could comfort one's grief, "people of a manly nature guard against making their friends grieve with them" (1171a. 35–1171b. 8–9). Cicero, however, argues that one of the greatest advantages of friendship is that it allows one to "dare discuss anything as if you were communing with yourself" (131). Elyot says that a nobleman must be particularly careful in choosing the friends to whom he may "saufely committe . . . his secretes" (189), while Dorke says that nothing is more comforting to a pensive mind "than to powre out the plaints thereof into the secret bosome of a sincere friend" (sig. A3ʳ). The anonymous *The Mirrour of Friendship* (trans. Thomas Breme [London: 1584]) says that "to a true and assured friend, a man may discover the secrets of his hearte, and recounte to him all his griefes, trust him with things touching his honor"; therefore, "great consideration is to be had in the choyce and election of such a one, least thou finde thy selfe deceived in thy trust, in uttering thy secretes to him" (sigs. Bivᵛ-vᵛ). Sir Francis Bacon, in his essay "Of Friendship," also emphasizes the friend's role as confidant (see *The Works*, 6:437–43).

10. Daniel Tuvill advises that "every man ought to be somewhat nice and scrupulous in this kind and not impart anything that may import [i.e., gravely concern, be important to] either himself or his friend but with sufficient caution. For, as the Italian proverb witnesseth, . . . 'He makes himself a servile wretch to others evermore, / That tells his secrets unto such as knew them not before'"; see his *Essays Politic and Moral and Essays Moral and Theological*, ed. John L. Lievsay (Charlottesville: University of Virginia Press, 1971), 49–50. Thus Ralegh advises his son to choose social betters as friends, in part because "they will be more careful to keep thy counsel because they have more to lose than thou hast" (Wright, *Advice to a Son*, 19).

11. Cicero writes that in breaking off friendships of the ordinary kind, "you must indeed be on your guard lest friendships be changed into serious enmities, which are the source of disputes, abuse, and invective" (187). Montaigne advises "prudence and precaution" in the conduct of most friendships, since "the knot is not so well tied that there is no cause to mistrust it. 'Love him,' Chilo used to say, 'as if you are to hate him some day; hate him as if you are to love him'"; see *The Complete Essays of Montaigne*, trans. Donald M. Frame (Stanford, Cal.: Stanford University Press, 1958), 140.

A passage from Jonson's *Discoveries* discusses the idea that familiarity breeds contempt: "There is a greater Reverence had of things remote, or strange to us, than of much better, if they be neerer, and fall under our sense. Men, and almost all sort of creatures, have their reputation by distance" (H&S 8:609). Jonson himself told Drummond that Sir Thomas "Overbury was first his friend. then turn'd his mortall enimie" (H&S 1:137). Ironically, it is partly because Drummond kept written records of their private conversation that Jonson has sometimes proven unattractive to later readers.

12. Cicero writes that "varied and complex are the experiences of friendship, and they afford many causes for suspicion and offence" (197).

13. See *Moralia*, trans. Frank C. Babbitt, Loeb Classical Library (1927–69), 1:264–395; for the passages referred to, see 267 and 275.

14. Plutarch, 1:273; 277; 281; 309–11; and 319. Ralegh claims "flatterers have never any virtue; they are ever base, creeping, cowardly persons. . . . But [he continues] it is hard to know them from friends, so are they obsequious and full of protestations; for as a wolf resembles a dog, so doth a flatterer a friend" (Wright, *Advice to a Son*, 24).

15. See Plutarch, 1:275. Cicero writes that "No one, to be sure, unless he is an utter fool, fails to detect the open flatterer, but we must exercise a watchful care against the deep and crafty one lest he steal upon us unawares. For he is very hard to recognize" (205). Elyot says much the same thing (190), and Ralegh warns that "even the wisest men are abused" by flatterers (Wright, *Advice to a Son*, 23); see also Tuvill, 47, and Thomas Churchyard, *A Sparke of Friendship and Warme Goodwill* (London, 1588), sig. C2ʳ. Knowing that even the wisest can be deceived might further erode confidence and promote suspicion and insecurity.

16. See Plutarch, 1:293, 295, 299, 301, 319, 329, 333, 345, 359, 375, 381.

17. Elyot discusses how flatterers shift their tactics and usurp the traits associated with good men (185). See also Churchyard (sig. B4ᵛ).

It seems worth noting that for Plutarch as for others, spotting flattery is often a matter of determining that a behavioral trait seems *excessive*: one must not be *too* self-deprecating nor *too* easily agreeable, etc. Inevitably these criteria raise questions of interpretation; excess, insufficiency, and balance are pliable concepts. What seems excessive to one observer might not to another. Once again the effort to establish sure criteria introduces new complications.

18. Elyot writes that flatterers often back up their tales with "othes, adjurations, and horrible curses, offringe them selfes to eternall paynes except their reporte be true" (190). He seems to assume that people who do this are deliberate and conscious liars, but Erving Goffman, in *The Presentation of Self*, makes the more interesting point that social performers are often taken in by their own acts (80–81).

19. Plutarch, 1:285; 311. Tuvill tells a remarkable tale of Alcibiades, who, to test his friends, supposedly "conveyed the image of a man into the darkest part of his house; and, thither having brought his friends, one by one, he told them he had slain a man and withal desired that by their aid and counsel he might be so assisted as that the murder might be concealed. All of them deny to be partakers with him in so great a fact [deed, crime]. Only Callias willingly condescends to satisfy his demands by doing him the best offices which in that case he possibly could, being as yet altogether ignorant of the verity of the thing. Whereupon he made no difficulty to embrace him ever after as his bosom friend and confidently to impart unto him the utmost and inmost of his secrets; yet, in those things by which his life might become questionable, he would not trust his mother for fear she might mistake the black bean for the white" (49).

20. As Edward Jones writes in his book *Ingratiation*, "In focusing on the ingratiator's tactical problems—his self-presentational dilemmas—we at the same time illuminate the obverse problems of one who wishes to present

himself with sincerity and to convey valid information to another concerning his feelings and opinions" (16). See also Goffman, *The Presentation of Self*, 66. Plutarch discusses some of the problems that can arise in attempting to avoid being charged with flattery (1:353). A passage in Jonson's *Discoveries* implies that modesty may sometimes be mistaken for flattery (H&S 8:566). For discussion of the special emphasis on the concept of sincerity in the Renaissance, see Lionel Trilling, *Sincerity and Authenticity* (Cambridge, Mass.: Harvard University Press, 1972), 12–25.

21. Jonson insisted to Drummond that "he would not flatter though he saw Death" (H&S 1:141), that he "never esteemed of a man for the name of a Lord" (H&S 1:141), and that "half of the Preachers of England were Plain ignorants for that either in their sermons they flatter, or strive to show their owne Eloquence" (H&S 1:142). He claimed that "of all stiles he loved most to be named honest, and hath of that ane hundreth letters so naming him" (H&S 1:150). Presumably Jonson valued the letters so much because they confirmed that the image he sought to project had been successfully projected and widely accepted. As the remark to Drummond suggests, the letters would also provide useful evidence further confirming his public image and self-respect.

22. See Aristotle, 1168b. 28–1169b. 2.

23. "How to Tell a Flatterer from a Friend," 1:301; 331; 351.

24. Plutarch advises that the flatterer "always presents himself in a cheerful and blithe mood, with never a whit of crossing or opposition." Then he continues: "But that is no reason why persons who express commendations should instantly be suspected of being flatterers" (1:271). More pragmatically, Tuvill warns that "to distrust without a cause is very dangerous: I do but teach another to deceive by fearing overmuch myself to be deceived" (52).

25. See, for example, Cicero, 137–41.

26. For discussion of the possible personal connections between Jonson and the spies he mentions here, see Mark Eccles, "Jonson and the Spies," *Review of English Studies* 13 (1937): 385–97. In his forthcoming biography of Jonson, David Riggs intriguingly notes that "The possibility that [Jonson] was—even here—indemnifying himself against a charge of libel by alluding to spies whose names could also refer to animals (poll, parrot) only heightens the feeling of insecurity." Joseph Loewenstein also discusses this feeling, and speculates interestingly about connections between the tone of the poem and Jonson's own involvement in espionage, in "The Jonsonian Corpulence; or, The Poet as Mouthpiece," *ELH* 53 (1986): 491–518; see esp. 501–3.

27. In a note on this poem, Richard S. Peterson remarks that "Jonson did not always live up to his own ideal of conviviality"; he then quotes the text of a letter written by James Howell, who reported to Sir Thomas Hawkins that he "was invited yesternight to a solemne supper by *B.J.* where you were deeply remembred, there was good company, excellent chear, choice wines, and joviall wellcome; one thing interven'd which almost spoyld the relish of the rest, that *B.* began to engrosse all the discourse, to vapour extreamly of himselfe, and by vilifying others to magnifie his own *muse*; *T. Ca.* busd me in the eare, that though *Ben* had barreld up a great deale of knowledge, yet it seemes that he had not read the *Ethiques*, which among other precepts of morality forbid self commendation, declaring it to be an ill favoured solecism in good manners; It made me think upon the Lady who having a good while given her guests neat entertainment, a capon being brought upon the table, instead of a spoon she took a mouth full of claret and spouted it into the poope of the hollow bird; such an accident happend in this entertainment you know—

Proprio laus sordet in ore; be a mans breath never so sweet, yet it makes ones prayses stink, if he makes his owne mouth the conduit pipe of it; But for my part I am content to dispense with the Roman infirmity of B. now that time hath snowed upon his pericranium." For the full text of the letter, see H&S 11:419–20; for Peterson's note, see *Imitation and Praise in the Poems of Ben Jonson,* 144n. In his valuable discussion of "Inviting a Friend," Thomas M. Greene nicely summarizes the work's impressively balanced tone: "The poem shows us how to be humble without servility, how to promise without promising, how to mingle playfulness with deference, how, possibly, to deflate the reverend gravity of an important acquaintance without offense to good breeding." See *The Light in Troy,* 281.

28. Ian Donaldson, *Ben Jonson,* 661. Roger Cognard offers, in one respect, a more convincing explication of these lines. "Jonson," he writes, "is referring to the common practice of using the pages of unsold books as wrappings in bakers' shops"; see "Jonson's 'Inviting a Friend to Supper.'" *The Explicator* 37, no. 3 (1979): 3–4. But he does not deal with the idea of a surprise reading, which seems to be implied (as Donaldson suggests) in line 26.

29. Drummond, in his intriguing concluding assessment of Jonson, wrote (among other things) that he was "given rather to losse a friend, than a Jest" (H&S 1:151). Ralph S. Walker, in his edition of *Ben Jonson's Timber or Discoveries* (Syracuse, N.Y.: Syracuse University Press, 1953), says that "this is a piece of self-criticism which Drummond naively repeats; it was satirically applied to Jonson by himself in *The Poetaster*" (125). Yet the phrase is proverbial, going back at least to Quintilian (H&S 9:424). It is the kind of charge that was frequently made against Jonson during the poetomachia, the kind of charge he defends himself against in *Poetaster.*

30. Several years after the tribute to Shakespeare, Jonson in *The Staple of News* implicitly mocked some "ridiculous" Shakespearean phrasing (H&S 8:584; 11:231–33). In the famous "Ode to Himselfe" appended to *The New Inn* in 1629, he specifically attacks *Pericles* as an example of the "mouldy tale[s]" popular on the English stage (H&S 6:492).

31. See Ian Donaldson, "Jonson's Ode to Sir Lucius Cary and Sir H. Morison," *Studies in the Literary Imagination* 6, no. 1 (1973): 151–52.

32. See Cicero, 141–43; see also Maus, 118–19.

33. For a discussion of psychological ambivalence in Jonson's published and conversational comments on Donne, see Roger B. Rollin, "The Anxiety of Identification: Jonson and the Rival Poets," esp. 139–42. Since Donne was not a professional poet—and since, for his own reasons of self-advancement, he did not want to be thought of as one—he was not a competitor of Jonson's in the same way as Daniel, Dekker, Drayton, Shakespeare, and others were. In general Jonson's closest literary friends were those least obviously in competition with him—including, on the one hand, his younger followers or "sons" and, on the other, contemporaries whose interests were not primarily poetic, such as Selden, Camden, and Cotton.

Chapter 7. The Masques and Entertainments

1. See Orgel, *The Jonsonian Masque;* the introductory essay to Orgel's edition of Jonson's *Complete Masques* (New Haven: Yale University Press, 1969); the introductory essays in Orgel's collaboration with Roy Strong, *Inigo Jones: The Theater of the Stuart Court,* 2 vols. (Berkeley and Los Angeles:

University of California Press, 1973); and Orgel's *The Illusion of Power* (Berkeley and Los Angeles: University of California Press, 1975). For other helpful scholarship, see for instance D. J. Gordon's *The Renaissance Imagination*, ed. Stephen Orgel; the essays printed in *Renaissance Drama*, n.s., 1 (1968), especially the essay by Orgel; John C. Meagher, *Method and Meaning in Jonson's Masques* (Notre Dame, Ind.: University of Notre Dame Press, 1966); Enid Welsford, *The Court Masque* (Cambridge: Cambridge University Press, 1927); Jeffrey Fischer, "Love Restored: A Defense of Masquing," *Renaissance Drama*, n.s., 8 (1977): 231–44; W. Todd Furniss, "Ben Jonson's Masques," in *Three Studies in the Renaissance: Sidney, Jonson, and Milton*, ed. B. C. Nagle (New Haven: Yale University Press, 1958), 89–179; Graham Parry, *The Golden Age Restor'd: The Culture of the Stuart Court*; and *The Court Masque*, ed. David Lindley (Manchester: Manchester University Press, 1984). Inga-Stina Ewbank helpfully surveys earlier approaches in " 'The Eloquence of Masques': A Retrospective View of Masque Criticism," *Renaissance Drama*, n.s., 1 (1968): 307–27.

2. Marcus's extraordinary series of essays led to her important book, *The Politics of Mirth*. For general statements of her positions, see " 'Present Occasions' and the Shaping of Ben Jonson's Masques," *ELH* 45 (1978): 201–25, and "Masquing Occasions and Masque Structures," *Research Opportunities in Renaissance Drama* 24 (1981): 7–15. For particular applications of her approach, see "The Occasion of Ben Jonson's *Pleasure Reconciled to Virtue*," *Studies in English Literature* 19 (1979): 271–93, and "City Metal and Country Mettle: The Occasion of Ben Jonson's *Golden Age Restored*" in *Pageantry in the Shakespearean Theater*, ed. David M. Bergeron (Athens: University of Georgia Press, 1985), 26–47.

Other recent approaches to the politics of the Jonsonian masque include David Norbrook, "The Reformation of the Masque," in David Lindley, ed., *The Court Masque*, 94–110, and Norman Council, "Ben Jonson, Inigo Jones, and the Transformation of Tudor Chivalry," *ELH* 47 (1980): 259–75. Both of these essays discuss Jonson's subtle critique of the nostalgia some Jacobeans felt for the martial ideals they associated with the Elizabethan era. Both essays deal insightfully with the works written to celebrate Prince Henry; on this topic, I have also benefited greatly from an essay by Mary C. Williams, "Merlin and the Prince: The Speeches at Prince Henry's Barriers," *Renaissance Drama*, n.s., 8 (1977): 221–30.

3. On this kind of opposition in Jonson's works generally, see Anne Barton, *Ben Jonson, Dramatist* (Cambridge: Cambridge University Press, 1984) and Alexander Leggatt, *Ben Jonson: His Vision and His Art* (London: Methuen, 1981).

4. See D. J. Gordon's essay "Poet and Architect" in *The Renaissance Imagination*, 77–101.

5. For the latter view see, for instance, Delora Cunningham, "The Jonsonian Masque as a Literary Form," *ELH* 22 (1955): 108–24. In a recent essay ("Forms of Ceremony in Ben Jonson's Masques," in *Modern Critical Views: Ben Jonson*, ed. Harold Bloom [New York: Chelsea House, 1987], 223–38), Marijke Rijsberman sees Jonson not as a flatterer in the masques but as an increasingly sardonic satirist of King James. Yet the evidence offered for this view (236–37) does not seem unequivocal. The whole issue of flattery in Jonson's works has been more stringently reviewed by Philip Edwards in *Threshold of a Nation: A Study in English and Irish Drama* (Cambridge: Cambridge University Press, 1979), 131–

73. On flattery in the masques, and on the political ambivalences this entails, see David Lindley, "Embarrassing Ben: The Masques for Frances Howard," *English Literary Renaissance* 16 (1986): 343–59.

6. See Willson, *King James VI and I*, 425–47. See also the very useful essay by Sara Pearl, "Sounding to Present Occasions: Jonson's Masques of 1620–5," in *The Court Masque*, ed. David Lindley, 61–77.

7. See, for instance, *The Court of the Most Illustrious and Most Magnificent James, the First* (London, 1619), esp. 16–18, 29, and 78.

8. In his article "Why Jonson Wrote Not of Love" (*Journal of Medieval and Renaissance Studies* 12 [1982]: 195–220), Lawrence Venuti interestingly discusses the dearth of comment on this subject in Jonson's nondramatic poems; but part of the humor of Jonson's lyric "Why I Write Not of Love" (*For.* 1) depends on the reader's realization that love was a constant topic in the masques. On this point, see Judith Dundas, " 'Those Beautiful Characters of Sense': Classical Deities and the Court Masque," *Comparative Drama* 16 (1982): 166–79, esp. 170–71.

9. For a fuller discussion of Jonson's attitude toward and manipulation of Plutus in this masque, see the second chapter of Leah S. Marcus's *The Politics of Mirth*. See also the valuable article by Jeffrey Fischer cited in note 1.

Chapter 8. The Plays

1. My thinking about Jonson's plays in their social contexts has been stimulated by a number of books and essays, but especially by Helgerson's *Self-Crowned Laureates* and by Judd Arnold's *A Grace Peculiar: Ben Jonson's Cavalier Heroes*, Penn State University Studies, no. 35 (University Park: Pennsylvania State University Press, 1972). See also J. A. Bryant, Jr., *The Compassionate Satirist: Ben Jonson and His Imperfect World* (Athens: University of Georgia Press, 1972); Lawrence Danson, "Jonsonian Comedy and the Discovery of the Social Self," *PMLA* 99 (1984): 179–93; Richard Dutton, *Ben Jonson: To the First Folio* (Cambridge: Cambridge University Press, 1983); Jonathan Haynes, "Festivity and the Dramatic Economy of Jonson's *Bartholomew Fair*," *ELH* 51 (1984): 645–68; Alvin Kernan, *The Cankered Muse: Satire of the English Renaissance* (New Haven: Yale University Press, 1959); L. C. Knights, *Drama and Society in the Age of Jonson* (New York: George W. Steward, 1937); Joseph Loewenstein, "The Script in the Marketplace," *Representations* 12 (1985): 101–14; Maus, *Ben Jonson and the Roman Frame of Mind*; Timothy Murray, "From Foul Sheets to Legitimate Model: Antitheater, Text, Ben Jonson," *New Literary History* 14 (1983): 641–64; Parfitt, *Ben Jonson: Public Poet and Private Man*; George E. Rowe, "Ben Jonson's Quarrel with Audience and its Renaissance Context," *Studies in Philology* 81 (1984): 438–60; John Gordon Sweeney, III, *Jonson and the Psychology of Public Theater* (Princeton: Princeton University Press, 1985); and Don E. Wayne, "Drama and Society in the Age of Jonson: An Alternative View," *Renaissance Drama*, n.s., 13 (1982): 103–29. In addition, see Marcus, *The Politics of Mirth*. For a sophisticated discussion of the problem of "subversion" in Jonson's dramatic writings, see Richard Burt, " 'Licensed by Authority': Ben Jonson and the Politics of Early Stuart Theater," *ELH* 54 (1987): 529–60.

2. Carl Bridenbaugh estimates that between 1605 and 1634 the population of the city grew from around 224,275 to perhaps 339,824; of these people, perhaps 90 percent were artisans and the urban poor. See his *Vexed and Troubled Englishmen: 1590–1642* (New York: Oxford University Press, 1968), 164, 166.

On London at this time, see, for instance, F. J. Fisher, "The Development of London as a Centre of Conspicuous Consumption in the Sixteenth and Seventeenth Centuries," in *Essays in Modern History*, ed. Ian R. Christie (London: Macmillan, 1968), 75–90, and Frank F. Foster, "Politics and Community in Elizabethan London," in *The Rich, the Well-Born, and the Powerful: Elites and Upper Classes in History*, ed. Frederic Cople Jaher (Urbana: University of Illinois Press, 1973), 110–38. Fisher emphasizes, incidentally, the heavy influx of "rusticke" gentry into the capital.

3. See Cook, *The Privileged Playgoers*. For discussion of Martin Butler's challenge to Cook's arguments, see chapter 5, note 5, above. Arnold's *A Grace Peculiar* discusses Jonson's efforts to prove appealing to the "gallants."

4. Sweeney provides the fullest discussion of these tensions, but see also Rowe.

5. On the tensions in this speech, see Robert C. Jones, "The Satirist's Retirement in Jonson's 'Apologetical Dialogue,'" *ELH* 34 (1967): 447–67.

6. For an interesting juxtaposition of *Volpone* and *Sejanus*, see Dutton, 54–74.

7. On this point, see Maus, 130–32.

8. See Jonas Barish, *Ben Jonson and the Language of Prose Comedy* (Cambridge, Mass.: Harvard University Press, 1960), 88–89.

9. See the chapter on Jonson in Jonas Barish's *The Anti-Theatrical Prejudice* (Berkeley and Los Angeles: University of California Press, 1981).

10. See especially the first chapter of *A Grace Peculiar*. For further discussion of Jonson's relation to the railers, see Helgerson, 134–38. Sweeney, however, usefully warns against making excessively neat or definite distinctions between Jonson and his angry characters (208).

11. On this point, see Don E. Wayne, *Penshurst*, 153.

12. Maus (41–42) relates Jonsonian "self-irony" to stoic traditions.

13. Howard Felperin writes that in *Volpone*, "for example, [the] several plotters form a hierarchy of imaginative accomplishment that mounts towards and finally implies Jonson's own accomplishment in the play itself." See his "Quick Comedy Refined: Towards a Poetics of Jonson's Major Plays," *Southern Review* (Adelaide) 13 (1980): 153–69, esp. 158. In a splendid book published while mine was in press, Robert N. Watson carries this sort of approach to its logical conclusion by detailing not only the ways in which Jonson achieves mastery over his characters but also the methods by which he parodies the works and assumptions of his play-writing competitors. Although Watson does not discuss very extensively the patronage context of Jonson's career, his book is full of implications for the kind of arguments I have been developing in this chapter. See *Ben Jonson's Parodic Strategy: Literary Imperialism in the Comedies* (Cambridge, Mass.: Harvard University Press, 1987).

14. On the distinction between true and perverse artists, see Gabrielle Bernhard Jackson, *Vision and Judgment in Ben Jonson's Drama* (New Haven: Yale University Press, 1968), 30.

15. On the general instability of Jonson's conception of the social self, see Danson's valuable article.

16. On the importance of trials in Jonson's drama, see Maus, 126–28.

17. For a fine discussion of this aspect of the play, see Joyce Van Dyke, "The Game of Wits in *The Alchemist*," *Studies in English Literature* 19 (1979): 253–69.

18. For valuable discussions of Jonson's work in its larger ideological con-

texts, see, for instance, Kelly, "Ben Jonson's Politics"; Goldberg, *James I and the Politics of Literature;* Patterson, *Censorship and Interpretation;* Dollimore, *Radical Tragedy;* Norbrook, *Poetry and Politics;* and Butler, *Theatre and Crisis, 1632–1642.* Obviously there is no way finally to separate micropolitics from the ideological context in which it occurs; the difference is mainly a matter of focus and emphasis.

Bibliography

Akrigg, G. P. V. *Jacobean Pageant: or The Court of King James I*. Cambridge, Mass.: Harvard University Press, 1962.

Aristotle. *Ethica Nicomachea*. Vol. 9 of *The Works of Aristotle*. Translated by W. D. Ross. Oxford: Clarendon Press, 1908–52.

Arnold, Judd. *A Grace Peculiar: Ben Jonson's Cavalier Heroes*. Penn State University Studies, no. 35. University Park: Pennsylvania State University Press, 1972.

Auberlen, Eckhard. *The Commonwealth of Wit: The Writer's Image and His Strategies of Self-Representation in Elizabethan Literature*. Tübingen: Gunter Narr Verlag, 1984.

Aulicus Coquinariae. In Vol. 2 of *The Secret History of the Court of James the First*. Edinburgh: John Ballantyne and Co., 1811.

Ayres, Philip J. "Jonson, Northampton, and the 'Treason' in *Sejanus*." *Modern Philology* 80 (1983): 356–63.

Bacon, Francis. *The Works of Francis Bacon*. Edited by James Spedding et al. 14 vols. London: Longmans, Green, 1862–1901.

Bald, R. C. *John Donne: A Life*. New York: Oxford University Press, 1970.

Bamborough, J. B. *Ben Jonson*. London: Hutchinson, 1970.

Barish, Jonas. *Ben Jonson and the Language of Prose Comedy*. Cambridge, Mass.: Harvard University Press, 1960.

———. *The Anti-Theatrical Prejudice*. Berkeley and Los Angeles: University of California Press, 1981.

Barton, Anne. *Ben Jonson, Dramatist*. Cambridge: Cambridge University Press, 1984.

Becker, Ernest. *The Birth and Death of Meaning*. 2d ed. New York: Free Press, 1971.

Bennett, H. S. *English Books and Readers 1558 to 1603*. Cambridge: Cambridge University Press, 1965.

Bentley, G. E. *The Jacobean and Caroline Stage*. 7 vols. Oxford: Clarendon Press, 1941–68.

Berger, Peter L. *The Sacred Canopy: Elements of a Sociological Theory of Religion*. Garden City, N.Y.: Anchor Books, 1969.

———, and Thomas Luckmann. *The Social Construction of Reality: A Treatise in the Sociology of Knowledge*. Garden City, N.Y.: Anchor Books, 1967.

Berringer, Ralph W. "Jonson's *Cynthia's Revels* and the War of the Theaters." *Philological Quarterly* 22 (1943): 1–22.

Bevington, David M. *Tudor Drama and Politics: A Critical Approach to Topical Meaning.* Cambridge, Mass.: Harvard University Press, 1968.

Birch, Thomas, ed. *The Court and Times of Charles the First.* London: Henry Colburn, 1849.

——, ed. *The Court and Times of James the First.* 2 vols. London: Henry Colburn, 1849.

Blau, Peter M. *Exchange and Power in Social Life.* New York: Wiley, 1964.

Blissett, William, ed. *A Celebration of Ben Jonson.* Toronto: University of Toronto Press, 1973.

Bloom, Harold. *The Anxiety of Influence: A Theory of Poetry.* New York: Oxford University Press, 1973.

Bond, Ronald Bruce. "A Study of *Invidia* in Medieval and Renaissance English Literature." Ph.D. diss., University of Toronto, 1972.

Bone, Quentin. *Henrietta Maria: Queen of the Cavaliers.* Urbana: University of Illinois Press, 1972.

Bowen, Catherine Drinker. *Francis Bacon: The Temper of a Man.* Boston: Little, Brown, 1963.

——. *The Lion and the Throne: The Life and Times of Sir Edward Coke.* Boston: Little, Brown, 1956.

Bradbrook, M. C. "Social Change and the Evolution of Ben Jonson's Court Masques." *Studies in the Literary Imagination* 6, no. 1 (1973): 101–52.

Brady, H. Jennifer. "Ben Jonson's 'Works of Judgment': A Study of Rhetorical Strategies in the 'Epigrammes.'" Ph.D. diss., Princeton University, 1980.

——. "'Beware the Poet': Authority and Judgment in Jonson's *Epigrammes.*" *Studies in English Literature* 23 (1983): 95–112.

——. "Jonson's 'To King James': Plain Speaking in the *Epigrammes* and the *Conversations.*" *Studies in Philology* 82 (1985): 380–98.

Brewer, John S., ed. *The Court and Times of King James the First.* 2 vols. London: Richard Bentley, 1839.

Bridenbaugh, Carl. *Vexed and Troubled Englishmen: 1590–1642.* New York: Oxford University Press, 1968.

Bryant, J. A., Jr. *The Compassionate Satirist: Ben Jonson and His Imperfect World.* Athens: University of Georgia Press, 1972.

Burt, Richard. "'Licensed by Authority': Ben Jonson and the Politics of Early Stuart Theater." *ELH* 54 (1987): 529–60.

Butler, Martin. *Theatre and Crisis, 1632–42.* Cambridge: Cambridge University Press, 1984.

Cain, William E. "The Place of the Poet in Jonson's 'To Penshurst' and 'To my Muse.'" *Criticism* 21 (1979): 34–48.

——. "Self and Others in Two Poems by Ben Jonson." *Studies in Philology* 80 (1983): 163–82.

Cartwright, Dorwin, ed. *Studies in Social Power.* Ann Arbor: University of Michigan, 1959.

Cartwright, William. *The Plays and Poems of William Cartwright.* Edited by G. B. Evans. Madison: University of Wisconsin Press, 1951.

Cecil, David. *The Cecils of Hatfield House: An English Ruling Family.* Boston: Houghton Mifflin, 1973.

Cecil, Robert. *An Answere to Certaine Scandalous Papers, scattered abroad under colour of a Catholicke Admonition.* London, 1606.

———. "The State and Dignity of a Secretary of State's Place, with the Care and Peril Thereof." In vol. 5 of *Harleian Miscellany*, 166–68. London: R. Dutton, 1808–11.

Chamberlain, John. *The Letters of John Chamberlain.* Edited by Norman Egbert McClure. 2 vols. Philadelphia: American Philosophical Society, 1939.

Chapman, George. *The Poems of George Chapman.* Edited by Phyllis B. Bartlett. London: Oxford University Press, 1941.

Churchyard, Thomas. *A Sparke of Friendship and Warme Goodwill.* London, 1588.

Chute, Marchette. *Ben Jonson of Westminster.* New York: Dutton, 1953.

Cicero. *De Senectute. De Amicitia. De Divinatione.* Translated by W. A. Falconer. Loeb Classical Library. 1923.

Coakley, Thomas M. "Robert Cecil in Power: Elizabethan Politics in Two Reigns." In *Early Stuart Studies: Essays in Honor of David Harris Willson*, edited by Howard S. Reinmuth, Jr., 64–94. Minneapolis: University of Minnesota Press, 1970.

Cognard, Roger. "Jonson's 'Inviting a Friend to Supper.'" *The Explicator* 37, no. 3 (1979): 3–4.

Cook, Ann Jennalie. *The Privileged Playgoers of Shakespeare's London, 1576–1642.* Princeton: Princeton University Press, 1981.

Cope, Jackson I. "Jonson's Reading of Spenser: The Genesis of a Poem." *English Miscellany* 10 (1959): 61–66.

Council, Norman. "Ben Jonson, Inigo Jones, and the Transformation of Tudor Chivalry." *ELH* 47 (1980): 259–75.

The Court of the Most Illustrious and Most Magnificent James, the First. London, 1619.

Cubeta, Paul M. "A Jonsonian Ideal: 'To Penshurst.'" *Philological Quarterly* 42 (1963): 14–24.

———. "Ben Jonson's Religious Lyrics." *Journal of English and Germanic Philology* 62 (1963): 96–110.

Cunningham, Delora. "The Jonsonian Masque as a Literary Form." *ELH* 22 (1955): 108–24.

Curtis, Mark H. "The Alienated Intellectuals of Early Stuart England." In *Crisis in Europe: 1560–1660*, edited by Christopher Hill, 309–31. New York: Doubleday, 1967.

Danby, John. *Poets on Fortune's Hill.* London: Faber and Faber, 1952.

Danson, Lawrence. "Jonsonian Comedy and the Discovery of the Social Self." *PMLA* 99 (1984): 179–93.

Davis, Joe Lee. *The Sons of Ben.* Detroit, Mich.: Wayne State University Press, 1967.

Davis, Tom. "Ben Jonson's Ode to Himself: An Early Version." *Philological Quarterly* 51 (1972): 410–21.

Dekker, Thomas. *The Dramatic Works of Thomas Dekker.* Edited by Fredson Bowers. 4 vols. Cambridge: Cambridge University Press, 1953.

De Luna, Barbara N. *Jonson's Romish Plot: A Study of* Catiline *and its Historical Context.* Oxford: Clarendon Press, 1967.

Dickens, A. G., ed. *The Courts of Europe: Politics, Patronage and Royalty: 1400–1800.* New York: McGraw-Hill, 1977.

Dictionary of National Biography. Edited by Leslie Stephen and Sidney Lee. 22 vols. Oxford: Oxford University Press, 1885–1913.

Ditton, Jason, ed. *View from Goffman.* New York: St. Martin's, 1980.

Dollimore, Jonathan. *Radical Tragedy: Religion, Ideology and Power in the Drama of Shakespeare and His Contemporaries.* Chicago: University of Chicago Press, 1984.

———, and Alan Sinfield, eds. *Political Shakespeare: New Essays in Cultural Materialism.* Ithaca, N.Y., and London: Cornell University Press, 1985.

Donaldson, Ian. "Jonson's Ode to Sir Lucius Cary and Sir H. Morison." *Studies in the Literary Imagination* 6, no. 1 (1973): 139–52.

[Dorke, Walter.] *A Tipe or Figure of Friendship.* London, 1589.

Dryden, John. *Of Dramatic Poesy and Other Critical Essays.* Edited by G. Watson. 2 vols. London and New York: Dent, 1962.

Duncan, Hugh Dalziel. *Language and Literature in Society: A Sociological Essay on Theory and Method in the Interpretation of Linguistic Symbols With Bibliographical Guide to the Sociology of Literature.* Chicago: University of Chicago Press, 1953.

———. *Symbols in Society.* New York: Oxford University Press, 1968.

Duncan, Owen. "The Political Career of Sir Henry Neville: An Elizabethan Gentleman at the Court of James I." Ph.D. diss., Ohio State University, 1974.

Dundas, Judith. " 'Those Beautiful Characters of Sense': Classical Deities and the Court Masque." *Comparative Drama* 16 (1982): 166–79.

Dunlap, Rhodes. "Honest Ben and Royal James: The Poetics of Patronage." *Iowa State Journal of Research* 57 (1982): 143–51.

Dutton, Richard. *Ben Jonson: To the First Folio.* Cambridge: Cambridge University Press, 1983.

Eccles, Mark. "Jonson and the Spies." *Review of English Studies* 13 (1937): 385–97.

———. "Jonson's Marriage." *Review of English Studies* 12 (1936): 257–72.

Edwards, Philip. *Threshold of a Nation: A Study in English and Irish Drama.* Cambridge: Cambridge University Press, 1979.

Eisenstadt, S. N., and L. Roniger. "Patron–Client Relations as a Model of Structuring Social Exchange." *Comparative Studies in Society and History* 22 (1980): 42–77.

———. *Patrons, Clients, and Friends: Interpersonal Relations and the Structure of Trust in Society.* Cambridge: Cambridge University Press, 1984.

Elias, Norbert. *The Court Society.* Translated by Edmund Jephcott. New York: Pantheon, 1983.

Elsky, Martin. "Words, Things, and Names: Jonson's Poetry and Philosophical Grammar." In *Classic and Cavalier: Essays on Jonson and the Sons of Ben,* edited by Claude J. Summers and Ted-Larry Pebworth, 91–106. Pittsburgh, Pa.: University of Pittsburgh Press, 1982.

Elton, G. R. *Studies in Tudor and Stuart Politics and Governments*. 3 vols. Cambridge: Cambridge University Press, 1983.

Elyot, Thomas. *The Governour*. Everyman's Library 227. 1907.

Epstein, Joel. *Francis Bacon: A Political Biography*. Athens: Ohio University Press, 1977.

Esler, Anthony. *The Aspiring Mind of the Elizabethan Younger Generation*. Durham, N.C.: Duke University Press, 1966.

Evans, Robert C. "Ben Jonson's *Epigrammes* 1–3." *The Explicator* 45, no. 2 (1987): 7–10.

———. "Ben Jonson's 'To Edward Allen.' " *The Explicator* 43, no. 1 (1985): 19–21.

———. "Defending the Father: Jonson's 'Sons' and the Poetry of Power." *Iowa State Journal of Research* 61 (1987): 347–58.

———. "Frozen Maneuvers: Ben Jonson's Epigrams to Robert Cecil." *Texas Studies in Literature and Language* 29 (1987): 115–40.

———. "Jonson, *Satiromastix*, and the Poetomachia: A Patronage Perspective." *Iowa State Journal of Research* 60 (1986): 369–83.

———. "Jonson's 'Epistle to Sir Edward Sacvile.' " *The Explicator* 43, no. 3 (1985): 7.

———. "Jonson's Epitaph on the Countess of Shrewsbury." *The Explicator* 44, no. 3 (1986): 15–17.

———. "Literature as Equipment for Living: Ben Jonson and the Poetics of Patronage." *College Language Association Journal* 30 (1987): 379–94.

———. " 'Men that are Safe, and Sure': Jonson's 'Tribe of Ben' Epistle in its Patronage Context." *Renaissance and Reformation*, n.s., 9 (1985): 235–54.

———. "Strategic Debris: Ben Jonson's Satires on Inigo Jones." *Renaissance Papers* 1986: 69–82.

Ewbank, Inga-Stina. " 'The Eloquence of Masques': A Retrospective View of Masque Criticism." *Renaissance Drama*, n.s., 1 (1968): 307–27.

Felperin, Howard. "Quick Comedy Refined: Towards a Poetics of Jonson's Major Plays." *Southern Review* (Adelaide) 13 (1980): 153–69.

Ferry, Anne. *All in War with Time*. Cambridge, Mass.: Harvard University Press, 1975.

Finett, John. *Finetti Philoxensis*. London, 1656.

Finkelstein, Richard. "Ben Jonson's Ciceronian Rhetoric of Friendship." *Journal of Medieval and Renaissance Studies* 16 (1986): 103–24.

Fischer, Jeffrey. "*Love Restored*: A Defense of Masquing." *Renaissance Drama*, n.s., 8 (1977): 231–44.

Fish, Stanley. "Authors-Readers: Jonson's Community of the Same." *Representations* 7 (1984): 26–58.

Fisher, F. J. "The Development of London as a Centre of Conspicuous Consumption in the Sixteenth and Seventeenth Centuries." In *Essays in Modern History*, edited by Ian R. Christie, 75–90. London: Macmillan, 1968.

Fogle, French R., and Louis A. Knafla. *Patronage in Late Renaissance England*. Los Angeles: William Andrews Clark Memorial Library, 1983.

Foster, Frank F. "Politics and Community in Elizabethan London." In *The Rich,* the Well-Born, and the Powerful: Elites and Upper Classes in History, edited by Frederic Cople Jaher, 110–38. Urbana: University of Illinois Press, 1973.

Foucault, Michel. *The Archeology of Knowledge and the Discourse on Language.* Translated by A. M. Sheridan Smith. New York: Pantheon, 1972.

———. *Power/Knowledge: Selected Interviews and Other Writings 1972–1977.* Edited by Colin Gordon. New York: Pantheon, 1980.

Fowler, Alastair. "The 'Better Marks' of Jonson's *To Penshurst.*" *Review of English Studies,* n.s., 24 (1973): 266–82.

Furniss, W. Todd. "Ben Jonson's Masques." In *Three Studies in the Renaissance: Sidney, Jonson, and Milton,* edited by B. C. Nangle, 89–179. New Haven: Yale University Press, 1958.

Gardiner, Judith Kegan. *Craftsmanship in Context: The Development of Ben Jonson's Poetry.* The Hague: Mouton, 1975.

Gardiner, Samuel R. *History of England from the Accession of James I to the Outbreak of Civil War.* 10 vols. London: Longmans, Green, 1883–84.

Garrison, James D. *Dryden and the Tradition of Panegyric.* Berkeley and Los Angeles: University of California Press, 1975.

———. "Time and Value in Jonson's 'Epistle to Elizabeth Countesse of Rutland.'" *Concerning Poetry* 8 (1975): 53–58.

Gaunt, William. *Court Painting in England from Tudor to Victorian Times.* London: Constable, 1980.

Goffman, Erving. *Interaction Ritual: Essays on Face-to-Face Behavior.* Garden City, N.Y.: Anchor Books, 1967.

———. *The Presentation of Self in Everyday Life.* Garden City, N.Y.: Anchor Books, 1959.

———. *Strategic Interaction.* Philadelphia: University of Pennsylvania Press, 1969.

Gold, Barbara K., ed. *Literary and Artistic Patronage in Ancient Rome.* Austin: University of Texas Press, 1982.

Goldberg, Jonathan. *James I and the Politics of Literature.* Baltimore: Johns Hopkins University Press, 1983.

———. "The Politics of Renaissance Literature: A Review Essay." *ELH* 49 (1982): 514–42.

Gordon, D. J. *The Renaissance Imagination: Essays and Lectures by D. J. Gordon.* Edited by Stephen Orgel. Berkeley and Los Angeles: University of California Press, 1975.

Gotch, J. Alfred. *Inigo Jones.* London: Methuen, 1928.

Great Britain. Historical Manuscripts Commission. *Report on the Manuscripts of Lord De L'isle and Dudley.* 6 vols. London, 1925–66.

———. Historical Manuscripts Commission. *Report on the Manuscripts of the Marquess of Downshire.* 4 vols. London, 1924–40.

———. Public Record Office. *Calendar of State Papers Domestic, James I, 1611–18.* Edited by Mary Anne Everett Green. London: Longman, 1858.

———. Public Record Office. *Calendar of State Papers, Venetian.* 38 vols. London, 1864–1947.

Green, Richard Firth. *Poets and Princepleasers: Literature and the English Court in the Late Middle Ages.* Toronto: University of Toronto Press, 1980.

Greenblatt, Stephen. *The Power of Forms in the Renaissance.* Norman, Okla.: Pilgrim Books, 1982.

———. *Renaissance Self-Fashioning.* Chicago: University of Chicago Press, 1980.

Greene, Thomas M. "Ben Jonson and the Centered Self." *Studies in English Literature* 10 (1970): 325–48.

———. *The Light in Troy: Imitation and Discovery in Renaissance Poetry.* New Haven and London: Yale University Press, 1982.

Hacket, John. *Scrinia Reserata: A Memorial Offer'd to the Great Deservings of John Williams, D. D.* London: Samuel Lowndes, 1692.

Hagestad, William Thomson. "Restoration Patronage." Ph.D. diss., University of Wisconsin, 1966.

Hamilton, Elizabeth. *Henrietta Maria.* New York: Coward, McCann and Geoghegan, 1976.

Handover, P. M. *The Second Cecil: The Rise to Power, 1563–1604, of Sir Robert Cecil, Later First Earl of Salisbury.* London: Eyre and Spottiswoode, 1959.

Harington, John. *Nugae Antiquae.* Edited by Thomas Park. 2 vols. London: Vernor and Hood, 1804.

Harrison, G. B. *Jacobean Journal.* London: G. Routledge, 1946.

———. *A Second Jacobean Journal.* Ann Arbor: University of Michigan Press, 1958.

Hauser, Arnold. *The Social History of Art.* Translated by Stanley Godman. 2 vols. New York: Knopf, 1962.

———. *The Sociology of Art.* Translated by Kenneth J. Northcott. Chicago: University of Chicago Press, 1982.

Haynes, Jonathan. "Festivity and the Dramatic Economy of Jonson's *Bartholomew Fair.*" *ELH* 51 (1984): 179–93.

Heinemann, Margot. "Middleton's *A Game at Chess:* Parliamentary-Puritans and Opposition Drama." *English Literary Renaissance* 5 (1975): 232–50.

———. *Puritanism and Theatre: Thomas Middleton and Opposition Drama Under the Early Stuarts.* Cambridge: Cambridge University Press, 1980.

Helgerson, Richard. *Self-Crowned Laureates: Spenser, Jonson, Milton, and the Literary System.* Berkeley and Los Angeles: University of California Press, 1983.

Herendeen, W. H. "Like a Circle Bounded in Itself: Jonson, Camden, and the Strategies of Praise." *Journal of Medieval and Renaissance Studies* 11, no. 2 (1981): 137–67.

Hibbard, G. R. "The Country House Poem of the Seventeenth Century." *Journal of the Warburg and Courtauld Institute* 19 (1956): 159–74.

———, ed. *The Elizabethan Theatre, 4.* Hamden, Conn.: Archon Books, 1974.

Hill, Christopher. *Economic Problems of the Church.* Oxford: Clarendon Press, 1956.

———. "Parliament and People in Seventeenth-Century England." *Past and Present,* no. 92 (1981): 100–24.

Hirst, Derek. "The Place of Principle." *Past and Present,* no. 92 (1981): 79–99.

Hobsbaum, Philip. "Ben Jonson in the Seventeenth Century." *Michigan Quarterly Review* 16 (1977): 405–23.

Holzknecht, Karl J. *Literary Patronage in the Middle Ages.* New York: Octagon Books, 1967.

Howard, Jean E. "The New Historicism in Renaissance Studies." *English Literary Renaissance* 16 (1986): 13–43.

Hoy, Cyrus. *Introductions, Notes, and Commentaries to Texts in 'The Dramatic Works of Thomas Dekker.'* 4 vols. Cambridge: Cambridge University Press, 1981.

Hurstfield, Joel. *Freedom, Corruption, and Government in Elizabethan England.* Cambridge, Mass.: Harvard University Press, 1973.

———. "Robert Cecil, Earl of Salisbury, Minister of Elizabeth and James I." *History Today* 7 (1957): 279–89.

Hutchison, Barbara. "Ben Jonson's 'Let Me Be What I Am': An Apology in Disguise." *English Language Notes* 2 (1965): 185–90.

Ingram, R. W. *John Marston.* Boston: Twayne, 1978.

Ives, E. W. *Faction in Tudor England.* London: Historical Association, 1979.

———. *The Political Works of James I.* Edited by Charles Howard McIlwain. Cambridge, Mass.: Harvard University Press, 1918.

Jackson, Gabrielle Bernhard. *Vision and Judgment in Ben Jonson's Drama.* New Haven: Yale University Press, 1968.

Javitch, Daniel. *Poetry and Courtliness in Renaissance England.* Princeton: Princeton University Press, 1978.

John, Lisle Cecil. "Ben Jonson's 'To Sir William Sidney, On His Birthday.'" *Modern Language Review* 52 (1957): 168–76.

Johnson, Richard. *Remembrance of the Honours Due to the Life and Death of Robert Earle of Salisbury.* London, 1612. Reprint. Newcastle: S. Hodgson, 1818.

Johnston, George Burke. *Ben Jonson, Poet.* New York: Columbia University Press, 1945.

Jones, Edward E. *Ingratiation: A Social Psychological Analysis.* New York: Irvington, 1975.

Jones, Robert C. "The Satirist's Retirement in Jonson's 'Apologetical Dialogue.'" *ELH* 34 (1967): 447–67.

Jones, W. J. "Ellesmere and Politics, 1603–17." In *Early Stuart Studies: Essays in Honor of David Harris Willson,* edited by Howard S. Reinmuth, Jr., 11–63. Minneapolis: University of Minnesota Press, 1970.

Jonson, Ben. *Ben Jonson.* Edited by C. H. Herford and Percy and Evelyn Simpson. 11 vols. Oxford: Clarendon Press, 1925–52.

———. *Ben Jonson.* Edited by Ian Donaldson. New York: Oxford University Press, 1985.

———. *Ben Jonson: The Complete Poems.* Edited by George Parfitt. New Haven: Yale University Press, 1982.

———. *The Complete Masques.* Edited by Stephen Orgel. New Haven: Yale University Press, 1969.

———. *The Complete Poetry of Ben Jonson.* Edited by William B. Hunter, Jr. New York: Norton, 1963.

———. *The Poems of Ben Jonson.* Edited by Bernard H. Newdigate. Oxford: Basil Blackwell, 1936.

————. *The Works of Ben Jonson.* Notes and a memoir by William Gifford. Edited by Francis Cunningham. 3 vols. London: Chatto and Windus, 1897–1903.

Kamholtz, Jonathan Zachary. "Ben Jonson and the Poetry of Praise." Ph.D. diss., Yale University, 1975.

————. "Ben Jonson's *Epigrammes* and Poetic Occasions." *Studies in English Literature* 23 (1983): 77–94.

Kay, W. David. "Ben Jonson, Horace, and the Poetomachia: The Development of an Elizabethan Playwright's Public Image." Ph.D. diss., Princeton University, 1968.

————. "The Shaping of Ben Jonson's Career: A Reexamination of Facts and Problems." *Modern Philology* 67 (1970): 224–37.

Keast, William R., ed. *Seventeenth Century English Poetry: Modern Essays in Criticism.* Rev. ed. London: Oxford University Press, 1971.

Kelly, Joseph John. "Ben Jonson's Politics." *Renaissance and Reformation,* n.s., 7 (1983): 192–215.

Kernan, Alvin. *The Cankered Muse: Satire of the English Renaissance.* New Haven: Yale University Press, 1959.

————. *The Playwright as Magician: Shakespeare's Image of the Poet in the English Public Theatre.* New Haven: Yale University Press, 1979.

Kerr, Mina. *Influence of Ben Jonson on English Comedy 1598–1642.* New York: Phaedon, 1967.

Kerrigan, William. "Ben Jonson Full of Shame and Scorn." *Studies in the Literary Imagination* 6, no. 1 (1973): 199–217.

Knapp, Peggy. "Ben Jonson and the Publicke Riot." *ELH* 46 (1979): 577–94.

Knights, L. C. "Ben Jonson: Public Attitudes and Social Poetry." In *A Celebration of Ben Jonson,* edited by William Blisset et al., 168–87. Toronto: University of Toronto Press, 1973.

————. *Drama and Society in the Age of Jonson.* New York: George W. Steward, 1937.

————. "On the Social Background of Metaphysical Poetry." *Scrutiny* 13 (1945): 37–52.

Kocher, Paul. "Francis Bacon and His Father." *Huntington Library Quarterly* 21 (1957): 133–58.

Koppel, Catherine Constantine. " 'Of Poets and Poesy': The English Verse Epistle, 1595–1640." Ph.D. diss., University of Rochester, 1978.

Korda, Michael. *Power! How to Get It, How to Use It!* New York: Ballantine Books, 1975.

Laffitte, Susan Miller. "The Literary Connections of Sir Thomas Egerton: A Study of the Influence of Thomas Egerton Upon Major Writers of Renaissance Literature." Ph.D. diss., Florida State University, 1971.

Lamb, Mary Ellen. "The Countess of Pembroke's Patronage." Ph.D. diss., Columbia University, 1976.

Lanier, Douglas M. "Brainchildren: Self-representation and Patriarchy in Ben Jonson's Early Works." *Renaissance Papers* (1986): 53–68.

Laslett, Peter. *The World We Have Lost.* 2d ed. New York: Scribner's, 1971.

Lee, Jongsook. "Who Is Cecilia, What Was She: Cecilia Bulstrode and Jonson's Epideictics." *Journal of English and Germanic Philology* 85 (1986): 20–34.

Lees-Milne, James. *The Age of Inigo Jones*. London: B. T. Batsford, 1953.

Leggatt, Alexander. *Ben Jonson: His Vision and His Art*. London: Methuen, 1981.

Lemly, John. "Masks and Self-Portraits in Jonson's Late Poetry." *ELH* 44 (1977): 248–66.

Lindley, David, ed. *The Court Masque*. Manchester: Manchester University Press, 1984.

———. "Embarrassing Ben: The Masques for Frances Howard." *English Literary Renaissance* 16 (1986): 343–59.

Linklater, Eric. *Ben Jonson and King James*. London: Jonathan Cape, 1931.

Livingston, Mary L. "Ben Jonson: The Poet to the Painter." *Texas Studies in Literature and Language* 18 (1976): 381–92.

Lockyer, Roger. *Buckingham: The Life and Political Career of George Villiers, First Duke of Buckingham 1592–1628*. London: Longman, 1981.

Lodge, Edmund. *Illustrations of British History, Biography, and Manners*. 3 vols. 2d ed. London: John Chidley, 1838.

Loewenstein, Joseph. "The Jonsonian Corpulence; or, The Poet as Mouthpiece." *ELH* 53 (1986): 491–518.

———. "The Script in the Marketplace." *Representations* 12 (1985): 101–14.

Low, Anthony. *The Georgic Revolution*. Princeton: Princeton University Press, 1985.

Lundquist, Eric N. "The Last Years of the First Earl of Salisbury, 1610–1612." *Albion* 18 (1986): 23–41.

Lytle, Guy Fitch, and Stephen Orgel, eds. *Patronage in the Renaissance*. Princeton: Princeton University Press, 1981.

Lytle, Guy Fitch. "Religion and the Lay Patron in Reformation England." In *Patronage In the Renaissance*, edited by Guy Fitch Lytle and Stephen Orgel, 65–114. Princeton: Princeton University Press, 1981.

MacCaffrey, Wallace T. "Place and Patronage in Elizabethan Politics." In *Elizabethan Government and Society: Essays Presented to Sir John Neale*, edited by S. T. Bindoff et al., 95–126. London: University of London, Athlone Press, 1961.

McCall, George J., and J. L. Simmons. *Identities and Interactions*. New York: Free Press, 1966.

McClung, William A. *The Country House in English Renaissance Poetry*. Berkeley and Los Angeles: University of California Press, 1977.

McEuen, Kathryn. *Classical Influence Upon the Tribe of Ben*. New York: Octagon Books, 1968.

Maclean, Hugh, ed. *Ben Jonson and the Cavalier Poets*. New York: Norton, 1974.

———. "Ben Jonson's Poems: Notes on the Ordered Society." In *Seventeenth Century English Poetry: Modern Essays in Criticism*, edited by William R. Keast, 174–200. Rev. ed. London: Oxford University Press, 1971.

McMillin, Scott. "Jonson's Early Entertainments: New Information from Hatfield House." *Renaissance Drama*, n.s., 1 (1968): 153–66.

McPherson, David. "Ben Jonson's Library and Marginalia: An Annotated Catalogue." *Studies in Philology* 71, no. 5 (1974): i–xii, 1–100.

Manningham, John. *The Diary of John Manningham of the Middle Temple, 1602–03*. Edited by Robert Parker Sorlien. Hanover, N.H.: University Press of New England, 1976.

Marcus, Leah S. "City Metal and Country Mettle: The Occasion of Ben Jonson's *Golden Age Restored*." In *Pageantry in the Shakespearean Theater*, edited by David M. Bergeron, 26–47. Athens: University of Georgia Press, 1985.

———. "Masquing Occasions and Masque Structures." *Research Opportunities in Renaissance Drama* 24 (1981): 7–15.

———. "The Occasion of Ben Jonson's *Pleasure Reconciled to Virtue*." *Studies in English Literature* 19 (1979): 271–93.

———. *The Politics of Mirth: Jonson, Herrick, Milton, Marvell, and the Defense of Old Holiday Pastimes*. Chicago: University of Chicago Press, 1986.

———. " 'Present Occasions' and the Shaping of Ben Jonson's Masques." *ELH* 45 (1978): 201–25.

Marotti, Arthur F. "All About Jonson's Poetry." *ELH* 39 (1972): 208–37.

———. "John Donne and the Rewards of Patronage." In *Patronage in the Renaissance*, edited by Guy Fitch Lytle and Stephen Orgel, 207–34. Princeton: Princeton University Press, 1981.

———. *John Donne: Coterie Poet*. Madison: University of Wisconsin Press, 1986.

Martial, Marcus Valerius. *Epigrams*. Translated by Walter C. A. Ker. Loeb Classical Library. 2 vols., 1919–20.

Marwill, Jonathan. *The Trials of Counsel: Francis Bacon in 1621*. Detroit, Mich.: Wayne State University Press, 1976.

Matchett, William. *The Phoenix and the Turtle: Shakespeare's Poem and Chester's Love's Martyr*. The Hague: Mouton, 1965.

Maus, Katherine Eisaman. *Ben Jonson and the Roman Frame of Mind*. Princeton: Princeton University Press, 1984.

Meagher, John C. *Method and Meaning in Jonson's Masques*. Notre Dame, Ind.: University of Notre Dame Press, 1966.

Messinger, Sheldon L., with Harold Sampson and Robert D. Towne. "Life as Theater: Some Notes on the Dramaturgic Approach to Social Reality." In *Drama in Life: The Uses of Communication in Society*, edited by James E. Combs and Michael W. Mansfield, 73–83. New York: Hastings House, 1976.

Miles, Rosalind. *Ben Jonson: His Life and Work*. London: Methuen, 1986.

Miller, Anthony. "Ben Jonson's 'Epistle to Elizabeth Countesse of Rutland': A Recovered MS Reading and Its Critical Implications." *Philological Quarterly* 62 (1983): 525–30.

Miller, Edwin Haviland. *The Professional Writer in England: A Study of Nondramatic Literature*. Cambridge, Mass.: Harvard University Press, 1959.

Mills, Laurens J. *One Soul in Bodies Twain: Friendship in Tudor Literature and Stuart Drama*. Bloomington, Ind.: Principia Press, 1937.

Miner, Earl. *The Cavalier Mode from Jonson to Cotton*. Princeton: Princeton University Press, 1971.

The Mirrour of Friendship. Translated by Thomas Breme. London, 1584.

Moir, T. L. *The Addled Parliament of 1614*. Oxford: Clarendon Press, 1958.

Molesworth, Charles. "Property and Virtue: The Genre of the Country-House Poem in the Seventeenth Century." *Genre* 1 (1968): 141–57.

Montaigne, Michel de. *The Complete Essays of Montaigne*. Translated by Donald M. Frame. Stanford, Cal.: Stanford University Press, 1958.

Montrose, Louis Adrian. "Celebration and Insinuation: Sir Philip Sidney and the Motives of Elizabethan Courtship." *Renaissance Drama*, n.s., 8 (1977): 3–35.

———. "The Purpose of Playing: Reflections on Shakespearean Anthropology." *Helios*, n.s., 7 (1980): 51–74.

Mulder, Mauk. *The Daily Power Game*. Leiden: Martinus Nijhoff Social Sciences Division, 1977.

Murray, Timothy. "From Foul Sheets to Legitimate Model: Antitheater, Text, Ben Jonson." *New Literary History* 14 (1983): 641–64.

Neale, J. E. "The Elizabethan Political Scene." In his *Essays in Elizabethan History*, 59–84. London: Jonathan Cape, 1958.

Newton, Richard C. " 'Ben./ Jonson': The Poet in the Poems." In *Two Renaissance Mythmakers: Christopher Marlowe and Ben Jonson*, edited by Alvin Kernan, 165–95. Baltimore: Johns Hopkins University Press, 1977.

———. " 'Goe, quit 'hem all': Ben Jonson and Formal Verse Satire." *Studies in English Literature* 16 (1976): 105–16.

———. "Jonson and the (Re-) Invention of the Book." In *Classic and Cavalier: Essays on Jonson and the Sons of Ben*, edited by C. J. Summers and Ted-Larry Pebworth, 31–55. Pittsburgh, Pa.: University of Pittsburgh Press, 1982.

Nicholl, Charles. *A Cup of News: The Life of Thomas Nashe*. London: Routledge and Kegan Paul, 1984.

Nichols, J. G. *The Poetry of Ben Jonson*. New York: Barnes and Noble, 1969.

Nichols, John. *Progresses, Processions, and Magnificent Festivities of King James the First*. 4 vols. London: J. B. Nichols, 1828.

Norbrook, David. *Poetry and Politics in the English Renaissance*. London: Routledge and Kegan Paul, 1984.

———. "The Reformation of the Masque." In *The Court Masque*, edited by David Lindley, 94–110. Manchester: Manchester University Press, 1984.

O'Farrell, Brian. "Politician, Patron, Poet: William Herbert, Third Earl of Pembroke, 1580–1630." Ph.D. diss., University of California, Los Angeles, 1966.

O'Neill, James Neil. "Queen Elizabeth I as Patron of the Arts: The Relationship Between Royal Patronage, Society, and Culture in Renaissance England." Ph.D. diss., University of Virginia, 1966.

Orgel, Stephen. *The Illusion of Power*. Berkeley and Los Angeles: University of California Press, 1975.

———. *The Jonsonian Masque*. Cambridge, Mass.: Harvard University Press, 1965.

———, and Roy Strong. *Inigo Jones: The Theatre of the Stuart Court*. 2 vols. Berkeley and Los Angeles: University of California Press, 1973.

Parfitt, George. *Ben Jonson: Public Poet and Private Man*. London: Dent, 1976.

———. "History and Ambiguity: Jonson's 'A Speech according to Horace.'" *Studies in English Literature* 19 (1979): 85–92.

Parry, Graham. *The Golden Age Restor'd: The Culture of the Stuart Court, 1603–42.* Manchester: Manchester University Press, 1981.

———. "Lady Wroth's *Urania*." *Proceedings of the Leeds Philosophical and Literary Society* 16, no. 4 (1975): 51–60.

———. *Seventeenth-Century Poetry: The Social Context.* London: Hutchinson, 1985.

Partridge, Edward. "Jonson's *Epigrammes*: The Named and the Nameless." *Studies in the Literary Imagination* 6, no. 1 (1973): 153–98.

Patterson, Annabel. *Censorship and Interpretation: The Conditions of Writing and Reading in Early Modern England.* Madison: University of Wisconsin Press, 1984.

———. "Jonson, Marvell, and Miscellaneity?" In *Poems in Their Place,* edited by Neil Fraistat, 95–118. Chapel Hill and London: University of North Carolina Press, 1987.

———. "Talking About Power." *John Donne Journal* 2 (1983): 91–106.

Pearl, Sara. "Sounding to Present Occasions: Jonson's Masques of 1620–5." In *The Court Masque,* edited by David Lindley, 61–77. Manchester: Manchester University Press, 1984.

Pearlman, E. "Ben Jonson: An Anatomy." *English Literary Renaissance* 9 (1979): 364–94.

Peck, Linda Levy. "'For a King not to be bountiful were a fault': Perspectives on Court Patronage in Early Stuart England." *Journal of British Studies* 25 (1986): 31–61.

———. *Northampton: Patronage and Policy at the Court of James I.* London: George Allen and Unwin, 1982.

Pembroke, William [Herbert], Earl of. *Poems Written by the Right Honourable William Earl of Pembroke.* Edited by Gaby E. Onderwyzer. Los Angeles: Clark Memorial Library, 1959.

Peterson, Richard S. *Imitation and Praise in the Poems of Ben Jonson.* New Haven: Yale University Press, 1981.

Pigman, G. W., III. "Suppressed Grief in Jonson's Funeral Poetry." *English Literary Renaissance* 13 (1983): 203–20.

Plutarch. *Moralia.* Translated by Frank C. Babbitt. 16 vols. Loeb Classical Library. 1927–69.

———. *Moralia.* Translated by Philemon Holland. New York: Dutton, n.d.

Price, David C. *Patrons and Musicians of the English Renaissance.* Cambridge: Cambridge University Press, 1981.

Rabb, Theodore K. "The Role of the Commons." *Past and Present,* no. 92 (1981): 55–78.

Randall, Dale B. J. *Jonson's Gypsies Unmasked: Background and Theme of* The Gypsies Metamorphos'd. Durham, N.C.: Duke University Press, 1975.

Rathmell, J. C. A. "Jonson, Lord Lisle, and Penshurst." *English Literary Renaissance* 1 (1971): 250–60.

Rebhorn, Wayne. *Courtly Performances: Masking and Festivity in Castiglione's "Book of the Courtier."* Detroit, Mich.: Wayne State University Press, 1978.

Reinmuth, Howard S., Jr., ed. *Early Stuart Studies: Essays in Honor of David Harris Willson*. Minneapolis: University of Minnesota Press, 1970.

Richmond, Hugh M. "Personal Identity and Literary Personae: A Study in Historical Psychology." *PMLA* 90 (1975): 209–221.

Riddell, James A. "The Arrangement of Ben Jonson's *Epigrammes*." *Studies in English Literature* 27 (1987): 53–70.

Rijsberman, Marijke. "Forms of Ceremony in Ben Jonson's Masques." In *Modern Critical Views: Ben Jonson*, edited by Harold Bloom, 223–38. New York: Chelsea House, 1987.

Rivers, Isabel. *The Poetry of Conservatism, 1600–1745: A Study of Poets and Public Affairs from Jonson to Pope*. Cambridge: Rivers Press, 1973.

Roberts, B. Dew. *Mitre and Musket: John Williams, Lord Keeper, Archbishop of York, 1582–1650*. London: Oxford University Press, 1938.

Roberts, Clayton. *Schemes and Undertakings: A Study of English Politics in the Seventeenth Century*. Columbus: Ohio State University Press, 1985.

———, and Owen Duncan. "The Parliamentary Undertaking of 1614." *English Historical Review* 93 (1978): 481–98.

Rollin, Roger B. "The Anxiety of Identification: Jonson and the Rival Poets." In *Classic and Cavalier: Essays on Jonson and the Sons of Ben*, edited by Claude J. Summers and Ted-Larry Pebworth, 139–56. Pittsburgh, Pa.: University of Pittsburgh Press, 1982.

Rosenberg, Eleanor. *Leicester: Patron of Letters*. New York: Columbia University Press, 1955.

Rowe, George E. "Ben Jonson's Quarrel with Audience and its Renaissance Context." *Studies in Philology* 81 (1984): 438–60.

Russell, Conrad. *Parliaments and English Politics, 1621–1629*. Oxford: Clarendon Press, 1979.

Saunders, J. W. "From Manuscript to Print: A Note on the Circulation of Poetic MSS in the Sixteenth Century." *Proceedings of the Leeds Philosophical and Literary Society* 6, pt. 8 (1965): 507–28.

———. *The Profession of English Letters*. London: Routledge and Kegan Paul, 1964.

———. "The Social Situation of Seventeenth-Century Poetry." In *Metaphysical Poetry*, edited by D. J. Palmer and Malcolm Bradbury, 237–60. Stratford-Upon-Avon Studies, 11. London: Edward Arnold, 1970.

———. "The Stigma of Print: A Note on the Social Bases of Tudor Poetry." *Essays in Criticism* 1 (1951): 139–64.

Savage, James E., ed. *The "Conceited Newes" of Sir Thomas Overbury and His Friends*. Gainesville, Fla.: Scholars' Facsimiles and Reprints, 1968.

Schmidgall, Gary. *Shakespeare and the Courtly Aesthetic*. Berkeley and Los Angeles: University of California Press, 1981.

Schmidt, Steffan W. et al., eds. *Friends, Followers, and Factions: A Reader in Political Clientism*. Berkeley and Los Angeles: University of California Press, 1977.

Schochet, Gordon J. *Patriarchialism in Political Thought: The Authoritarian Family and Political Speculation and Attitudes Especially in Seventeenth Century England*. New York: Basic Books, 1975.

Schoeck, Helmut. *Envy: A Theory of Social Behaviour.* Translated by Michael Glenny and Betty Ross. New York: Irvington, 1966.

Scoufos, Alice-Lyle. *Shakespeare's Typological Satire: A Study of the Falstaff–Oldcastle Problem.* Athens: University of Ohio Press, 1979.

The Secret History of the Court of James the First. 2 vols. Edinburgh: John Ballantyne and Co., 1811.

Seneca. *Moral Essays.* Translated by John W. Basore. 3 vols. Loeb Classical Library. 1958.

Shapiro, I. A. "Jonson's *The May Lord.*" *Harvard Library Bulletin* 28 (1980): 258–63.

———. "The 'Mermaid Club.' " *Modern Language Review* 45 (1950): 6–17.

Sharpe, Kevin, ed. *Faction and Parliament.* Oxford: Clarendon Press, 1978.

———. "The Politics of Literature in Renaissance England." *History* 71 (1986): 235–47.

Sharpe, Robert Boies. "Jonson's 'Execration' and Chapman's 'Invective': Their Place in Their Authors' Rivalry." *Studies in Philology* 42 (1945): 555–63.

———. *The Real Wars of the Theaters.* Boston: D. C. Heath, 1935.

Sheavyn, Phoebe. *The Literary Profession in the Elizabethan Age.* 2d ed. New York: Barnes and Noble, 1967.

Shils, Edward. *The Intellectuals and the Powers and Other Essays.* Chicago: University of Chicago Press, 1972.

Shire, Helena Mennie. *Song, Dance and Poetry of the Court of Scotland Under King James VI.* Cambridge: Cambridge University Press, 1969.

Short, Raymond W. "Jonson's Sanguine Rival." *Review of English Studies* 15 (1939): 315–17.

———. "The Patronage of Poetry Under James First." Ph.D. diss., Cornell University, 1936.

Simpson, Percy. "Jonson's Sanguine Rival." *Review of English Studies* 15 (1939): 464–65.

Small, Roscoe. *The Strange Quarrel Between Ben Jonson and the So-Called Poetasters.* New York: AMS Press, 1966.

Smith, Bruce R. "Ben Jonson's *Epigrammes*: Portrait-Gallery, Theater, Commonwealth." *Studies in English Literature* 14 (1974): 91–109.

Smith, David Nichol. *Characters from the Histories and Memoirs of the Seventeenth Century.* Oxford: Clarendon Press, 1918.

Smuts, R. Malcolm. "The Culture of Absolutism at the Court of Charles I." Ph.D. diss., Princeton University, 1976.

Spencer, T. J. B. "Ben Jonson on his beloved, The Author Mr. William Shakespeare." In *The Elizabethan Theatre, 4,* edited by G. R. Hibbard, 22–40. Hamden, Conn.: Archon Books, 1974.

Steele, Mary Susan. *Plays and Masques at Court During the Reigns of Elizabeth, James, and Charles.* New Haven: Yale University Press, 1926.

Stone, Lawrence. *The Crisis of the Aristocracy, 1558–1641.* Oxford: Clarendon Press, 1965.

———. *Family and Fortune: Studies in Aristocratic Finance in the Sixteenth and Seventeenth Centuries.* Oxford: Clarendon Press, 1973.

————. *The Family, Sex and Marriage in England 1500–1800*. Abridged ed. New York: Harper and Row, 1979.

————. "The Fruits of Office: The Case of Robert Cecil, First Earl of Salisbury, 1596–1612." In *Essays in the Economic and Social History of Tudor and Stuart England*, edited by F. J. Fisher, 89–116. Cambridge: Cambridge University Press, 1961.

Stroud, Theodore A. "Ben Jonson and Father Thomas Wright." *ELH* 14 (1947): 274–82.

————. "Father Thomas Wright: A Test Case for Toleration." *Recusant History* 1 (1951): 189–219.

Summers, Claude J., and Ted-Larry Pebworth. *Ben Jonson*. Boston: Twayne, 1979.

————, eds. *Classic and Cavalier: Essays on Jonson and the Sons of Ben*. Pittsburgh, Pa.: University of Pittsburgh Press, 1982.

Summers, Joseph. *The Heirs of Donne and Jonson*. London: Oxford University Press, 1970.

Sweeney, John Gordon III. *Jonson and the Psychology of Public Theater*. Princeton: Princeton University Press, 1985.

Taylor, Dick, Jr. "Clarendon and Ben Jonson as Witnesses for the Earl of Pembroke's Character." In *Studies in the English Renaissance*, edited by Josephine Bennett, 322–44. New York: New York University Press, 1959.

————. "Drayton and the Countess of Bedford." *Studies in Philology* 49 (1952): 214–28.

————. "The Masque of the Lance: The Third Earl of Pembroke in Jacobean Court Entertainments." *Tulane Studies in English* 8 (1958): 21–53.

————. "The Third Earl of Pembroke as a Patron of Poetry." *Tulane Studies in English* 5 (1955): 41–67.

Taylor, Jennifer Reynolds. "Lucy Countess of Bedford, Jonson, and Donne." Ph.D. diss., McMaster University, 1979.

Teague, Francis. "Ben Jonson's Poverty." *Biography* 2 (1979): 260–65.

Tedeschi, James T., Barry R. Schlenker, and Thomas V. Bonoma. *Conflict, Power, and Games: The Experimental Study of Interpersonal Relations*. Chicago: Aldine, 1973.

Tedeschi, James T., ed. *The Social Influence Processes*. Chicago: Aldine; New York: Atherton, 1972.

Tennenhouse, Leonard. *Power on Display: The Politics of Shakespeare's Genres*. New York and London: Methuen, 1986.

————. "Sir Walter Ralegh and the Literature of Clientage." In *Patronage in the Renaissance*, edited by Guy Fitch Lytle and Stephen Orgel, 235–58. Princeton: Princeton University Press, 1981.

Thomas, Peter. "Two Cultures? Court and Country Under Charles I." In *The Origins of the English Civil War*, edited by Conrad Russell, 168–93. New York: Barnes and Noble, 1973.

Thomson, Patricia. "The Literature of Patronage, 1580–1630." *Essays in Criticism* 2 (1952): 267–84.

————. "The Patronage of Letters Under Elizabeth and James I." *English* 7 (1949): 278–82.

Tourneur, Cyril. *The Works of Cyril Tourneur.* Edited by Allardyce Nicholl. London: Franfrolico Press, 1929.

Trexler, Richard C., ed. *Persons in Groups: Social Behavior as Identity Formation in Medieval and Renaissance Europe.* Binghamton, N.Y.: Medieval and Renaissance Texts and Studies, 1985.

Trilling, Lionel. *Sincerity and Authenticity.* Cambridge, Mass.: Harvard University Press, 1972.

Trimpi, Wesley. *Ben Jonson's Poems: A Study in the Plain Style.* Palo Alto, Cal.: Stanford University Press, 1962.

Turner, James. *The Politics of Landscape: Rural Scenery and Society in English Poetry 1630–1660.* Cambridge, Mass.: Harvard University Press, 1979.

Tuvill, Daniel. *Essays Politic and Moral and Essays Moral and Theological.* Edited by John L. Lievsay. Charlottesville: University of Virginia Press, 1971.

Urban, Raymond. "The Somerset Affair, the Belvoir Witches, and Jonson's Pastoral Comedies." *Harvard Library Bulletin* 23 (1975): 295–323.

van den Berg, Sara J. *The Action of Ben Jonson's Poetry.* Newark: University of Delaware Press, 1987.

———. " 'The Paths I Meant unto Thy Praise': Jonson's Poem for Shakespeare." *Shakespeare Studies* 11 (1978): 207–18.

van Dorsten, Jan. "Literary Patronage in Elizabethan England: The Early Phase." In *Patronage in the Renaissance,* edited by Guy Fitch Lytle and Stephen Orgel, 191–206. Princeton: Princeton University Press, 1981.

———. "Mr. Secretary Cecil, Patron of Letters." *English Studies* 50 (1969): 545–53.

Van Dyke, Joyce. "The Game of Wits in *The Alchemist.*" *Studies in English Literature* 19 (1979): 253–69.

Van Fossen, R. W., ed. *Eastward Ho.* By George Chapman, Ben Jonson, and John Marston. Baltimore: Johns Hopkins University Press, 1979.

Venuti, Lawrence. "Why Jonson Wrote Not of Love." *Journal of Medieval and Renaissance Studies* 12 (1982): 195–220.

Walker, Ralph S., ed. *Ben Jonson's Timber or Discoveries.* Syracuse, N.Y.: Syracuse University Press, 1953.

———. "Literary Criticism in Jonson's Conversations with Drummond." *English* 8 (1951): 222–27.

Walton, Geoffrey. "The Tone of Ben Jonson's Poetry." In *Seventeenth Century English Poetry: Modern Essays in Criticism,* edited by William R. Keast, 479–96. Rev. ed. London: Oxford University Press, 1971.

Walzer, Michael. *The Revolution of the Saints.* New York: Atheneum, 1973.

Watson, Robert N. *Ben Jonson's Parodic Strategy: Literary Imperialism in the Comedies.* Cambridge, Mass.: Harvard University Press, 1987.

Wayne, Don E. "Drama and Society in the Age of Jonson: An Alternative View." *Renaissance Drama,* n.s., 13 (1982): 103–29.

———. "Mediation and Contestation: English Classicism from Sidney to Jonson." *Criticism* 25 (1983): 211–27.

———. *Penshurst: The Semiotics of Place and the Poetics of History.* Madison: University of Wisconsin Press, 1984.

———. "Poetry and Power in Ben Jonson's *Epigrammes*: The Naming of 'Facts' or the Figuring of Social Relations." *Renaissance and Modern Studies* 23 (1979): 79–103.

Weber, Kurt. *Lucius Cary: Second Viscount Falkland.* New York: Columbia University Press, 1940.

Welsford, Enid. *The Court Masque.* Cambridge: Cambridge University Press, 1927.

Wentworth, William. "Sir William Wentworth's advice to his son." In *Wentworth Papers, 1597–1628.* Edited by J. P. Cooper. Camden Society Publications, 4th ser., vol. 12. London: Royal Historical Society, 1973.

Whigham, Frank F. *Ambition and Privilege: The Social Tropes of Elizabethan Courtesy Theory.* Berkeley: University of California Press, 1984.

———. "The Rhetoric of Elizabethan Suitors' Letters." *PMLA* (1981): 864–82.

White, Stephen D. *Sir Edward Coke and "The Grievances of the Commonwealth," 1621–1625.* Chapel Hill: University of North Carolina Press, 1979.

Whitlock, Baird W. *John Hoskyns, Serjeant-at-Law.* Washington, D.C.: University Press of America, 1982.

Wilbraham, Roger. *The Journal of Sir Roger Wilbraham.* Edited by Harold Spencer. The Camden Miscellany 10. London: Royal Historical Society, 1902.

Williams, Mary C. "Merlin and the Prince: The Speeches at Prince Henry's Barriers." *Renaissance Drama,* n.s., 8 (1977): 221–30.

Williams, Raymond. *The Country and the City.* London: Chatto and Windus, 1969.

Willson, David Harris. *King James VI and I.* New York: Oxford University Press, 1956.

———. *The Privy Councillors in the House of Commons, 1604–1629.* Minneapolis: University of Minnesota Press, 1940.

Wilson, Gayle Edward. "Jonson's Use of the Bible and the Great Chain of Being in 'To Penshurst.'" *Studies in English Literature* 8 (1968): 77–89.

Winner, Jack D. "Ben Jonson's *Epigrammes* and the Conventions of Formal Verse Satire." *Studies in English Literature* 23 (1983): 61–76.

———. "The Public and Private Dimensions of Jonson's Epitaphs." In *Classic and Cavalier: Essays on Jonson and the Sons of Ben,* edited by Claude J. Summers and Ted-Larry Pebworth, 107–19. Pittsburgh: University of Pittsburgh Press, 1982.

Womack, Peter. *Ben Jonson.* London: Basil Blackwell, 1986.

Wright, Louis B., ed. *Advice to a Son: Precepts of Lord Burghley, Sir Walter Raleigh, and Francis Osborne.* Ithaca: Cornell University Press, 1962.

Wright, Thomas. *The Passions of the Minde in Generall.* Introduction by Thomas O. Sloan. Urbana: University of Illinois Press, 1971.

Wroth, Lady Mary. *The Poems of Lady Mary Wroth.* Edited by Josephine A. Roberts. Baton Rouge: Louisiana State University Press, 1983.

Wykes, David. "Ben Jonson's 'Chast Booke'—*The Epigrammes.*" *Renaissance and Modern Studies* 13 (1969): 76–87.

Zagorin, Perez. *The Court and the Country: The Beginning of the English Revolution.* New York: Atheneum, 1971.

Index